RADICAL UNIONISM
IN THE MIDWEST,
1900–1950

**THE WORKING CLASS
IN AMERICAN HISTORY**

Editorial Advisors
James R. Barrett
Alice Kessler-Harris
Nelson Lichtenstein
David Montgomery

*A list of books in the series appears
at the end of this book.*

Radical Unionism
in the Midwest,
1900–1950

ROSEMARY FEURER

UNIVERSITY OF ILLINOIS PRESS
URBANA AND CHICAGO

© 2006 by the Board of Trustees
of the University of Illinois
All rights reserved
Manufactured in the United States of America
1 2 3 4 5 C P 5 4 3 2 1

♾ This book is printed on acid-free paper.

Library of Congress Cataloging-in-Publication Data

Feurer, Rosemary.
Radical unionism in the Midwest, 1900–1950 / Rosemary Feurer.
p. cm.—(The working class in American history)
Includes bibliographical references and index.
ISBN-13: 978-0-252-03087-1 (cloth : alk. paper)
ISBN-10: 0-252-03087-7 (cloth : alk. paper)
ISBN-13: 978-0-252-07319-9 (pbk. : alk. paper)
ISBN-10: 0-252-07319-3 (pbk. : alk. paper)
1. Labor unions—United States—History—20th century.   2. Labor
unions—Middle West—Political activity—History—20th century.
3. Industrial relations—Middle West—History—20th century.
I. Title.   II. Series.
HD6508.F35   2006
331.880977'09041—DC22   2006006962

For Dave

CONTENTS

ACKNOWLEDGMENTS

It is a great pleasure to be able to acknowledge the assistance given over the course of this project.

I am particularly grateful, as someone who was a first-generation college student, to those who helped initiate me into the world of ideas at Southern Illinois University-Edwardsville. Here I would like to acknowledge especially Ellen Nore and Rod Wright. Ellen Nore introduced me to the study of social history and the connection between the intense work of social history and intellectual issues. Rod, though a low-paid adjunct, was an extraordinary professor who helped me to connect the realities of the experience of class in the present to politics and the past and who took the time to convince me that I could contribute something despite my insecurities.

I learned the craft of history from Henry Berger and Mark Leff at Washington University. Henry's introduction to the rapidly changing field of labor history directed me toward this topic. Mark's thorough critiques coupled with his own stellar example made me aspire to become the master craftsman he already had become. Others at Washington University including Iver Bernstein, Howard Brick, Richard Davis, and Andrea Friedman gave valuable critiques of my dissertation or other work. I was also fortunate to meet and dialogue with Dave Roediger while in graduate school and was grateful that he agreed to be a member of my dissertation committee. His warmth and politically engaged scholarship are a source of inspiration. I thank him for his generosity and the numerous ways he has helped me.

This project started with the intention of researching the CIO in one location, but when I was sorting through the papers in the basement of William Sentner Jr., the significance of District 8's role in the CIO soon became apparent. But it was only with the encouragement and advice of Ronald Schatz and Steven Rosswurm that I took up District 8's story and abandoned the earlier project. Both of them contributed important insights and models that guided my search. I formulated some of my initial perspectives on this subject in response to Steven's critique. He read the manuscript carefully in an earlier stage and provided probing and difficult questions that I fear I have not fully answered, but I am glad he asked them.

I encountered the scholarship of David Montgomery as a graduate student and labor activist and read everything he wrote. His work directed me to take the study of power relationships seriously, looking at both workers' and employers' roles in class struggles. I had heard stories of his generosity, but it never dawned on me at the time that I might benefit. His extended critique of this work and his guidance of it as a University of Illinois Press reader have been a significant resource for me. Similarly, I am indebted to another scholarly model, James Barrett, whose work I held in such awe and who agreed to be the second reader for the University of Illinois Press, even in the midst of a very busy schedule. Laurie Matheson and Richard Wentworth provided vital support and assistance as editors of the University of Illinois Press.

I want to acknowledge as well other scholars who read all or part of the manuscript in various stages and commented or asked good questions. These include Iver Bernstein, Bill Douglas, Susan Hartmann, Andrew Hurley, Howard Kimeldorf, Allan Kulikoff, Staughton Lynd, Roger Ratliffe, Gerda Ray, John Schacht, Harvey Smith, Shelton Stromquist, and Joe William Trotter. James Schmidt, my colleague at Northern Illinois University, gave a thorough reading that was extraordinarily helpful.

Staughton Lynd deserves special mention for affecting my conceptualization of this project, though it is certain that he will object to some parts of the final work. Staughton's commitment to combining intellectual debate and labor activism was an inspiration long before I met him and Alice Lynd. But engaging in dialogue with Staughton, Alice, and the folks in Youngstown directed me to questions about the importance of community-based organizing and helped me to see more clearly what the radicals of District 8 were doing.

This book would have looked very different had it not been for the many people from whom I learned valuable lessons or provoked debates that made me think seriously about the possibilities of labor as a social movement. The rich milieu of activists I learned from needs to start with the inestimable Bob Tibbs, who together with his wife Shirley communicated that one could "keep the faith" and stay radical even as one ages in the working-class struggle. Bob's spirit, humor, and intellectual depth were a source of inspiration to all who knew him. Other activists who inspired questions or imparted important lessons that helped to shape the questions I brought to this history were Mark Albrecht, Judy Ancel, Willie Braswell, Marcia Cline, Bill Dettleff, Dave Dowling, Peter Downs, Anne Feeney, Norma and Gary Gaines, Don Giljum, Steve Maason, Kevin Madden, Ora Lee Malone, Peter Rachleff, Terry Reed, Bob Reinhold, Randy Reynolds, Eddie Starr, Jerry Tucker, Dave Vitoff, Roz Sherman Voellinger, Mark Waldemer, Hershel Walker, and John Webb. The many conversations I had with Staley activist Dan Lane, who questioned the strategy for the Staley workers' struggle in the mid-1990s, were extraordinarily powerful during the formative time of this book.

This book used more than one hundred collections from various archives and personal homes, and I benefited from the many archivists who facilitated my research and pointed to possible leads for materials or helped facilitate the depositing of records that I collected. Several in particular deserve special mention. James Cassedy of the National Archives and Records Administration is among the most valuable labor archivists in the country. His assistance and patience with numerous requests are deeply appreciated. He steadfastly went beyond the call of duty to hunt down materials, seemingly lost, and to help navigate the federal records. David Rosenberg of the UE Archives at the University of Pittsburgh endured many visits but managed to punctuate every visit to the archives with a plethora of jokes and wise assistance. Zellie Fischetti and Kenn Thomas at the Western Historical Manuscripts Collection, University of Missouri-St. Louis, were especially helpful in securing the depositing of numerous other archives. Mary Bennett of the State Historical Society of Iowa provided some important leads and allowed access to materials before they were officially open. Mark Smith of the Iowa AFL-CIO allowed use of interviews that he commissioned. Others that deserve special mention are Patricia Adams, Linda Belford, Doris Wesley, Duane Sneddecker, Dina Young, Carole Prietto, Gina Walker, Hans Brosig, and Beverly Cross.

I am indebted to the dozens of people who shared their memories with me, some of them enduring the revival of "old ghosts," as Antonia Sentner put it. Each person provided insights that informed my understanding or gave me important clues and other leads. I especially treasure my time with early UE activist Lloyd Austin, who became a friend and whose hope that this book would "tell the real story" so that the memory of District 8 would not be lost inspired me. Conducting interviews with the many people who informed the project was an enriching experience for me, one for which I will forever be thankful.

In the course of this project, a number of people agreed to donate or share their personal collections. They include Frank Abfall, Lloyd Austin, Charles Berger, Alice Click, William "Red" Davis, Ed Fitzgerald, John Logsdon, Gladys Slate, Charles Slezak, Eugene Paul, David Phillips, Duane Raab, Betty Raab, and William Reidel. Others generously shared information gleaned from their research or directed me to other materials or interviewees, including Merle Davis, Jeannette Gabriel, Tom Verdot, Wilson Warren, Samuel White, and Doug Wixson. Peter Gilmore of the United Electrical Workers union alerted me and allowed access to the St. Louis edition of the *People's Press*. The richest source of information was the collection from William "Billy" Sentner Jr., who was very generous with his time and assistance. He kept much of his father's records intact over the years, saving them from a flooded basement and towing them across the country. Billy was born in the eye of the storm, during the Maytag strike of 1938, and endured the torments of coming of age in the worst period of what came to be known as the McCarthy era, experiencing the threat of losing his mother to deportation and his father to jail and the torment of going to school in the midst of all these travails, all without succumbing to bitterness. His generosity of spirit communicated to me his family's strong humanity.

Other friends or family who provided assistance of various kinds include Tim Sears, Mary Ann Feurer, Rochelle Rathke-Simmons, Beth Shulman, and Gene Zitver and his family. Their assistance saved me considerable research expense.

I would also like to acknowledge the financial support of Northern Illinois University, which funded the publication of photographs in this book as well as the website at www.radicalunionism.niu.edu with additional photographs and other materials.

The largest debt I have, both personal and scholarly, is to Dave Rathke, to whom the book is dedicated. Discussions as well as debates with him over history, politics, and strategy have informed much of my life and many of the questions I brought to this work. Our journey together was a wise and fortunate choice for me, one that took me on a path that enriched my life immeasurably. I am thankful to have such a wonderful soul mate. Together with our sons Benjamin and Joseph, he has brought the deepest meaning to my life.

Portions of chapter 2 were previously published as "Crossing the Boundaries between Community and Union: The Nutpickers Union in St. Louis, 1933–1934," in Staughton Lynd, ed., *We Are All Leaders: The Alternative Unionism of the Early 1930s* (Urbana: University of Illinois Press, 1996), and are used with permission of the publisher. An earlier version of a portion of chapter 5 was previously published as "'River Dreams': St. Louis Labor and the Proposal for a Missouri Valley Authority, 1944–1948," in Andrew Hurley, ed., *An Environmental History of St. Louis* (St. Louis: Missouri Historical Society Press, 1997), and is used here by permission of the publisher. Segments of "William Sentner, the United Electrical Workers, and 'Civic Unionism' in St. Louis, 1933–1945," in Steven Rosswurm, ed., *The CIO's Left-Led Unions* (New Brunswick, N.J.: Rutgers University Press, 1992), are also used throughout the text, with permission of the publisher.

INTRODUCTION

This study explores the efforts of working-class activists during the 1930s and 1940s to develop a style of unionism that would be a force for social transformation. It is the story of District 8 of the United Electrical, Radio and Machine Workers of America (UE) and its battles with fiercely antiunion companies in the electrical and metal trades industries of the Midwest. District 8 originated in St. Louis but eventually comprised locals in Missouri, Iowa, Indiana, Illinois, Arkansas, and Kansas. During World War II, the district expanded to more than fifty thousand workers. The activists who shaped trade union policy in District 8 sought to develop a way to effectively confront corporate power and to make the workers' movement a force for social transformation on the local, regional, and national levels.

Radical activists were key organizers in the district's formation and held many of its leadership positions. During 1937–48, workers elected William Sentner, an open member of the Communist Party (CP), as president. Sentner and other radicals built a base of support among workers who, at the beginning of the 1930s, were distant from the radical traditions in the electrical and metal trades industry that are usually said to account for the emergence of left-wing leadership in the UE in other areas of the country.

The desire to link union and community concerns to a far-reaching critique of corporate power and capitalism animated the organizing, collective bargaining, and broad-based planning visions of the district throughout the period. District 8 confronted many obstacles, including the recalcitrant antiunionism of employers, workers' social and political divisions, and ties to the CP that tarnished the strongly democratic radical vision the Left promoted. Nevertheless, community-level organizing in an effort to democratize workplace and community spaces defined radical activists' contribution to the workers' movement of this era.

The companies that District 8 confronted were fiercely antiunion "independents" on the periphery of the industry, but they were central to establishing the open shop and gaining control of the urban labor market as well as the shop floor regime. These employers remained intransigently opposed to unions and are a vital and often overlooked part of the labor history of the 1930s. They revived community-based strategies when challenged by workers' movements and critically shaped the outcome of the movement.

In concentrating on workers' battles with companies on the periphery, this study departs from the main narrative about the 1930s' union movement—the emergence of nationally organized industrial unions in the Congress of Industrial Organizations (CIO) and their confrontation with major multiplant corporations.[1] Attention to the unionization of larger corporations has seemed appropriate. The great drama of the 1930s was the confrontation with the large corporations, beginning with the national strike against General Motors (GM). Clearly, workers themselves saw the capitulation of the giants, such as General Motors, General Electric, and U.S. Steel, as major victories of that era. Lizabeth Cohen, in telling the story of Chicago's workers between World War I and World War II, concluded that "despite minor variations, there was one national story to be told" even when studying a single community. For Cohen, the simultaneous failure of major corporations' internal labor strategies and the local ethnic-based welfare organizations in Depression-era Chicago drove the effort to build national unions that could fight for national political representation of the working class. The heroic part of the Left in this story is that it selflessly helped to organize workers to develop the ability to do this effectively. The story of the 1930s becomes the triumph of national-oriented union strategies.[2]

This study starts from the premise that uneven capitalist development made the local terrain an essential arena of struggle and an important site of class power formation even within the context of national and international markets and national and international unions. It places the development of District 8 within the context of longer struggles over control of the local labor market. Employers used the local terrain to achieve what David Harvey calls capitalists' "spatial fix"—building the landscape for accumulation through localized struggle and taking on a group of workers one at a time. From 1900 to 1935, the "independents" of the electrical industry acted collectively and ideologically at the local level to construct the conditions in the Midwest that allowed them to exist on the periphery of unevenly developing capitalism. This group of employers established a regional labor market based on low wages and defended it vigorously. In the 1930s, these companies, facing a challenge from a revived radical-influenced labor movement, again sought to revive these arguments and strategies through networks and ideological campaigns at the local level. While the changed nature of state power prevented some of the full implementation of these strategies, we can nevertheless see how critical the local arena of struggle remained. It was against this backdrop that District 8 sought to organize workers to confront this concerted power.[3]

This study also suggests that the local level can yield insights on the role of radicals in the 1930s' labor movement. Historians have usually credited radicals with helping to build the 1930s' labor movement but have also sometimes concluded that radicals' trade union behavior in the 1930s did not differ significantly from traditional trade unionists. A number of studies of the UE have contributed to this interpretation. Ronald Schatz's important book, *The Electrical Workers: A History of Labor at General Electric and Westinghouse, 1923–1960*, found that the prominence of Communists and other radicals in the UE developed from the legacy of earlier worker struggles in the electrical industry and the communities in which the industry located. These key groups of union activists, many attracted to the CP as the main organization of the Left in the 1930s, helped to build the UE. Schatz noted that "members of left-wing parties had skills which equipped them to organize. Unlike most workers, they knew how to call a meeting, distribute literature, and speak on their feet." Radicals' dedication and commitment, not a Communist conspiracy, allowed them to be of service to building the union. Schatz also argued that the main social base for radicalism was among the higher-paid skilled workers—but these were the very workers in decline in an industry based on mechanization.[4] Summarizing Schatz's work, Harvey Levenstein has observed that the leftist leaders in the UE "owed their strength to the survival of a radical nuclei in the industry, the flotsam and jetsam of years of sinking radical dreams" that preceded the CIO era.[5]

Schatz and others have argued that the political perspectives of the radicals in leadership positions held little importance for the trade union behavior of the UE. The challenge to capitalism that supposedly lay behind radicals' allegiance to the CP did not have much influence on day-to-day shop floor matters such as piecework, incentive wages, and seniority. Schatz notes with evident disappointment that "by the mid-1940s . . . wage increases had become the primary—in reality almost the sole—goal of the UE in its negotiations with GE [General Electric] and Westinghouse." In fact, Schatz's study suggests that the Cold War era conflict between the UE and its rival, the International Union of Electrical Workers (IUE), was based not on distinctions regarding trade union issues but on "social differences which lay beneath political factions" and foreign policy positions. Schatz found that older skilled workers seemed to have more of a propensity toward sympathy for the UE than younger semiskilled workers who entered the industry during the war.[6] The irony of a left-wing leadership that suffered the McCarthyism of the Cold War period without differing substantially from mainstream trade unionists was not lost on historian Ronald Filipelli, who concluded that UE leaders gained and held legitimacy through their trade union effectiveness on "bread and butter" issues. Therefore, "they tended to view ideology as a handicap rather than as an asset."[7]

These views on the UE coincide with the conclusions of many other studies that stressed that while Communists were products of a genuine "American" radical tradition, their political viewpoints made little difference in the policies and strategies of the trade union movement. Assessing the literature on the CIO, David Brody observed that "it is remarkable how little difference [radicals] made on the direction of the . . . unions they controlled." He concluded that left-wing unionists were unable to act other than as "essentially conventional trade unionists."[8]

In explaining why radicals "were held captive to a trade union agenda that they did not set themselves," some scholars have pointed to the shortcomings of the programmatic approach of the CP in the CIO,[9] but most, in the end, have contended that the conservative nature of American workers limited any radical potential for the ferment of 1930s' labor activism and placed limits on the progressive direction of the CIO. In sobering analyses, historians contend that workers were limited by their parochial concerns for the security and stability of their families and communities, which drew them to a shrewd, pragmatic, and cautious approach and to disinterest in workers' control issues that had animated the militant earlier generations of skilled workers.[10] These scholars see deeply conservative tendencies in workers' consciousness that emanated from family, community, and ethnocultural influences—influences that stressed security and insulated workers from radical ideas. Workers' quest for economic security and stability perpetuated a focus on a narrowly conceived "job consciousness" that radicals could not overcome.[11] Lizabeth Cohen's influential study of the CIO in Chicago concluded that workers in the 1930s were motivated by what they viewed as betrayal by paternalistic employers, who abandoned the security guarantees embodied in corporate welfare programs of the 1920s. Workers wanted to restore that security by forcing employers to fulfill the promise of "moral capitalism" that they had guaranteed through those programs. Workers, Cohen argued, "did not demand a fundamental redistribution of power such as a role in hiring, firing, work and wage assignments, and production decisions" and never transcended the conservative influence of family and community concerns. Gary Gerstle has asserted that the "elusive radical spirit" did not stir the mass of workers; "radicalism was generally confined to small groups of skilled workers with long histories of trade union and political activities." In order to appeal to workers, he and others argued, radicals had to couch their ideas and beliefs in a patriotic language. During World War II, that patriotic language was easily turned in a more conservative direction that preceded the penultimately conservatizing influence of the Cold War. Michael Kazin has concluded that CP members "enjoyed some success in the CIO precisely because they *were* opportunists—committed organizers who talked about socialism only in private."[12] The conservative direction of the CIO, then, was the inevitable outcome of the conservative goals of workers.[13]

In recent years, this perspective has been challenged by the resurgence of an interpretation suggesting that the crucial memory we should have of trade unionists associated with the CP is that they were part of a worldwide conspiracy that aided and abetted a murderous, totalitarian regime. Communists were illegitimate trade unionists because the CP, as demonstrated by the archives of the former Soviet Union, was controlled by a foreign power.[14]

This study suggests that District 8 constructed one of the most democratic labor organizations in the country by the time of its demise and developed a style of unionism that was anything but conventional in that the key organizers continually sought a way to advance workers' power in a contest against employers who sought to limit that power. It borrows from David Montgomery's insights about the way that social history sometimes obscures the "decisive role" of the "militant minority"—the "men and women who endeavored to weld their workmates and neighbors into a self-aware and purposeful working class"—to argue that the role of radicals mattered critically in District 8, and not just because they were skilled organizers. It borrows insights from social movement literature to understand that, as Kim Voss puts it, "workers are not the only participants in the process of class formation" and that their aspirations and possibilities are shaped critically by other actors in the process, which cautions us not to read consciousness from outcome.[15] Here I find that the determination of a "militant minority" of employers to constitute themselves as a class and operate collectively at the local level to eradicate radical impulses was a critical factor in shaping the landscape of possibilities. Those possibilities were also critically shaped by the state as well as by an international landscape of war and revolution. Particularly important here is the rise of the revolution that brought the Soviet Union into existence. This made the Soviet Union a focus of radical aspirations and also the focus of a bitter Cold War. These factors fatally affected District 8's movement in the Midwest.

The Left in District 8 developed a focus on community-based organizing as the starting point for challenging the control of the political economy that had been carefully constructed in the previous era. I trace this impulse to the unemployed and union organizing struggles of the early 1930s. This experience was transferred and expanded in the years of organizing the independent electrical and machine shops. Throughout, the quest for wages, security, and community in the district was deeply intertwined with workers' challenge to management rights. District 8 activists used the concepts of "human rights over property rights" and "civic unionism" to express their goals and sought to connect workplace and community concerns; challenge management rights; mitigate social divisions based on skill, race, and gender; and suggest that workers might have a role in planning for a local and national economy. They also linked the quest for human rights to attempts to argue that radicals, including members of the CP, might have a political right to expression in the CIO. Through their layers of experience gained over time, they developed a deepening commitment to community-based organizing as the basis for this struggle for the soul of the CIO union movement. The Left in District 8 did not see the community focus of their organizing as parochial but rather as the basic starting point for a national and international movement for social transformation. This was directly contrary to the centralizing tendencies of the CIO, which saw the national-level campaigns and elite New Deal networks as the key operating procedure. By World War II, such insights led the district to the sort of coalitional politics that presented grassroots strategies for organizing for economic planning.

There would never be an acceptance of Communists in the ranks of labor as there had been for Socialists in the early twentieth century, and much of this was justified by their blind refusal to see the Soviet state for all its brutal realities. After 1945, District 8's Left came under siege. It was a campaign that developed from multiple motivations, including principled anticommunism, but whose own coalitional politics were reactionary. The Left was initially able to prevail against attacks that were aided by the national and local CIO, employers, and a congressional committee. Only when the CIO set up new unions to compete with the eleven it expelled for being Communist-dominated did the right-wing coalition prevail, splintering the district and dealing a fatal blow to the democratic, community style of unionism that the Left had nurtured.

The first two chapters set the context for the emergence of District 8. Chapter 1 shows how St. Louis electrical "independents" managers secured the open shop and their position in the industry through an agenda of local strategies that was equally focused on shop floor control and securing the larger spatial arena of the labor market, such as the community wage that businesses in St. Louis struggled to define and that workers negotiated daily. In order to do this, they aimed at eliminating the radical challenge from metal trades unionists who sought to build a movement from the community outward. While much has been written about the radical impulses of metal trades workers, employers in St. Louis were thoroughly effective in eliminating that tradition by the 1920s, despite evidence of worker discontent. Chapter 2 considers the early Depression years and electrical workers' renewed attempts to organize—attempts that failed and thus provided an opening for the Left. Radical activists were critically influenced by the early 1930s' drives among the unemployed and the attempts to build alliances between employed and unemployed; in particular, the African American working class helped to develop a vision of unionism grounded in linking workplace and community struggle. This experience was not simply a prelude to the CIO. Rather, it was the critical grounding that built a community-based social movement that later became associated with the CIO drive and defined radical unionism. It also argues that a fair assessment has to credit the CP as the midwife to the rebirth and growth of a radical vision of unionism in St. Louis but that these were also tied to older working-class traditions.

Chapter 3 explains how a cadre of activists successfully launched a sit-down at Emerson Electric and shows how the Left's critical understanding of the local political economy as well as the strategies developing out of the early 1930s were employed to break the open shop of the St. Louis electrical independents as part of the nationwide CIO movement. The chapter also portrays the building and structure of District 8 and its philosophy. In the formative period of the district, William Sentner and the leftist leadership were able to deflect anticommunism and influence the development of a movement that challenged employers' control of the shop floor and the community labor market.

The backlash against District 8 and the Left that occurred in the wake of the 1937–38 recession is the subject of Chapter 4. Employers revived community-based strategies in an effort to turn back the tide in the context of New Deal political retreat and anticommunist factional developments within the CIO from 1939 to 1941. The district's response revealed how leftist unionism was distinguished from the general CIO response in this period. Ultimately, the CP policy of alliance with the Democratic Party, which Sentner and the Left followed, reinforced tendencies that made their challenge vulnerable to forces on the Right. Further, the CP's ties to the Soviet Union, especially in the aftermath of the Nazi-Soviet Pact, allowed anticommunism to lurk in the background as an effective weapon, even if the direction of District 8 was toward more democratic structures.

As World War II and the international coalition between the United States and the Soviet Union muted anticommunism, the community-organizing strategies of the Left developed into a full-fledged "civic unionism" that sought to build a challenge to employer power even in the context of the no-strike pledge. This is the subject of Chapter 5, which describes the community-based version of the industry council proposals famously proposed by CIO leader Philip Murray. District 8 developed this concept of grassroots movements for economic planning when it organized and critically structured the campaign for a Missouri Valley Authority. The vision showed a great deal of promise until it was snuffed out by the postwar battles over the role of Communists in the coalition and by the betrayal of key Democratic Party players. During this time, the district also distinguished its style of unionism by a deepening commitment to racial and gender equality that was part of a thorough critique of the political economy of capitalism and the structure of CIO unions.

Chapter 6 evaluates this postwar anticommunist drive, which focused on Sentner; explains how the district's leftist coalition was able to defeat these challenges; and traces the resurgence of the right-wing campaign in 1948 in the context of national and international developments. This campaign climaxed in Evansville, where the marginalized right wing was resurgent due to political support from reactionary forces and was able to conflate the district's contest over the community wage and management rights with Communist subversion. But it was only with the establishment of the IUE and an even more vigorous CIO campaign against the UE that the faction triumphed. The conclusion summarizes and assesses the findings and discusses the long-term consequences for the defeat of the Left.

RADICAL UNIONISM
IN THE MIDWEST,
1900–1950

The Militant Minority in the St. Louis Electrical Industry and the Political Economy of Control, 1900–1935

From 1900 to 1935, electrical employers, acting collectively and ideologically at the local level, eradicated the radical impulses of metal trades workers in St. Louis. Their efforts helped to secure a place for their companies, which became known as "independents," in the electrical industry, an industry dominated by large companies such as General Electric (GE) and Westinghouse. The independent electrical managers worked together with businessmen in other industries to establish a regional labor market based on low wages that would allow them to exist in the political economy of uneven capitalist development. This story frames the background to the opening battles of the 1930s.

St. Louis electrical employers organized as part of a "militant minority" of antiunion businessmen who relied on an agenda of local strategies to secure the open shop and their position in the industry. The term "militant minority" is borrowed from twentieth-century syndicalists who used it to describe "the men and women who endeavored to weld their workmates and neighbors into a self-aware and purposeful working class."[1] The term is also useful to conceptualize the group of *businessmen* who urged fellow managers and owners to act collectively to control the labor market and to eliminate radical influences among workers. Other studies have shown that employers won control of regional labor markets only through tremendous collective action and ideological drives against labor. Interestingly, small- and medium-sized employers often played a decisive role in organizing the urban landscape of unevenly developing capitalism to stave off labor's demands.[2] The narrative that follows allows us to see that as the electrical independents acted to establish patterns of dominance, shop floor control tactics were finely interwoven with the local political economy of control, which describes the broader means of controlling labor beyond the internal plant-based programs, such as welfare and personnel programs. The local business strategies were clearly geared toward controlling the larger spatial arena of the labor market, such as the community wage that businesses in St. Louis struggled to define and that workers negotiated daily.

The St. Louis Electrical Industry

Between 1890 and 1930, St. Louis emerged as a center of the electrical industry independents, small- and medium-sized companies that were on the margins of the highly concentrated electrical products markets. GE and Westinghouse, headquartered in New York City and Schenectady, respectively, controlled the production of large generators, turbines, and huge motors, the core products of the industry, as well as some of the key manufacturing components such as copper. Wagner, Emerson, and Century, companies that came to be known by the 1930s as the "big three" of the St. Louis independents, carved out a niche in smaller motor and electrical products. They owed that success to their ability to maintain staunch antiunion policies throughout the region's labor market.[3]

Closely tied to the St. Louis financial elite, Wagner Electric organized the local open shop drive until the 1920s. Herbert Wagner came to St. Louis in 1887 to set up a power plant turbine for Westinghouse. In 1890, bankrolled by "old money" financiers of the dry goods and warehouse industry, Wagner and engineer Francis Schwedtman founded Wagner Electric. August Samuel, the director of the city's largest bank, became president of Wagner Electric in 1900, but Schwedtman was connected to National City Bank of New York.

Wagner Electric's first products were single-phase, alternating current motors used to power small appliances; the company also patented a range of electrical products, including transformers. Wagner expanded from a small shop in downtown St. Louis to a burgeoning local enterprise with national market outlets. By 1913, its Wellston plant in St. Louis's northwest industrial corridor was proclaimed the third largest and the most modern in the country. Wagner engineers also developed electrical components for automobiles, eventually producing generators, starters, and ignition and lighting devices. The company was one of the largest employers in St. Louis's diverse manufacturing base, growing to forty-five hundred workers thanks to war production contracts during World War I.[4]

By the 1920s, Emerson Electric and Century Electric had joined Wagner to form the "big three" of the independents, but they were much smaller enterprises until World War I. Emerson Electric was established in 1890 by brothers Charles and Alexander Meston, leaders in motor development. In 1892, railroad magnate Herbert Parker bought controlling interest in a partnership with the Mestons. Parker was president and then general manager until 1920. Emerson started as a producer of fractional horsepower alternating current motors, but by the 1920s, with almost twenty-five hundred employees, it was "one of the largest manufacturing plants making electric fans in the U.S." Fans remained its most important consumer product line until World War II. Emerson remained in St. Louis's downtown manufacturing corridor, in the area around its main plant facility.[5]

Two former Wagner and Emerson managers who patented repulsion type motors, a major innovation used to power small factories, founded Century Electric in 1902. Century's engineers developed innovations in smaller-size direct current motors that facilitated the initial development of many household appliances. The company also had a line of ceiling fans by 1911 and the first successful automatic electric refrigerator motors in the 1920s. Along with Wagner, it produced motors built to specification for factories, from St. Louis to China. After 1914, the company operated out of several multistory facilities in the vicinity of 19th and Pine in the downtown business corridor, a short walk from Emerson's main plant. Its workforce reached more than two thousand in the late 1920s.[6]

The experience of these three companies illustrates that despite the ongoing consolidation of the industry and the huge research laboratories of GE and Westinghouse, smaller companies and entrepreneurs could carve out a role in the electrical industry. Several small-niche electrical and machine producers grew in the diverse St. Louis economy. Moloney Electric by the 1920s employed more than fifteen hundred workers to produce transformers, but others, such as Superior Electric and Baldor Electric, employed one hundred or fewer workers. Some speculated that GE and Westinghouse allowed such companies to survive because they served a useful purpose—an excuse to keep workers' wages lower. By the late 1920s, there evolved a gentlemen's agreement: as long as the smaller companies did not compete on price—that is, undercut the price of the products that competed with GE and Westinghouse—their existence would not be contested. The larger independents even had an international trade, as St. Louis businessmen pushed to create markets, especially in Latin America, for their surplus products. Emerson and Century ceiling fans graced the dining halls and offices of many Latin American cities.[7]

At the turn of the century, metal trades employers such as the electrical manufacturers depended on skilled workers, many of them members of craft unions who had won some control over their trade; the skilled workers lodge of the International Association of Machinists (IAM) claimed to have organized 98 percent of the trade by 1900. Many smaller companies simply conceded to the various metal trades' union shop rules (such as restrictions on operating more than one machine at a time and insistence on union control over the payment plan) and hired from the craft union's ranks under its apprenticeship rules, which limited the supply of skilled workers and thus the flexibility of the companies to utilize the labor market at will. Emerson refused to recognize the union, but its "policy was to pay [the] current scale" of the crafts. Wagner Electric placed itself out front in the battle against these restrictions; in 1898 it withstood a boycott by several crafts unions over the company's refusal to abide by union shop rules. As a result, it found its supply of skilled labor limited.[8]

St. Louis electrical independents developed control over the labor market through the Metal Trades Association (MTA) of St. Louis. Wagner Electric managers were the main organizers of the MTA and remained the driving force until the 1920s. F. C. Schwedtman, Wagner's general superintendent, headed the MTA from 1899 until 1913, when Waldo Layman, Wagner's new president, succeeded him. The MTA was affiliated with the National Metal Trades Association (NMTA), which Layman led as president from 1913 to 1914.[9]

In 1904, the MTA began the open shop drive in the local metal trades industry. By the 1920s, they won the contest. The open shop drive, a response to developments within the local labor movement, reached beyond shop floor control issues and was made in concert with employers outside the metal trades. To understand the MTA perspective, we need to look at the broad challenge that the St. Louis labor movement posed to business during this period. To the local leaders of the MTA, the workers' movement had radical implications that could only be met by a grand collective local drive for control.

St. Louis Labor's Challenge to Business Control

In the years between the turn of the century and World War I, the St. Louis labor movement seemed poised to transcend the organizational limitations of the American Federation of Labor (AFL), to be more reflective of the entire working-class community, and to present a broad challenge to business at the community level. The ascendancy of the AFL, organized around craft-based unionism, was counterbalanced by networks of activists, many of them socialists, who continued to agitate to reshape the AFL at the local level. Some of these activists had experienced the tumult of the 1877 general strike, when workers had organized effectively, if momentarily, on a community basis. Many activists also carried the perspective of the Knights of Labor into the AFL. Organized on an inclusive, community-wide basis, the Knights of Labor saw themselves as much an egalitarian citizens' reform effort as a workplace-based organization. Systematic repression organized by employers' associations spelled decline for the Knights of Labor and brought about the AFL, organized with more limited goals of craft unionism.[10] But the most influential unions over the next generation in the local St. Louis Central Trades and Labor Union (CTLU), the citywide central body of the AFL unions, were those that originated with the Knights of Labor and carried forward some of its ideals. One, the Brewery Workers Union (BWU), became the largest and strongest local union in St. Louis. Its members and leaders included many Socialists, and it was the most influential local advocate of industrial unionism, that is, organizing all workers within the industry, not just the crafts.[11] Strong links between labor and radicals also advocated powerfully for inclusivity in an organizational apparatus founded on exclusivity. The German immigrant community provided the main base for leftist politics and unionism.[12] Socialists were influential in St. Louis trade unions, and some were leaders of the CTLU, advocating a form of industrial unionism within the AFL's structure. The BWU modeled such an industrial unionism structure in the local breweries by 1910 after engaging in jurisdictional battles with local and national unions.[13]

The Federated Metal Trades Council of St. Louis and Vicinity (FMTC) represented another model, the attempt to bring together craft unions in order to set up shop committees to bargain with employers across crafts and to include the unskilled. St. Louis had been the headquarters of radical anarchist metal trades unionism in 1886.[14] The International Progressive Machinists' Union, which split with the IAM when the IAM set up a color bar, continued to agitate in St. Louis in the 1890s, and though it folded after originally being part of the FMTC, its effects were still felt into the early 1900s. In 1900, the FMTC offices were not only union headquarters but also a center of activity for socialists and anarcho-syndicalists who debated strategies for achieving social justice. Workers entering there might just as well encounter a Socialist meeting as a union meeting. Activists had begun encouraging a movement to organize less-skilled workers and to include them within the FMTC. The Amalgamated Metal Mechanics, a union of unskilled and semiskilled workers, was booming, and the Foundry Workers International Union, led by Socialist George Bechtold, set up offices in the FMTC building to recruit unskilled foundry laborers, including black workers. (The workforce of the electrical companies was almost exclusively white, so such developments profoundly countered the exclusive tendencies of AFL unions such as the IAM, which was the main union in the electrical and metal trades industry.) By 1900, shop committees composed of workers from the different trades were functioning in many St. Louis metal trades shops. These shop committees sought to address the kinds of conditions that shocked observers such as Frank O'Hare, whose commitment to socialism grew when he encountered St. Louis metal trades workers in 1901: "To say I was appalled is putting it mildly. I never knew before how and under what conditions the working people of St. Louis worked," where even unionized metal polishers died from inhaling dust and those without unions were fodder for a gristmill of unsafe conditions and poverty.[15] As these men gathered in this milieu, they sparked the idea of a community-based drive to contest the boundaries of the labor market.

In March 1900, the FMTC issued a call to workers in the electrical and metal trades of St. Louis to launch a local drive for a minimum wage and a nine-hour workday. A circular signed by representatives of machinists, brass workers, pattern makers, molders, and core workers argued that the limits to craft organization were being revealed, given the "tendency of modern methods to specialize all trades and tradesmen," to the extent that the "'all around' mechanic is fast disappearing." They argued that it was actually ironic and supremely unjust that employers paid the "specialist" (less-skilled worker) less than the "all-around mechanic" on the grounds that "the specialist is not worth as much as the 'all around' man," when, in fact, "measured by his product" and the "steadier work" he performed, the specialist is "worth more than the average 'all around' man." The employers only paid the all-around mechanic more, the circular asserted, to "arouse craft pride, and prevent a combination of both for their mutual bene- fit." The activists viewed the craft unions' attempt to organize only the skilled worker as narrow-minded. Noting the local arena of struggle, the appeal urged expanding bonds of solidarity as the basis for broader efforts at control of the labor market, even on the national level. A fight for the minimum wage and a shorter workday in a concerted local drive and in other large cities could open the way for a broader national movement.[16] At the bottom of the circular there was a ballot for workers to vote to join the movement. The ballot was to be returned to the shop committees, operating in defiance of traditional national craft union structures where lines of authority descended from national unions.

The call was indeed adopted by a vote of workers in shop committees and crystallized a moment of possibility and direction within the context of local developments in the St. Louis labor movement as well as nationally. St. Louis workers had been inspired by the call of Chicago metal trades workers for the nine-hour workday, a movement that sparked a national campaign. But the cir- cular was first and foremost the product of the careful development of local sol- idarities. It was not a coincidence that the circular was issued in the midst of a community-wide drive in support of streetcar workers, whose strike polarized the entire city along class lines and whose target was the key political power in the city.[17] For radicals in the FMTC, it was natural to draw a link between wages and hours and the broader power struggle.[18]

In March 1900 industry leaders in the NMTA and top officials of the IAM attempted to settle this local ferment by agreeing to uniform national limits on hours of work. But when the St. Louis employers of the NMTA refused to agree to St. Louis machinists' demand to raise their wages to compensate for the reduction in hours and objected to their demand that the NMTA negotiate with shop committees, that agreement began to unravel. This marked a turning point in the NMTA strategy. The NMTA refused to arbitrate the issue at the national level; thereafter, they insisted on the local determination of wages and other conditions, for St. Louis as well as other cities.[19]

In the following years, electrical and machine manufacturers consciously constructed their own community-based antilabor campaigns, despite the steady development of national markets and the increasingly oligopolistic char- acter of the industry. The NMTA served mainly as a clearinghouse for those locally developed strategies. In 1910 the NMTA helped defeat a strike in Lynn, Massachusetts, and noted that "if the strike had been lost at Lynn, it would have meant the presentation of like unreasonable demands the next week, probably in Boston, and the week after in Fitchburg, and finally all over the country." Large companies, some members complained, recognized how they benefited from these local battles but avoided identification with them in order to escape negative publicity, while the small- and medium-sized companies were on the front lines.[20]

The St. Louis Metal Trades Employers and the Open Shop Drive

In order to gain control of the labor market in a diverse industrial base such as St. Louis, the "militant minority" of metal trades employers, who orchestrated the antiunion drive, allied with other local employers. They found key allies among leading businessmen who shared their perspective on St. Louis's role in the expanding capitalist system. These men viewed themselves as civic leaders determined to keep control of the local labor market. Key developments contributed to their shared perspectives. First, St. Louis's diverse economy and geographical location nurtured "independents" in other industries, such as important chemical, steel, and auto companies, that were primarily single-plant operations. These companies tended to rely on lower wages in order to compete with the larger or dominant firms in their industries or attract capital to the area. St. Louis's multiplant shoe companies established dominance of the market over eastern shoe companies through a relentless drive for cheap labor that led them to reliance on child labor and, beginning in the 1910s, decentralization of their plants to impoverished rural towns that guaranteed union-free conditions. Lower wages to win the market from eastern capital was the key to the growth of the local garment and hat industry as well.[21] Second, St. Louis employers felt that they were at a disadvantage because the city did not have a low-wage labor supply of new immigrants to the extent that other cities did. By the second decade of the twentieth century, St. Louis had one of the lowest immigrant populations among industrial cities. Third, St. Louis capitalists confronted higher railroad freight rates for shipments west of the Mississippi. This drew large-scale multiplant industry financed by eastern capital to the Illinois side of the river. For this reason St. Louis businessmen continually argued, in a perverse boosterist fashion, that lower wages were compensation for higher freight rates. Fourth, despite many differences separating them on issues, leading St. Louis capitalists shared a vision of growth for St. Louis that linked control of civic affairs and the labor market with market dominance of their southern economic periphery and the foreign trade market in Latin America. This worldview promoted the interdependence of low local wages for unskilled workers, the utilization of labor from the southern geographical periphery, the drive to compete with or transfer capital from the East, and imperialist exploitation.[22]

Within this broad context, a key group of businessmen and capitalists acted as a militant minority, giving leadership to other employers for effective community-based labor strategies. Wagner's managers were prominent in the campaign, no doubt acting on behalf of their capital interests. The group initially gathered to lay plans for labor strategies during the World's Fair. Then the 1900 streetcar strike struck the tinderbox of political, ethnic, and class tensions. Socialists in the labor movement had initiated that organizing drive not only to help the much-abused streetcar workers but also to contest the center of elite power in the city, which had facilitated a monopoly for the company, and to spark a mass organizing drive among workers in the city. All recognized the implications of the streetcar strike. The strike revealed the unions' spatial base of power in the community, as working-class neighborhoods effectively shut down the lines. Although the strike was eventually lost, it inaugurated a period in which St. Louis labor remained at the center of the antimonopoly campaigns, the most important opposition movement to business in the Progressive Era. During the strike, the business elite formed a posse comitatus, an exhibition of their determination to protect property rights. Understanding that the labor movement was a threat beyond the workplace, they viewed control of the urban labor market as linked to larger issues of political and cultural power. The strength of the working-class community as demonstrated in the 1900 streetcar strike inclined employers to tread carefully. Over the next two decades, business attempted to meld civic interests with business interests. The local MTA negotiated generous agreements that satisfied the craft unions, thereby undermining the more radical strategies of the FMTC. But with the conclusion of the World's Fair, these employers aimed to reestablish the open shop.[23]

These "World's Fair bargainers" eventually formed the Citizens' Industrial Alliance (CIA), an organization that sought to give ideological and strategic leverage to employers' community-based campaigns and targeted especially labor strategies based on local solidarities such as the boycott. The national organization was originally named the National Industrial Association. The St. Louis affiliate used the appellation "Citizens," which the national organization then appropriated, in shameless reference to the famous Populist campaigns of the previous era, but also because it was a relentless local campaign that the national organization promoted. James W. Van Cleave, a stove manufacturer and founder of the national CIA, which fostered other city-based organizations, coordinated the St. Louis branch.[24] St. Louis MTA employers helped to organize and coordinate the CIA, both locally and nationally. F. C. Schwedtman of Wagner Electric was known as Van Cleave's "right hand"; in 1910 Schwedtman became president of the local association and was a national CIA leader and the National Association of Manufacturers' leader as well.[25]

In 1904 the St. Louis CIA initiated its open shop drive, in coordination with the MTA and other local business groups such as the shoe and garment employers' organizations. The MTA refused to meet with craft unions to negotiate agreements for 1905 and instead announced that it would operate only under a new set of shop rules—no restrictions on output, no limits on apprentices, and no union control over the type of wage payment plan. Machinists responded righteously: "They do not consult their employees, nor stop to consider whether it is right or wrong, but acting on" the belief "that the Lord in His infinite wisdom gave to the employers the right to lay down laws, rules and conditions and fix prices under which honest men should toil, adopt a set of shop rules and tell us to accept them, whether we like them or not."[26] Workers bitterly recognized "the hand of Mr. Ferdinand Schwedtman," who, they charged, aimed "to force all other employers to be as unfair to their employees as he is to his." The "men and women who have sacrificed their positions to make this world a better place to live in" were all threatened by the CIA's designs. The machinists promised a fight and even threatened a general strike but reneged when it was evident that they were not organized strongly enough.[27]

The diminished role of the workers' FMTC lent an advantage to the employers. The FMTC's radical goals had succumbed to the AFL crafts' success during the honeymoon period of World's Fair. The FMTC came increasingly into conflict with the national officers of craft unions, who compelled the locals to secure approval for strike votes, thereby preventing sympathy strikes based on local solidarities and undermining the means to respond in kind to the locally driven strategies of the NMTA. Polarization between the FMTC leadership and the craft unions became more apparent by 1905, when the FMTC elected a member of the Industrial Workers of the World (IWW), the radical rival to the AFL, as treasurer. In reaction, local machinists—the largest trade union—withdrew from the FMTC, and the FMTC soon withered away.[28]

From 1904 to 1920, the CIA and the local NMTA coordinated the policies of local industries toward labor, employing a diverse array of strategies. They used blacklists and spied on their employees to weed out union agitators. They established Ranken Technical, a training school, to replace the apprenticeship programs of craft unions; established employment bureaus to screen union advocates and to serve as an alternative to the crafts clearinghouse for skilled and semiskilled workers; and secured police and judicial cooperation in strikes. The CIA's legal department provided a critical support service in regard to injunctions and prosecutions of strikers. They also fought a legal and political battle to constrain unions' use of the boycott. The crowning victory of this campaign was the *Buck's Stove and Range* case, a landmark employers' judicial victory that essentially outlawed the boycott.[29] Through these efforts, St. Louis employers won political and legal battles that constricted workers' leverage in the urban labor market.

Over time, the CIA and the NMTA grew more sophisticated in their approach to labor issues and focused on enlisting public support for business objectives. The CIA hosted a series of lectures and civic events meant to remove the negative publicity surrounding its strategies. Gradually, the CIA put a progressive veneer on its organization, gathering ministers and priests and even N. O. Nelson, one of the nation's foremost proponents of profit sharing, as a way to prevent unionization. At the same time, employing what Michael Rogin has called

the American "countersubversive tradition," the CIA waged a full-fledged propaganda campaign to label unions as the base of foreign ideas that would destroy
the community. It worked to define unions as impediments to civic progress,
to negate any sympathies between the middle class and workers, and to paint
labor as violent and needlessly disruptive of the urban order. It argued that the
association between labor and socialism had chaotic consequences for capital
accumulation in the urban context, in that the quest for higher wages would
destroy the special advantages for capital investment in the city and cause that
investment to be placed on the east side of the Mississippi instead of the west.
Throughout this time, the organization continued to employ its repressive
repertoire of strategies.[30]

In 1907, machinists, shoe workers, and other workers who had experienced
the CIA's assault countered the CIA campaign with a series of strikes. For the
metal industry, the IAM demanded the reestablishment of its wage scale and
shop rules. Radicals sought to organize a general strike but were foiled by
the trades' rules. The machinists secured agreements at some companies, and
others accepted the wage scale but refused to recognize the shop committees.
The key MTA firms held out successfully against the IAM drive, using spies,
"gun squads," and imported scabs. Wagner stood firm as the bastion of the open
shop.[31]

Wagner: Shop Floor and Labor Market Control

Victory in these battles enabled the leading NMTA and CIA firms to wield more
control over the shop floor and to more effectively utilize the regional labor
market.[32] Wagner boasted that its policy "encourage[s] speed, and slow men are
discharged at the option of the foremen." Managers implemented payment systems of their choice, including "hourly rate, premium system, piece work, contract, or such other system as we may devise in each individual case." Production
manager C. B. Lord's hated slide rule was used to institute a premium piecework
system that managers touted as "scientific" as Wagner speeded up production.
Wagner's premium system encouraged speed by paying workers a low base rate
and then half of any amount workers produced over the standard.[33] De-skilling
was coupled to a policy of hiring only workers from the "countryside between 16
and 22 years old" and avoiding hiring native St. Louisans, who Wagner felt were
too heavily influenced by local "radical" union culture. Management proclaimed St. Louis "an excellent market for intelligent, green help from Arkansas,
Tennessee, Oklahoma, Kansas, Iowa, Texas, Southern Illinois, as well as the more
western states. They are trained readily, are subject to discipline, and [are] loyal
Americans."[34] De-skilling also gave them access to a labor market of young
women: "We consider girls superior to boys but inferior to men, and cheaper
than either," Lord proclaimed. By 1917, almost five hundred women (one-fifth of

the production workforce) worked as timekeepers or punch press operators or in small arms war production.[35]

Using the interdependent levers of de-skilling operations and the utilization of the surplus labor market, by World War I Wagner had helped to establish a lower community wage standard in the St. Louis area. The community wage was the counterpart to, and significantly lower than, what craft unions referred to as the prevailing rate, a wage rate that, in fact, was a goal rather than the actual norm. The premium wage system favored by Wagner management and all MTA firms theoretically held out promise of limitless pay advances if workers produced more than a management-determined standard. But in fact, workers learned that if they worked harder and thereby produced more, the job would be retimed to reduce overall wages to the going rate in the area. In an article explaining personnel methods of the company in 1917, C. B. Lord acknowledged this, too: "As to wages, local conditions must control."[36]

Wagner's experiments with welfare programs were linked to their desire to create a positive public image and utilize the labor market. Its programs rivaled those of GE and Westinghouse. Extensive recreation and sports programs were used to attract young workers, especially boys interested in extending high school sports experience. Young girls also had exclusive access to a resort along the Meremac River. Wagner touted its Employees Mutual Benefit Association, a sick and death benefit program established in 1910, as an alternative to unionism. The company justified the "considerable expense" on the grounds that the programs attracted workers to the company, especially younger workers.[37] It is clear that in the local context, workplace welfare programs were a response to labor's challenge to the local political order as well as to internal plant order. It is significant that the only local company with more extensive programs than Wagner's was the streetcar company, which endured political and union challenges throughout the Progressive Era.[38]

Wagner's welfare programs did little to reduce complaints about low pay (thirteen cents an hour base rate for women, twenty-two cents for men), speedup, and long hours (fifty-four-hour weeks). Workers described Wagner as a "penitentiary" rather than the model factory the company's managers portrayed. Recurrent evidence of rebellion among workers was centered on departments most subject to speedup and reduced wages. Several walkouts occurred in 1916, led by young boys in the motor winding department. Wagner fired and blacklisted the strikers and hired more spies. In 1917, the company attracted "captive" workers by using its influence to exempt their workers from the draft. Conversely, "troublemakers" found themselves high on the draft list.[39]

Wagner and the MTA pressured other electrical and metal trades employers to maintain labor market control. Wagner became one of the key St. Louis "war babies," securing lucrative war contracts that resulted in a 200 percent increase in profits in 1917. With its financial ties and its ability to distribute subcontracts during World War I, the MTA figures were indeed powerful, particularly as World War I brought a tight labor market. For example, in the face of a local drive for the eight-hour day led by the machinists in 1916, the MTA warned smaller firms to resist workers' demands. George Fritz of Fritz Foundry came to an IAM union meeting to plead that if he agreed to the eight-hour demand at his plant, the MTA would "ruin him."[40] When Century Electric's workforce walked out of the plant in support of the eight-hour-day drive in 1916, the company easily secured injunctions and imported workers from "the countryside," including substantial numbers of women and a small number of black workers. Century management stood outside the plant gates and directed the police in mass arrests by pointing out leading "agitators." The police openly recruited strikebreakers for the company.[41] Despite rising profits and the tighter labor market, workers' wages held to the employers' wage standard. With rising wartime inflation, workers' buying power decreased rapidly. Anger over such inequities percolated in the working-class community. Yet Wagner's management remained confident: "The probable war conditions are not troubling us," C. B. Lord wrote in September 1917.[42]

World War Upheaval and Defeat

Yet within six months of Lord's statement, Wagner workers were at the center of another upheaval. The catalyst was another streetcar workers' strike, in February 1918. Like the 1900 strike, it gathered tremendous working-class community support. Fearing the collapse of wartime production without adequate worker transportation, leading capitalists, even the most fervent defenders of the open shop, pressured the United Railways Company to recognize the union.[43] St. Louis workers regarded recognition of the streetcar workers' union as a siren call to organize. Enthusiastically they joined the CTLU's drive to organize "100 percent of St. Louis workers." A strike wave began at the end of February when five thousand department store clerks walked out, escalating until more than thirty thousand St. Louis workers were on strike, and made St. Louis one of the most turbulent cities as far as strikes were concerned.[44] Unskilled workers, women, African Americans, and others long outside labor's ranks joined and, in some cases, led the movement. The strikes were widely interpreted as a community uprising as well as a workplace-based organizing drive. "There is a serious situation here in the industrial world," mediator W. H. Rodgers alerted his Department of Labor superiors.[45] The *St. Louis Labor* newspaper, on the other hand, declared sanguinely, "St. Louis is in the midst of an industrial war—the biggest and most serious since the memorable days of [the] 1877 [general strike]."[46]

Observers agreed that the Wagner Electric strike was the central conflict of that upheaval, in large part because of Wagner's leadership of the MTA and the CIA. Unionists claimed that St. Louis workers and the entire southwestern labor movement were carefully watching its outcome. The strike tested the leanings toward inclusivity that had grown in the prewar period. One signal of this was that it was women workers at Wagner who led the parade of strikers who gathered outside the plant, "waving flags and blowing horns" in a spirited display of unity.[47] Although metal trades workers never reestablished the FMTC that focused on building local solidarities in the way the earlier organization had done, the influence of radical ideas and industrial unionism continued to foster this inclination. A new Metal Trades Council, an attempt to coordinate actions, was established by the AFL and began to act cooperatively in the prewar period. The IAM had made changes in response to the IWW's challenges even while denouncing it. A strong chapter of the Women's Trade Union League and the unifying effect of a local campaign for the eight-hour day fostered solidarity. In 1916, the IAM organizer declared, "We hold that woman shall have the same rights as man, industrially, politically, and socially." The Machinists union lowered dues to attract unskilled workers, including women. This impulse was more limited in respect to black workers. The East St. Louis Race Riots of 1917 indicated how easily race could divide workers. St. Louis socialist-influenced unions made extraordinarily limited overtures to blacks who came across the river in the riot aftermath, mainly seeking to blame employers and police indifference for the tragedy. This seemed to reinforce the interpretation that black workers were merely employer pawns rather than potential comrades. Nevertheless, the shop committee system was reestablished, briefly flourishing during the war period, to foster cooperation between trades and even the unorganized to bargain together as a unit. In at least one steel plant, a black worker led the shop committee. Beginning in 1915, the machinists' and electricians' unions, the most keenly affected by these influences, agreed to launch a joint campaign to organize all the workers in the electrical plants. Their main target was Wagner. The Wagner walkout became a test of whether the AFL could effectively unite workers within the community to contest leading capitalists' power.[48]

Wagner workers demanded union recognition, an eight-hour day, wages based on a "union standard," the end to premium piecework, and disbanding of the Mutual Aid Society.[49] Management especially denounced the call for "union" wages, contending that "the prevailing scale is the open market price for labor."[50] Union officers countered that the government boards were bound to ratify union wage standards.[51] The War Labor Policy Board had earlier declared that "in fixing wages, hours and conditions of labor, regard should always be had to the labor standards, wage scales and other conditions, prevailing in the localities affected." The contracts the government had awarded to Wagner and the other war industries specified an eight-hour day and called for the prevailing rate of wages.[52]

Expectations of justice were soon dashed. The Ordnance Department representative sent in to mediate the dispute persuaded workers to return to work and then orchestrated a campaign to paint the strikers as unpatriotic while sanctioning business's wage and shop floor practices as the prevailing community standard. (The mediator by 1919 became vice president of the St. Louis Employers Association, the successor to the CIA.)[53] Workers found a more sympathetic ear at the National War Labor Board (NWLB); however, all but one St. Louis employer refused to appear before the board. The NWLB concluded that there was a "conspiracy" orchestrated by Wagner Electric management "to prevent the National War Labor Board from functioning." One NWLB official declared that the "intransigence" of St. Louis business, determined to retain its low-wage status, was among the worst in the nation.[54] In the end, only one strike of the entire St. Louis NWLB caseload was settled in favor of the workers; the other cases were dismissed without ruling because employers refused to appear. Strikers concluded that the NWLB "can't do nothing for them and won't do nothing for them."[55]

The 1918 uprising anticipated the decisive battles between labor and capital that occurred in St. Louis and across the United States from 1919 to 1922. In September 1919, a Department of Labor mediator observed that St. Louis employers, still operating through a solid united front, were "defiant," "arbitrary," and "generally favorable to controversies." The postwar Depression gave employers enviable leverage. Local employers took up with enthusiasm the "American Plan" that portrayed unions as "anti-American," a plan that simply expanded upon the CIA's earlier ideological campaigns. The CTLU put up a valiant fight against the open shop campaigns in printing and railroads, the established unions in St. Louis survived, but dreams of "100 percent unionism" and real contests for power that had escalated during the war period gradually faded.[56]

The postwar years took a heavy toll on the Left's influence in the labor movement, affecting the conceptualization of the union movement as a contest for local power. The decline of the Left as a vital factor in the local labor movement was, of course, related to national and international developments. The Bolshevik Revolution and the domestic anticommunism that followed cannot be underestimated. Factional battles between Socialists and Communists contributed to the declining influence of both groups in the local AFL, although the Communist Party (CP) remained numerically insignificant in St. Louis. Throughout the 1920s, many of the old Socialists in St. Louis labor declared any chance for the socialist project over. In the 1920s, the kind of linkages between radical groups and labor that had been such an integral component of the local labor movement faded into memory.[57] As a new working class drawn from St. Louis's rural and southern periphery emerged, the connections between labor and the leftist community that had been based in the German immigrant working class, a vital part of St. Louis labor before the war, were lost. In 1927, Gottlieb Hoehn, a member of the German labor Left, remarked that there was a palpable "tired feeling" in the central body: "[T]he regular monthly meetings of the Central Trades and Labor

Union are gatherings of the Old Guard. It is indeed surprising to observe the absolute absence of the younger generation. Out of about 200 delegates you hardly find three men or women below thirty years of age.... Lively debates and prolonged deep discussions are as rare as banana trees in Arctic regions."[58] Unions with leftist influence and oriented toward industrial unionism declined further in the 1920s economy. With Prohibition, brewery workers lost the leading role in the St. Louis CTLU. On the other hand, the conservative building trades maintained a more stable membership due to the building boom of the 1920s. Moreover, national unions and the AFL conclusively reasserted control over both local unions and the city central bodies in the 1920s.[59]

It is within this context that the IAM abandoned its two-decades-long drive to organize the leading MTA firms, surrendered any notion of broadly addressing the political economy of control, and embraced antiradicalism and racism. William Fitzmaurice, the head of IAM District 9, is representative of that transformation. He began the decade as a major force in the local Conference for Progressive Political Action (CPPA) campaign to build a labor party and ran on the American Labor Party ticket in 1922. He joined the Trades Union Educational League (TUEL), which originated in St. Louis as an organization to fight the employers' open shop campaigns of the early 1920s, and developed community-based union campaigns in the printers and railroad strikes of the early 1920s. The group organized on a ward-by-ward basis for political activity and included members and their wives in strategic boycotts.[60] Fitzmaurice was also part of a pressure group in District 9 that continued to coax the international to organize on an industrial basis and to lower dues for unskilled workers. The significant defeats of the early 1920s, factional battles over the CPPA, the disastrous decisions of the CP that demonstrated Soviet Union control over the organization, and hyperpatriotism led him and others toward antipathy to radicalism. As the hopes of the early 1920s faded, Fitzmaurice and other Catholic influentials in the TUEL such as Mary Ryder of the Printers Union (the TUEL's dynamo), and O. E. Jennings, the International Brotherhood of Electrical Workers representative who had enthusiastically endorsed the organization of women at Wagner, veered toward the more conservative trade unionism represented by the renamed Trades Union Promotional League, which descended into mere promotion of local charity works and buying union label goods. Ryder declared that unions would bring about the "consumer commonwealth," not the "socialist cooperative commonwealth."[61] The 1920s construction boom led Fitzmaurice to narrow business unionism; skilled, loyal, white card-carrying union members could secure jobs in construction and machine shops only through him. Fitzmaurice focused on jurisdictional disputes with other construction trades rather than organizing the unskilled to contest for power. He built a prominent place for himself in the CTLU after he abandoned the labor party idea. His vituperative antiradicalism eclipsed the voices of socialists in the local body. By the early

1930s, Fitzmaurice, now a Republican, was elected president of the CTLU, conclusively signaling the end of the earlier era.[62]

While in the early part of the century electrical and metal workers were part of a radical milieu and workers' culture that manifested itself prominently in workers' institutions, the new working class that entered the electrical manufacturing plants confronted the political economy of control in isolation from radical influences. In other parts of the country, radicals quietly remained in the industry. In St. Louis, both the union and the companies continued to purge radicals and "troublemakers."[63]

Electrical Workers in the New Era

Electrical manufacturers benefited considerably from the labor market they had helped to forge even as they were eclipsed by the eastern-based oligopoly in the postwar era. Wagner had anticipated expansion and growth but instead found itself in a serious financial crisis. It never reached wartime employment levels again until World War II, and only through contracts with auto companies for brakes and starters in the mid-1920s did the number of employees reach prewar levels. Emerson and Century also experienced financial crises after the war. Emerson's difficulties began when it raised capital for expansion in 1919 and then could not fulfill its obligations during the postwar period, and Century's goals of foreign expansion ran head-on against global contraction. St. Louis companies acquiesced in the larger companies' command of the national market but through the National Electrical Manufacturers Association (established in 1926 with the support of the St. Louis independents) sought a certain portion of the national market for themselves. They made a gentlemen's agreement that allowed the independents and niche producers to remain in the market, as long as the price for products was determined by the large companies, which aimed to stabilize the industry as well as to ensure their control. Through this stabilizing factor, the local electrical industry kept pace with the accelerated national growth rate of the electrical industry in the 1920s. By 1930, it was St. Louis's second largest manufacturing industry (after automobiles, which rose quickly as St. Louis became an assembly center).[64]

The St. Louis independents' workforce was mostly white men, although Wagner Electric hired a substantially larger number of women and black men. Women made up one-fourth of Wagner's labor force during the 1920s, and management encouraged marriage between employees. Wagner sometimes employed entire families and financed housing for them. Some workers remarked that the entire family had to work to survive on Wagner's low wages. Wagner Electric also hired African American men during and after World War I, especially in their foundry divisions and as laborers, increasing their numbers to roughly 10 percent of the company's workforce. Century Electric kept many of the women the company had hired during the 1916 strike and augmented their numbers slightly during the 1920s, but less than one-quarter of the production workforce were women. In 1929 Century Electric established a separate foundry facility on Spring and Grand avenues and hired more than 150 black workers for that plant. Emerson Electric, on the other hand, employed only a few women in production until the mid-1930s, but men's wages on jobs that women held at Wagner and Century paid substantially less. Other smaller companies such as Maloney and Superior hired men almost exclusively. All plants continued to place a strict prohibition on hiring African American women.[65]

As St. Louis became more integrated into the national and international economy, businesses such as the electrical manufacturers considered the city's lower community wage an essential asset. The agricultural and mining depressions of the 1920s brought a flow of young rural migrants to the city. The "rural districts [supply] a constant flow of the hard-working classes," boasted a Chamber of Commerce advertisement.[66] Business boosters touted St. Louis's "southern" characteristic of cheap unskilled labor but also advertised flexible skilled labor that some southern cities lacked. The Chamber of Commerce promised that "starting rates for beginners, both male and female, are . . . lower than in other large industrial centers. . . . Common labor rates here are slightly higher than those farther south, attracting to this district the more ambitious and intelligent class of workers."[67] Census bureau statistics confirm these impressionistic statements. St. Louis wages averaged thirteenth out of the largest fifteen industrial areas but were third among these industrial areas in the ratio of value added by manufacture to average wages. Taken together, these statistics indicate that among large industrial cities, St. Louis was one of the most exploitative.[68]

In terms of the labor market and the political economy of control, there developed a certain mutuality of interest between local and national capitalist goals. During the postwar Depression, business successfully enlisted city funds to advertise and promote St. Louis "as an economic point of fabrication and distribution" of hemispheric trade. The courting of national corporations was advocated not only to promote St. Louis's economic growth but also as part of a strategy to diversify local industry in order to act as a "ballast" against labor unrest. The independents relied on a production workforce that was highly flexible, using the labor market as a reservoir from which to accommodate a more erratic production schedule than Westinghouse's or GE's. For their part, national firms such as GE and Westinghouse, which established small divisions in St. Louis during the 1920s, paid the community wage and followed local wage practices rather than setting them. To the independents, low wages and speedup remained the key to competing with the larger firms; they relied on this more than on larger scale or systematized production for their profit margins. During the 1920s, despite their varying fortunes and competition between each other on certain product lines, the independents united behind the "going wage rate in the community."[69] Workers in the St. Louis electrical industry were among the lowest-paid industrial workers in the country. It was common for women electrical workers to earn fifteen dollars or less per week. To Frank Abfall, who earned ten dollars for a forty-eight-hour week in 1926 at Emerson, there was not much difference between Emerson and the sweatshop garment factories located nearby. Abfall, studying a 1929 picture of his coworkers in the field winding department, pointed to four people with physical handicaps in order to illustrate his point that "people who did stay had to stay for one reason or another." Abfall's small income along with his widowed mother's wages as a washerwoman and his sister's weekly pay of two to three dollars for housekeeping allowed them to eke out a living, but years later he remembered the painful hardships they endured. Margaret Entrikin, a Wagner Electric worker who had started work there at age fifteen in 1918, echoed Abfall. To work at the electrical plants "you had to be the type who would have to work or not eat." But in explaining why she and others stayed, she added that "there wasn't very many places to go and they all paid just about the same."[70] Low pay rates thus seemed more immutable because they were, if not universal, preponderant in the community. Charlie Slezak recalled that he stayed at Emerson because "working conditions especially in factories was rough all over," even in the 1920s. St. Louis manufacturing unemployment remained high until 1924 declined briefly, but started to increase again in 1927. Scores of people waited outside of factories for jobs in the late 1920s as the unemployment rate climbed even before the Great Depression.[71]

St. Louis's labor market structure and electrical companies practices provide a clear basis for David Montgomery's argument that "the relative stability of employment" for skilled workers during the 1920s "was possible only because of the flexibility provided by this unskilled force in meeting the unstable demands of the market." Census data indicate that skilled workers' average pay was close to that of other industrial cities, unlike the case with unskilled workers.[72]

All three companies structured their policies to build loyalty among core groups of workers, especially skilled and selected semiskilled workers. Those who were cultivated for loyalty were promised the benefit of steady employment, a type of seniority system (though still based on the foreman's sometimes arbitrary oversight), and a week's vacation with pay. The companies hired young temporary workers for peak production periods and selected from that group to promote to more steady employment. Century Electric claimed a workforce of two thousand; actually it hired three thousand workers during peak production, and most of its fifteen hundred steady employees experienced regular layoffs and a precarious employment situation.[73] In 1923, when Roy Hoffman was hired at Emerson during the seasonal upswing, his foreman warned him that the company filled its "regular" positions with those workers who had the "best work habits." "Once you were twenty years old," Hoffman attested, "and had demonstrated that you could control your habits and cooperated with the foreman in terms of production," there was more steady employment.[74]

Emerson used a complicated system of employee levels to determine pay rates and other policies. Frank Abfall remembered that about ten coworkers were in Group One; these workers were almost never laid off and got the highest pay. A larger number were in Group Two, which got less pay. Group Three had the largest and lowest-paid group of workers. "When they were real busy," Abfall said, he was transferred from Group Three to Group Two but then would be moved back when work was slack. Group Three workers were laid off more often, while Group One workers were shifted around to lower skilled positions when work was slack, but at Group One pay.

Layoffs were the ideal time for foremen to reduce the number of "troublemakers." Foremen kept the grade system secret, though it determined which people were recalled from layoff; shifted people from group to group when work was slack; and selected people to be placed in the higher groups. Grades were not necessarily demarcated according to skill; many people in Group Two, for instance, were doing the same work as those in Group One.[75] Workers were often frustrated to know that the person next to them, doing the same work, might get a higher base rate or that the complex system gave them an unpredictable job rate. Abfall later discovered that his foreman had two books, "one for the guys he liked and one for those he didn't," and used it to recall and lay off selectively. According to Charles Slezak, who was hired in 1918, the foremen were the "absolute masters." The practice of cultivating a portion of loyal workers who received steady employment and favorable treatment while relying on a steady influx of new workers who had to prove themselves or who considered their stay as temporary made practices based on solidarity difficult.[76]

Low pay and few opportunities made the tendency to "self-exploit ourselves" more difficult to control. At Emerson, the company instituted a program called "Beat the Best Time," rewarding workers who speeded up production. According to Lloyd Austin, who started in the fan machining department in 1926, some workers attempted to influence their workmates to stick together to prevent speedup, but "people just wouldn't get together and unite and work against" the company's agenda. Charles Slezak said that while constantly changing time requirements and "false promises" of the companies were a regular source of grievance, workers knew that they were being spied on by foremen and others.[77] Photos kept by Wagner's personnel department indicate management's sense of the unevenness of power: one photo of an assembly line is labeled "Speeding Up Work." Signs in the factory declared "Boys and Girls, You Have Done Fine!" amidst charts that evidenced the human element behind enormous productivity increases. Wagner was not hesitant to document the human cost in its personnel photographs, including dozens of photos of severed fingers. In another, a boy with an arm severed at the shoulder looks on blankly, followed by a photo of a sign on a machine that reads, "This is a dangerous machine."[78]

The independents' managers continued to lead the local NMTA and remained active in the national organization, while the Merchants and Manufacturers Association, established in 1921, assumed the CIA's programs. The local and national NMTA advocated "enlightened" personnel management and welfare capitalism in the 1920s but continued their practices of blacklists, spies, and foremen empires.[79]

Interestingly, despite the association of the 1920s with welfare capitalism, there was a marked decline in the emphasis on welfare programs, since the programs showed that they could build loyalty among only a small section of the workforce. Management lost faith in welfare's usefulness as a control mechanism and antiunion device during the war period but could not risk abandoning the programs altogether. So, for example, one hundred of Century's most skilled, older workers had some stock in the company through the company's stock investment plan.[80]

All three companies experimented with what was touted as "industrial democracy," an employee representation plan or works council, in response to the wartime union drive. The plans claimed to give workers a voice without the "outside interference" of unions. Workers for a time used them as vehicles for their grievances, but when the union drive was crushed, Wagner and Century abandoned their plans. Emerson, however, retained its plan, believing it useful to contain worker discontent and as a vehicle for explaining the company's perspective to its workforce.[81]

Signs of discontent among St. Louis electrical workers continued, manifested in short-lived strikes among portions of the workforce at Emerson in 1925 and 1929, at Century in 1926 and 1928, and at Wagner in the mid-1920s.[82] Frank Abfall remembered his feelings of powerlessness as he and other workers watched "from the window" with sympathy for the winders who walked out of Emerson in 1929. Workers later vouched that "morally, the whole shop supported the strike, but there was no organized leadership to coordinate the action." A company union leader "sweet-talked" the men into giving up shortly thereafter, reminding them that the company could transfer the work to women for lower wages if they weren't happy.[83]

Lloyd Austin remembered "learning the ropes" at Emerson in the 1920s as a time of confused bitterness. "I remember learning about this stuff in high school, about the great American system, you know. Then, I went to work [at Emerson] and I started to see right away that what I had been told was a lot of bunk. . . . I knew something was wrong. But it wasn't until we started organizing [in the 1930s], when I met people like Bill Sentner and Bob Logsdon and Lou Kimmel . . . , that I could understand it, make sense of it. It was like a lot of bitterness, but nothing to do about it."[84]

Austin's comments reflected the eradication of the alternative visions from the industry and from public life in St. Louis. Electrical industry representatives, the "militant minority" that had been so essential to that campaign, no doubt felt that they had done what was best for the city and for their own prosperity by erecting their own wall of solidarity. While unions survived into the new era, employers had stamped out the kind of trade union vision that suggested that workers should contest broad power connections between the workplace and the community. The victory had been won with the acquiescence and support of local, state, and federal government and despite the obvious discontent and vigorously sustained—though hardly unified—protest of a significant number of workers. While much has been written about the radical impulses of metal trades workers, employers in St. Louis were thoroughly effective in eliminating that tradition by the 1920s, despite evidence of worker discontent. When the Left was reborn in the 1930s, it was under totally different circumstances and arose in significant degrees from outside the industry.

CHAPTER 2

A Vision of Unionism Takes Shape

A close look at the early 1930s is essential to a full understanding of the origins of the vision of unionism that animated District 8. Workers in the electrical industry produced plenty of indications that they were dissatisfied with the status quo. But it was in a parallel movement of unemployed organizing and union drive among African American nut pickers that we can see the rebirth of a style of unionism that would challenge the political economy of control. This experience was not an "inchoate prelude" to the Congress of Industrial Organizations (CIO) drive, the national effort to organize all workers on an inclusive basis. Rather, it was the critical grounding that built a community-based social movement that later became associated with the CIO drive and defined radical unionism.[1]

For electrical workers, discontent rose sharply as the economy spiraled downward with the Great Depression. Between 1929 and 1933, wages were cut in half as the labor force worked harder than ever before. Smaller numbers of workers were steadily employed as management struggled to use the labor market to gain contracts. Wage rates plummeted to fifteen cents an hour for women's jobs. Men's rates were as low as a base rate of nineteen cents. Often workers found that they could not make the job's time standard. With every new rehiring (after layoffs), managers had an opportunity to institute a grueling base time for each job. Workers who protested were told that "they should either take it or go home." Still, this strategy did not save any of the independents from decline. By 1932, Emerson had only one hundred workers left. When new contracts came in, workers stood in large groups outside each company's gate. By March 1932, Emerson workers in the Employees Representation Plan (ERP) passed a motion: "[E]mployees feel that they have sacrificed to the utmost in the loss of wages and time, and feel that they can stand no more decrease in wages under the existing conditions."[2]

Workers were hopeful when the New Deal's National Recovery Administration (NRA) sought to end the downward spiral. The NRA established "codes of fair competition" to bring stability through industry self-regulation of wages and prices. In August 1933, with great fanfare and promise, St. Louis industry pledged to enforce the NRA. But the NRA's goal of national standards threatened the position of the St. Louis industry. The large companies' wages were already above the minimum wage mandated by the code; however, St. Louis industry was forced to bring its lowest wages up to a minimum wage of thirty-five cents. St. Louis independents circumvented the minimum wage from the beginning, despite their pledge of compliance. Managers averaged wages over a monthly period so that workers could make, as managers explained, "somewhere near" thirty-five cents an hour. On many jobs workers were paid much less than the minimum, and in some weeks their average wages might be much less than the thirty-five-cent mandate. Meanwhile, electrical industry managers resolved to modernize production methods to catch up with the larger companies, a decision that workers experienced as speedup.[3]

While they found little promise in the NRA, these workers joined thousands in the city and across the country who drew new hope from section 7a of the National Industrial Recovery Act (NIRA), the enabling legislation for the NRA that promised the right to organize and bargain collectively. In the next three years, workers' activism prompted the National Metal Trades Association (NMTA) firms to revive their repressive strategies and spend large sums of money on spies and stool pigeons in an effort to squelch this campaign. Wagner was successful. But at Century and Emerson, two of the most important organizing campaigns in St. Louis during the early Depression originated in response to the legislation.

Century Electric Workers Organize

The campaign at Century seemed to be the most promising. After the NIRA became law, small groups of workers began to meet to form a union. Workers were determined to end the monthly averaging of NRA rates and address other grievances. Like many workers across the country, they sought help from established labor organizations. By spring 1934 more than twelve hundred Century workers had signed petitions that asked the International Association of Machinists (IAM)/American Federation of Labor (AFL) leader William Fitzmaurice to represent them.[4] Each department elected a representative to a "committee of 46," and in late June 1934, these workers attempted to negotiate. Management refused, and the workers walked out. Fitzmaurice convinced workers, on the request of Century's managers, to return in order to make another attempt to bargain. Century's managers were nettled by the democratic impulse among workers. One manager, faced with a roomful of workers insistent on bargaining, stammered repeatedly. Another "made several attempts to make a clean getaway" during negotiations and then declared them over. Workers sensed management's vulnerability and walked out on strike again, cheering as they surrounded Century and as operations ceased.[5]

The Century strike turned into a battle that in some respects recalled the war period. Women were more involved in representing and prosecuting the strike, sometimes in fierce ways. In one instance, four women used "billies made of cakes of soap wrapped in cloth" to beat a woman who had crossed the picket line. The commitment to inclusiveness, however, did not extend to black workers. Black workers at Century's foundry, excluded from membership in the IAM, crossed the picket lines; white workers made no effort to organize them.

Century's determination to retain control recalled the wartime response of St. Louis employers. Through the NMTA, Century hired three hundred strikebreakers and threatened to fire workers if they remained on strike. Melees on the picket line resulted in dozens of arrests. Strikers followed workers to their homes in order to plead with or threaten them if they returned. Meanwhile, Fitzmaurice, wary of the democratic impulses of the self-organized workers, took a vacation to Florida. The NRA's regional labor board persuaded Fitzmaurice to call off the strike and wait for a government decision on the case.[6] But Century's management, citing NMTA policy, refused even to meet with the labor board, despite direct hints that to do so would have meant a decision in their favor. The company even managed to get an injunction preventing the labor board from calling a hearing on the strike, although the injunction was later withdrawn. "The resistance of the Company to all efforts so far as this Board was concerned was certainly the most pronounced and most studied and the most evasive that this Board has ever experienced," the labor board noted in a decision against the company in August 1934. By that time, the vice president of the IAM local was a Century spy.[7] The regional board ordered the company to reinstate the strikers without discrimination, but when the case went to the National Labor Board (NLB), the ruling was overturned in Century's favor because, the NLB argued, there was not enough evidence that Century had refused to bargain. Century triumphantly announced that it "has always operated under the open shop and it will continue under that plan as long as it is in business."[8] A year later, three hundred of the most active workers were still laid off. While many of these eventually were offered their jobs back, resistance had paid off for Century. It had squelched the momentum of workers' self-organized drive in the electrical plants in the city.[9]

Emerson Electric, the Company Union, and Worker Organizing

At Emerson a smaller but more tenacious movement developed that provided the center for the later CIO drive. Here, workers' continued attempts at self-organization signified their rejection of management's efforts to convince them that their conditions were a product of market forces and community-wide conditions that workers were powerless to change. It signaled their repudiation of Emerson's company-sponsored Employers' Reprensentation Plan (ERP), which had been fostered and promoted by management since the wartime upheaval.

Initially the ERP, formed in 1918, was structured as a unicameral body, with one management representative and one worker representative from each department, and its chair was the president of the company. Continued threats to organize in the war period caused management to modify the plan to a bicameral body, creating one of the more progressive of the employer-endorsed plans of the 1920s.[10] Some prounion workers participated. Frank Schlieman, who joined Machinists Lodge 41 in 1915, recalled that Emerson's production superintendent "convinced workers" to try the plan or face repression. Schlieman became an ERP representative and even served as an early secretary of the ERP.[11]

Workers elected departmental representatives to their own body, the Board of Representatives. Departments could meet to discuss their problems outside of the board meeting, but meetings of more than one department were forbidden. The ERP also had an arbitration procedure to resolve grievances, although Schlieman attested that important "book" provisions were never used. When the board voted for wage increases or protested speedups, for instance, the General Committee, a body dominated by management, turned them down. When asked why workers did not pursue their grievances during much of the time that the ERP existed, Schlieman replied, "We didn't seem to have the power to do that." By 1920, management had fired many of the union "troublemakers" or, alternatively, had promoted some of the leaders of the union drive to foremen. The economic downturn in 1921, not satisfaction with the ERP, finally crushed the wartime unionization drive.[12] By the early 1920s, workers' hopes for meaningful representation through the ERP were put aside, along with any realistic prospects for unionization.

Emerson, unlike Wagner and Century, did not drop the plan after the threat of unionization had passed.[13] The ERP did not represent a more progressive management philosophy but did represent an addition to management's repertoire of strategies to control its labor force. The company used the ERP meetings to try to "indoctrinate" its employees, according to Charles Slezak, who began work at Emerson in 1918 and was regularly elected to the board. Throughout the history of the ERP, management sought to convince workers that their interests were mutual and that conflicts were "due to the lack of facts or a lack of understanding" of management's position in the industry.[14] Even the smallest matter could be a means to educate workers on management's perspective. Slezak recalled when workers complained that the toilet tissue was inadequate, "thin and delicate, the cheapest grade." Management "brought to our attention the yearly cost [of toilet paper] and told us to be more conservative; instead of two or three [sheets], use only one—it does the job." Management emphasized the perils of the marketplace and the risks of selling and sought to convince workers that they shared these burdens. They rejected worker wage demands, explaining that Emerson paid the "going rate" for similar work in the community.[15] Emerson's management also utilized the ERP as a mechanism to gain information about discontent on the shop floor. According to Slezak, workers "representing our departments began to realize the unfairness, getting nowhere with complaints, using us to their advantage to get firsthand information as to [workers'] activities in regards to their unfair decisions."[16]

By the mid-1920s, most workers had come to view the ERP as a management tool. Schlieman acknowledged that many found the ERP "rather a joke." To them, "it was an afternoon spent smoking a cigarette or so, and they were being paid for it, so why not go to it." Schlieman sheepishly admitted that he took the ERP "rather serious[ly], but couldn't get so far with it." He tried to get incentive rate times adjusted for his fellow tool and die makers and was sometimes successful, "but often too late for a particular job." "Aggressive" representatives knew that they courted retaliation. Frank Sulzer, a staunch unionist, was elected as a representative of the machining department in the late 1920s, but the company laid him off when he became outspoken for workers' rights.[17]

Schlieman's and Sulzer's experiences support Charles Slezak's contention that most ERP representatives were not necessarily "company-minded" but, like him, participated "in the hope of some miracle to change this company-controlled plan." The company failed in its unrelenting effort to persuade workers of a mutuality of interest. While the company had hoped that the ERP would be an effective tool, in the end the ERP functioned as the rope in a tug of war between workers—sometimes it was a vigorous contest, but most times it was an uneven match. Thus it should not be surprising that among the key figures in the CIO drive at Emerson were those who had been active at one time or another in the ERP. The experience of these workers with the company's version of "industrial democracy" would actually make some more receptive to the need for "outside" representation and leftist leadership.[18]

The Emerson ERP was, however, a means for workers to gather and discuss their mutual complaints and remained an instrument that management had to deftly control. Sporadic attempts at self-organization during the mid-1920s, as well as a field winders strike in 1929, indicated discontent that was not contained by the ERP. On occasion, workers clearly indicated their displeasure with the limits of the ERP in collective fashion. For example, after Frank Sulzer was laid off, his department refused to elect any representative. Others protested by returning blank ballots at election time. In the early 1930s, as the management of the company unilaterally implemented pay cuts and speedup, the ERP became a means through which workers expressed protest, although they risked retaliation by the company. The ERP enabled workers from different departments to meet to pass resolutions favoring thirty-hour work-week legislation, protest against speedup, vote to have jobs retimed, and question numerous other policies and practices of management. By allowing the ERP to exist, management sought to make it a credible vehicle so that workers would participate yet also sought control of discontent. When management questioned representatives about why some did not attend the board meetings, one responded that they were "afraid of discrimination if they bring up questions for argument and consideration during these times; suppression of the men in various departments during these times will not bring us to a better understanding."[19]

While workers explored the limits to representation under the company's ERP, a continuous dynamic for workers' self-organization developed from 1933 to 1936. The dynamic was fueled by the tenacity of rank-and-file workers whose hopes were raised by the passage of section 7a of the NRA and then the Wagner Act, which gave workers firmer legal protection for their right to organize and bargain collectively, and by Emerson's financial crisis, which caused managerial and production changes and aggravated workers' long-standing grievances.

Emerson's financial troubles predated the Depression crisis. Desiring to expand in the post–World War I era in 1919, the Parker family had issued two million dollars in preferred stock to finance Building D, a new fan and motor assembly site at 2012–18 Washington Avenue. In 1921, as the postwar economic downturn found the owners unable to pay their obligations to the preferred stockholders, this refinancing reduced the power of the original family owners. The problems of meeting these obligations continued in the 1920s and became endemic after 1928. The old owners held on to their control until September 1933, when the preferred stockholders were able to name a new manager. They selected thirty-five-year-old Joseph Newman, a member of their board since 1928, as president. Newman had no experience in the electrical industry, having been a vice president of Lesser-Goldman, a cotton brokerage company. Newman's contract gave him bonuses on gross sales per year, a condition that would fuel his drive to increase sales and volume rather than concentrate solely on profits.[20] The condition reflected the board of directors' agreement that the future of the company lay in "modernizing" production and entering into competition with the large companies in the industry.

When Newman assumed control in September 1933, sales were at their lowest point ever, and only one hundred workers were steadily employed. He was determined to replace the company's niche manufacturing with modernized mass production of cheaper fans and other products. Newman pleaded with workers to cooperate in order to increase sales, promising that this would bring about steady employment and higher wages. He also promised to restructure production methods at Emerson to the standards of the larger electrical companies. At Emerson, male workers still wound motors by hand, whereas at General Electric (GE) and Westinghouse women workers tended the machines that wound the motors.

Newman implemented a mass production system at the plant. Managers and engineers laid out an assembly line system for motor production. Motor components were machined and assembled on the same floor of Building D, with all operations connected by conveyors. The process eliminated some bench operations, increased output by fifty motors per hour, and brought in the first substantial numbers of lower-paid women, up to four hundred (22 percent of the workforce) by 1936.[21] But the new markets for cheaper fans that Newman had counted on never materialized, and fans actually caused a loss for the company. In motors, Emerson found that the "big boys" (as they called GE and Westinghouse) would not permit a price reduction that might create the niche Newman desired. Though the NRA was dead by 1935, tacit quotas remained the industry norm in the mid-1930s.[22]

For workers, Newman's attempts to restructure the company fueled discontent, especially aggravating motor assemblers and tool and die workers, the groups of workers whose loyalty had been assiduously cultivated in the 1920s. Frank Abfall recalled the resentment of the men over the "modernization" in the department: "We used to do the complete motor, wind the coils, insulate, everything. But the company broke everything down, into separate operations, so the easy stuff was taken away from us. They were taking our work and giving our work away to women at half the wages." On the other hand, the women who were hired for the line assembly soon developed their own resentments at the low wages they earned—some took home paychecks of under five dollars for a week's work, and speedup was a constant complaint. "Oh, it was a sweatshop, that's what we called it!" exclaimed Marie Strathman, who wound motor coils. "We had to suffer for them to make money," Strathman added, describing women who came in before 7 a.m., well before starting time, to be able to make the required output and bandaged their entire hands to endure the work. Turnover among women was 100 percent during the year.[23]

In mid-1933, Emerson workers initiated another organizing drive. Newman appealed to workers to cooperate with him in rebuilding the company, as he had just assumed the presidency.[24] Management tried to renew workers' faith in the ERP. They rehired Frank Sulzer and asked him to resume his duties as ERP representative. But such gestures weren't enough to stymie the union drive. Inspired by the Century workers and the clashes taking place across the country, ERP representatives voted to have Fitzmaurice of the IAM represent them as well. Management refused. Then, after the strike failure at Century, the IAM and the AFL were completely discredited at Emerson.[25]

Disillusioned because of their experience with conservative unionism and realizing that the government's section 7a guarantees were meaningless, Emerson workers redoubled their efforts to make the ERP a vehicle for addressing their grievances and winning wage increases. The company, trying to thwart the union drive, found that when they granted any demands, this merely inspired workers to escalate their efforts for more meaningful representation. Meanwhile, pressures to remain profitable brought continued speedups and some wage decreases.[26]

Throughout 1934 and 1935, workers tested the limits of the company union. They passed motions to grant wage increases. They continually asked for retiming of jobs and passed motions for the company to "stop simplifying jobs to lower wages." They protested the company's methods of hiring and firing.[27] Contesting management's rhetoric, which called for harmony between workers and employers, they passed a motion declaring that "in order to promote harmony, the practice of employees working before the starting bell in the morning, at noon time and during the rest period be discontinued."[28] In 1935, when the company announced that the "most serious [accidents] in our history" had occurred in the previous six months, the ERP board passed a resolution stating that the company's speedup was responsible.[29] When told that new sales programs required cheaper fans and more simplified methods, the workers voted that management consult them about sales programs before implementation. They proposed a plan for reorganizing fan production so that it would be spread out over the course of the year.[30] Workers' challenges were broadly defined and mounted to the point that the company sometimes felt it necessary to alter the meeting minutes in order to conceal the level of discontent among its employees.[31] Workers had begun to articulate a challenge to management rights.

But ERP representatives were still among the most privileged. The company's strategy of cultivating loyalty remained appealing. For instance, in October 1935, the ERP succeeded in its demand that the company rescind its Depression-initiated practice of "rating the job rather than the man," thereby returning to the complicated system that privileged a section of the workforce for higher pay and steadier work. Moreover, the company union never constituted a forum for the grievances of the women employees, who were not represented. In April 1936, just months before the CIO drive began and at a meeting that was notable for worker contentiousness, the ERP unanimously agreed "that representatives be confined to male employes only." The company union also defined its rebelliousness in racial terms when it passed a motion demanding "that a more accessible toilet be assigned to colored help" and that separate shower facilities be set up for black workers.[32] The question of representation for black workers was not even a point of discussion.

In late 1935, workers active in the ERP met either to form "a club or to affiliate with some union." Their organizing meeting attracted more than five hundred Emerson workers, and soon the group was considering unions. A leading "company-minded" ERP representative came to a meeting and read a letter to the workers asking them to wait four or five months and promising to "take care of us." But by mid-1936, no raises were forthcoming. Later, workers suggested that the group had suffered from "passive leadership."[33]

Workers' rejection of Emerson's version of "industrial democracy" produced the firm belief that they needed a broader movement. Management's invective that their standards conformed to the "community standard" and that their wages were "equal to our local competitors" also made them recognize the limits of a fight that focused only on Emerson. St. Louis's community wage, managers explained, was part of the "special advantage" of St. Louis industry that allowed it to compete with the eastern companies. At least three times between 1933 and 1936, Emerson's managers, confronted with workers' wage demands, sent a "fact-finding" committee from the Board of Representatives to research the wage rates of other electrical companies in the area. These groups of workers reported their findings and confirmed the company's claims—that the "policy of the company is to pay the going wage in the community."[34]

Electrical workers issued continual challenges to management, but it was a parallel movement of the early 1930s that sparked the beginnings of a new trade union movement in St. Louis. Left-wing activists, initiated into the unemployed movement of the early 1930s, brought forward from this an experiential basis that was critical in forging a coalition that could effectively challenge the political economy of control in the electrical industry.

The Unemployed Council and Neighborhood Organizing

The Left was given a clear field for unemployed agitation in St. Louis when the Central Trades and Labor Union (CTLU) reined in Mary Ryder and a group of women delegates who sought to organize the unemployed. While a few rallies were held as unemployment escalated in 1929, by early 1930 the CTLU had voted to abandon the effort.[35] The St. Louis unemployed movement was born when a group of mostly black workers protested at city hall for jobs and relief. After the protest, they formed into an Unemployed Council (UC). The councils, set up across the nation in 1929–30 by the Communist Party (CP), were the most important vehicle for local agitation in the early 1930s.[36] The UC program of direct action to obtain relief and its demand for concrete reforms, as well as its style of community mobilization and protest, drew an array of activists into the orbit of the CP. Certainly the CP had not found fertile ground for expansion in St. Louis before this point. Descended from the 1919 Socialist Party (SP) split, by the late 1920s barely more than twenty activists held the group together. Across the country, the CP had survived in cities with high foreign-born populations, but St. Louis had the lowest percentage of foreign-born workers of any industrial city. As workers migrated from the rural hinterland and as antiradical sentiment ruled the day, there were few prospects to build from this core. The party survived in gatherings and discussions at the Labor Lyceum, at 1421 North Garrison, located near the Jewish-settled neighborhoods on the near north side of St. Louis. The area was also close to the segregated black neighborhoods in the central corridor of the city, but until the early 1930s the CP, whose members were mostly small shopkeepers, clerical workers, and housewives, had no black membership and no inclination toward mobilizing this group.[37] But the party's fledgling efforts at organizing the unemployed on a community basis and targeting the St. Louis relief system made it into a viable radical voice in St. Louis.

According to a 1931 Russell Sage Foundation study, St. Louis's relief system during the early years of the Great Depression was among the most miserly in the country. The relief system epitomized the whole ensemble of local class relations. Run by private agencies, the system was dominated by elite and business interests even after the city began to contribute funds to the system.[38] Control by St. Louis's elite resulted in a regressive method of funding the constituent private charities that distributed relief. Businesses pressured employed workers to contribute to the drives. More of its funds were drawn from employed workers than from any other source, and there was no mechanism to ensure that the wealthy contributed.[39] The St. Louis Citizens Committee on Relief and Employment (CCRE) spent less per capita on relief than any other city of its size and aided fewer people; the amount given to the poor was 38 percent less than in other cities. Civic boosters claimed that these statistics demonstrated that St. Louis had fared better during the Depression than other areas. But such claims only masked the extreme suffering of many people, in particular African Americans, during these years.[40]

The UC challenged the relief system, exposed the degree of neediness, and extracted more relief from the system for its followers. They called for jobs at union wages instead of paltry relief. They contended that a just relief system should be governed by the unemployed themselves and called for a redistributive basis for collection of funds, whereby the wealthy would pay a greater share. Further, they called for federal legislation to fund a national relief system.[41]

The UC attracted an almost entirely new leadership and membership to the orbit of the CP. UC activists were a diverse group who sought to distance themselves from the foreign reputation of the CP.[42] Among the most active members and leaders of the St. Louis UC were young women activists, dubbed "girl agitators" by the press, whose youthful defiance of prescribed roles drew much attention. The police even designated the women as "ringleaders" of the movement. Fannie Goldberg recalled that "whenever the police would see a leaflet, or some meeting was called, they'd pick [a key woman activist] up and put her away!" But Goldberg, who led at least one city hall demonstration herself, added pointedly, "There was no major leader in St. Louis; we were just a group of people who believed in the same thing."[43]

African Americans also became an important part of the UC membership and its leadership. This development arose from the party's veteran organizers' efforts in the early 1930s to get St. Louis in line with national party policy on the integration of the black working class into their work as well as from neighborhood-based agitation. The UC constituted the first integrated protest movement in St. Louis. Since African Americans were the group worst hit by the Depression in St. Louis (they were one-tenth of the population but one-fourth of the unemployed and were the largest group on relief but received a lower allotment than whites), they were an important base for agitation. They became prominent in many of the demonstrations and sometimes outnumbered whites. By 1933 they constituted one-third of party membership in St. Louis. Hershel Walker came from Arkansas via Memphis searching for a job but, encouraged by his brother, soon joined the Unemployed Council. He recalled the moving effect of "black and white demonstrating together before city hall, going to jail together, and getting food to eat together" in a city that was still fully segregated.[44]

The activism of women and African Americans, as well as the party's "weakness" in shops and factories, reinforced the strategy of mobilizing through neighborhood activities. This neighborhood-based unemployed activity for the CP represented, according to one scholar, a "resurgence of a familial-based conception of solidarity." Personal and familial networks always played an important role in black workers' and women workers' organizational efforts.[45] UC activists concentrated on mobilizing neighborhoods to obtain relief or to prevent evictions. Fannie Goldberg remembered that "we would take members of the council and instead of a person going to the relief station alone, we went with them. And on evictions, if we heard someone was being evicted, we would gather a group and get there and put the furniture back in." The boundaries of racial divisions were bridged when integrated groups of workers helped each other keep a roof over their heads.[46] They also helped to mobilize the residents of the swelling Hooverville along the Mississippi to demand relief. Built of ramshackle makeshift housing, by 1931 it was home to five hundred black and white residents; later it would stretch a mile long.[47]

Through these experiences, activists revived forms of protests that are usually associated with labor activism in the later part of the decade. In January 1931, the UC held the first sit-down of the 1930s in St. Louis. It began with a huge march, one contingent coming from the south and one from the north sections of the city, the symbolic unification of the two historic divisions and racial boundaries of the citizenry. By the time they came to city hall, their ranks had grown to five thousand. They demanded ten million dollars in aid to the unemployed, reduction of relief administrators' salaries, and taxing corporations and the wealthy for relief funds. A delegation of the crowd entered city hall and refused to leave until their demands were heard and acted upon by the Board of Aldermen. The outcome was predictable; police clubs and tear gas prevailed in a bloody melee.[48] The repression these activists met, including repeated long-term jailings for a substantial number, prevented a high level of activity; it also provoked in the group arguments about civil liberties, citizenship, and constitutional rights. Already by 1932 CP activists were carrying the American flag as well as the red flag of revolution in their demonstrations.[49]

Through community organizing, the UC scored a major victory in July 1932. They were hitting their stride just as the St. Louis relief system reached a crisis point. In June the CCRE started rejecting new relief applicants and announced the imminent cutoff of fifteen thousand families from the rolls.[50] One candid relief system employee remarked, "All through the Depression we have had the poor sharing with the poor. We have almost come to the limit of that."[51] On July 8, after two weeks of neighborhood public hearings and house-to-house canvassing, the councils led a mass demonstration to city hall, forcing the mayor to grant immediate relief to one thousand unemployed workers who had previously been denied assistance. Three days later, another mass demonstration turned into a violent confrontation when police fired tear gas and bullets into the crowd, killing at least four people and wounding others. The panic-stricken mayor called an extraordinary meeting that restored relief, appropriated $2 million of city funds, and recommended issuing bonds for a $4.6 million loan from the federal government's Reconstruction Finance Corporation.[52]

Ralph Shaw, the young activists' main contact with the national CP, reinforced the emphasis on community and neighborhood agitation but also sought to get the party involved in factory organizing. Shaw, thirty years old, was an experienced organizer. His grounding was in the union battles of the southern Illinois coalfields of the 1920s. There radical union strategies, especially those focused on community mobilization, flourished in the 1920s.[53] Toni Radosovitch, the daughter of a Croatian coal miner, described these as centered around familial involvement: "the whole family was involved. . . . Women would wrap up the kids and take them to the picket line." Radosovitch recalled having to hide Shaw "in a great big haystack" to escape local law enforcement and vigilantes during this period. Shaw survived and thus was able to carry forward radical working-class community-based strategies. As the unemployed movement developed, Shaw began to spend more time in St. Louis, helping to develop the skills of the novice organizers.[54] One of the young organizers Shaw influenced was William Sentner, who later became president of District 8. Sentner had already been initiated into radicalism through his experiences in the merchant marine. But joining a movement that was developing a focus on community-level struggle and bonds, he developed a vision of trade unionism that he would carry into the United Electrical, Radio and Machine Workers of America (UE).

William Sentner

Sentner was born in New York in 1907 but grew up in St. Louis. He was the son of Russian Jewish immigrants who worked in the rapidly expanding St. Louis garment district that centered on Washington Avenue. The struggle to improve the family's life through the garment unions was central to Sentner's childhood in a working-class Jewish community.[55] He was extraordinarily bright (he graduated at age sixteen from Central High School on the city's near north side) and ambitious. "From the time he was a kid he wanted to go to college," noted his wife Toni, adding that of the family's six children, only two completed high school. He enrolled in Washington University's School of Architecture in the fall of 1924, still only sixteen years old.

Sentner's trajectory was redirected by his college experience and by his meager finances. He was surprised by the class biases of most of his classmates. "What he found in college disappointed him," said Toni. A quiet, unassuming young man, he felt ostracized even by Jewish groups and students "because he was poor and working his way through. This really hit him." Sentner was befriended by an intellectual who introduced him to Karl Marx's writings and political theory. When Sentner's finances fell short in the spring semester of 1927 as a result of his father's death, he decided to "study by experience" with his friend, who had already graduated as an electrical engineer; they hit the road, walking, riding the rails, and hiking across the country. After they parted ways, Sentner decided to join the merchant marine.

The seeds of Sentner's political commitments were planted firmly in his experiences with the merchant marine. For the next four years he intermittently signed out as a laborer and fireman from the ports of New York, San Francisco, and Galveston, traveling to Europe and the Near East. Seamen were among the most exploited U.S. workers, but they also had a rich tradition of labor struggles. On board ship, in addition to a harsh and grueling work regimen, Sentner studied Marx and labor history and discovered the radical syndicalist milieu of the merchant seamen; at port, he studied architecture. "When he came out of that he was pretty well versed on economics and politics," remarked Toni Sentner. Other acquaintances later told the Federal Bureau of Investigation (FBI) that he "became enthusiastic toward the communistic movement while a seaman." While these experiences may have radicalized Sentner, he had not yet joined the CP.[56]

Sentner mixed the sailor's life with more conventional jobs, and he continued to try to further his education. His steadiest job was with Sol Abrahams Construction Company in St. Louis, where he worked as laborer, timekeeper, carpenter and draftsman off and on over a period of eight years. After his final stint at sea, he returned in 1932 to work for Abrahams as an architectural draftsman.[57]

As the Depression wore on, Sentner's questioning of the system and commitment to socialism deepened. During this time he became part of the rich leftist artistic milieu centered on the riverfront, where "wharf workers and artists mixed in an atmosphere thick with cigarette smoke, jazz music, and the smell of bootleg gin." There he would have engaged in debates with a diverse and often motley group of the disaffected, including his old grade school friend, the house painter-turned-artist Joe Jones, as well as novelist Jack Conroy, author of the acclaimed autobiographical novel *The Disinherited*. Sentner was increasingly drawn into the CP's activities. In February 1933, he joined the local John Reed Club, the CP-influenced organization for leftist intellectuals, writers, and artists committed to making a difference in the real world of working-class struggle. Here a "cultural front" of the Left was in formation, one that helped to sow the seeds of a social movement in the city.[58] Meanwhile, the more practical work of the unemployed movement had led to a union drive among African American women nut pickers. Soon, Sentner became a central player in the union campaign.

The Nut Pickers' Union: Crossing Boundaries between Community and Workplace Struggles

The UC began to agitate among the women nut pickers as early as 1931.[59] Nut picking, along with chicken cleaning and rag sorting, comprised the very bottom of the submarginal industries in St. Louis, those that fed on the political economy of control described in chapter 1. There were more than fifteen hundred women in St. Louis's nut-shelling sweatshops who picked, sorted, and packed pecans brought to St. Louis from the Mississippi Valley. Funsten Nut Company was the largest single employer, with four plants dispersed around the city and three in East St. Louis, Illinois. White women were hired for the main storefront, especially in sorting and weighing, but the greatest part (perhaps 80 percent) of its workforce was black women. This seasonal work never provided a living wage and fell below the common rate of manufacturing work, but during economic downturns, wages and conditions became Dickensian. In 1933 weekly average earnings were three to four dollars for blacks and four to six dollars a week for whites. Black women also worked longer hours. It is not surprising that more than 40 percent of Funsten's workers were on relief, and it was from the relief struggles that the initial contacts and organizing began.[60]

The organizing drive was guided by Ralph Shaw, under the official aegis of the Food Workers Industrial Union (FWIU), an affiliate of the Trade Union Unity League (TUUL). The TUUL was the party's dual union federation, organizing on an industrial rather than a craft basis, especially where the AFL unions were moribund or nonexistent. It aimed to link the struggles of the employed and unemployed. There was no better place than with the nut pickers, who were poised between employment and relief.[61]

Over the course of the two-month drive, the core of black women developed confidence that they could launch and win a union campaign at Funsten, despite earlier failed attempts. Meetings galvanized the ranks with the conviction that their struggle was a fight for a living wage and a challenge to the political economy that consigned black women to a life of misery. Carrie Smith, an older religious woman who had worked at Funsten since at least 1918, became the leader of the drive. The workers demanded a wage increase, equal wages for black and white workers, and union recognition. An elected committee of twelve presented the demands to the company on April 24. They waited three weeks for an answer,

meanwhile developing organization in the other factories through personal networks and urging white women to join their struggle. Superintendents "got to
trembling" when two hundred women massed in management's office to make
their demands. When the company refused to negotiate, the shop committee at
the fully organized plant staged a well-planned walkout.[62]

The Funsten strike was defined by mass picketing, roving strike brigades,
group arrests, and the mobilization of community support. It was later urged as
a model by the CP national office. It was a notable contrast to another strike at
the same time in St. Louis by the Amalgamated Clothing Workers of America,
where the leadership refused to engage in "mass pickets." Picketing began every
morning with demonstrations around the main plant. A commissary fed twelve
hundred picketers daily. A truckload of food arrived from the Workers International Relief organization in Chicago. The CP and the UC mobilized all their
forces behind the strikers; white women from the UC were especially strategic
on the picket line, as their presence encouraged white Funsten workers to join
the strike.[63] On the second day of the strike, two hundred white women from
the main factory joined the five hundred black women. A cascade of solidarity
developed, bringing almost the entire industry workforce on strike within a
week.[64] At a mass meeting at Carr Park, a "white girl" declared that "we were all
Funsten's carpet-rugs. He kept us apart so's he could beat us as he pleased."[65]
When police brought strikebreakers to and from work in patrol wagons and
taxis, the women and their supporters formed a "sandwich parade," forcing
scabs to dare to pass their line of bricks, bats, and other objects. There were one
hundred arrests.[66]

The strikers took their plight to various groups to build community pressure
on Funsten to settle. The bakery workers' union took up a collection and sent a
delegation with bread. The women called on personal networks of support from
the African American community, including their churches.[67] Soon ministers as
well as husbands and children dotted the picket line. Shortly after the strike
began, a delegation of two white and two black strikers appealed to the St. Louis
Social Justice Commission (SJC), a self-styled mediation group made up of
clergy and academics. The SJC was organized in 1931 by Rabbi Ferdinand Isserman of Temple Israel in St. Louis and Bishop William Scarlett of the East Missouri Diocese of the Episcopal Church, both social and theological liberals
"noted as champions of . . . social and economic justice." In 1933, the SJC
included fifteen clergymen and ten professors from Washington University and
St. Louis University and boasted that it had "settle[d] a number of industrial
difficulties."[68] Accompanying them were Irving L. Spencer, an attorney for
American Civil Liberties Union, and J. Clark Waldron, a teacher at Beaumont
Night High School. (Spencer was also an attorney for the International Labor
Defense, a legal defense group associated with the CP, and Waldron was an SP
member, though these affiliations were not noted publicly.) At the meeting the

strikers testified about the horrible working conditions and dramatized their low wages by opening pay envelopes showing $1.50–$2.00 for four days' work. "All we want is a living wage," Sentner told the press. "We think we are entitled to live as other folks live," declared Smith.[69]

A delegation of nut pickers asked the new mayor, Bernard Dickmann, to arbitrate the strike. Dickman contended that the strike was a "private matter." Sentner countered that the city was "subsidizing the Funsten Company" because so many of the workers received relief, so it was a "municipal matter." The mayor agreed to appoint a committee of seven, with four black representatives, to negotiate. The mayor and the Urban League attempted to get the nut pickers to denounce Sentner and the Communists and to negotiate without them, but the women resolutely refused.[70]

The strikers' ever-widening circles of support and their innovative tactics took Funsten officials by surprise and rapidly depleted their resolve to defeat the strike. After an all-day hearing and negotiations, and after Rabbi Isserman of the SJC asked the company to open its books to prove that it couldn't pay more, the company agreed to a settlement, which the mayor announced after unwittingly following the strikers to the Labor Lyceum (CP headquarters). After Dickman congratulated the workers and their leaders for the nonviolent approach and thanked the CP for bringing the conditions of the nut pickers to the city's attention, the strikers applauded him and the strike leaders thanked him "for his interest and assistance." The ten-day strike brought the workers nearly all their demands except union recognition, including doubling of their pay and equal pay for black workers.[71]

The model of the strike was electrifying in St. Louis's black working class and to activists across the country. Writer Jack Conroy, inspired by the events to think that a new labor movement was possible, used it for material in his second novel, *A World to Win*.[72] In St. Louis, the nut pickers were the inspiration and support network for a TUUL organizing drive among the most marginal workers in the St. Louis area. Sentner led these organizing drives as an FWIU and TUUL organizer. In July 1933, for instance, black women at rag-making plants waged a successful strike using all of the same components, including the mayor's arbitration committee. At around the same time, the nut pickers successfully struck another nut company. Enough alarms were set off that NRA federal authorities ordered Sentner's arrest and held him for several days, until "unpleasant publicity" for President Franklin Roosevelt's new recovery program brought his release.[73]

Perhaps even more significant than the nut pickers' victory is the union's survival in the year following the strike. During the strike and shortly afterward, fourteen hundred nut pickers, including workers in the East St. Louis plants, joined eleven locals of the FWIU. Political activism around relief became a mainstay of union activity, as the union argued that it was in the city's interest to get companies to pay a living wage, and only by supporting the workers during economic downturns could activists bring this about. This political struggle combined with cultural activities (including integrated ball teams) fostered a remarkable degree of loyalty, gaining leverage to struggle against the familiar employer weapon of selective layoffs of activists. The *Daily Worker* declared that the St. Louis FWIU was "one of the best [labor] organization[s] in the U.S."[74]

All of this paid off when, in early October, Funsten laid off five hundred workers in an effort to break the union. Building on mass actions, seven hundred picketers surrounded the factory, demanding the guarantee of reemployment for those laid off. Funsten had planned mass arrests to settle a score, but the union garnered further public support, especially from black newspapers that applauded their nonviolence. On October 8, the nut pickers held a "public trial" with a "workers' jury" composed of thirty-five workers from the nut shops, clothing shops, striking miners from Southern Illinois, and "many other members of the AFL." Dean Sweet, one of the original May strike arbitrators, and other well-known liberals took part in the trial. The committee visited Mayor Dickman and NRA officials and demanded their presence at the trial. The "jury" found the company "guilty of violating the NRA pledge, misusing the NRA signs, and . . . deceiving the public in an effort to further speed up the work and cut down the [work]force."[75]

Meanwhile, relief office protests won the guarantee of immediate relief for the laid-off workers. When officials did not fulfill their pledge, an integrated group of union supporters marched on the relief offices, charging that the CCRE was complicit in "starv[ing] out the workers." Seventy-five were arrested, and Sentner faced false charges of attempting to incite a riot.[76] Meanwhile, the rest of Funsten's workers went on strike in solidarity with those laid off. Within four days, the newly created mediation board of the NRA produced a settlement. The Funsten workers had won their demands for reinstatement.[77]

Reflecting the intersection of work and community agitation, the nut pickers, in a set of demands submitted to the Pecan Shelling Code Authority of the National Recovery Administration, called for the establishment of an unemployment fund with the equivalent of 5 percent of wages paid by the employer, to be administered by an employees' board of trustees, and requested that the government immediately establish unemployment insurance at the "expense of bosses and the state."[78] The FWIU hosted a conference in November 1933 to launch a drive for national unemployment insurance and a city relief ordinance. The conference elected a committee to continue protests around relief issues in conjunction with the UC and resolved to try to attract more labor unions and churches to the relief work.[79] By June 1934, FWIU members were at the center of agitation at the local relief offices and before city hall. The UC's agitation resulted in passage of a resolution by the Board of Aldermen favoring the Lundeen Bill, a strong unemployment insurance bill then before Congress.[80]

The FWIU's approach underscored the relationship between the workplace and the community in the local political economy. Fannie Goldberg, the UC activist whose apartment was the location for the strike's leaflet writing, credited Sentner with "[coming] up with the idea [that] we have to prove to the city that the city was supplementing the livelihood of these people" and "subsidizing the company" and therefore should pressure the company and side with the strikers as a key strike strategy, contrasting this approach with the "raw," "fighting" approach of the early unemployed movement.[81] Through the party, Sentner and Shaw were also familiar with the unemployment fund demands of the TUUL's Fur and Leather Workers' Union (FLWU) in New York.[82] It is not surprising that African American women were central to the development of this approach.[83] Race and gender issues made the boundaries of the nut pickers' struggle fluid, and the nut pickers became the core group of a nascent working-class–based civil rights movement in St. Louis. In 1934 the FWIU was one of the major constituent organizations to launch a local "Bill of Rights for Negroes" campaign under the aegis of the League of Struggle for Negro Rights, which included attempts to desegregate St. Louis parks. The FWIU thus became, for a brief moment, the basis for a working-class civil rights movement in St. Louis.[84]

Networks and Obstacles

The Funsten strike and subsequent organizing efforts allowed Communists to "come out with prestige" within the black working class and to utilize a growing network of contacts to organize black workers excluded or ignored by the AFL: ragpickers, laundry workers, longshoremen, metalworkers, and steelworkers. The practice of breaking down racial barriers was a transformative aspect of Sentner's experience, as he became an organizer of these campaigns for the TUUL. Toni Radosovitch Buneta, at the time a packinghouse worker who became involved in TUUL organizing and married Bill Sentner in 1935, emphasized the lasting experience of breaking racial barriers through the TUUL's house-to-house organizing efforts, which brought white workers into black workers' homes and vice versa: "this was a taboo in St. Louis that we really broke down" through the TUUL organizing drives. Hershel Walker agreed, remembering this period as a "real breakthrough."[85]

But the TUUL remained largely a black workers' movement, an organization that faced overwhelming obstacles. The marginality of many of the industries in which black workers were dominant, their isolation resulting from racial segregation, and their association with the CP impeded organizational stability and expansion. The effects of what Sentner referred to as "Jim Crow and Red Scare" were apparent by April 1934, as the TUUL unions began to experience serious defeats in strikes.[86]

The TUUL was isolated from the mostly white workers who organized in the aftermath of section 7a, including local electrical industry workers. These workers joined the AFL, many under AFL "federal union" status, while others affiliated with established unions. During the Century Electric strike of 1934, the TUUL organizers, and quite possibly Sentner himself, issued leaflets to strikers on the picket line counseling workers that their only hope for victory "lies in spreading the strike to Emerson's and Wagner's!!" The leaflet urged Century workers to organize a community base of supporters through delegations to other shops to "call a conference of all organizations of working people in St. Louis" and warned them against depending on the labor board. While there is no record of Century workers' response, the leaflets stirred IAM representative William Fitzmaurice to action. He gave a copy to representatives of the National Labor Board of St. Louis, and this provoked the board's first real intervention in the strike in order to get "the men and women off the streets" and thereby "avoid possible interference with radical elements." Workers accepted the board's offer to settle the case but were disappointed by it. TUUL activists found little solace in the fact that by 1934, these workers were also experiencing strike defeats and finding the existence of their new organizations threatened, as they confronted the hard reality of business intransigence and a precarious position within the house of labor.[87]

The inability to connect effectively into a citywide or national movement made the formal disbanding of TUUL unions by the national CP in 1935 anticlimactic. Four of the St. Louis TUUL unions were absorbed into the AFL. The nut pickers were not among them. After 1934, nut pickers' union activities declined. The struggle necessary to sustain the union had overwhelmed the initial potential. Funsten's multiplant apparatus gave the company leverage. By 1935 the companies, facing competition from Texas where wages and conditions were even worse, closed several plants and began to mechanize its remaining processes. However, it is important to remember that the TUUL unions, despite their association with the CP and the vigorous attacks on them, had fared better during this trying time than many of the union efforts associated with the AFL in St. Louis.[88]

The UC and TUUL experience had constituted an important chapter in St. Louis labor history. That chapter drew upon the critique of the political economy of control that the unemployed movement had ignited. It had also shown the potential of community-based mobilizations and alliances that prefaced the later 1930s in ways that confound traditional perceptions of the early 1930s' CP as a period of "extremism" based on party doctrine that eschewed alliances with other radicals and liberals. As activists learned to be effective organizers, among some there developed a degree of willingness to work in genuine coalition from 1932 onward. Sarah Shaw recalled that these ties really began to develop after the

July 1932 "riot," when she convinced an American Civil Liberties Union attorney to come to the St. Louis courts to listen to the "railroading" of activists. Initially skeptical, the attorney eventually provided the bail for many of those rounded up. Later these connections were used to develop part of the community base that supported the Funsten strikers. In fact, there was a growing recognition of the need to work with churches and liberal and political organizations during this period that came into play more fully after the official Popular Front was announced.[89]

The UC and the TUUL gave organizational expression to a contest over power relations in the workplace and outside that had been eradicated by the electrical corporations in the previous generation. The unemployed movement's parades and demonstrations often marched by Emerson and Century plants, and it seems this activity had some influence. Worker representatives to Emerson's company union protested pressure to donate to the CCRE's United Relief campaign from 1932 to 1935; Emerson management acknowledged "opposition in our factory to the United Charities."[90] In 1934, Century worker Earl Brown wrote to the National Labor Board, explaining his understanding of the connections between power relations in the workplace and the community, when he suggested that Century preferred "to get men or women on $12 or $14 a week, [and] work them like slaves, for 4 or 5 months out of the year. Peak Production they call it. And after that they lay them off for the Local or Federal Relief Agencies to feed for the remainder of the year. I know Century is not the only Firm that does this."[91] Nevertheless, electrical workers remained distant from the parallel movement that met success through the interaction of radicals and the St. Louis black working class.[92]

By late 1934, while the UC and TUUL were in decline, new groups furthered the concept of community-based mobilization. In particular the Missouri-based American Workers Union (AWU), formed in late 1934 by SP members, modeled itself on the UC. The AWU sought to organize the unemployed and to mobilize community support on picket lines to obstruct the use of the unemployed as scabs. In 1935, the foundering UC merged with the AWU. The AWU was able to gain a tremendous following, claiming more than eighty thousand members in St. Louis and thus outdistancing the Workers' Alliance, the major national organization of the unemployed in the mid-1930s. Many small merchants decided to endorse it, and in some cases the NRA blue eagle was replaced by the AWU symbol on merchants' windows. With UC influence, the AWU became a racially integrated coalition and included women nut pickers in its leadership ranks.[93]

The AWU provided key support for strikes among newly organized workers in the AFL. In key federal labor union strikes of 1935–36, the AWU helped collect food, provided critical assistance, and forced city agencies to give relief to strikers—all strategies begun by the nut pickers' union.[94] The AWU constituted more than an alliance between Communist and Socialist activists. It produced cooperation among the unemployed, trade unions, churches, small merchants, social workers, and professional associations and even black community groups such as the Urban League. A well-organized Ministerial Alliance was a moral force behind many of the activities of the AWU, and its interactions with relief and union activists gave those organizations a degree of legitimacy and moral authority that had eluded the UC. It was this movement that made the sit-down tactic familiar to St. Louis workers. Workers hosted sit-ins in relief offices on a regular basis. In April 1936, for instance, a racially integrated group of women and men, mostly members of the AWU, took over the city's Aldermanic Chambers, refusing to leave until the city agreed to withdraw the threat to cut off relief to fifteen thousand families.[95]

These community and workplace struggles had created alternative networks among workers outside the AFL. During 1935 and through 1936, the AWU continued to play a key role in raising consciousness of the need to unite the unemployed and the employed as well as work and community issues. Thus, the Left's trade union approach was distinguished from the AFL's in the period before the CIO, not just by industrial versus craft unionism per se but also by the effective linkage of workers' struggle with community-based mobilizations.

The possibilities raised by these connections affected the aspirations of radical activists such as Sentner. Sentner's involvement with the nut pickers and other black workers was transforming. The CP's focus on the black working class had helped to revive radical traditions and models for the labor movement, a vision of unionism that propelled Sentner into a lifetime of activism, where he sought to realize democratic, inclusive possibilities in the labor movement. That the CP was also an organization based on authoritarian and hierarchical principles antithetical to democratic ideals was a paradox that Sentner would never fully confront or resolve. But there is little doubt that to Sentner, the party would be an instrument to bring about a democratic, socialist future. "Every bone in his body was about democracy," avers Toni Sentner. "He lived and breathed the idea that the more democracy, the more power for workers. That was what socialism meant to him."[96]

These experiences sealed Sentner's commitment to the CP, though he did not join officially until 1934, after he "was beat up pretty badly in the police station, and it kind of shook my faith in a few things."[97] For most of 1935, Sentner was vice-chair of the St. Louis CP, and Shaw was local chair. (Before that point Shaw was continually diverted to the southern Illinois coalfields organizing.) Sentner's willingness to sacrifice and his allegiance to the party certainly was in part based on a romantic perception of the Soviet revolution and state. Like many others of his generation, he sought to make the Soviet Union reflect his own hopeful images. Sentner was attracted to the idea of being a part of an international movement tied to the leading revolutionary state. For someone like Sentner, with serious aspirations to change society, there was much of value in the

CP milieu that had kindled the fires of social transformation. Comrades such as Shaw carried forward radical traditions of struggle that had foundered in the 1920s. Sentner also learned from Alfred Wagenknecht, a "very warm and friendly person" affectionately known as "Wagonwheels," who became a district organizer in 1935. Wagenknecht, a former national chairman of the Socialist Party who had condemned World War I and gone to prison with Socialist leader Eugene Debs for these objections, became a Trades Union Educational League leader in the 1920s and learned labor-organizing strategies directly from the party's brilliant labor strategist, William Z. Foster. Foster had used industrial organizing strategies in the Chicago packinghouses and later the nationwide steel strike of 1919. Foster had taught Wagenknecht his commissary (food distribution) system and put him in charge of it in the battles of the coalfields in the 1920s in Pennsylvania, the Passaic textile strike of 1925–26, and the Gastonia textile strike of 1929. "Relief can lose a strike as well as win it," Wagenknecht advised, urging that relief only be used to support mass action.[98] Sentner later utilized the knowledge in the Emerson sit-down as well as in numerous other battles, perfecting strategies introduced in the nut pickers' strike.

These veterans found Sentner the most promising hope for a moribund St. Louis party, which during 1934 had foundered.[99] Party official Bill Gebert remarked to Earl Browder on the "heroism" of Sentner and others for their efforts to build the St. Louis party, which he called remarkable for "the art of starvation" of its organizers. Indeed, Toni Sentner remembered this time as one of extreme deprivation, of eating donated and spoiled food that contributed to the onset of her husband's ulcers and of walking twenty miles because he didn't have the money for bus fare to go to an organizing meeting in East St. Louis. The deprivation was tempered by Sentner's ever-plentiful supply of humor and wit and a significant degree of help from liberal friends who admired his work and gave him food and other financial support.[100]

Later, Sentner remembered that when he joined the party, he thought that "we would have a revolution," but from the beginning Sentner recognized that any social transformation would have to come out of American experiences.[101] Sentner's work with CP women activists such as Caroline Drew and women workers such as herself, Toni Sentner asserted, also turned him into a feminist in this period. In 1935, Drew proclaimed to fellow party activists in St. Louis that they would "teach men how to cook and women how to be leaders."[102] Sentner was by nature pragmatic, and coalition work with women activists probably influenced him to eschew perceptions of a macho, "romantic and heroic perception of violence" that Elizabeth Faue has detected among leftist labor activists during the 1930s.[103] In fact, FBI reports give examples of Sentner's restraint in the face of mass arrests. In July, 1933, he led 150 demonstrators to protest the jailing of rag company strikers. "Special officers remained at the door with drawn revolvers" as Sentner, according to the FBI, "protested stating he had led his friends peacefully to the station to protect them from what he termed 'police brutality.'" Sentner demanded the release of the women "because they were being held without cause in violation of the Constitution." The police captain treated their demands as "ridiculous" and told him that by bringing the mass demonstration, he was "advocating mob violence and intimidation against the constituted legal law enforcement agencies." Sentner dispersed the gathering when notified that the captain intended to use force to break up the crowd.[104] Nonviolence would remain a central tenet of Sentner's organizing and union activities, even in the most provocative of situations.

Sentner's politics by the time he became involved in the CIO drives were a hybrid fitting with the Popular Front: a blend of ideas from his own experiences and from writings by party leaders, advice from comrades such as Shaw, and Sentner's own inclinations and historical studies that developed an idealized conception of worker solidarity rooted in late-nineteenth-century visions of American populist democracy blended with feminist and antiracist amendments. In mid-1935, on the heels of the national party's decision to build the Popular Front, Sentner urged his comrades to remember the struggles of St. Louis workers in 1877 and beyond:

> In our District our Party is the inheritors of the splendid labor traditions and revolutionary backgrounds as laid by John Brown of Kansas, the correspondents of Marx and early abolitionists of St. Louis and Missouri, and the heroic farmers of Arkansas who led the premature Green-Corn rebellion during the world war in their attempt to turn it into a civil war. Yes, comrades, we can say that we are the inheritors of all that is good in the history of the gateway to the southwest. . . . This is the language and traditions of the workers and the farmers of our district that we must again revive.[105]

On May Day 1936, Sentner, speaking as marshal of the parade that included radicals and a few fledgling unions, insisted that "common folks" knew how to run the government, as demonstrated by the workers' history of the St. Louis region. "He was a St. Louis patriot!" recalled Robert Logsdon, who admired Sentner's love for and detailed knowledge of St. Louis and its history. (Sentner's intense interest in St. Louis history preceded his politicization. As a teenager, he was once fired as a Sunday School teacher for taking the children on a tour of St. Louis history without permission.) Now, however, he sought to awaken workers to the rich historic legacy long buried. Sentner liked to recount stories of the Knights' local struggles, and he embraced the political language of the Knights, filled with references to citizenship. With Sentner, the language was never a convenient veneer for an attempt to build a "Soviet America."[106]

While Sentner was trying to build the party, he continued to be involved in the AWU and some of the key labor struggles of the period. He organized janitors and became a representative of the Building Service Workers in the CTLU, "working within the AFL to break down the color line." He helped to establish the Negro Workers Council and to create an alliance between the black working class and the Urban League. From his position in the AFL, he became part of an ad hoc group organized within the local CTLU to promote organizing; this committee would become the base for the local CIO. Leaders of the brewery workers, the old Socialists linked to the St. Louis labor movement's radical past, reestablishing themselves in the aftermath of the repeal of Prohibition, regarded him as an extremely effective organizer. He also established wider regional contacts, such as those from the network of radicals associated with Commonwealth College, established in the early 1920s as one of a series of movement schools whose curriculum was designed to produce grassroots organizers committed to radical change, break down racial divisions, and connect southern labor concerns with the rest of the labor movement. (The model was used to establish a St. Louis Labor College in the 1930s as well.)[107]

In mid-1936 Sentner was hired for the CIO's Steel Workers Organizing Committee. He and Ralph Shaw began a union drive at Scullin Steel, which had a high percentage of black workers. Initially the drive drew large numbers of black and white workers, but racial unity proved tenuous. Scullin management enticed black workers away from the drive by placing them on jobs formerly preserved for white workers, leaving the union drive compromised. If Sentner had intended to help launch the CIO drive by organizing a base of black workers, this experience may have tempered his ambitions.[108]

By the beginning of the CIO drive, Sentner had a wealth of organizing experience, many contacts in the area, and an understanding of the local political economy. In a mid-1936 letter to John Brophy, head of the organizing drive for the newly established CIO, Sentner introduced himself as someone "with wide friendship in the labor movement as well as among liberal people generally." Rather than support the CIO national leadership's plan to organize steel first, Sentner urged the CIO to concentrate on organizing the electrical industry in St. Louis, a plan he had initially proposed to the CP in late 1935: "[I]t is my opinion that this industry, if organized . . . would revitalize the entire St. Louis labor movement."[109] Sentner's prediction would be proven correct, but not because the national CIO acted on Sentner's advice. While the national leaders of the CIO kept their focus on the steel drive, a self-organized core of electrical workers at Emerson Electric and the local Left brought results at Emerson.

The ability of the Left to emerge as leaders among the electrical workers, discussed in chapter 3, underscores the importance of the early 1930s wherein two parallel threads of development emanated from the failures of the previous era. First, workers' contentiousness indicated the potential to challenge employers' power in the electrical industry. However, employers were able to keep the new insurgency from threatening their ability to control their enterprises through instruments that had worked effectively since the World War I era. Breaking through this industry would resonate with the St. Louis working class, under-mining the political economy of control. Understanding the community basis of employer power was essential to any organizing strategy in the 1930s, as it had been in the previous generation. Second, worker radicalism, thoroughly con-quered in the earlier era, reemerged in the early 1930s in organizing that began with the unemployed movement. This movement became a vessel for the les-sons of earlier generations, including the incorporation of community-based strategies. The legacy of the earlier era, when radical impulses had been squelched, could not, however, be erased. And while a fair assessment has to credit the CP as the midwife to the rebirth and growth of a radical vision of unionism in St. Louis tied to older working-class traditions, the fact that it grew within an organization reviled as "foreign" and tied to the Soviet Union would make the project of radicalizing workers in the 1930s fraught with problems from the outset.

CHAPTER 3

"Human Rights over Property Rights"
Forging Movement Unionism in District 8

A self-organized workers movement at Emerson Electric, the strategic role of radicals in the local plants, and the nationwide workplace upheaval of late 1936 and early 1937 broke the open shop of the St. Louis electrical independents and created District 8 of the United Electrical, Radio and Machine Workers of America (UE). The strategies and styles that had been constructed in the early 1930s' struggles now resonated among electrical workers in 1937. Workers used a community-based strategy tied to a nationwide movement and a dramatic plant occupation that became the second longest sit-down in the United States. In the formative period of the district, William Sentner and the leftist activists were able to deflect anticommunism and influence the development of a movement that challenged employers' control of the shop floor and the community labor market.

The strategic role of the left-wing activists can only be viewed against the background of self-organization attempts among electrical workers, including those that culminated in the disappointing Century and Emerson drives of 1933–35. Just as the Emerson company union was floundering in mid-1936, these activists, committed to building the Congress of Industrial Organizations (CIO), began to organize in the St. Louis electrical industry.

The Emerson Drive

The local Communist Party (CP) sent young activists into the St. Louis electrical industry based on the party's policy of "concentration," which Sentner defined as paying "special attention to a specific project and . . . relat[ing] all other work to the success of this project." Sentner and other party activists' analysis was based on their understanding of the local political economy: "the wages paid in this industry set the pattern for the community and almost all other industries." The electrical industry was the open shop stronghold: "the industry was almost totally home-owned and had direct ties through their managements with banks and other industrial establishments." It had become a major industry in the area, composed of many semiskilled and unskilled workers as well as a large group of skilled metal workers. Given this, local CP activists and leadership "decided that the key to the organization of the unorganized in this area was the organization of the electrical industry, and in particular the three main plants, Emerson, Century and Wagner." Sentner and local CP activists knew of the attempt to form an independent union at Emerson in 1935 and were thus aware of the previous efforts to organize.[1]

This "colonizing" of plants was not the stuff of intrigue depicted in later House Un-American Activities Committee hearings and movies about the CP, where portrayals suggested highly coordinated cells tied to a national network of Soviet agents. The strategy was the product of more than a year of dialogue and debate and was not derived centrally from New York, where both the CP and the UE were headquartered. Those affiliated with the party in the UE's top leadership were hardly aware of what was going on in St. Louis until the fall of 1936, months after the local campaign was under way. National party leaders were interested in providing organizers for the Steel Workers Organizing Committee (SWOC) campaign, the major focus of John L. Lewis and the new CIO leadership.[2] What emerges from the evidence is testament to the important role of the local Left in putting in motion the plan for organization. Their plan was based on their understanding of the local political economy.

CP member Bob Manewitz was hired at Emerson in February 1936. Manewitz's father had been a local CP leader in the 1920s. Manewitz remembered growing up in a home that was "sort of the neighborhood center"; the "whole atmosphere" was one of "a feeling in regard for people." Manewitz joined the Young Communist League (YCL) at the age of fourteen and the CP in 1935. He was active in the relief protests and in labor support work of the early 1930s, including the nut pickers' struggles and the American Workers Union (AWU) campaigns.[3]

Around May 1936 Manewitz contacted Lou and George Kimmel, two Emerson paint shop workers he knew from relief organizing. Both brothers worked as spray hands in the fan line in Emerson's Building H, where Manewitz worked on the assembly line. The Kimmel brothers' father had been a socialist union activist in the Granite City, Illinois, Lodge 8 of the Amalgamated Association of Iron Steel and Tin Workers, which in the prewar era had advocated industrial unionism and socialism; he had been blacklisted for his activities. George Kimmel got a job at Emerson around 1925, and Lou started work there a few years later. Lou married in 1935 and, with his wife Fritzi, became active in the movement. "Lou and I were searching for a better way," Fritzi Kimmel remembered. In the early 1930s, they circulated among a variety of groups, including the St. Louis socialist discussion group the Utopia Club, and were active in the AWU. Sometime during the course of the Emerson organizing drive, both brothers joined the party. The two were well known among Emerson workers not for their politics but for their boxing talent. (Lou held the light heavyweight amateur championship for the Missouri Valley for two years, but George "wrecked his arm" at Emerson as a spray gun operator.) The union's initial meetings were held in the Tower Athletic Club in northern St. Louis where the Kimmels were training for the Golden Gloves matches. The brothers were "extremely effective as organizers, probably the most effective in there," according to Bob Logsdon, the fourth key organizer at Emerson.[4]

Logsdon came from Junction, Illinois, a small coal town. He excelled in high school and won a scholarship to Illinois College in Jacksonville. His family, however, could not afford to send him, a disappointment he still felt years later. In 1923 he joined the rural youth migration of the 1920s to St. Louis. After a number of temporary jobs, he was hired at Western Union where he worked his way up to assistant building manager. Just before Christmas 1931, he was laid off. He moved back with his parents for a while and for a time worked for farmers. Eventually he came back to St. Louis to search again for a job. "I started to go to the library on Jefferson and Lafayette. Read a little of *The Nation, The New Republic.* . . . I think they also had *The Daily Worker.* . . . And I got interested in that sort of business." Logsdon became involved politically to the extent that the first date with his future wife, Fern, was to hear Socialist Norman Thomas speak. Sometime during this period, Logsdon joined the Socialist Party (SP).[5]

When Logsdon was hired on the refrigerator motor assembly line at Emerson in 1934, he began a very erratic employment experience that was frequently punctuated by layoffs. He soon decided to start organizing a union: "And I thought, well, I'll go to the Socialist headquarters, they'll know where the unions were." But, as Logsdon recalled with amusement, he took a wrong turn. "I went to the Carpenters Hall and asked them if this was Socialist Headquarters," he laughed. "They looked at me! . . . So nothing happened there." Logsdon dropped plans for organizing: layoffs made any plans difficult to carry out. He had "nothing to do" with the company union. But the other key activists recognized him from his association with the SP and the AWU. When Lou and George Kimmel asked him in the spring of 1936 if he wanted to come to the meeting with them, he eagerly joined them.[6]

Thus it was actually from unemployed movement networks that the core organizers found each other. Manewitz invited Sentner to the first meeting, and from this point, though he was assigned at the time as an SWOC organizer, Sentner guided the organizing strategy.[7] Years later, Sentner chastised a CP activist who wrote a leaflet giving sole credit to "a handful of communists" for organizing Emerson. Sentner reminded him of the "movement from below" that propelled the drive. But for machine shop worker Lloyd Austin, who had seen other organization attempts easily put down by management, these left-wing activists were "the light at the end of the tunnel, come to show you the way out."[8]

Over the course of the summer, the key organizers slowly built their ranks, attempting to get a member from each of the departments. In July and August, Manewitz reported a high degree of enthusiasm for the drive among key Employees Representation Plan (ERP) representatives, three of whom joined the group. Together they determined that "about 28 of the 30 representatives [could] be won over to an industrial union in the plant." While seasonal layoffs made a big organizing push inadvisable at the time, twenty-one workers chartered Local 1102 in August, electing Oscar Debus as president of the group. Debus, a ceiling fan assembly line worker for seventeen years, had remained active in the ERP, where he had been secretary pro tem. He had also been involved in the 1935 effort to form an independent union. Debus needed little persuading to join the CIO and responded well to the strategies set forth by the leftist organizers, marking a pattern that would be followed by others associated with the company union. While waiting for employment levels to resume, workers attended classes organized by the St. Louis Labor College, a "school for workers" modeled on and using instructors from Commonwealth College. There Emerson workers attended sessions on topics such as political economy, the basics of industrial unionism, and organizing.[9]

At Emerson, semiskilled and unskilled workers were the most receptive to the industrial union drive, as would be the case in most of the locals of District 8 over the course of the next ten years. The organizers were most successful in the assembly departments, comprised of mostly unskilled and semiskilled workers, where some of the key prounion ERP representatives held influence. (The key exception was the small motor line assembly, with large groups of women.) By October 1936, those departments were completely organized. Skilled workers, on the other hand, were initially reluctant to join the UE. In December, Manewitz reported that the organizers had "persuaded the tool and die and machining [departments] to work with us," but they "were not the backbone of the effort." UE secretary-treasurer Julius Emspak told Manewitz that the local's experience was typical in the broad experience of the UE except that "in one instance, [tool makers and machinists] provided the initiative to organize."[10]

That skilled workers climbed to some of the leading positions in the union drive probably had more to do with the acceptance of the political realities of coalition building than with a proclivity among skilled workers toward organizing unskilled workers into an industrial union movement. The skilled workers' pivotal role in the manufacturing process made their position strategic in the coalition that was necessary for success. Skilled workers were the key to shutting down a factory; their positions gave them authority in the plant. The assembly line workers who initiated the drive coaxed representatives of the tool and die workers and other skilled workers into leadership roles in the UE. When tool and die maker and International Association of Machinists member Frank Schlieman agreed to join the CIO in the late fall of 1936, he moved quickly into a leadership position. Schlieman's authority also derived from his status as an elder worker, from his association with the company union movement and with the failed independent union drive of late 1935–early 1936. In December 1936, when the union decided to run union candidates for the ERP board, Schlieman was elected president. This was an achievement mirrored in countless struggles in the 1930s. The tug toward exclusivity among skilled workers remained a factor in the history of District 8, as it was elsewhere in the UE and throughout the CIO.[11]

With coalition building as the goal, radicals placed recruitment of women among the highest priorities. After the executive board reduced dues for women and after some women leaders signed up, others joined steadily. The company union had excluded women and had not been concerned about women's low pay rate. Now a woman was elected to a leadership position in the organizing committee. The small number of black workers also soon gained a representative in the organizing committee. By late November the union had 150 signed members, and the following month the group elected its slate of workers to the ERP.[12]

Manewitz wrote to the UE national office several times, urging them to send an experienced organizer to help build the kind of community coalition that was necessary to win a strike. The lack of a functioning committee at Century, and only a fledgling one at Wagner, was most troublesome. But the UE's few resources were concentrated in trouble spots in the East. Emspak pleaded a lack of resources but promised to send an organizer as soon as it was possible.[13]

Recognizing the potential of the drive, the local leftist leadership increased their involvement. Sentner began to devote more of his time to the drive despite his official position as an SWOC organizer. Clara Warnick, who was district director of the local YCL and recently had been an organizer in the famed cotton pickers' strike in Arkansas, got a job at Century. She was soon "discovered" and fired.[14]

Henry Fiering replaced Warnick as the "colonizer" at Century. Fiering came from a working-class radical background. His father, a Socialist who initially sided with the left wing but then dropped out after 1919, had been blacklisted in Ohio for his union activism. Fiering grew up in New York and had been generally apolitical until 1931, when rounds of unemployment and youth activism in New York jolted him. He became active in the CP, he remembered, because Communists were "action-oriented, results-oriented," and "had the biggest thing going." Fiering came to St. Louis because of his romantic attachment to Warnick (whom he would later marry). For a time he was involved in the unemployed movement and the American Youth Congress, but by late 1936 he was one of the local CP activists hired for the SWOC drive as an organizer at American Foundry. But when Fiering was needed at Century, leaving SWOC was not a difficult decision. He recalled the local SWOC director's methods as less than satisfying: "My work was to sign cards. They had their own MO [modus operandi] as far as organization was concerned. I would be assigned to go out to visit people individually and sign them up. There was no such thing as the kind of organization I had looked forward to."[15]

As the drive intensified and as Emerson workers approached a high level of organization, the UE national office began to pay attention to its outpost. UE officers were impressed with the way that the local was methodically building its ranks. Finally, in January 1937, after the Emerson workers passed a resolution demanding it, Sentner was appointed field organizer for the UE on a part-time basis. Theoretically, he was to continue organizing for the SWOC part-time. But Sentner soon completely abandoned that position as he and the workers were swept up in the CIO momentum that was played out in the electrical industry in St. Louis.[16]

In late 1936, the CIO movement was given an enormous boost when workers at General Motors (GM) plant in Flint, Michigan, launched a sit-down that catalyzed, within a month, into a nationwide strike against GM. St. Louis's GM plant shutdown was accomplished by a community coalition, composed of AWU members, Emerson union activists, miners from southern Illinois, and other local activists. They congregated at the plant gates and successfully appealed to auto workers to remain outside.[17] Across the country, such community-based actions combined with shop floor drama gave hope and momentum to workers. The UE organizers initiated radio broadcasts and a "flying squad" of fifteen workers to distribute organizing material at the other plants. Workers' enthusiasm for action mounted. The landmark victory of GM workers at Flint in mid-February 1937 brought scores of Emerson, Century, and Wagner workers to a CIO mass meeting.[18]

Despite the CIO's rising tide, Emerson's managers were confident that they could defeat the union drive. On the eve of the CIO drive, in July 1936, Emerson managers joined other local metal trades businessmen, under the aegis of the National Metal Trades Association (NMTA), in a meeting designed to formulate strategies. The NMTA had lost some of its local focus in the years since World War I, the kind of focus that had been aided by the Citizens' Industrial Alliance. During the Depression, employers associated with the NMTA had relied on the poor economic situation rather than local strategic coordination to keep workers in line. To be sure, there was a local committee, headed by the management of the "big three," but most personnel matters had been generally left up to each individual plant. At the meeting, managers expressed regret that "in the past six years Management has paid very little attention . . . to keeping the support and loyalty of its working personnel." (They apparently dismissed the thousands of dollars they had spent on spies and stool pigeons during the earlier organizing drives from 1933 to 1936, expenditures later revealed by the Senate's LaFollette Committee.) Meanwhile, "radicals and malcontents . . . ha[d] organized as never before." The participants agreed to work together on the local level, across industries, and to explore many possible personnel programs. They agreed that

the programs could vary as long as they did not allow "putting some of the powers of management into the hands of the workers"; there would be "no hint of
any such relinquishment." Among the programs suggested was one of posting
comparative community wage rates in the factory to discourage workers from
believing that they were entitled to wage increases.[19]

NMTA operatives and stool pigeons kept the companies, and especially
Emerson, abreast of the CIO drive. In October 1936, the NMTA reported that
Sentner had urged Emerson workers to "slow down the tempo of their work"
and "passively resist any attempts at speed-up," as part of the strategy to build
support for the union among workers. But NMTA spies were confident that the
union drive was mostly isolated to the Emerson plant. Further, the company's
attorneys, like others across the country, assured Emerson's Newman that the
Wagner Act (which gave workers legal rights to organize and an enforcement
agency, the National Labor Relations Board, to investigate and punish violations
of the act) was unconstitutional; if management could hold the union drive at
bay until the Supreme Court ruled unfavorably on the act, they would best the
core activists' strategy. Reflecting forty years of experience in defeating union
drives, the company thus proceeded with a certain degree of impassivity.[20]

Ironically, Emerson's strained financial status was considered its trump card
to outmaneuver the union. Emerson was entering another capital crisis just as
the workers' movement was escalating. In early 1937, to provide leverage in the
event of a strike, the company began to build a modest inventory of fans to fill
orders. A short strike under these circumstances could actually be beneficial to
the company, allowing it to avoid wage payments. Workers would return
demoralized, having been let down by misleading promises from the radical
organizers.[21]

Still, through threats and cajoling, supervisors sought to divide the coalition.
They talked to "200 of the older employees," especially skilled workers, reminding them of the steady work they had obtained from Emerson over the years.
They reminded women of the men's initial opposition to their employment.
Foremen demanded that women sign cards professing regret that they had
joined the CIO in order to keep their jobs. While a few women did sign the
cards, this strategy was also a failure. Then, in the midst of what would normally
be the company's busy season, and just after the GM strike, the company laid off
more than two hundred workers. Management suggested that a strike might
cause the company to close. But workers seemed immune to the threats and
warnings; years of broken promises steeled them in their resolve.[22]

By March 6, Local 1102 was on the "threshold of 100% organization" at Emerson. Sentner reported that while he hoped the company would yield to the overwhelming numbers, the union had "greased our machinery for strike action." A
steward system was operational and ready to take charge of a strike, and they
had already put together the "necessary apparatus for the raising of local

finances as well as relief." James Carey, the young president of the UE, immediately wired back, pleading with Sentner not to strike. The national union's funds were stretched, with uncoordinated strikes taking place in response to the CIO national drive.[23]

But by the time Carey's telegram arrived, it was already too late. At noon on March 8, Emerson's workers had launched a sit-down strike at the main plant, surprising the UE national office as well as NMTA spies and the managers who hired them. Most workplace sit-downs in the 1930s were orchestrated by strategic groups of workers in key departments. As Ronald Schatz has noted, electrical plant production generally defied this tactic. But Emerson's workers were so well organized that they took over the plant simultaneously at every level. Two hundred of the youngest workers (many of them with relatively short records of employment, and all but fifty of them without family obligations) occupied the Washington Avenue offices. They went floor-by-floor escorting foremen out the door.[24]

A "picnic atmosphere" prevailed among the sit-downers and their supporters on the first day and for much of the duration of the strike. "Just think of that— us workers telling the bosses to get out of the plant!" said Gilbert Kamp, recalling the audacity more than fifty years later. While the sit-downers set up facilities to prepare for occupation, hundreds of workers and sympathizers paraded outside, arms linked and singing songs. When asked if he could remember what he thought on the first day that events unfolded, Lloyd Austin recalled that at the time he thought "we had laid down the gauntlet." For what? "For freedom."[25]

Emerson Sit-Down Strike

During the initial weeks of the strike, the leadership sought to solidify its own ranks, mobilize community support, and prepare to extend the strike to other electrical plants. A flurry of activity could be witnessed at strike headquarters on a daily basis. A picket system kept eighty strikers and supporters on the lines every day. Women workers and some wives and children of strikers, as well as unemployed movement activists and other community supporters, joined the picket line on daily assignments, singing songs and leading cheers outside the plant. "I walked the picket line every day I possibly could," recalled Marie Strathman, who was inspired by the effectiveness and organization to do even more to win. Socialist Party leader Norman Thomas and Pulitzer Prize–winning novelist Josephine Johnson as well as less well known ministers and liberals joined workers on the line to show support. Groups of strikers paid visits to workers at their homes to sign them up and get them involved. A team of twenty-five doctors sympathetic to labor issues agreed to provide free medical care to the strikers and their families. A welfare committee helped strikers' families meet bills and fend off bill collectors. A cafeteria owner across the street from the plant turned over his operation as a union commissary. Teams of workers solicited food from bakers and merchants in the strikers' neighborhoods. Six food squad leaders collected the supplies. A newsletter, the *Emerson Equalizer,* was produced by a team of workers. Classes were organized by the St. Louis Labor College for sit-downers and strikers. Union members chose some of the topics to be explored, and classes were followed by open forums.[26]

Sentner recognized that the UE needed to spread the strike to the three large independents. A "well-functioning organizing committee of 25 people," led by five men and two women worked toward this end. Throughout March, Emerson workers conducted handbilling and marches on the two other main plants, and the organizing committee developed more contacts at the plant from workers' own networks.[27]

The strategy developed in the Emerson strike established a pattern that would be replicated throughout all of District 8's struggles: building as much support as possible by tying the struggle to the community and using this support and other tactics to keep reactionary forces at bay. Sentner and the committee contrived ways to get news stories to keep up strikers' morale, and two of the three major papers gave favorable coverage. Several local reporters covering the strike were themselves close to the labor movement, as they were taking part in an organizing drive of the Newspaper Guild, and at least one was a member of the CP.[28]

Throughout the strike, Sentner stressed the connection between workers' immediate demands and the issues of community and power, both to the strikers and the public. He linked the struggle to the city's welfare: "Our organization, which is primarily interested in the economic welfare of the working people, is however also interested in the effects of their economic status on our community."[29] The strikers placed the struggle not only in the context of the nationwide CIO drive but as part of a challenge to the local political economy and local control of the labor market: "You are not striking for yourselves alone," he declared. "This is a civic strike because if everybody in this town received the pay scale you get St. Louis would be a shanty town."[30] "It is this low wage scale which has given St. Louis the black name of an open shop Southern labor town."[31] The Emerson sit-down strike "is important," Sentner stressed, "because it represents the first effort to organize electrical workers of the St. Louis area to prevent employers from using St. Louis as a low-wage field, thereby cutting down wage standards which have been established by the CIO in other areas."[32]

"We have been able to make the whole issue a civic one involving the mayor and forcing him to demand a settlement," Sentner reported to the national office on March 27. The campaign began with a visit by a striker/CIO delegation who asked Mayor Dickmann to set up conferences with the company. The mayor, engaged in another election campaign (almost exactly four years after the Funsten strike), agreed. But Newman had left town on a "goodwill tour" (to explore marketing and trading arrangements) of the South organized by the St. Louis Chamber of Commerce. This played perfectly with the union's portrayal of the company as lacking the "civic concern" that might end the strike.

A bit of theater conveyed their judgment. When the train that carried New-man pulled in, groups of strikers and supporters, half of whom were women, greeted him carrying a funeral wreath and placards declaring that the company union was dead and that "We Can't Go South on 25 Cents an Hour—We Demand 50 Cents an Hour." An embarrassed Newman stayed on the train rather than confront the paraders. Thereafter, Newman's continued refusal to allow the mayor to set up conferences and his insistence that the workers could not dissolve the ERP received a great deal of coverage in St. Louis newspapers. "Mr. Newman," Dickmann told Ethan Shepley, an Emerson board member, "cannot sit in his office and ignore this strike. It is a serious matter, and will have serious consequences." Newman's rejection of the mayor's mediation attempts "strengthened our position in the public eye," Sentner reported.[33] Meanwhile, on election day, sit-down strikers elected a "Mayor of Emerson" from among their ranks, theatrically and comically fashioning their intentions for represen-tation in the company and connecting representation to the city's welfare.[34]

As the union appealed for public support, it also worked to prevent a reac-tionary response to the radical tactic of the sit-down. Sentner announced to the press that workers had vowed "no violence" during the sit-down. Sentner and other CIO officials made an arrangement with the police chief that allowed workers themselves to patrol the plant area on the promise that the union would ensure order, thus "giving us control of the strike in and about the plant." This would of course also ensure that the company would be unable to marshal a back-to-work movement by the NMTA. This arrangement was aided by sympa-thetic contacts between local United Automobile Workers leaders and the police that had developed when a hired GM "thug" brutalized the son of a police ser-geant in the aftermath of that strike. It marked a significant departure in rela-tions between St. Louis workers and the police.[35]

The Emerson strike inspired other sit-downs and organizing drives in St. Louis factories. As Sentner commented in late March, "It is my opinion and this has been confirmed by others . . . that OUR STRIKE at EMERSON has aroused the workers in the other Electrical plants as well as in other plants in about the same manner as Flint aroused the auto workers." Shoe, warehouse, furniture, hotel and restaurant personnel, clerks, and many other workers in small shops in St. Louis's central manufacturing district were suddenly answering the CIO call, whereas they had remained hesitant even after the auto workers' victory. Sentner trained dozens of workers in hastily arranged organizing classes that could hardly accommodate the demand. Emerson workers aided these other strikes and organizing efforts. As was the case across the country during the height of the CIO surge, workers marched on other workers' picket lines and helped to shut down the plants in the ferment that developed in the aftermath of the Emerson sit-down. Sentner concluded that "the whole future of the CIO organizations in this entire district [was] wrapped up in this fight."[36]

Workers at some small metal trades plants, including Johnston Tin-Foil, a subsidiary of a Pittsburgh company located in Carondelet in the far southern area of St. Louis, joined the movement en masse and quickly made plans for sit-downs. Management locked out these workers before they could implement their plans, but the company conceded and began to negotiate with the union. It was the first clear UE success in the area. Baldor Electric, a plant of just 120 workers who produced small machinery, transformers, and motors, also organized completely in the weeks after the Emerson strike.[37]

The financing of the Emerson strike, which became more urgent as days turned into weeks and as the possibility of a general strike in the industry developed, involved a great deal of community-wide appeals and organizing by rank-and-file workers. In order to continue to build support for their struggle, workers visited other unions and organizations. As with Funsten, unopened pay envelopes were used as evidence of the low wages of Emerson's workers, particularly those of women. Over the course of the strike the local collected a total of twenty-five thousand dollars. Only a small amount of that money came from the UE nationally, and none came from the national CIO, which was still pouring its money into the steel drive. The most substantial money came from the brewery workers and the southern Illinois Progressive Miners, neither of which was in the CIO.[38]

Just as in the nut pickers' struggle, the strikers decided to force local relief officials to rescind their practice of refusing relief to strikers, a policy that had been issued and left unchallenged during the GM strike. A "strikers' welfare committee" led by George Kimmel protested to the mayor, who agreed that "the best policy is to give relief to strikers" but noted that only the state administration could force a change in the local policy. Kimmel led groups of strikers to the governor's office and to the state administrator of relief, who informed the St. Louis office that there was no state prohibition of relief to strikers. When the St. Louis relief administrator refused to budge on the issue, a racially mixed group of people, including Emerson strikers and supporters, strikers from other plants, and unemployed activists from the Workers' Alliance (which had merged with the AWU to become the new umbrella group of the unemployed), staged a two-day sit-down in the St. Louis relief offices. The St. Louis relief board finally reversed its policy. In reaction, four relief board members associated with the St. Louis financial and social elite resigned in protest. An Urban League observer felt the CIO movement was "more than just an organizational campaign" when workers "lock arms with their fellow white workers in the picket line; sit down with them; and comb the community together soliciting food and funds."[39]

Throughout March and early April, the Emerson Electric Company waited for the strikers' momentum to fade. The company's policy was guided not only by advice from the NMTA but in particular by one member of Emerson's board of directors, Alroy Phillips. Phillips represented the interest of his sister Gertrude Meston, the widow of Emerson's former director Tom Meston, a younger brother of the Emerson founders. Phillips had important connections to some American Federation of Labor (AFL) officials that dated from his role as a lead attorney in the fight for workman's compensation legislation. He still served as an attorney for several AFL unions. Phillips steered management's course of action, hoping to defeat the new CIO union without resort to violence and negative publicity. Using stool pigeons and advice from AFL officials, he laid plans with Newman to defeat the strike even before workers called it. Phillips advised Newman to take the goodwill tour, and even when that turned into negative publicity, he continued to think that the company would prevail.[40]

The strategy devised by Phillips, Newman, and the NMTA to wait while workers tired of the battle was based on the advice of Phillips's AFL "labor friends," who counseled him that the strike must be allowed to "run its course." One of Phillips's AFL confidants, ironically, was O. E. Jennings, the head of the electricians' union, who had represented the Wagner strikers during the 1918 battle and who at the time had pressed for amalgamation and for organizing women. That vision was now forgotten; Jennings was glad to do his part to prevent any new eruption of industrial organizing under the CIO. On March 19, he advised company officials to be patient and dryly remarked to Phillips that "the strike needs another week" to begin to decline.[41] Ten days later, a different AFL official repeated the same advice. Whatever else they advised, Phillips felt confident that the company's relatively passive response to the strikers was the best approach.[42] Meanwhile, Phillips and Emerson management were buoyed by the rivalry between the AFL and the CIO: "[AFL president] Green has done all I want by asking AFL members to get out of CIO unions," Phillips wrote in one diary entry. Green and William Frey, head of the AFL metal trades federation, chose St. Louis as the launching point of their five hundred thousand-dollar campaign to organize metal fabricating plants. Sentner was convinced that the drive was launched in response to the Emerson sit-down.[43]

As the strikers' momentum continued to build, management's doubts about their strategy deepened. Both sides understood that spreading the strike to other electrical plants was the key to union victory. Century and Wagner raised wages in an attempt to stifle the union drive, and Wagner hastily organized a company union.[44] Newman counted on these other two factories to hold back the tide. Phillips noted in his diary entry for March 29 that "Newman thinks [the] Century walkout will be [a] failure and when it fails our men will give up."[45]

Indeed, NMTA operatives reported that few workers had signed membership cards. Century had formed a company union to circumvent the drive, and its officers and supporters were tool and die workers, who were key to any walkout. In early April the company union conducted a poll and claimed that 90 percent of workers voted against "outside" representation. Henry Fiering, the UE's lead organizer, was fired in March along with eight other UE supporters. Fiering noted that "by the time of the Emerson strike, only fifty-two people had signed union cards."[46]

Still, as Fiering relates, when 650 Century workers came to a meeting and voted to join the strike, the leadership decided to move. Fiering explained that "it's indicative of the temper of the working class at the time. In a shop you've got 4 percent of the people signed up on cards, not really organized, and a good portion of them, eight out of fifty-two, fired, that you can dare to call a strike and expect to win." More than 1,500 workers from other shops, especially Emerson, as well as other supporters massed on the Century entrances to close its doors. A car with a loudspeaker circled the plant encouraging workers to show class solidarity by joining Emerson workers in taking on the electrical open shop. Works manager Robert Hill, frantically pointing to hundreds of workers who moved back and forth on the sidewalk in front of the building, announced to the press and to police, "I never saw most of those people before!" To Century managers, according to Fiering, it was clear who was responsible: "I remember this Bob Hill telling the police, 'Get that redheaded red son of a bitch, that's the guy!'"[47]

Fiering attested that a "veritable war" was fought to keep the plant shut down. Despite scores of arrests, each day more of Century's employees refused to cross the line. On the first day of the strike, around 450 employees remained in the plant. On the second day, only 150 went to work. On the third day, the company decided to close the plant and whitewash its windows. More than 1,200 workers joined the union in the next week.[48] At Century's foundry, leaflets called for interracial unity and promised that the mistakes of the 1934 strike would not be repeated. Century management, fearing an interracial occupation of the plant, welded shut the steel doors to the foundry.[49]

Century workers had the good fortune to strike the company on the day before the Supreme Court declared the Wagner Act constitutional. Across the country, managers woke up to the news and bemoaned the political tide that was moving toward them, now even in their cherished preserve, the courts. "No longer can the Joe Newmans and the Pillsburys [of Century Electric] deny the rights of their workers under the flimsy excuse that the Wagner Act is unconstitutional!" the union's strike bulletin gleefully declared. Legal scholar Jim Pope has shown that the determination of workers such as those in Local 1102 to occupy plants in defiance of employers' property rights claims influenced the court's Wagner decision.[50]

Despite the Supreme Court ruling, Century was not ready to give up. Management decided to bring in scabs provided through the NMTA and petitioned for an injunction, which was also signed by workers who had backed the Works

Council.[51] But as the union succeeded in shutting down the plant, these workers, in a dramatic moment that signified the shifting tide, withdrew their names from the injunction and joined the CIO. One of the workers, tool and die maker Fred Riethmeyer, explained that "everybody was jittery, so we signed" the injunction. Now, though, he and others could see, according to Fiering, that "this was not going to be another 1934."[52]

The reversal took Century managers by surprise and aided the union's case against the injunction. Century's management was then outraged when the judge refused to allow them to prove that Sentner was a Communist. The St. Louis assistant chief of police described Sentner as a leader who controlled "hotheads" during labor strife and applauded the peacefulness of the Emerson sit-down. The judge finally granted Century its injunction on April 20 but allowed 50 picketers at each plant entrance, hardly the barrier to mass action that Century had desired. When the company tried to reopen the plant, only 150 workers returned. The injunction was still a threat, and Century workers were still prosecuted under it. But it was not enough to dash the newfound confidence that had been rekindled among a segment of Century's workers. Two hundred workers became the nucleus of a force that, Sentner reported on April 25, gave promise that "we will win the battle" against Century.[53]

Community and state forces and momentum were clearly with the electrical workers. Emerson's management had miscalculated when they relied on Century to hold back the tide. In his April 12 diary entry, Alroy Phillips noted with an air of resignation that he "read [the] Wagner Labor Relations Act decision the rest of the afternoon." Looming over the company was the prospect of hearings on unfair labor practices that the National Labor Relations Board (NLRB) was ready to begin, hearings that would prove embarrassing and reveal its financial troubles. On April 15, Emerson was able to stave off the hearings by conceding to bargain. Newman and the company attorneys had wanted to insist on plant evacuation as a precondition to bargaining, as typically was the case in many CIO sit-downs, but Phillips persuaded them otherwise. In any case, the sit-downers quickly served notice that they would not leave until the company signed an agreement with full recognition of the UE. As Schlieman explained, workers had heard promises for "35 years in the Emerson plant and then nothing was ever done."[54]

Newman, who had earlier vowed to government officials that he would not attempt to forcibly evict workers from the plant, now considered a concerted counterattack employing red-baiting and injunctions to evict the sit-downers. He wanted to establish a strategy of "continuing along" in negotiations until "an investigation" of the CIO might give management the upper hand.[55] Newman particularly was repulsed by the idea of negotiating with a Communist and hoped that an NMTA "exposure" of Communists in the CIO might salvage victory after the Supreme Court decision. The local NMTA mailed out the right-wing tract

Join the CIO and Help Build a Soviet America, which made the charge that the CIO was riddled with Communists, to all employees of metal trades firms.

Sentner responded in the union newsletter by reminding workers that "OURS IS A DEMOCRATIC ORGANIZATION, an American organization based on TRUE DEMOCRACY," which includes all workers "REGARDLESS OF THEIR RELIGION, COLOR, CREED OR POLITICAL BELIEF." In the weeks that followed, Newman's plans to use red-baiting were foiled by the NLRB, which refused to allow the issue to be brought forward in any of the proceedings regarding worker representation. Furthermore, the LaFollette Senate Civil Liberties Committee had already begun to issue records of the numerous abuses by employers, shocking revelations that rendered red-baiting less effective.[56]

Alroy Phillips, still seeking to avoid a direct confrontation and under pressure from Emerson stock underwriters to help bring about an end to the strike, made overtures to other CIO leadership. He sought out Max Michelson, the head of the Amalgamated Clothing Workers of America (ACWA) and leading official of the CIO in St. Louis, to intervene. Michelson agreed that "quick settlement" was best.[57] Then, a local newspaper reporter suggested to Phillips that Emerson officials meet UE president James Carey, who was visiting the St. Louis strikers to prepare for negotiations, "to dispel their negative perceptions of the CIO." Phillips arranged for Newman to meet Carey. Afterward Phillips noted in his diary, with obvious delight, that the two "became chummy."[58] This was not the last time that District 8 leftists used Carey to present a moderate face of the UE.

Workers summarily rejected the CIO's plan for a quick settlement, while Sentner proved unwilling to sacrifice workers' allegiance to become a "responsible" CIO leader. Carey took center stage in the negotiations, however, and agreed to a settlement that called for little more than union recognition and continued negotiations on wage issues after workers returned. This was in fact a typical CIO sit-down settlement, but it shows why many UE workers distrusted him in negotiations. According to Phillips's diary, in the negotiations prior to Carey's entry into the bargaining site, Newman and Sentner had rejected each other's proposals for evacuation, though Newman had agreed to several points in the union's proposal. Carey then made a proposal "more satisfactory to Newman than his own," without checking with Sentner and the executive committee, who then were in an awkward position of rejecting their president's negotiations. Carey left town that night.

The next morning, April 22, the committee secured a few provisions that were more favorable and, under pressure from Michelson, agreed to settle on a simple CIO-style contract as the basis for ending the second longest sit-down on record. The basis for bargaining was critically influenced by Michelson, whom Sentner had known since 1933 when they met during the Funsten strike. During the TUUL period, Sentner and other activists from the party were very involved in picket line and community support for strikes for the ACWA. During the initial electrical organizing drive, when Sentner was essentially disobeying top CIO policy by organizing electrical instead of steel workers, Michelson had loaned the fledgling UE office space. Michelson was progressive, having been one of the young radicals who organized the garment industry in the 1910s. He admired Sentner, but not the CP. But Sentner refused to recommend the proposal to the membership when speakers from the ranks vowed not to give up the plant until the wage issue was settled.[59] "There is no trust of the company amongst the workers" because of the long history of unfulfilled promises, Sentner reported to James Matles, UE's director of organization. Sentner was encouraged that "the vote consolidated the strike and forced the company to reopen wage negotiations."[60]

In the aftermath of this vote, the union and the company agreed to supervised negotiations under the NLRB, which began on April 26. The entire union committee, without national CIO officials, engaged in the bargaining.[61] Newman had hoped that he could work out a settlement with the leadership of the CIO without dealing with Sentner or Emerson workers. Now, in intense negotiating sessions that included a woman and an African American worker, he felt more directly the potential democratic thrust of the CIO movement. Phillips began to lose influence over Newman, who decided to file an injunction to forcibly remove the sit-downers.[62] News of the injunction suit, which spoke of "the malicious, wicked and unlawful acts" of the union and called for eviction and complete prohibition of picketing, reached Sentner and the union committee in the midst of a negotiation session. Plant manager John Driy, however, mindful of the company's bargain with the NLRB, asked for negotiations to continue during injunction proceedings. Sentner retorted, "On the basis of tear gas, Mr. Driy? A little tear gas and a police force?" Sentner expressed bitterness that he had ever "had faith" that the company would bargain. "I am glad the brains of the employees of Emerson prevented themselves from making a mistake. . . . I must admit I certainly had one foot on the wrong side, believing that everything was going in good faith." Sentner left with a warning that "we are going to fight for our jobs!"[63]

In a hastily called union meeting, Sentner urged workers to be "ready for action." He reminded workers that "an injunction meant fight in New England, Chicago, California and other places. It means the same thing here." He assured the strikers of "wide CIO support" and aid from Illinois coal miners if "trouble was forced upon them. . . . They may send me and the other leaders to jail before this is over, but other leaders will take our places and the fight will go on until this company takes a licking. We have sought to be peaceful, but this move by the company would even prohibit peaceful picketing." Meanwhile, strikers called on Mayor Dickmann and Chief of Police McCarthy and charged that the company was trying to "disrupt the peace of the community." Meanwhile, the union increased the picket line to four hundred strikers and supporters.[64]

Without full CIO support, however, the UE's ability to fight an injunction was vastly compromised—Sentner learned that the CIO leadership would oppose it. Of particular importance was the counsel of Max Michelson. Phillips later recalled, "I relied a whole lot on Mr. Michelson's advice, and I looked to him in a advisory capacity in this matter." Phillips told Michelson that he was disappointed that Sentner "seem[ed] unable to control" the sit-downers and to get them to evacuate. Sentner had made it clear to both Phillips and Michelson that he did not want to be a party to more "face saving" measures by the company.[65]

But a backlash against sit-down strikes was mounting across the country. Only days before the U.S. House Labor Committee had passed a Senate resolution condemning sit-downs. Sit-downers in the 1930s relied on their ability not only to keep strikebreakers from entering the plant but also to prevent police from successfully enforcing an injunction. If Emerson workers held their ground, they would be the first group of sit-downers to have done so over the issue of wages rather than the more fundamental issue of recognition. It would be difficult to hold public support when Emerson had announced its intention to bargain, no matter if workers realized that the vow was insincere. Recognizing this, as the hour for the hearing on the injunction came closer, management made a wage offer that amounted to a 2.5 percent increase, an offer Sentner characterized as a "slap in the face," done for publicity and not for real bargaining purposes. The union countered with an offer to evacuate if the company pledged not to start operations until a contract was agreed upon, which the company refused. Then, in another meeting, the company, taking advantage of the weakened position the union was in, noted that it considered sole recognition of the UE as a negotiable point.[66]

In the face of these pressures, Sentner and the union negotiating committee agreed to prevail on the sit-downers to evacuate, but Sentner now depended on Michelson to do the dirty work. Michelson orchestrated a special CIO meeting that resolved to call on the workers to evacuate the plant. Five years later, when Michelson and Sentner had become factional enemies, Michelson chided Sentner about that role: "You cannot erase the part we played in your Emerson sit-down strike, and the getting out of the strikers from the plant." It took much cajoling to convince the sit-downers to relent. Sentner later noted that the bitterness was so intense that some workers threatened to "blow up the plant" rather than leave it. But the threat of the loss of CIO support for their strike was persuasive, and workers were told that they would be subject to full state and federal prosecution if they remained. Forty-five minutes before the injunction was due to be heard on April 29, the sit-downers decided to leave the plant. William Reidel, the workers' "mayor" of Emerson, said that the sit-downers "yielded to the advice of CIO leaders."[67]

Whatever their misgivings, it was a "laughing, cheering group of sit-downers" who evacuated the Emerson plant and joined two thousand other workers and allies waiting outside on April 29. Workers had held the plant for fifty-three days, four short of the record for such an occupation. Their stance indicated unity and determination rather than any signs of defeat. As they marched through downtown streets, they carried banners indicating unity and loyalty to the CIO. They raised their arms and shook their fists as they passed by Emerson offices. As they turned south on Eighteenth Street and passed Century Electric, they loudly booed the small number of Century scabs who were in the plant.[68]

If continued occupation of the plant was risky, evacuation was also a gamble. Judge Robert Kirkwood had postponed strike injunction proceedings for only a week to give negotiations another chance. On the other hand, in exchange for the evacuation, NLRB officials agreed to begin the unfair labor practices hearings they had earlier postponed in return for the promise of negotiations. The hearings were due to begin the following week, a prospect that deeply disturbed Newman and Emerson officials, given the potential to reveal the company's internal and financial problems.[69]

Throughout the next week and beyond, negotiations continued to stall over the wage issues, and wages indicated the larger issues of the power clash over the local "community wage." Lou Kimmel explained to management that "past history" made workers determined that "they must have that settled definitely before they go back." George Kimmel told Emerson's managers that the drive had awakened workers to the wage rates of other companies outside the area that manufactured similar product lines. Logsdon remarked that workers in the small town of Newton, Iowa, made "30% more than your company."[70] Plant manager Driy objected that they could not keep up with companies such as General Electric (GE), because "we are not big enough to control the motor prices" the way that the larger companies were.[71] Sentner countered that even with the wage increases workers were asking, the St. Louis companies would have a substantial wage advantage. He warned: "This low rate of yours, if allowed to remain, would affect . . . workers in other places. . . . We are interested in equalizing wage standards in the industry."[72] Another member of the negotiating committee added that "if the manufacturers cannot run their business so they can pay wages which are enough for a man to live on they might as well quit."[73] Sentner declared that "we don't have any intention of having the factory operate here at 32 cents an hour. It is just not going to happen. Now the Emerson Company might as well get it in their mind that we do live in this country and we are out to establish half way decent working conditions and wages."[74] Management tried to dismiss concerns about its low minimum rate by noting that it mostly affected "girls," but the union made it clear that the low minimum rate was its main target.[75] The union policy insisted on a "flat increase of 10 cents an hour" in order to "help those on the bottom of the wage scale" instead of a percentage increase, which favored higher-paid workers.[76] Whereas the company had sought to use the labor market to secure the loyalty of a select group of workers at the expense of the rest of the employees, the new CIO union had turned that bargain upside down. An increase in women's substandard pay was a part of this bargain.

The following exchange between Sentner and Driy illustrates the sharply conflicting views of the labor market that were brought forth in negotiations:

Sentner: You have almost 600 people who . . . are keeping families on that [low rate]. . . . You have girls who are keeping a mother and father and a couple of sisters or brothers on it.

Driy: I don't see how the sisters and brothers come into it.

Sentner: Have you ever visited the homes of those that work for the Emerson [company]? . . . Did you ever go down to South Ninth or South Tenth Street, to the twelve dollars a month, fourteen dollars a month houses[?] You see, it is just as much to us a civic question as a question of just the Emerson Company. . . . [T]he wages that are established at [the] Emerson Company actually affects the wages . . . of the whole city.[77]

Schlieman, echoing others, pointed to the way that the low wage levels affected all workers in the city and accused Emerson of forcing some workers to depend upon charity. When one worker suggested that the company needed to consider workers' welfare first, Driy countered that the question was one of "a point of view." Sentner rejoined, "That is right. It is quite a point of view. A question of human rights over property rights. It has not been settled yet."[78]

The strike had not yet been settled, either, and negotiations continued to bog down. As the day of the injunction hearing neared, the CIO, and especially Michelson, pressured the union to settle the case. Michelson apparently even schemed with Judge Kirkwood to have Kirkwood order Michelson replace Sentner in negotiations in return for not issuing the injunction.[79]

Sentner sought to use NLRB hearings to pressure the company and thwart the injunction.[80] The union let the company know that its case would expose the long history of the NMTA, its attempts at intimidation of workers, and the company's looming insolvency. The union began a series of radio broadcasts exposing these and announced a plan to "have a voice in a meeting of Emerson stockholders," using a few of the older employees who owned some stock.[81] On May 10, the NLRB hearings finally began, with riveting testimony carried in the media. With this momentum, six members of the union executive committee, as well as Sentner and Michelson, also met with Judge Kirkwood. They gained another delay in the injunction hearings.[82] The following day, the union called on the company to "open its books" to a commission, consisting of a worker representative, a management representative, and a third representative selected by workers and management, to audit the company's financial records.[83]

This proposal, together with the pressures of the NLRB hearings and the pressure to settle the strike in order to secure financing of a stock underwriting, caused Newman, who, Phillips wrote, "has not slept for several days," to suggest that the company "bring in the AFL electrician's union" to break the strike. Michelson, hearing of this from Phillips, reacted with rage, given his efforts to conclude the strike. He warned that the entire CIO would turn on Emerson if they brought in the AFL and, according to Phillips, "threaten[ed] violence, and [a] fight which will cost the company $100,000." Newman quickly lost his enthusiasm for the only alternative left for negotiation with "the Communist."[84]

Within two days, a tentative agreement was ratified by the membership. It called for a general 5 percent wage increase. Then, after five months, workers receiving less than fifty cents an hour would receive another 5 percent wage increase. The wage bargain represented a compromise between the union goal of wage solidarity and the company's desire to reward its higher-paid employees through percentage increases. Other provisions in the contract, including plantwide seniority, a steward, grievance and arbitration provision, and a no-strike and no-lockout clause, were settled in the following weeks. The contract was ratified in June.[85]

Forming District 8, UE-CIO

Century Electric and Wagner Electric settled on similar terms with the UE around the same time. The NLRB brought charges against both companies, who agreed to elections in order to avoid NLRB hearings. Century workers voted for the union by a four hundred-vote margin.[86] By May 1, UE supporters at Wagner established a shop steward system that was handling workers' grievances. At a meeting of Local 1104, three thousand workers joined and two thousand of them voted to strike, just as the NLRB was filing unfair labor practices against the company. Wagner had used armed guards and its influence with county police to disrupt union meetings, had spied on workers, and had fired more than a dozen leading activists. Wagner management consented to an election rather than expose the company to scrutiny in labor board hearings but pressed the labor board to allow the company union on the ballot. Meanwhile, St. Louis County "special deputies" under Wagner influence arrested two union activists for distributing union literature near plant property, held them in jail, and refused to release them. The company announced that it had fired the workers. Backed by strong condemnations from the local branch of the American Civil Liberties Union, the union held protest rallies outside the sheriff's office and requested investigation from the Senate's Civil Liberties (LaFollette) Committee, which was revealing its findings regarding violations of rights. NLRB officials reported that this "upset [the] company and they contacted our office," agreeing to "still" the uproar by reinstating with back pay not only the two activists fired but all seventeen of those it had fired for union activities over the course of the union campaign. The combination of NLRB and workers' actions sent a bolt of lightning into the union campaign. Workers "will be paid for the time spent in jail!!" declared a Local 1104 leaflet. The union won the election in early June by a vote of 1,800 to 740. By July, with a signed contract, "#3 of the big boys is under our belt," Sentner reported.[87]

In addition to the "big three," a number of smaller electrical and metal products shops such as Superior Electric, Johnston-Tin Foil, Baldor Electric, Medart, Benjamin Air Rifle, and the Perfection Company reached agreements with the UE. The keen attention necessary for the Emerson struggle, on the other hand, had allowed some companies to successfully establish company unions such as at Maloney Electric and Knapp-Monarch. And while a number of smaller tool and die and machine shops were organized during this period, others quickly reached agreements with AFL unions, especially the machinists and electrical workers' unions, in order to prevent workers from organizing under the UE.[88]

Nevertheless, no one could miss the significance of what had been accomplished. The UE, in conjunction with a new national movement, had faced down the antiunion stronghold in St. Louis, challenged the control exerted by the "big three," and won. Only shortly before, Emerson's managers would have found their situation inconceivable. But as workers and managers each assessed in the aftermath of the signed contract, the question of where this worker's movement would lead remained for both sides.

The means to workers' victory determined to some extent the parameters for future struggle. Four factors in particular merit discussion: the degree of worker militancy and tenacity, the style of organizing, the role of the state, and the CIO coalition. Phillips's diary confirms workers' wisdom in distrusting the company. Even after the Supreme Court decision on the Wagner Act, management sought a way to circumvent the law. If the sit-downers had not remained adamant about gaining a solid agreement, they would have reentered the plant on weaker grounds. During the struggle, a number of workers had raised their expectations of the movement and of themselves as activists. While they had to fight intensely for a contract that fell far short of their goals, there was no limit, as management could tell, to workers' desires. Management feared what workers could want under radical influence. As Driy told Sentner in one of the negotiations meetings, "I have never seen them [workers] satisfied."[89]

Driy's remarks give a significant amount of insight into the dance between consciousness and control. The degree of workers' militancy and the limits of their aspirations were not the products of some predetermined level of class-consciousness. Rather, it was the result of their somewhat pragmatic assessment of the chance for success with the forces of repression and repercussion waiting in the wings.[90] The moment in the events described above that illustrates this best is when the key actors in the Century Works Council suddenly withdrew from the injunction petition and joined the CIO, acknowledging that their fear had held them back from class solidarity. According to Henry Fiering, several of those workers subsequently joined the CP. If the strategy to use a community-based coalition to shut down the plant had not been deployed, future historians would have placed these workers among those consigned by Melvyn Dubofsky to having "assimilated the values of business civilization." Lloyd Austin, in discussing such historical moments and explaining why Emerson workers held on for so long, reflected that "workers will follow you if they know you mean business, that you won't leave them hanging."[91]

The role of the state was also a determining factor in the settlement. The NLRB and the LaFollette Committee, in particular, led workers to believe that agencies of the federal government would counter the repressive forces of local government, such as police and judicial injunctions, that had often served the interests of business. In the case of Wagner Electric, the sense that the NLRB backed workers' rights gave workers courage to stand up. Sentner was undoubtedly relieved that the NLRB officials went to significant lengths to prevent the company from using red-baiting. This was a significant change from the past. Sentner recognized the dangerous aspect to the seductive role of state support of the movement, however, as he explained in the middle of negotiations when he told the company that he did not "like to tie their bargain too much to the NLRB," precisely because "political factors could swing the other way," leaving workers powerless if they grew too dependent on the government. Indeed, labor law and state intervention would come to define the boundaries for many of the goals of this workers' movement. The NLRB, even in its most supportive moments, sought to channel workers' actions into strictly defined limits. Sentner was also aware that the degree of support for him from the NLRB was dependent on his behavior as a "responsible" trade unionist. Workers learned all too soon that limited government support for organizing came with significant costs.[92]

The electrical workers' victory was bound intricately with the fate and direction of the entire CIO movement in the region and ultimately would be tied to the rather conservative goals of the top leadership of the CIO. The CIO is usually portrayed in terms of the establishment of strong national industrial unions to contest the giants of industry. But as is exemplified in the St. Louis CIO drive, at the base it depended on local solidarities, worker and coalition networks. In the spring and summer of 1937, the community-based movement that the Emerson Electric strike was a part of helped to further develop a viable St. Louis area CIO.

The base of activists and organizers recruited from the UE drives contributed significantly to the St. Louis CIO. It was the hub of CIO activity in the St. Louis area. Throughout the summer of 1937, Sentner taught a weekly class for organizers, with fifty people on average attending. The local UE financed three organizers who were "occupied with general CIO work only" and covered expenses for "volunteer organizers." At this critical point, before the 1937–38 recession, these organizers developed successful organizing drives among department

CIO leader
conservative

store, warehouse, and furniture workers and in numerous other industries. Many of the workers in these organizations requested affiliation with the UE. Instead, the UE dutifully relinquished locals it had organized outside the CIO-defined jurisdiction or had them directly affiliate with the CIO. Without the jurisdictional boundaries set by the CIO, the UE would have been overwhelmingly the largest union within the St. Louis CIO. Even with the jurisdictional boundaries, Logsdon described the UE offices as a place where people, whether in unions or not, "would drift in and drift out. They didn't have to be members, they'd just stop and talk about things that were going on, about places to organize," and debate issues about the direction of labor.[93]

The dominant forces that created the CIO at the top, with connections to the political elite of the New Deal, were more conservative than the local impulses that gave it life. As Robert Zieger has shown, in the summer of 1937 the CIO defined a structure based not on "mass regional mobilization that would have recalled the Knights of Labor" but rather on a federation structure based in international unions with relatively narrowly defined and top-down jurisdictions. Further, top leadership of the CIO demonstrated a distinct desire to ensure that the movement defined its goals within limits acceptable to the New Deal political elite. They "stood for stable contractual relations that were committed to taking labor disputes off the streets and into the courtrooms and negotiating chambers." The top leadership in the local CIO reflected these desires, as was evident in the role of Max Michelson during the sit-down. Moreover, most top CIO leaders were uncomfortable with the fact that CP radicals were an integral part of the base of activists in their ranks.[94]

Nonetheless, there were alternative paths even within the CIO. The UE created a structure and recruited leadership most conducive to an alternative path, embodying more of the qualities of the decentralized local movement that gave life to the CIO than most other CIO internationals did. Each local union of the UE was relatively autonomous from the district and the national office. District directors were elected by the district convention rather than appointed, as in some other CIO unions. Further, the UE's constitution contained provisions ensuring the right to membership regardless of political beliefs (as well as regardless of race, religious affiliation, etc.). Radicals such as Sentner were secure from the type of top-down purge that occurred in unions such as the SWOC, where centralized control resided in the top hierarchy of the CIO.[95]

The union victories in the spring and summer of 1937 established St. Louis as the hub of District 8 of the UE. District 8's geographical territory, established by the fall 1937 convention, initially included Missouri, Iowa, and Kansas. The St. Louis UE also served as a hub of regional organizing within the CIO's jurisdictional guidelines. In April 1937, when Maytag workers called on the CIO for an organizer, Bob Logsdon went to Newton, Iowa. Almost overnight, that drive brought more than seventeen hundred more members. During the summer and fall of 1937, while the UE held the utilities organizing franchise in the CIO, utilities workers from Iowa also poured into the UE's ranks. (Later, utilities were given their own CIO international.) By October, District 8 represented ten thousand to sixteen thousand workers at peak production under contract. The size of the district reflected the geographic concentration of electrical plants in the Northeast. As the district leadership looked at the types of companies in its territory, both those already organized and those potentially to be organized, it was apparent that District 8 would be the district of the "independents." GE and Westinghouse had few major plants west of Ohio at the time. Without them (the main targets of the national union), District 8 was considered one of the least important districts to the strategic aims of the international union whose priorities, like the CIO in general, were focused on national contracts with the giants.[96]

Philosophy and Practices

Sentner, elected president of District 8 at the first district convention in August 1937, viewed the small part of the CIO he had helped to organize in all its multiple possibilities: a movement built on a community coalition of workers and supporters with a range of political and social perspectives, a movement whose direction was not yet determined. The Emerson sit-down strike had awakened the aspirations of workers in St. Louis and demonstrated the possibilities of unity and claims to rights. The central project for the Left was to extend workers' rights on the shop floor and in the community and the nation without bringing the repressive forces of management and government into play.[97]

The extension of workers' rights was something that was central to the district's agenda. Sentner articulated the stance of "human rights above property rights," initially expressed during the Emerson sit-down and negotiations, as a guiding philosophy of the movement. This philosophy was framed by the sit-down itself, which expressed spatially the idea that workers had ownership in their jobs and that management was violating these rights by unilateral implementation of rules and wages. The occupation of the plant was simply a visual representation of that ownership. The decision to elect a mayor of Emerson was both theater and philosophical assertion of the ties between citizenship rights and union rights. Sentner stressed that the contracts that had been won were the product of workers' current power. While they had signed contracts that included no-strike and (weak) management rights' clauses, the union should not be permanently reconciled to such clauses, and the agreement was simply a way to trade one sort of power for another. A further challenge to management prerogatives was a key part of the union's program, though that goal was not always blared from trumpets. It was "the bosses' myth that workers have no executive ability," but workers had shown otherwise. It is clear that a variety of ideas and strategies, not just CP doctrine, were influencing the young activists. Sentner took some cues from Max Michelson, the local ACWA official, regarding how to gain power in an industry typically driven to sweat its profits out of its workforce. Since the 1920s, the ACWA had sought to trade no-strike and no-lockout clauses in order to assume managerial functions to reduce the cutthroat competition that led both profits and wages into downward spirals. But whether or not Sentner was willing to bend to accommodate the recognition that a trade union organizing drive was not a revolution, one of the cardinal principles that separated the district philosophy from the ACWA was that increased use of machinery would not be a means to further reduce workers' wages.[98]

Thus the challenge to management rights did not separate wage issues from issues of power. The battle for the "just share of the increased profits of industry" was articulated as an integral part of the quest for power in the capitalist political economy. Wages were seen as a major component of this—not something set apart from management rights but linked to them and to struggles on the shop floor and in the community.[99]

Sentner argued that the CIO was part of a historic struggle for "industrial democracy." At a May Day rally sponsored by the CIO during the Emerson strike, Sentner pointed out to the crowd that the rally was held near the site of the first AFL May Day hours protest in St. Louis and that the CIO was the renewal of that historic project for workers' rights. Sentner proclaimed that the CIO was "not just another labor campaign" but a "crusade to free the American working people from wage bondage and to open the way to [an] industrial democracy guaranteeing a more abundant and happy life to the working people of our great nation."[100]

For Sentner, the term "industrial democracy" was a dynamic, expansive concept whose ultimate direction was toward workers' control of industry. Bandied about since the 1890s, the term accommodated a range of perspectives, including simple collective bargaining. Gary Gerstle argues that radicals in the 1930s and 1940s used the term to express their goals in a consensual, patriotic American idiom: "Embedded in the phrase 'industrial democracy' was the kernel of a truly radical idea—the democratization of industrial enterprise—that helped [radicals] communicate . . . their far-reaching plans for social reconstruction" of capitalism. For them, the key meaning was that democracy, taken for granted in the political sphere, should expand into the industrial sphere and that socialism was the most advanced form of industrial democracy. This term also fit well with the rhetoric surrounding the Popular Front. The CP's national leader, Earl Browder, even proclaimed that "Communism is twentieth century Americanism." Gerstle argues that radicals also viewed the language of patriotic Americanism as a way to overcome local parochial, ethnic, and religious concerns that they felt impeded workers' willingness to countenance a radical agenda.[101]

While Sentner utilized this kind of patriotic Americanism language some-times, more often he employed the conceptualization of the union as a civic organization in the context of a local as well as a national contest for power. Any attempt to build shop floor power, Sentner argued, was dependent on the devel-opment of the union as a key civic organization in the community. The idea was to impede the ability of companies to repress workers and use community coali-tions as the building block for power, not an impediment to it. In contrast to Gerstle's depiction, the Left in District 8 did not see the community focus of their activism as parochial but rather as the basic starting point for any move-ment for social transformation.

Such a conceptualization also emphasized the need for inclusivity within labor's ranks; the union needed to be reflective of the community in order to build alliances. Sentner reminded workers from different locals in mid-1937 that their gains were due to industrial unionism, the "fruit of labor unity," that united the "aristocrats of the plant" with the hundreds of production workers on the line. He called on them to nurture that unity and inclusiveness. He urged them to consider the rights of African American workers and also to "pay more attention to involving our girl and women members in the life of the union and in its leadership." The district's Education Committee sent speakers who "urged women to come to the Front in the CIO" and who spoke on the evils of "racial theories."[102]

The impulse to make the union a civic organization was evident at the first St. Louis district convention. Sentner noted approvingly that district locals had begun to participate in "movements for better housing and other civic endeav-ors to make St. Louis a healthier place in which to live and work." At the New-ton, Iowa, subdistrict meeting, Sentner remarked that Newton members "are just beginning to realize the importance of their union and the fact that it is the largest single group of people in Newton and will take on an increasing civic responsibility for the well being of Newton."[103] The union established contacts between the CIO and the ministerial coalition that had been involved with the unemployed movement. Victor Pasche, who became an organizer for the dis-trict, acknowledged that "it was Bill Sentner who taught me how to build alliances with the clergy" and that such coalitions were strategic aspects of building the necessary alliances to stave off red-baiting, build workers' power, and effectively contest for power. When Sentner sent Emerson worker Art Meloan to organize in Evansville, he advised him to make contacts simultane-ously with workers and local clergy. District 8's Education Committee also sponsored talks by progressive ministers on "religion and labor." Henry Fiering years later still relished the memory of his reception as the "fair-haired boy" by some clergy in the Catholic Church in 1937.[104]

District 8's developing philosophy reflected the legacy of the nut pickers' experience, the Left's ideology, workers' own impulses, and, in part, the nature of the companies with which District 8 dealt. These companies had relied on local control over the labor market to maintain their position in the national and international markets. Sentner expressed the union's philosophy; its practice was broadly accepted and became meaningful through the actions of the workers themselves, in particular the "militant minority" who came to view the union as their life. They sought to use the rights won in the contract to transform their daily lives, and the starting point was the shop floor. Workers understood their ability to improve their lives on the job and in the community by constricting management's ability to unilaterally implement decisions. Management, in the aftermath of unionization, came face-to-face with the potential direction of the new movement, which sought a redistribution of power.

A strong shop steward system was central to the style of unionism established in the aftermath of the 1937 agreements. It was designed to be the "backbone of the union" for workers' new assertion of shop floor rights in which the "leadership [was] able to carry out the democratic will of the membership." District 8's contracts established a steward for each department or foreman, or at least one for every fifty workers. The stewards would collect dues directly and achieve the "cooperation of all members" so that the union could function to "*continue* to raise the standards of pay and maintain and improve the working conditions in the shop." Sentner stressed that the stewards should not be considered "the fall guys who take care of everything, thus relieving the union membership of its responsibility. Nothing is further from the truth."[105]

In the months after the contracts were signed, workers and management tested the limits of their powers under the new conditions. During negotiations, Sentner had warned Driy that many areas of contention would be ironed out between workers and bosses on the shop floor.[106] In early June, Sentner reported that the locals were "battling to enforce the contracts [they had] signed" as management tested the allegiance of workers to their new union. The workers' assertion of new shop floor power resulted in sit-downs that District 8 leadership supported. In mid-June, Emerson workers found that the company had decided to "chisel on the 5% general wage increase promised" and issued a circular suggesting that the union had agreed in negotiations that the increase would be given to only the highest-paid workers. Shop stewards gathered the circulars from workers and threw them on the foremen's desk, and the company relented.[107] When Century officials reneged on their promise of bonuses to workers, Fiering led shop stewards in a successful sit-down.[108] When Maytag placed an antiunion agitator in its assembly department, workers walked out and ultimately forced the worker to join the union. Maytag's chiseling on overtime pay for Saturday work ended after three sit-downs in five days.[109]

Sentner negotiated between the desire for shop floor control by workers, acting on pent-up grievances, and the potential catastrophe for the union that might result from this unleashed shop floor volatility. At Wagner Electric, for example, a promotion grievance in August led to a five-hour sit-down in the punch shop, resulting in the firing of three workers. Sentner noted that while five hundred workers, including "some of our best people out there," supported the sit-down, it ended abortively and was "the culmination of a series of movements attempting to force a strike situation of the organization out there." Sentner felt that sometimes the militancy was "instigated by individuals . . . directly controlled by the company, or [by] selfish interests," and that it was necessary to "eliminate irresponsibility of our leadership" in order to ensure that the spontaneous actions of the sort at Wagner were replaced by "a most rigid discipline in our local organizations."[110]

Grievance procedures and even arbitration, often viewed as instances of decreased power and bureaucratic unionism, were considered a means of increasing workers' power in this period. Management viewed arbitration as a serious threat to their control. Sentner told management during the Emerson negotiations that "we believe in arbitrating matters. In other words, instead of allowing things to come to a head we like to have the cases placed before the management and try to settle it amongst ourselves." Sentner, no doubt drawing on the nut pickers' experience with community juries and boards, suggested that if there was no settlement, the union preferred to involve "leading citizens of the city" such as "Bishop Scarlett, Dean Sweet, people of this nature." Employment manager L. T. Arnold replied, "It is awful hard for me to imagine such a situation arising," adding that the board of directors would never allow arbitration. The provision was, however, included in the new contract, and the union sought to expand its meaning in the year after the contract was in place.[111]

In July 1937, Emerson workers began to use the arbitration clause to win rights not explicitly stated in the contract. In particular, they used it to challenge times on incentive rates for jobs. This was particularly important when management received new orders that necessitated some changes in production. In the past, management faced no organized challenge to the new rates. Now workers could contest the new rates and thus control speedup on the job. Arbitration became a means of expanding workers' ability to challenge what had been perceived as unilateral management rights. "Our arbitration feature was the club over their head which held reductions to a minimum during the past year," Logsdon reported in summer 1938.[112]

Emerson's assistant factory manager complained in May 1938 that one-third to one-half of his time daily was spent dealing with grievances. Foremen complained that workers were "more belligerent" and "argumentative about everything." In particular, managers attested that workers continually challenged the timing on jobs, asserting their rights to have a particular job retimed in the presence of their steward, as provided for in their contracts. Some managers and foremen could not adjust to the regime. Emerson's employment manager, L. T.

Arnold, left the company in the fall of 1937, a departure for which the union took full credit.[113]

The Left viewed the shop steward system as the way to expand the core of activists committed to the union, as workers who experienced the power of challenging management successfully could develop a deeper consciousness. At Emerson, George Kimmel and Bill Cortor, both CP members, were chair and secretary of the shop stewards, respectively. Henry Fiering built what were dubbed "shock troops" through educating and activating shop stewards. "We built a machine you couldn't beat!" he exclaimed when asked about the first year after the strike. Stewards challenged management to the limits of the contract and beyond, especially on issues of timing and on disciplinary matters.[114]

Shop stewards also asserted their presence in the shops in educational ways, not just direct action, by challenging managerial positions and ideology. One means to do that was through shop bulletins, which were distributed by stewards. In one typical article, unions were defined as one means for workers to challenge capitalism's tendency to use labor-saving devices to lower wages and to inaugurate speedups on the job.[115] Management perceived these bulletins as a serious threat to their authority, as demonstrated in October 1937 when Emerson officials declared that the shop paper could not be distributed at the plant. Shop stewards defied the order and distributed the bulletins in front of management. The company set an example by firing two of the most active shop stewards. When every shop steward marched out of the plant in unison, and the union threatened to send the case to an arbitrator, the company reinstated the workers and allowed for distribution of the bulletins in the plant. Distribution of union literature would remain a thorn in the side of Emerson from that point forward.[116]

Shop stewards were also conceived as politicized "shock troops" for the entire St. Louis labor movement. Through education sessions in every available setting, the leftist leadership sought to build a core group of workers who would move the entire labor movement of the area in a progressive direction, the base of community-wide solidarity actions. That management felt threatened by this possibility was clear in the dispute over the firing of William Cortor. Emerson fired Cortor after he was listed as one of several persons arrested for marching on the Ford workers' picket line in November 1937, complaining that Sentner had encouraged workers to think that they even had the right to leave the plant in order to assist other workers' struggles. Cortor countered that he had the "perfect liberty as an American citizen to do anything I saw fit to do on my own time." When management would not allow the case to go through the grievance and arbitration procedure of the contract, the union decided to take it to the NLRB.[117]

Cortor's firing marked the onset of a concerted drive to regain shop floor and labor market control by the company, a campaign that intensified as a recession took hold in late 1937. In November, the company issued a new "Employees

Book of Rules" that asserted its rights to discipline workers. For example, the company asserted the sole right to discipline or dismiss workers who through "inefficiency" or "inability" failed "to attain standard work quality and quantity" or who were found to be "coercing or intimidating another employe." It also restricted workers from entering other sections of the plant and thus reduced the ability of stewards to police the plant for grievances.[118] Foremen required workers to sign an agreement to the rules in back of the booklet and asserted the company's "right to promulgate and apply administrative policies for effective control and efficient operation." Driy warned that "the management of the company never intends to surrender its right to run the business." Local 1102 responded: "We . . . stand ready to fight for THE RIGHT TO HAVE A VOICE AND VOTE ON ALL RULES that may be established. . . . No, Mr. Driy, IT ISN'T THE COMPANY THAT WILL DO THE POLICING OF THE COMPANY POLICIES. . . . IT WILL BE US." Most workers threw away the books, refused to sign them, or gave them back to their foremen en masse.[119]

That the union intended to have a voice on all policies seemed clear to management when, in early 1938, the union demanded the right to codetermine wages on a new line of motors the company was getting ready to build. Workers argued that the rates on the new line should be higher because the motors would yield higher profits for the company. Shop steward Clarence Erbe argued in the initial grievance that workers were "entitled" to more of the "larger margin of profit" that would be realized from larger motors.[120] Later the union argued that since workers had been the victims of "simplified" operations, when the company reduced the rate of pay or transferred work to a department with lower pay, as they had in creating the 41 line (the motor-winding assembly line), they should benefit when the company stood to gain more from new operations. Management saw this as the final straw. Claiming that such matters were the "sole function of management to decide," Emerson refused to arbitrate.[121]

By early 1938, Emerson management viewed arbitration as the greatest threat to their control of the company. In refusing to arbitrate any of the cases above, the company was acting on behalf of the NMTA, of which Joseph Newman had become the local leader in 1937. Even more intolerable to management were Sentner's expansive views on the potential limits to questions subject to arbitration: "Mr. Sentner in one of these conferences did state that he thought that if they didn't like the color of the paint on the wall they could put a grievance in on that and leave it up to arbitration if we didn't paint the wall the color they wanted!" complained the company's attorney.[122]

The Left in District 8

Off the shop floor, leftist leadership encouraged the development of activities that promoted the union as the cultural and social center of workers' lives. In the year after District 8 was established, each of the locals sponsored a range of such activities, many of them geared toward youths. The district established a sports program, consisting of boxing, wrestling, corkball, and baseball. Dances were frequently held by each of the locals.[123] Local 1108 developed a youth group program that included theater, group singing, and public speaking. Other events, including picnics, were geared toward "making the union a family affair." The activists pushed for the establishment of "ladies auxiliaries" as politically and socially functioning organizations. The auxiliaries in several locals were the foundations for a consumer cooperative that began to function during the spring of 1938.[124]

The Left encouraged these activities to be based on inclusiveness, but this goal was not always realized. The Emerson local held dances that excluded black workers and their wives. District 8 education director Raymond Koch vouched that "these locals did organize black and white, but it doesn't mean they got rid of racism, any more than it meant they got rid of male sexism by organizing women. I went to a meeting at Wagner, where they had a special entertainment, and they had a stripper! And the women who were in the local were at that meeting. I was shocked. The women didn't even complain openly." Addressing these attitudes would not be automatically accomplished, Koch and others stressed. It was a project to which the Left devoted considerable time and discussion. While district leadership pushed the locals to abide by a policy of inclusivity, at least one cultural event encouraged by Sentner in particular reinforced gender relationships in attempting to build class-consciousness. The Queen of the UE contest and ball, which lasted until World War II, was a popularity and beauty contest that mocked the Veiled Prophet Ball, the leading elite social event in St. Louis.[125]

Throughout the history of District 8, most of those who identified with the Left came from the ranks of workers in the organized shops who were attracted to a vision of unionism that Sentner articulated. As district educational director Ray Koch put it, Sentner "could stir a vision in workers, without a lot of involved dogma. He went beyond. . . . [H]ow do you stir a vision in people if you don't go beyond the facts of their lives?" Koch remembered that "every one of the plants had a few people who were class-conscious. They had gone beyond trade union consciousness to feel that the workers' movement could be a spark, not only for spreading trade unionism, organizing the unorganized, but also to form some sort of alliance with the neighborhood people and with other organizations, including black people's organizations, churches, white churches."[126] Sentner sought to encourage self-development among these workers into a movement force and to cultivate their understanding of connections between shop problems and larger questions. In the course of organizing and establishing the union, most of these workers did not join the CP. But James Click, who was later to be the leader of the anticommunist faction at Emerson, attested that the

"Communist issue" did not "disturb" a large number of the younger workers at this time. He believed that as many as one hundred Emerson workers joined the party in the course of the strike or organizing.[127]

While it is important to stress that membership in the CP was not the definition of the Left in the UE, looking closely at the workers who did join the CP calls into question the view that "radicalism took root more easily" among the strata of skilled workers "than among the more closely supervised, lower paid production workers." Most had little union or radical family background, and all were a reflection of working-class formation in the 1920s and 1930s. Of twelve identifiable CP members in the UE who came from the electrical shops, only the Kimmels came from a radical family tradition.[128] At Johnston Tin-Foil, assembly line worker James Payne, born in Oklahoma and raised in Arkansas and Missouri, was drawn to the Left at the same time as he was drawn to the union and to an expansive conception of unionism. Wagner workers Orville Leach and Zollie Carpenter, both from Arkansas rural backgrounds, joined the CP after the Wagner drive and helped organize the local. Zollie was a skilled worker, and Leach was not. For Leach the decision to join the CP was connected to antiracist feelings that had surfaced during his formative years in Arkansas.[129]

Henry Fiering noted no special affinity for radicalism by skilled workers among the Century workers he recruited. On the one hand tool and die maker Fred Riethmeyer joined the party, but a stronger member was John Nordman, who had never held anything but an assembly line job. Fiering's recollection was that it was not any easier and in many cases more difficult to recruit radicals from the ranks of the skilled long-term production workers. "There was a guy fresh out of the hill country," he recalled, smiling. "He didn't know how to spell 'communism,' but I was one, and if it was good enough for me it was good enough for him!" For this worker, Fiering, who had been a source for change in the power equation in the shop, became a source for an alternative perspective not only on labor issues but for a new outlook on the world.[130]

Emerson worker William Cortor was among those who joined the party. Cortor was born in 1912 in rural Missouri, and his parents came to St. Louis in 1921. Eight years later he went to work at Emerson, where he was placed on various low-skill jobs. There was little hint of any radical direction for him in those days. But the union drive of 1936–37 and the activities around the sit-down changed Cortor. He became vice-chair of the sit-downers and, after the strike, secretary of the shop stewards' council for the local. In the course of working together with Henry Fiering on the joint strike committee during the whirlwind strike and organizing period around April 1937, Cortor said, Fiering "asked me if I had ever given any thought with working with the Communists." Cortor responded that "I was willing to listen to anyone." He joined the YCL and then joined the CP in September 1937. For Cortor, the Kimmel brothers, and several others, the fact that their wives joined was decisive for whether they remained in the party.

"When these people came in, into the YCL, they all came in, husbands and wives," Fiering remembered.[131]

CP members in the St. Louis UE operated in a relatively open fashion. Sentner's politics were fairly well known among workers, from the earliest days of organizing. CP members at Emerson sought to function as an open political faction within the union and distributed issue-oriented leaflets.[132] Lou Kimmel, who joined the party and became chief shop steward in the aftermath of the union victory, and Bob Manewitz were well known as party members. They helped to organize a leftist caucus that held meetings and distributed issue-oriented leaflets. One leaflet given out to Local 1102 members at the shop gates reminded workers that "many of the Charter members of Local 1102, who worked day and night together with brothers and sisters to establish Local 1102 are COMMUNISTS. We are happy that our work was not in vain and pledge to continue to willingly join hands with everyone to win more and more concessions from Emerson in the form of better wages, hours and working conditions. ONE FOR ALL AND ALL FOR ONE is our motto."[133]

Shortly after the end of the Century strike, Henry Fiering revealed his membership in the CP to activists in the Century local. After attending a local YCL meeting where the issue of legitimizing leftists in labor was discussed, Fiering recalls, "I decided to make my politics public" at a meeting of fifty Century shop stewards. Although many already knew that he was a "red," Fiering, who had been elected financial secretary for the local, told the stewards that he was a CP member and then asked them to vote on whether he should remain the local's only paid officer. After "considerable uproar and debate," they voted to confirm him, excepting one Catholic member who afterward punched him in the nose.[134]

Fiering claimed that his openness actually eased his ability to recruit people to the CP. "After I had made this dramatic announcement about 'here I am, take me or leave me,' and they said they'd take me . . . I went out and blossomed. I brought forty people into the party." Fiering organized what was dubbed the "Century shock brigade," 150 of the most active unionists in the local. Fiering "appealed to them on issues of the basis of a better society, of class-consciousness," rather than with "theory and party doctrines," and involved the group in both shop floor strategies and community-based activism.[135] The development of an openly leftist leadership among workers deeply disturbed Century's management. Robert Hill, Century's works manager, called Al Meyer and two other of Century's local officers, who were Catholics, and tried to convince them that their allegiance to a Communist such as Fiering was inconsistent with their religion. Meyer replied with a question:

Meyer: Mr. Hill, have you ever been sick?

Hill: Yes, of course.

Meyer: And when you were sick, did you go to a doctor?

Hill: Why, yes.

Meyer: Well, that's exactly what we did. Henry's our doctor.[136]

With that, the men got up and left Hill's office and immediately repeated the encounter to Fiering himself.

Actual party membership did not define the Left in the district. Rather, Fiering's "shock troops" and Koch's definition of activists come closer. They were those dedicated to expanding the rights of workers and building the union in the community. CP membership was not a litmus test, but certainly the acceptance of CP members as part of the coalition was. Emerson worker Lloyd Austin never officially joined the party but was part of the leftist caucus in Local 1102. During the sit-down, Austin noticed that the group he respected the most in leadership huddled together occasionally. "I didn't know they were Communists at first, but that didn't matter to me. . . . People began to say, 'there are the Communists caucusing.'" Austin invited himself along on one of these occasions and found the meetings to be anything but the conspiracy meetings he expected. "They were just trying to keep the people together, putting their heads together to do it," and they welcomed Austin to the group. Austin had started a "basement club" on Saturday and Sunday nights for night shift workers during the union drive and invited the leftist caucus to use the facilities for meetings. The group sometimes met to strategize before union meetings in order to "move the union forward, in the right direction. . . . They got their heads together, to keep the ball rolling." For instance, they attempted to get Local 1102 to stop its discrimination against black workers at dances, a plan that eventually succeeded. The members planned their approach, including stationing themselves strategically in the meeting and outlining what each would say. Austin stressed that the goal was "for the membership to pick it up," in order for the idea to gather momentum. Of course, this sort of strategy was later targeted as a violation of the democratic process and showed that a Communist cabal was at work at the service of a foreign power, a notion that Austin rejected. Austin, a Catholic, viewed with some suspicion those who derided the "atheistic" Communists, and he suggested that people be judged in accordance with whether they advanced justice. Years later he still held these views, averring that many of the workers who fought the leftist leadership "wouldn't like Jesus Christ" either. In a 1938 letter to the editor, written under a pen name, he asked, "When the time is ripe for the round-up of communists I wonder if I . . . will be condemned for wanting to be treated in a Christian way as a believer of justice?" Austin also believed that Sentner made it clear that his "loyalty [was] to workers above the party," a critical part of his respect. When Alfred Wagenknecht, head of the St. Louis CP, chastised Sentner for promoting Bob Logsdon rather than a party member to a high position in the district, Sentner replied, before the group, "Look, you run your organization, and I'll run mine."[137]

Logsdon became the second most influential leader in the district, as district secretary and as an international representative. Logsdon's allegiance to Sentner led to charges that he was also a Communist or, if not, Sentner's pawn.[138] Such perceptions fall far short of understanding the dynamic relationship between the two leaders. In 1938, when Logsdon was charged with being a Communist by the AFL's arch red-baiter, John Frey, he replied in an article in the *St. Louis Star-Times,* "I'm not a Communist, but if I had to choose between Frey and the Communists, I'd take the Communists."[139] Logsdon was still a member of the SP when he became active in the district but at some point dropped his membership. Logsdon held socialist beliefs but never seriously considered joining the CP—"I ran away from them like the plague when they asked me to join, but I'd work with them"—and Sentner never pressured him to do so. Henry Fiering emphasizes that "Bob came to socialism on his own; he was a very free and independent soul, a very strong person."[140]

The leftist coalition was defined by its challenges to racist practices. They argued for the right of African Americans to all jobs in the plant and sought to break down racist cultural practices. Black activists such as Lee Henry—who was born in 1909 in Fairhope, Alabama, and started to work on the railroad at age thirteen and then had been hired at Wagner Electric in 1935—was part of the leftist coalition that started to challenge that company's racist hiring policies as well as those of the local union. Hershel Walker, who joined the UE in 1942, noted that Henry was one of the many black workers who had a shrewd eye for the "opportunity the CIO might afford" to advance the cause of equality. Henry understood that with the Left's support, "now companies couldn't fire you for agitating for racial justice" as they would have in the past. The involvement of workers such as Henry in the union influenced the views of white workers as well. Marian Barry, a white 41 line production worker, met black workers through union activities and identified with their view of the union as their opportunity for advancement after years of being held to certain jobs. Barry soon defined her view of "progressive unionism" through issues of race despite the fact that few black workers were employed at Emerson. Asked where she derived her progressive stance on race issues, she responded, "You know where I got them? I got them from Bill Sentner. He was a good guy! He used to get us the Communist Party paper. My neighbors would ask me, 'Are you a Communist?' I'd say, hell no, I ain't no Communist. But would you look at some of the things they're saying here—we need to know." Barry never joined the party, but she rejected the racist practices she associated with some of the anticommunists and thus defended the CP's right to involvement on these grounds alone. Sentner tried to get her husband Tom to join the CP, but according to Marian "he said, no, he couldn't see that. He agreed with him [Sentner] on a lot of the things he did and what he stood for," and Tom would read the *Daily Worker* "from cover to cover." But "we were both Catholic" and on those grounds refused to join the party. "A lot of things that Bill Sentner said was not Communist," she insisted, meaning that she felt this was not a "foreign" influence or "atheistic."[141]

Otto Maschoff defined his activism in the UE on race and gender issues. These positions were the product of a long process of education and experience. Maschoff had grown up on a hog farm near Breese, Illinois. Coming to St. Louis in search of a job during the Depression, he became an assembler at Century Electric and went on strike in 1934. Fired in March 1937 for union activity, Maschoff devoted himself to districtwide organizing. He became vice president of the local and then, in 1939, president. Maschoff's commitment to racial and gender equality grew as he became influenced by the Left. When Logsdon recommended Maschoff to James Matles for an organizer position for which he was hired in 1941, he described Maschoff as "not a member of any political organization. His outlook on politics and economics corresponds pretty well to mine."[142]

While there was no party membership requirement for staff jobs, the district leadership did hire some activists from outside the union and attempted to gather a staff that would promote their trade union agenda. Such was the case with the hiring of educational director and district newspaper editor Ray Koch. Koch's entire family was involved with Commonwealth College, the unconventional "workers' school" in Mena, Arkansas. The college's approach to developing workers as agents of social change continued to influence the district. Sentner became a nonresident board member of the college until it was shut down as subversive by Arkansas in 1941. Koch had left the college and come to St. Louis just before the Emerson sit-down began. He had been involved in relief demonstrations and other community activities. Koch was not a CP member in 1937, but he was sympathetic to the party. (He later joined the party, at least after World War II, although his employment with the district only lasted until 1939.) While Koch was certainly not the only appointment made by hiring outside the union membership, the vast majority of the organizers and staff of the district came from the ranks of workers in the plants. Sentner and Logsdon searched for and developed workers whom they could then promote to organizing positions in each plant. Between 1937 and 1945, fifty-three workers were recruited from District 8 to the national union as organizers and staff. "No other district comes close" to that figure, Sentner later reminded the national officials. Organizers such as Art Meloan, who were fully cognizant of Sentner's political affiliations, engaged in a dialogue and debate with him without fear of repercussions and proudly referred to themselves as the "boys Bill Sentner trained."[143]

According to Ray Koch, Sentner "could work with everybody. That was his genius. He was what I would call a mass leader, a mass organizer. He could enthuse people, he could focus their attention on the issues, and he could inspire them to go into action. And Logsdon was like a first sergeant who could help him carry it out." Koch emphasized that "Logsdon and Sentner felt the same thing when it came to issues: the workers were getting the dirty end of the stick, the corporations were getting too powerful." Logsdon understood that Sentner's "whole theory was based on the fact of having a bunch of people who would work with him, you know, who didn't have the same deal against them."[144]

The "deal against" Sentner, his open affiliation with the party, was indeed an obstacle to be overcome. There would never be an open acceptance of Communists in the ranks of labor as there had been for Socialists in the early twentieth century. As the leader of the district, Sentner was a target for reactionary forces among workers and management from the outset. But it is important to recognize that the first anticommunist caucus within the district developed in conjunction with layoffs and with the determination by the district to enforce policies against Jim Crow practices in the Emerson local.

Emerson's anticommunist faction developed, especially among some of the older male workers, in reaction to the strength of the Left and its openness in the local. The compromise between Left and Right was to let the Right hold most of the executive board positions while the Left concentrated within the shop steward structure. The district Left also made the caucus vulnerable when key organizers from the Left were pulled out of Emerson for district and international work. The right-wing faction that developed by the fall of 1937 was led by Earl White, a conservative skilled winder who had been among the first to join the union. As layoffs caused discontent, rumors spread that the company was refusing to deal with the union because of its leftist leadership. Also, the anticommunist drive came after the district leadership, in an effort to pressure Local 1102's executive board to comply with nondiscrimination policies of the district and international union, instigated an investigation of Local 1102 for its exclusion of black members from social events. In reaction, Local 1102's executive board threatened to withdraw from the UE and form an independent union. It passed a resolution withholding per capita tax on the grounds that the district constitution had not been procedurally approved. But the issue was only an "excuse," Sentner wrote, adding that the actions were the maneuvers of a "small clique" of the executive board "to sabotage [the] district program and attack me indirectly."[145]

Sentner sought to link the civil rights of the Left with those of African American workers in the letter he sent to all the locals on the issue, reminding them that the union was founded on nondiscrimination and the right to political beliefs. "The question of the particular political religious or racial qualifications of any member cannot concern our organization. Our national constitution based on sound democratic principles provides open membership for all workers in our industries regardless of their particular political allegiance."[146] Sentner called for a joint meeting of locals to discuss the issue. During the course of the meeting, James Payne openly charged that the issue raised over the constitution was a "smokescreen" for a larger agenda and asked "for those representing 1102 to say what they actually meant." Payne was backed by other local officials. White agreed to cease efforts at disaffiliation with the UE.[147]

Sentner, anticipating arguments about "Communist control," sought to make the District 8 president's position subject to referendum ballot election through each local. In other districts, presidents were elected at the district convention. The move reflected Sentner's faith in the democratic process, his belief that radical aspirations would not deter workers, and his faith in the leftist coalition that was then in formation.[148]

But the effort to expand workers' rights and the Left's position in the labor movement was severely tested by the economic downturn and political backlash that began in the fall of 1937. Rather than expansion into management rights, District 8 by late 1937 was confronting a drive waged by employers to force back the gains already made. Though they had won recognition from antiunion employers, the UE was soon confronted with employer campaigns aimed at stifling union growth. Years later, Robert Logsdon reflected that "it was a good thing we accomplished what we did up to that point. Because the forces of reaction, they were waiting in the wings for their chance. And they got that chance."[149]

Before considering that backlash, it is worthwhile to emphasize what had been accomplished during this period. The organization of electrical workers had revived a "militant minority" among the electrical independents, where the same had been completely vanquished in the previous generation. A coalition of workers dedicated to a new vision of expanded rights and power had appeared and had allies, even assisted for the time being by governmental powers that sought to neutralize the issue of communism. These factors had expanded the terrain on which workers could continue to mobilize for their rights. District 8 was clearly not establishing simple trade unionism. Rather, a segment of the electrical industry workforce had reconceived and reenvisioned the possibilities for unionism and their own role in their shops and in the community. It must have been astonishing for Emerson's John Driy to have to debate issues of political economy with Communists and the workers who revered or tolerated them. Compared to the early era, the world must have appeared to be turned upside down for electrical manufacturers. Driy understood clearly that there was no limit to workers' aspirations under radical leadership. Those limits would have to be set through other means.

CHAPTER 4

"This 'Red' Gave Them a Run for Their Money"

Backlash and Holding Ground, 1937–40

As an economic recession took hold, employers launched their own community-based efforts to roll back the Congress of Industrial Organizations (CIO) and the New Deal, campaigns that recalled the efforts of the Citizens' Industrial Alliance (CIA) in the previous era. District 8 developed strategies that countered these efforts. Sentner sought various means to expand workers' rights and assert another vision of the possibilities for the CIO during this troubled period. But the experiences of this era revealed the vulnerability of the coalition of forces that had come together in 1937, the limits of the Democratic Party support for the CIO, and how anticommunism lurked as an effective weapon for forces that aimed to constrain workers' assertion of power.

The 1938 Maytag Strike

As layoffs hindered workers' momentum in late 1937 and throughout 1938, District 8's greatest hope for demonstrating the potential of its vision of unionism developed in Newton, Iowa. But Maytag sought to contain the union movement that had taken it and the town by storm in mid-1937.

Maytag and the UE Local 1116

Maytag, which had started as a farm implement dealer, became a player in the electrical industry through an innovation in washing machines made by one of its employees. By 1929, 20 percent of all washing machines in the country were made in Newton, Iowa, located thirty miles east of Des Moines and now dubbed the "workshop of Iowa." While General Electric (GE) and Westinghouse made some washers, they did not dominate this market in the 1920s, when the washing machine industry was composed primarily of independents in the Midwest.[1]

Maytag's rise in the industry transformed the town of Newton. Fred Maytag and his family poured money into Newton at what seemed an astronomical rate, in part to attract and accommodate the increased number of workers who brought the town's population to nine thousand by 1937. The company built parks, a swimming pool, and a YMCA. It invested in housing for its workers and financed home loans for them. Maytag dominated local institutions, including banks and car dealerships, and Newton seemed to embrace Maytag's control. The farm families of German and Scandinavian descent were grateful for the boom that Maytag brought, and they accommodated the wishes of the Maytag family.[2]

In the 1920s, Maytag advertised its claim to have "the best cared-for factory workers of the middle-west," a model of welfare capitalism.[3] The company found a ready supply of transient labor from the declining mines and agriculture of the area. Maytag workers, who accounted for more than half the town's wage earners, earned more than St. Louis electrical workers, yet they considered their wages inadequate for family sustenance. Since the company did not hire any women and since there were few other wage-earning jobs open to women in Newton and surrounding areas (as there were in St. Louis, for example), working at Maytag required a "family wage." Maytag utilized the rural labor market as a reservoir to draw from during peak production times, when the company hired an extra four to five hundred workers and ran shifts of ten and sometimes fourteen hours. One worker claimed that some workers' average annual wages amounted to only five hundred dollars a year due to these practices. Many workers resented the "benevolent autocracy," which involved pressure to buy only through Maytag-affiliated car dealers and home loaning agencies, take out a membership in the Maytag YMCA, donate to various Maytag charities, and even buy from the designated milk delivery—what assembler Siebert Chestnutt later described as "direct tribute" for keeping a job. Workers did not easily endure the petty empires of foremen, who selected and fired workers and set piece rates unilaterally.[4]

Many Maytag workers resisted. The "farm boys" who came to work at Maytag seldom adjusted easily to the grueling work discipline they found at the company. The company also hired workers with experience in railroads and from declining Iowa mines who were "union-minded." A few of these led the drive to organize Maytag. While an early 1930s American Federation of Labor (AFL) union drive disintegrated rapidly, resistance continued sporadically. In 1936, Maytag assembly line workers engaged in at least one sit-down.[5] In April 1937, after hearing of the Emerson strike, twenty-five hundred Maytag workers called on the United Electrical, Radio and Machine Workers of America (UE) and organized Local 1116 within one week's time.[6]

Maytag agreed to a contract providing some wage increases, seniority protection in layoffs, and a grievance procedure. Fred Maytag, the founder, had died the previous summer, and workers sought to institute their own governing regime. When the company began to fire activists and violate contract provisions, workers staged sit-downs in June and July 1937.[7] Sentner worked with the local to establish the shop steward system, building a strong rapport with key activists who used the grievance and arbitration system to win rights that were not written in the union contract.[8]

After this rapid success, Maytag workers sought to make Newton a "model CIO town."[9] This drive resulted in the organization of every grocery store, the Montgomery Ward and Woolworth stores, every garage, and several cafes. The *Newton Daily News* successfully resisted the drive and became a main antiunion force. When the city council refused to enact an ordinance, desired by Maytag and the Chamber of Commerce, prohibiting mass picketing, it seemed that Maytag's grip on Newton was loosening. Nearly six thousand people attended the Labor Day celebration in September. Local 1116 experienced its first political victory when the local's candidate for the school board won election in the fall.[10]

In early 1938 Maytag decided to throw itself on the front lines of the corporate counteroffensive against the CIO, despite (or perhaps driven by) healthy profits of 42 percent for the previous year. Maytag had organized its niche in the washing machine market around surplus cheap Midwest labor and special patents that were due to expire at the same time new low-priced machine lines from GE, Norge, and Westinghouse were being introduced. The company's plans to develop a more efficient production method for the plant ran up against the new shop floor power of workers, which curtailed the company's flexibility.[11]

It is likely that Maytag was acting on behalf of National Metal Trades Association (NMTA) forces. The company hired attorneys who had guided the Republic Steel Company's antiunion drive, resulting in the infamous 1937 Chicago Memorial Day Massacre, in which ten workers were killed and many more were wounded. In early 1938, Maytag management refused to settle grievances and was hostile to all union contract proposals. Management sought to provoke a strike, initiated a drive for a company union, and forced the union to hold another election proving representation.[12]

The union drew up a plan to build community support, including friendly overtures to the police, and to strengthen its ties to the miners' union in the area.[13] One antiunion observer complained that prounion sentiments had "entered our public schools, our Board of Education, our churches, our Parent-Teachers Association, every organization in the town is affected by this union organization."[14] Eighty-one percent of the workers voted for the union in the April 23 election. Afterward, one thousand workers staged a triumphant parade around Newton's courthouse square and back to union headquarters. The marchers had a police escort and were led by the newly formed ladies auxiliary.[15] Sentner called it "one of the most enthusiastic meetings and torch light parades that I have seen in all time." Afterward, bands of workers made the rounds of local cafes, bars, and pool halls, "sometimes receiving free food and drinks." When workers plastered union stamps on shops, many merchants did not remove them.[16]

The union's new determination to entrench itself in the community was matched by Maytag's efforts to eradicate it, on behalf of a larger plan by the NMTA. The union wanted a new minimum of sixty-two and a half cents to replace the fifty cents per hour minimum (an increase to match GE and Westinghouse's eastern rates). It also wanted a guaranteed annual wage to force Maytag to rationalize its production from the workers' standpoint rather than relying on a floating labor supply of temporary employees. The company, determined to scale back union power, steadfastly demanded a 20 percent reduction in wages and the right to increase hours to fifty a week, dismantle the seniority system, and curtail the grievance procedure. It also rejected the union's demand for vacation with pay as "the equivalent of a wage increase." Finally, Maytag sought the rescission of the arbitration clause and suggested that the company "would not enter ANY AGREEMENT that would make any wage question subject to arbitration."[17]

Local 1116 Charts a Militant Strategy

Writing to the national UE office and describing Maytag's intransigence, Sentner posed the situation as one that presented an opportunity to offer alternatives to the CIO's recent loss of momentum. In the face of recession and employer intransigence, the steelworkers' union had agreed to wage reductions without a struggle, and the United Automobile Workers (UAW) was racked by internal turmoil that led to declining membership and conditions. The Maytag situation, waged as the front lines of a national corporate strategy aimed at rolling back the labor movement, begged the question, wrote Sentner, of "WHAT SHALL BE OUR POSITION RELATIVE TO THE DRIVE BEING NOW MADE AGAINST LABOR?" Sentner argued that the union needed to show that it was necessary to continue "engaging in battle where and when such engagements achieve" solidification of the ranks and maintain the organization. "I believe that at no time can we become negative in this situation. Wage reductions, in my opinion must be viewed from this light and no other." Local 1116, Sentner argued, was strong at the community level and thus capable of presenting a model for the CIO and other workers who were cowed. Sentner concluded that "I do not believe we should do anything other than strike. I believe that the entire labor movement everywhere should establish their determination through the strike weapon to fight the aggression of finance capital and thus in a real way exercise their economic power to lay the basis for a political victory in the fall elections."[18]

The political victory that Sentner referred to was of course the congressional midterm elections. In considering possibilities for extending workers' rights, Sentner was likely drawing on Communist Party (CP) ideas about the role of the Popular Front in moving the Democratic Party to take a stronger position on workers' issues. Beginning in 1936, the CP had decided to shelve its own party and its coalitions with third parties in order to throw its efforts behind working within the Democratic Party to make it a "people's party" and to extend the political rights of the New Deal. Sentner's interpretation of the doctrine was that the CIO would only have the momentum to fight politically for progressive outcomes for the 1938 elections if it could face down capital on the shop floor and in the community. This was somewhat different than the increasingly deferential role of national CP leaders in respect to the CIO.[19]

In early May, Local 1116 passed a resolution connecting its wage demands to the goal that "human rights and human welfare must be given precedent [*sic*] over property rights." The union prepared for what Sentner called "gorilla [*sic*] warfare, a la China Red Army." When the company cut wages by 10 percent on May 9, the stewards made "the inside of the plant a mad-house for management, with quickies and actions on any attempt to foist worsened conditions." Some departments staged sit-downs.[20] Sentner slyly noted that "the whole plant proceeded to bargain collectively with the foremen and everybody else in managerial capacity."[21] Taylor termed the actions "un-American" and told the union officers that "if they were going to strike, they should strike in the American way and not this foreign stuff." The company responded with a lockout, which the union expected would help them gain public support by placing "full responsibility on the company publicly for the conflict."[22]

Throughout May the union built community support. Strategies for preventing violence brought results when the mayor swore in eight Local 1116 members as a "special police force to prevent disorder." They "visited all the beer parlors and asked the managers not to allow our men to have too much to drink."[23] Sentner pointed to the company's prosperity and the difference between GE and Maytag's wages and what it might mean for the community to have higher wages at the plant, and he argued that Maytag's workers were on the front lines against the "howl for wage reductions as the cure-all for the Depression." Years later Maytag worker Ezra Cooper recalled that "he was an avowed communist, but he was a labor leader. I mean to tell you, he'd stand up there on the square and tell the people in no uncertain terms about the Maytag Company. And he told them the truth. He told them how they lived in Florida," not in Newton. Sentner "appealed to the citizens of Newton and its civic organizations, including churches," for help in getting a settlement and pledged nonviolence. Workers set up a committee to solicit the support of the county's ministers.[24] By June the women's auxiliary had large numbers of women attending and participating. One testified that the union "meant a lot to us women" and "enlightened our social life." Throughout the lockout, the auxiliary set up a thirty-minute performance that told the "story of the struggle of the Maytag workers from the wives' view point."[25]

Maytag sought to use its own community-based strategies and the language of community to combat union support. The company implemented a version of the "Mohawk Valley Formula," a set of antiunion tactics that gained notoriety after its exposure by the LaFollette Committee investigations. The "formula" was actually a distillation of previously developed strikebreaking strategies that were similar to those employed by the Citizens Industrial Alliance a generation before, "centered around ways to isolate the union from the larger community and to create community support for the owners." Labeling the CIO union movement itself as "foreign" to the community and its supporters as "outsiders" was essential to this strategy.[26] Thus, it reinvented the methodology of the American "countersubversive tradition," which suggested that all efforts to transform the social order or reduce employers' power were the work of foreign ideas and alien forces.[27]

The relief issue catalyzed the campaign. The union's commissary system, dubbed the "Union Commissariat," was based on Foster's 1919 steel strike model, but the union was determined to force county and state officials to provide aid to the workers despite the opposition of the county Board of Supervisors, which dispensed relief and was dominated by farmers who opposed unions.[28] On June 3, one hundred workers held a sit-down at the office of the county Board of Supervisors, demanding that Governor Nelson Kraschel intervene. Kraschel agreed that "food should be given to families in need," and the supervisors began to provide relief on an individual basis rather than automatically denying aid to workers who were on strike.[29] In response, Maytag helped to organize the Jasper County Farmers and Taxpayers Association, led by farmers with major debts to Maytag's banks, to oppose relief to strikers. On the day after the sit-down, the association issued a resolution opposing relief to strikers, calling the CIO a "selfish un-American institution opposed to the best interests of our county" that was "committed to a policy of violence and intimidation," and called for workers "to shake off these foreigners and talk for themselves. . . . [If] these outsiders, who have no real interest in the welfare of the men of the community as a whole, are dismissed, the whole problem will be more speedily solved."[30]

The company formed a back-to-work movement whose members petitioned for an injunction against the union and its leaders. County prosecutor Luther Carr, a close friend of Maytag management and the back-to-work movement's attorney, used his position as county prosecutor to bring the case for the injunction, which was issued by Judge Frank Bechly on June 10. The injunction indicated the extent of community outreach by the union in that it prohibited activists from visiting workers' homes or going to bars or churches to dissuade workers from crossing the lines. The injunction even prohibited appeals by "peaceful persuasion or attempting to educate workers away from the 'back to work' movement."[31]

At a mass meeting on the town square after the injunction was issued, Sentner told outraged workers, who recognized the hand of Maytag behind the turn of events, that the injunction violated the law and that "the judge who wrote that decision must have been asleep. It is not worth the paper it is written upon." He urged them to personally but peacefully picket the back-to-work movement leaders. He promised bonds for anyone who was arrested.[32]

The *Newton Daily News* was determined to label Sentner as a violent and dangerous force, despite his continued insistence on nonviolence, that was conspiring to control Newton. The paper accused Sentner of "inciting mob spirit, using vile language, threatening to blow up the town, and bragging about being in jail twenty-eight times." The editorial ended by asking, "Who is in charge in Newton right now? Is it William Sentner, who openly defies our courts and incites our citizens to violence?"[33] The *Newton Daily News,* which received a substantial amount of its revenue from Maytag advertising, had resisted workers' attempts to organize the year before by gaining an injunction against mass picketing with Luther Carr's help. Meanwhile, a local minister, L. B. Logan, urged citizens to force Sentner to leave town and suggested that the "Christian" way was "against unions." Workers could recognize the lies in the claims to violence, and Sentner wrote that "I do not believe that this has affected our ranks much; it has however driven the wedge further between the town people and our membership." Workers responded to claims that Maytag "had built the town" with retorts that their labor had built Maytag and the town and that their civil and human rights to expression were being denied to keep the company in power.[34]

On June 21, Judge Bechly issued a permanent injunction against mass picketing and interference with plant operations, making it possible for the plant to reopen. The following day, the union's special "peace officers" prevented entrance to the plant by Maytag's top officers and foremen. The company then won an injunction prohibiting more than three picketers at each entrance and any other interference with entrance to the plant. Through its connections on the city council, Maytag forced the resignation of Mayor F. M. Woodrow, who had cooperated with the strikers. An attorney with close ties to Maytag replaced him. The police chief, who had allowed special union deputies, was forced to take a thirty-day vacation, and he was replaced with another Maytag friend. Local 1116 president Wilbert Allison concluded that "the stage was set for the wholesale arrest and beating of our pickets."[35]

The Maytag Sit-Down

But the the union's strategy catalyzed on the morning of June 23. A group of back-to-workers marched toward the plant, and it appeared that union supporters who had given up the fight were joining them. But once inside the plant, union supporters, identified by blue flannel tied to their shirts, forced the outnumbered back-to-workers out of the plant. Union leader Hollis Hall yelled out, "We're taking over the plant!" Workers soon painted "CIO" on the plant's water tower.[36] It was a dramatic turn of events.

Sentner wrote to UE director of organization James Matles that "we are shooting the works." Maytag was completely confounded, Sentner added: "After we pulled the sitdown and took over the plant, they didn't know just what to do." The company wanted to pressure Governor Kraschel to use troops to force evacuation, but "they were leary [*sic*] of opening up an attack on us not knowing just where they stood legally and with public pressure being applied by us . . . we had them by the ——, so to speak."[37]

Sentner understood the risks, recognizing that the company would "start a campaign against the sit-downers and the 'illegality of sit-down strikes': all sit-downers subject to $500 fine and 6 months in the can for contempt, etc. After they whip this up, then I expect them to move via tear gas, etc, against the sit-inners." Sentner and other union officials played a "cat-and-mouse hiding game" to avoid being served for the injunction hearing and to avoid seeming to be directing the plot. Maytag worker John Griffith recalled that "I can remember . . . me and Web Allison got Sentner's clothes out of his room at the hotel and went to Des Moines and met him at the Union Station and handed him his suitcase. He jumped on the train and went to St. Louis. They was looking for him."[38] The union laid plans to bring in Iowa mine worker supporters so that, as Sentner wrote, "if an attack is made, it will be both an inside and outside affair. Hell nor high water could move those boys." One hundred more workers went inside the plant in defiance after a federal judge confirmed Judge Bechly's injunction. When antiunion minister G. B. Logan came to the plant and asked by what authority workers could control it, a worker pointed to himself and said, "I am the C.I.O. I am the law. Keep moving." District Attorney Luther Carr indicated that he was ready to imprison union supporters, charge them with kidnapping for holding foremen in the plant the first day, and even arrest the women's auxiliary members as "an accessory in crime" for getting meals to the plant, but the women expressed willingness to suffer these consequences. The sit-downers' families were removed from the county relief rolls in retaliation. The union started dramatic broadcasts from a Des Moines, Iowa, radio station. Sentner was energized: "Even if we lose, the son-of-abiches [*sic*] will have to confess that this 'red' gave them a run for their money."[39]

While support from fellow workers was needed, Sentner and the union calculated that only political leverage on Governor Kraschel would prevent him from using the National Guard against strikers. In Iowa, the labor movement was still mostly confined to a few industrial centers and mining areas. Up until 1932, the state was consistently Republican. The vast majority of the Democrats carried into office on Roosevelt's coattails in 1932 were conservative. Sentner later described Kraschel, elected in 1936 by a margin of only twenty-five hundred votes, as "by no means a New Dealer and as far to the right" as Iowa's Democratic senator, Guy Gillette. The union sought to convince the governor, who had made negative comments about the CIO in his 1936 election bid, that the electoral support of labor depended on not using the National Guard.[40] The fledgling Iowa Farmer-Labor party was very weak and torn by factionalism, but it had enough leverage, particularly among those miners who were willing to mass on the Maytag plant, to destroy Kraschel's election bid in the fall. Wallace Short, the party's candidate, expressed disgust with Governor Kraschel's waffling over labor issues. However, key allies of the Maytag local were active participants in the left wing of the Iowa Democratic Party and sought to use the threat from the Farmer-Labor party to keep Kraschel in line. Local 1116's struggle had significant support even from the AFL, whose leadership had opposed the split with the CIO. CIO regional director Don Harris helped the union to organize a joint meeting with the AFL, the CIO, and the railroad brotherhoods in the state. The meeting expressed support for the sit-downers, asked Kraschel to back their efforts to win a fair contract, and warned him against using troops. John Connolly, the union's attorney, was a key player in the Iowa Democratic Party. An Irish Catholic and a Democrat who worked with both the AFL and the CIO, he was key to insulating Sentner from anticommunist attacks. Sentner hoped that the extraordinary unity the union had already built with the AFL and key Democratic Party players would put enough pressure on Kraschel to ensure his support for the Maytag workers. The Iowa Farmers Union joined in a condemnation of any attempt to use troops.[41] On June 28 Sentner reported that "so far we have been able to stop any movement of the Governor for troops. It is quite apparent that any move on his part, unless he uses same to close down the plant, will boomerang for his defeat this August, and I don't think he'll take the chance. We are doing every thing possible inside and outside, pressure from within and pressure from without."[42]

In an attempt to counter negative public reaction to the sit-down, the union offered to submit the issues involved to arbitration, sending hundreds of petition cards, signed by workers and citizens of Newton, demanding arbitration under Iowa law.[43] Sentner thought that offering arbitration would mitigate the public opposition to sit-downs and also might "get the company into negotiations and force the governor to close the plant down in a truce until a settlement is made." Workers hung signs from the factory in the midst of occupation that read "Possession is nine tenths of law" but also "We the employees will submit differences to arbitration, ask the company if they will." Maytag's opposition to arbitration held to that of the NMTA and now the National Association of Manufacturers as well. Kraschel, however, refused the union's plea for a "disinterested group of ministers, college professors and other public spirited citizens to investigate the situation and present their findings to the people of Iowa."[44]

Pressure mounted daily on Kraschel to use troops to evict the sit-downers. Sit-down leaders sent out word that they would evacuate if troops kept the plant closed until a settlement was reached. On July 1, when the governor ordered the factory closed until the strike was settled, the union agreed to evacuate. After a union parade, Don Harris announced that "for the first time the Iowa governor's office has been used for the people and not for the vested interests." But Sentner wrote to Matles that "this was about the only move the governor could make, however I am not putting much stock in it, and neither are any of the boys."[45]

Keeping Antiunion Forces at Bay

Now the political pressure from the Right intensified. On July 5, Kraschel told National Labor Relations Board (NLRB) officials that he would not "stand for the God damn nonsense" of Maytag as a "laboratory for a national battleground" and recommended that the union accept the 10 percent wage cut in "the best interest of all parties concerned." The following day, two hundred back-to-workers, encouraged by the governor's pronouncement, tried to enter the plant. Union members "who felt as though they had been betrayed by the governor" successfully held back the reopening with a force of more than five hundred members and sympathizers from the region, violating the injunction against mass picketing.[46]

Meanwhile, the company and its community supporters focused on Sentner's politics. Sentner asked the UE national office to send President James Carey to Newton "because of the red scare" as well as growing "attacks on me for being a [J]ew. . . . Lets give them an Irisher and a [C]atholic—like our attorney Connolly." Speaking to workers at a union meeting, Carey said that "when they quit calling my boys Communists, I'm going to start looking to see what's the matter. They're not doing their job." Sentner wrote to Matles that Carey "was a big help and assisted in overcoming much racial and political prejudice."[47]

But on the night of July 6, Sentner was arrested and charged with violating the injunction and with criminal syndicalism. Criminal syndicalism statutes had been passed in thirty-four states during World War I and the red scare of the early postwar era. These laws made it a penalty to advocate or teach "by word of mouth the use of violent sabotage, crime, or other acts of terrorism to accomplish industrial or political reform." The U.S. Supreme Court overthrew the Oregon law in 1937, causing repeal in Oregon, Washington, and Idaho. Iowa's law remained in effect and carried a maximum penalty of ten years in jail and a fine of one thousand dollars. Prosecuting attorney Luther Carr cited Sentner's speech suggesting support for violation of Judge Bechly's injunction and Sentner's purported leadership of the sit-down strike as evidence of the "terror" necessary to indict him under the law, which, like the later Smith Act, necessitated only that speech and beliefs could result in violence.[48] When workers discovered that Sentner was in jail and that no bond was being accepted for his release, Carey had to persuade workers not to storm the jail to free him. A day later, Carr also charged Carey and Hollis Hall, vice president of Local 1116, with criminal syndicalism, a development that was obviously favorable to Sentner.[49]

Police and prosecutors in Jasper County from this point on had assistance from Fred Bender, a St. Louis-based antiunion operative formerly employed by the Railroad Audit and Inspection Company, a notorious strikebreaking agency. Bender, considered a "thug" by the LaFollette Civil Liberties Committee, had served a year in Leavenworth before being hired by St. Louis business interests to spy on radicals in the workers' movement. Bender wrote to Earl Shields, the sheriff of Jasper County, characterizing himself as an "investigator." The information that Bender offered played a considerable role in subsequent events: "I am inclined to believe that all recent disturbances in your district were instigated by Sentner and his Communist henchmen," he offered on the condition of confidentiality, adding that the policy of Sentner and the CP was "sit-down strikes, bloodshed and violence." As workers fought back, the authorities in Jasper County echoed Bender, characterizing the actions as part of planned "bloodshed and violence" on the part of the CP. The sheriff and mayor organized a posse of one thousand volunteers to squelch the rebellion, with a meeting in support of the idea that they "take shotguns and pitchforks and run the C.I.O. out of Newton."[50]

Workers escalated mass picketing in anticipation of an attempt to reopen the factory. Carloads of miners from Pershing, Iowa, and union supporters from distant Estherville traveled to Newton to prevent the plant from opening, employing what they called a "Minnesota picket line," or mass action. Eighty women, mostly wives of union workers, marched in a circle in front of the east gate. When L. A. McCall, the assistant police chief, attempted to drive a company official though a picket line at the east gate, the women and some men lifted the rear end of the car so that the wheels spun in the air. After McCall retreated, pickets tore up a brick sidewalk outside the plant, piled the bricks up, and distributed them among the strikers.[51]

In response, Governor Kraschel declared martial law "only for the benefit of the public," pledging that troops would keep the plant closed pending a settlement. He sent four state agents to keep him informed of developments and to assist local law enforcement officers. Finally, he agreed to appoint an arbitration board. In exchange, he asked the union to cease mass picketing; the union agreed but soon regretted that decision. In addition, the NLRB agreed to put off hearings scheduled to start in mid-July in order to await the governor's intervention results.[52]

Between July 8 and July 11, Newton police arrested most of the union leadership and scores of union members, charging them with violating the injunction. Some workers were also accused of kidnapping on the grounds that they had held foremen and company officials inside the plant for a time during the sit-down. All of the union leadership remained held without bail. They were released only after the intervention of the Iowa attorney general. On July 11, the governor's agents persuaded the mayor to stop the arrests.[53]

Days later, Judge Fuller, who replaced Judge Bechly, offered to quash the indictments if union leaders would end the strike. When they refused, Fuller reopened the trial to permit the cross-examination of each regarding their political affiliations, aiming to expose Sentner's Communist affiliation and using information gleaned from the antiunion operative Bender. A local attorney testified about "the coming of that black cloud from St. Louis" that had "torn the town apart." He argued that the union was a threat to community progress and revealed that Maytag was considering moving to Canada. Others openly worried that "the union program had entered the churches and the schools" and that workers were "misled by a confessed communist who bragged he had been in jail 28 times." When E. A. Ramige, pastor of the First Congregational Church, wrote a letter on behalf of the union and privately suggested to Maytag officials that the profit motive was un-Christian, his church board forced him to resign, and he was denounced as "a CIO tool" and an "outside agitator."[54]

Sentner acknowledged his membership in the CP and discussed his beliefs about socialism, arguing, however, that he aimed for a socialism that would be achieved democratically in the United States and that would undoubtedly be "far off in the future."[55] Carey, noting that he was a Democrat, defended Sentner's right to membership in the CP and the UE.[56] Maytag worker Ralph Seberg countered the company's rhetoric: "They talk about outside agitators, but the company also brought in outside agitators." William Cuthbert, a union steward who had worked at Maytag since 1925, countered the charge that Sentner and others were "outside agitators," arguing that this was what workers wanted and denying the charges of violence: "I have sat with William Sentner in many private meetings, and he has never done anything but stress law and order. He forbids us from using violence, not once but numerous times." Turning to the businessmen in the courtroom, he declared, "I believe Sentner is as good a citizen as any of you."[57]

On July 13, Fuller convicted the union leaders of contempt of the injunction, sentenced each to six months in jail, and fined each five hundred dollars. Fuller offered to lift the fines and sentences if the leaders would use their influence to persuade workers to go back to their jobs. He warned that if they refused, he would continue proceedings against all the others who had violated the injunction. On July 16, however, the Iowa Supreme Court placed a stay on their sentences.[58]

Inasmuch as the company was using the courts effectively, the union grew frustrated with NLRB foot-dragging on their appeals for a hearing. Meanwhile, to their dismay, the governor's arbitration board recommended that workers go back to work with no initial reductions in pay but with the provision for 10 percent reductions if no agreement was reached in sixty days. Only if Maytag's profits rose in 1938–39 would the wage cut would be restored.[59] Since Maytag refused arbitration, this was a meaningless basis to reenter the plant.

The decision buoyed the antiunion forces and showed the potential pitfalls of arbitration. On July 18, the county sheriff resumed arrests, jailing twenty-one unionists for violation of the injunction. When union members were brought before Judge Fuller, he repeated his offer to forgive the fines and release them if they would try to persuade Maytag workers to take the pay cut.[60] The sheriff called for 1,000 deputies, a move Sentner described as a strategy for "vigilante warfare."[61] Judge Fuller added fire when he warned that there would be an uprising in district court the next day when the men were arraigned. He told the governor that "this is not a case of capital against labor. It is communism versus the good people of Newton. If you'd send fifty men, I'll guarantee we'll put the fear of God into these fellows."[62] Meanwhile, 450 people had entered the plant by July 18. Sentner realized that the cessation of mass picketing had been "an error and we proceeded Tuesday morning to mend our ways." A day later workers and their families massed on the picket line. When workers intercepted Teamster truckers with Maytag parts on their way to Newton, the Teamsters abandoned the trucks on the highway. This successful halting of the trucks prompted an urgent request for troops.[63]

At a union rally on the night of July 19, a Pentecostal spirit took hold. An older worker testified that "I protest the ten percent cut in the name of my home, my crippled wife, in the name of not enough clothing, food, and poor houses. I protest that wage cut now and forever."[64] Sentner told the workers, "I can't tell you it would be right to accept the Judge's decision and go back to work and take the pay cut. You have a right to live happily if you can—a right which stands above every law." Accepting one thousand dollars from a Des Moines local, he pledged that "for that $1000 you gave us, we're going to do what you asked us, and stop anybody from going in the plant." He paused, then continued to waves of laughter from workers and supporters: "I am sure, that by peaceful persuasion, and within the confines of the injunction and the laws of Iowa and the U.S. we can do it."[65]

The meeting was interrupted with news that Kraschel had ordered the Iowa National Guard into Newton, declaring that the plant would remain closed under martial law until a settlement was reached. At a union meeting that night, workers were "sobbing with joy because a dream of unionism seemingly had come true," as they had forced the governor to choose sides. On July 20 as the troops arrived, fights broke out in the streets as the back-to-workers tried to enter the plant. Sentner surmised that it was a company "provocation" designed to "smear the Union. Some of our boys fell for the trick and some 10 or 15 scabs were given the works." Sentner still felt confident that the governor would take "a real honest to goodness chance to come thru for labor and the New Deal. We hope and of course are working to see that he don't muff his chances. . . . Of course we are also preparing for any mistake that the Governor attempts to make with a reopening of the plant before a settlement is reached. Towards this end we have and are fraternizing with the troops, keeping in touch with the officers (all of whom are good friends of our attorneys), etc. We have also connected with every influential person and organization in the state and the Governor no doubt knows where the New Deal forces stand on the question."[66]

Sentner argued that in the context of national politics and CIO politics, almost any settlement would still mean victory and would represent a CIO model of struggle. As one observer put it, "All eyes of organized Labor . . . was watching . . . and wondering just how far a community in Iowa, including the courts, would go to defeat a union of working men and women who was willing to risk losing their jobs and sacrifice their future for industrial freedom." Sentner urgently appealed for help from CIO national leaders and stated that "every national new deal force is thrown behind the demand that Gov K effects a settlement and does not use troops to break strike. . . . Any results from marshal [sic] law other than a settlement will throw the state [R]epublican this fall." Sentner suggested that national Democratic Party leaders advise Kraschel on the importance of the issue. "We must convince the administration forces that this situation can effect [sic] national politics."[67]

Throughout July the governor seemed to have crossed over to the CIO position. Under military order, he made relief available to the strikers, denouncing the attempt to deny it "as a means of clubbing the employes into going back to work." Asked again and again if he would consider using the National Guard to open the plant, he continually said that he would refuse to allow it.[68] Kraschel told Maytag officials as late as July 27 that the plant would remain closed until a settlement was made. Kraschel made an even more remarkable statement to the Democratic Convention in late July: "ownership of property by a non-striker does not exempt that property from its responsibilities to the worker who produced it."[69] Sentner was elated, interpreting this as a signal that the struggle had escalated the workers' claims to rights: "It's quite apparent that the gov will stick to his guns and make a real campaign issue out of the question of human rights versus property rights." But Sentner warned, "It is also apparent that the National Manufacturers' Association will try to use this situation to stump against the New Deal." The company was already planning to get a federal court injunction against the governor.[70]

The Maytag strike had become a conflict with national ramifications, a political football in state and national politics, but important ingredients for success were missing. The CIO nationally was very quiet. Its top leadership offered no endorsement of the kind of sit-downs that contained the kernel of a challenge to property rights discussed and acted upon by the Maytag workers. The CIO was now seeking to eliminate Communists from its ranks, and Sentner's open political affiliation (perhaps as well as the support he had among Maytag's workers) was no doubt embarrassing to its effort to present its movement as a respectable part of the New Deal coalition. The top CIO leadership seemed incapable of having anything more than an elite relationship with the top eche-lons of the Democratic Party. Meanwhile, foremen told the union that Maytag would keep the plant closed until election time, if necessary, to allow the Repub-licans to use the issue in the fall campaign.[71]

In line with the concept of a Popular Front, Sentner and union officials appealed for unity with Governor Kraschel at a late July Farmer-Labor party convention, where Kraschel's role in the strike was a central issue. Wallace Short, the iconoclastic Farmer-Labor candidate for governor, criticized Kraschel for recommending that the workers go back to work under the 10 percent pay cut and called for the repeal of the criminal syndicalism laws. But a delegation of Newton and state CIO unionists asked the convention to "do all in your power to defeat the Republican party in the state of Iowa." Delegates loudly applauded the appeal. While Short refused to withdraw, the appeal had its intended effect of defusing the third-party attempt.[72]

But conservative political forces within the Democratic Party were now set to act. The head of the National Guard and the military commission in charge of "keeping law and order" was Democrat General Matthew Tinley, the com-mander who had prevented the Iowa Farm Holiday Association road blockages in 1933. Tinley, taking seriously Bender's view of Sentner, now set in motion a plan to prevent the strike from benefiting the Republican Party. The commis-sion prevented workers' community-based public activities. One worker was imprisoned for three days and threatened with court-martial for shouting "scab" at another worker. Further, the military commission began hearings that focused on exposing Sentner's political affiliation and the negative influence of union "outsiders."[73]

The union was therefore elated when the NLRB announced that it would begin at last to hold hearings in Newton on charges of unfair labor practices. Workers hoped to counter the military commission hearings with the only public forum left to them. The hearings, which began in late July with hundreds of people in attendance, quickly turned into a devastating exposé of Maytag's maneuvers, including the company's sponsorship of the back-to-work movement, the Farm-ers and Taxpayers Association's practices, and the actions of judges such as Bechly and Fuller. The sensational testimony, which was a catharsis of justice for workers and their families who filled the rooms, appeared in major newspapers all over the state and the nation. The NLRB trial examiner refused to entertain issues of polit-ical affiliation as Maytag's lawyers urged. Fred Maytag was alarmed especially at the testimony from strikers' wives, saying that "it reminded him of Madame Lefarge and the women of the French Revolution."[74]

The hearings also provoked a powerful reaction from Tinley, who persuaded Kraschel to order them stopped on July 30 in a challenge to federal authority. Kraschel charged that the hearings were "a show and a spectacle" and were not "conducive to peace in the community."[75] The governor, appealing to conservative fears of federal power, announced: "You can tell the cockeyed world that there will be no Labor Relations Board hearing in the military district of Iowa." He declared martial law over the entire state to enforce his order. The NLRB, calling Kraschel's actions "illegal," then ordered the board to resume hearings in Des Moines on August 4, saying it would not subordinate national law to state authority.[76]

Krashel used the confrontation to renege on his promises. While the NLRB might resume hearings, the National Guard would reopen the plant under martial law, and the union, he ordered, must accept the company's proposal. Kraschel indicated that he was influenced by the conclusions of the military commission, which blamed "outside agitators" who "encouraged dissatisfaction and inflamed men's passions" for the inability to reach a compromise and recommended that one hundred workers be dismissed who had been influenced by these "outside agitators." Kraschel reduced the number to twelve workers.[77]

Workers debated for hours how they should respond. One worker proclaimed, "I never worked under bayonets, and I never will." But Sentner and other union leaders urged workers not to defy martial law, as it could only result in violence, and asked workers to return to the plant without accepting the contract. Sentner and others reminded them that they would go to the plant with bargaining rights, giving them continued ability to assert their shop floor power and to initiate sit-downs in the plant to gain leverage against Maytag. Connolly overtly discussed production restrictions: "[I]f you go back and give the company all the machines it wants, you'll be just plain nuts." Connolly pledged a general strike by the united forces of the CIO and AFL if the company tried to use strikebreakers.[78] At the end of the meeting, workers reluctantly voted to return to work with this resolution: "We only have our labor to offer to the Maytag Company at a fair price. Our wives, our homes, our children and the City of Newton depend upon our wages. We have no reserves—we cannot gamble with our wages against stock dividends. We stand firmly for the princip[le] that human rights take priority over property rights." The union emphasized that they were "returning to work under the compulsion of military force."[79]

The next morning, union members marched single file into the plant. They were surrounded by armored cars and guards stretched for two blocks around the plant gate; guardsmen on rooftops were armed with bayoneted rifles, tommy submachine guns, tear gas weapons, and automatic pistols. The night before, ten rounds of ammunition were distributed to each guardsmen, and the union hall was prohibited from having more than two people in it at a time.[80]

In the immediate aftermath of the strike, many acts of defiance were evident. In union meetings, Sentner urged workers to continue the battle on the shop floor— to employ direct action and engage in sit-downs if possible. Shop floor militancy was not, however, enough to force Maytag into significant concessions or a union contract until World War II. It was a dramatic contrast to the heady days in the summer of 1937, when workers had vowed to make Newton a "model CIO town."[81]

The Maytag strike was thus not a victory for the Left's strategies, as Sentner had hoped. Sentner had miscalculated on key issues during the strike. The Democratic governor was more susceptible to conservative forces in and outside the party than to workers' entreaties and their nascent influence in the Democratic Party. Sentner had followed CP ideas on how to advance the CIO into a political coalition that would allow a more militant trade union movement to develop. It is important to recognize how, from the local level, this seemed tenable, given the advocacy of John Connolly, who not only defended Sentner against anticommunism but also hoped to transform the Democratic Party into a workers' party. But that hope was misplaced. One can clearly see in hindsight that Kraschel turned away from workers' concerns as soon as the Farmer-Labor party convention was no longer a challenge to him. The CIO's refusal to back a third party was fatal to the Farmer-Labor party, which never again fielded a ticket and thereby reduced the kind of leverage that was possible against a wavering governor such as Kraschel. The Iowa CIO continued to attempt to salvage Kraschel from the forces of reaction, even campaigning in fall 1938, however weakly, for someone who had driven workers back to the plant with bayonets. There was little enthusiasm among politicized workers, and so it did not help. Iowans deserted Kraschel and the New Deal and would not elect another Democratic governor for twenty years.[82]

Still, it is important to recognize the extraordinary commitment of Local 1116 to the idea of expansion of human rights, using a plant occupation that illustrated their desire for more power. It was an occupation that tried to assert workers' rights to a job and their right to decision making about their future. Workers seeking to fulfill that vision were not significantly deterred by Sentner's political affiliations, and the ability to make charges of subversion was more difficult when the political affiliation was not secret. Sentner's solid base of support among workers had been won by tying bread-and-butter concerns to larger issues of power and control in the community and nation. Workers brought their own concerns of workplace security, family security, and a desire to be a more important force in the community. The fight over wages had brought workers face-to-face with raw power and the "right" of capital to lower wages unilaterally in a declining labor market. Sentner had tapped the subversive potential of "pragmatic" community and family concerns. Certainly the company had effectively tapped anticommunism as a counter strategy within the community and in the larger state and national arena. Connected to this was an argument forthrightly mobilizing the employers' property rights in the community in order to stifle workers' rights on the job. These assumptions were even more the case in Evansville, Indiana, where the district sought to contest a stridently antiunion sector of the industry.

The Evansville, Indiana, Organizing Drive of 1938–39

Servel and Evansville

Evansville, Indiana, a city of around 125,000 people located less than 150 miles from St. Louis near the Illinois border, shared with St. Louis a low-wage structure for the metal trades industries.[83] Appliance, furniture, machinery, farm implements, and auto industry companies dominated the city's industrial landscape, some migrating there to take advantage of the city's low wages. By 1938, major employers included Servel, Sunbeam, Hoosier Lamp, Bucyrus-Erie, Briggs Automotive, and Chrysler. Though Chrysler was the best-known company, it was clearly Servel that dominated the city's labor policy.

Servel's roots were in the Hercules Company, a gas engine manufacturer that moved from Cincinnati to Evansville in 1902. Hercules remained a small company until it merged with several others, including Servel, in 1925. Servel, a small Virginia-based company, became a vehicle of the Chase Manhattan Bank, acting on behalf of European capitalist interests, to become the exclusive U.S. manufacturer of Electrolux, gas- and kerosene-operated refrigerators, whose patent was held by a Swedish company. Electrolux manufacturing was moved to Evansville, bringing great growth in employment. By the late 1920s, Servel employed five thousand workers in Evansville, making it the largest employer in the city. The company's board of directors was more nationally and internationally based than was, for example, Emerson's or Maytag's, and it had better-established markets in South America. In addition to a Chase Manhattan director, the company's board included a Sears-Roebuck representative. Its major stockholders were in Europe and New York.[84]

Nevertheless, as had been the case in St. Louis and Newton, Iowa, the community was central to strategies. Servel also became the leader of a coalition of employers who, like the St. Louis independents and in alliance with them, sought community control for a competitive advantage in the national and international marketplaces. While St. Louis employers had been weakened in the mid-1930s, Servel's president, Louis Ruthenberg, emerged as the antiunion spearhead in Evansville as well as regionally and sought to contain the New Deal's nod toward workers.[85]

Early Organizing Drives

In response to section 7a of the National Industrial Recovery Act, Evansville workers, including those at Servel, had engaged in a spirited union organizing drive, joining AFL federal labor unions and seeking redress for a series of grievances that had been percolating since the 1920s. Workers complained about low wages and speedups at the various plants, whose production methods were predominantly assembly line operations. At Servel, for instance, workers were never told their daily output quotas, which determined their minimum wage. Group leaders were responsible for speeding up production, and every two weeks management posted bulletins stating what each group had made. Herb Lansden recalled working anywhere from eight to fourteen hours a day in brutal conditions. "In those days, we were told either do the job or someone else would have it."[86]

Several strikes in fall 1933 and spring 1934 were discouraging. Even where union elections were held and workers voted for the union in overwhelming numbers, management held firm. Most followed Servel's lead in refusing to acknowledge the legitimacy of the labor board. Wholesale firings and layoffs of union activists drained the organizing momentum.[87] Servel used strategically arranged wage increases to deflate the drive and instituted well-financed company unions. The Servel Workers Association included management, and workers paid no dues. After the Wagner Act declared such arrangements illegal, Servel simply modified the bylaws. But a later NLRB decision found conclusively that the "plan ha[d] been subject to substantially the same employer restraint, control and support, direct and indirect, which existed theretofore."[88]

Louis Ruthenberg and other Servel officials organized the Evansville Cooperative League, an organization that was similar to the earlier Citizens' Industrial Alliance. Hailed as a "new type of community organization to fight the New Deal, the Wagner Act and the CIO," Servel, Sunbeam, and Hoosier Lamp were especially prominent in the organization. The league sought to influence public opinion against unions with radio broadcasts and advertisements that suggested the CIO was controlled by Communists, and, as Bob Logsdon later quipped, it "did a good job."[89] Given that the management of these companies were also active in the NMTA (Ruthenberg was a leading national official, and Sunbeam and Hoosier Lamp officials ran the Evansville branch), it is likely that the league was the brainchild of that group. These managers also used industrial espionage, employing a series of operatives from St. Louis, to spy on workers. Evansville had "a very efficient blacklist across industries."[90]

Despite these obstacles, workers in several plants began another union drive in November 1936, in the aftermath of a Democratic sweep of local elections. Servel assembly line workers were especially active, responding to a series of wage cuts and charges of unfairness in shop floor changes. In early 1937, metal finishers on the assembly line launched a sit-down strike. These workers were immediately fired, and Ruthenberg proposed that each agitator "should be photographed and have his picture posted on every billboard and bulletin board in Evansville in order that the community might know who he was." Meanwhile, as in the earlier drive, Servel raised wages 10 percent.[91]

Logsdon noted that there was no community-based CIO organization in the city strong enough to counter that of the employers at this point. The UAW had gained representation at Chrysler during the nationwide strike, using a blitz card-signing campaign. But in March 1937 when a UE organizer from another district came to start a union drive, he found that the UAW refused to cooperate on a community drive. Logsdon noted that in contrast to St. Louis, there was no "educational" program undertaken and "no disposition of the leaders at that time to look to outside sources for advice," a faintly veiled reference to the CP and other leftist groups. It was clear that the CIO movement had failed to take hold when the "town was on fire" in 1937. The UAW had been able to organize because the Ruthenberg antiunion forces figured it would have little influence on the "city's labor policy itself."[92] Sentner, assessing the situation in late 1938 after he had spent some time in the city, noted that in contrast to auto companies, Servel "represent[ed] the Ruthenberg dynasty and political machine of the town—and this [wa]s a different matter affecting LOCAL power."[93]

In October 1937, Art Meloan, a former Emerson worker, began an organizing campaign. He established a shop steward system in some of the electrical plants and a citywide shop steward council, with the goal of building a CIO movement. He built bridges with the UAW forces by helping them to establish an effective shop steward system and "was largely instrumental" in a successful three-day strike in one auto plant. He assisted in organizing packinghouse workers and negotiated their first agreement. He countered the Evansville Cooperative League by developing the seeds of community alliances, carefully ferreting out stool pigeons, and building a labor board case against the company for violation of workers' rights. He made an alliance with clergy in the Church League for Industrial Democracy. After layoffs began in late 1937, Meloan and Thurlow Jones, Servel Local 1002's secretary, helped to organize laid-off workers to demand relief and Works Progress Administration (WPA) jobs through the Workers' Alliance. Up to five thousand Evansville workers attended Workers' Alliance meetings. But in the wake of the recession, Meloan was pulled out of Evansville. As the recession took firmer hold, the fledgling union campaign collapsed.[94]

The 1938–39 Organizing Drive

In late 1938 Logsdon and Meloan started another organizing drive at Servel, because Ruthenberg was the "lynchpin of local politics and police and thus the key to breaking open the Evansville independents."[95] By early 1939, shop stewards were functioning as a union in several key departments, and a core militant group had developed. In addition, the union reestablished its contacts with groups such as the Church League for Industrial Democracy and countered the Cooperative League's massive antiunion propaganda with its own radio broadcasts and open public meetings. Logsdon sought a means to achieve women's involvement and worried that they might be hesitant to come to the UE's offices, located in the same building as the UAW offices. The UAW was experiencing factionalism that had led to a descent into a union without much vision, with "slot machines" in the union hall. Sentner reported on "drunken street brawls, goon squads, whores and the likes" that tarnished the public image of the CIO overall. The UE needed a sustained community campaign to counter this.[96]

Servel wielded intimidation through private and community forces. When the union sought to marshal supporters to hold a union "card drive" outside the plant in October 1938, fifty Evansville policemen cordoned the plant.[97] Foremen, group leaders, and antiunion workers conducted a "careful but consistent campaign" of "union-baiting [and] rumor mongering." Foremen took down names of those who signed union cards and then harassed them inside the plant. Servel employed a private police force of thirty-five armed men who intimidated union supporters. Two of the armed men "constantly watched" the chief steward and followed him out of and back in the gate.[98]

Simply put, Servel power ensured that workers' citizenship rights in their own community were limited. They looked to the NLRB decision on their case—a reliance that Sentner and Logsdon warned against. While workers remained reluctant to sign union cards, they were ready to engage in shop floor actions. They hoped that public support could be generated from radio broadcasts and other union propaganda that exposed Servel's methods. Reports from sympathetic ministers indicated that these were helpful: "This seems to be the first time that the public is learning of what has been going on in the plant." In February 1939, the union pulled a stoppage among assembly line metal finishers, the most solid union supporters in the plant. Fifty policemen were sent into the plant after the company claimed that "a riot was going on." But Meloan called Indiana governor Maurice Townsend, "and he had [the policemen] out faster than they went in."[99] The following morning, there was a contingent of police at every gate and several carloads of police slowly circling the plant. But the fact that no one was fired was enough to propel the movement. A week later, two departments launched a sit-down after a union leader was laid off when he discussed Servel's private police force in a radio interview. Within fifteen minutes, fifty city policemen forced the sit-downers out of the plant, and management fired them. But when management learned that workers were considering an occupation of the entire plant, they agreed to rehire all, including the original person laid off.[100]

Workers were still considering a plant occupation when, in late February 1939, the U.S. Supreme Court handed down the *Fansteel* decision, which declared sit-downs illegal. Fansteel workers had occupied the plant in response to the company's violations of their rights under the Wagner Act, including the use of spies to provoke a traditional strike and replace them. As legal scholar Jim Pope has shown, the details of this decision made it clear that "the employer could violate the workers' statutory rights [illegal spying in violation of the Wagner Act] without sacrificing its property rights, while the workers could not violate the employers' property rights [through sit-downs] without sacrificing their statutory rights—a return to the hierarchy of values that predated the

Wagner Act." The decision certainly affected possibilities for District 8. A local judge threatened a severe injunction against the union if there was another sit-down at the plant.[101]

Logsdon, responding to clamors for a strike by union supporters, sought to reduce the police power wielded on behalf of Servel. The target was Louis L. Roberts, an attorney for Servel but also the city's director of Public Safety with control over city police, and a colonel in the National Guard. Logsdon joked that Roberts was the "handy man of the city." The union leadership and state CIO officers sought leverage from Governor Townsend, who presumably had authority over the National Guard in the city. Townsend, a former factory worker who was a stronger New Deal supporter than Kraschel, sent a state labor commissioner "to investigate . . . subversive company activities." The number of police cars circling the plant was reduced from nine to one, and the company withdrew the foremen who had been regularly posted around the gates. Logs-don reported that the morale of workers and "interest in the union" escalated.[102]

The 1939 Strike

Momentum for a strike grew, and workers expressed "desire for action of any kind." In addition to the metal division and foundry, the union had solid support of a portion of the box division, heavily dominated by women who had formerly avoided the union. Sentner and Logsdon believed that these constituted strategic groups of workers capable of shutting down the entire factory. Given that Servel was entering a high production period, the union planned for mass actions at the plant gates with the aid of community supporters and expected the governor's help in containing local police and Servel's private army.[103]

As soon as the strike was called on the morning of March 14, 1939, however, it was clear that Servel too had prepared well. The local radio station rejected the union broadcasts under influence from the company. Servel erected watchmen's shanties and installed spotlights (loaned from public parks) on building tops that followed cars as they approached the factory. Police were "thick as lice around the plant." That evening almost the entire Evansville police force was at the plant gates. Facing this intimidation, community supporters failed to show. According to Logsdon, even some of the most militant shop floor activists "lit out like scared rabbits," and many could not be persuaded to picket.[104] Then the governor balked at his promised intervention.

A countersubversion strategy was quickly put into play, coordinated with the help of St. Louis agents of the NMTA. Fred Bender, the agent who had assisted Maytag and was billed as a "private investigator" from St. Louis, spoke at an evening "Americanization" meeting arranged by the American Legion, whose commander was the Evansville chief of police. All local administration officials and key businessmen attended and endorsed Bender's speech. Bender spoke as an authority hired by St. Louis business interests to investigate Communist activity three years earlier, and he revealed Sentner's affiliation and claimed that Logsdon was a "left-wing Socialist" under Sentner's control. Telling the audience that Sentner was on his way to assist the strike (Sentner had arrived on the same train to Evansville as had Bender), he warned that Sentner's arrival would bring violence in the strike.[105]

As if on cue, violence broke out on the picket line that evening, initiating a chain reaction. It started when a company guard shot a union man in the leg, but police arrested the injured man and refused him medical care until he absolved Servel of blame. Meanwhile, provocations on the picket line brought minor fracasses and an opportunity to arrest all picketers on charges of assault. Judge Spencer ordered the police to jail Sentner, Logsdon, and Meloan without filing charges, and they were held until appeals were made to the Indiana attorney general. Spencer justified the arrests on the ground that violence had occurred and said that the union had violated its pledge. Actually, Spencer had told Logsdon and Sentner earlier that "there is going to be violence tonight" after they had assured him there would not be.[106] Spencer, whom Logsdon now recognized as being in on the entire scheme, announced the convening of a grand jury investigation to issue indictments of strikers and to discover the "organized movement" behind the "disorders." The first ruling of the grand jury resulted in a five hundred-dollar fine and sixty days in jail for one of the workers caught in the roundup of the picketers.[107]

The strike collapsed rapidly. The next morning more than 150 workers returned, and most others came to the union hall "disheartened." Most unionists refused to picket "because of the terrific amount of terror and intimidation." Two hundred police were stationed at the plant at shift change and were "running people into the plant, and calling for them at their homes." Even the Evansville Fire Department hauled workers to the plant. Foremen visited workers at their homes to persuade them to return to work. Servel influenced grocery stores to cut off the accounts of strikers. Meanwhile, the city ordered the cessation of leaflet distribution. The union charged that Servel hired an agency to conduct a campaign of window breaking in order to further discredit the union. The American Legion organized what Logsdon described as a "vigilante committee to finish up the job of intimidation and coercion." Servel organized a campaign for fraternal organizations such as the Shriners to pass resolutions against the union and the strike. Logsdon lamented that "apparently our talks of peace on the radio and our public statements over [the] period did not take with the people living here. Public sentiment developed strongly against the union right from the start. Headlines on arrests, shootings and violence did the rest."[108]

Sentner appealed to U.S. Attorney General Frank Murphy for a federal grand jury investigation to "stir into the mess that's being cooked up in Evansville" and threatened to file criminal libel charges against Bender for accusing Sentner of fomenting violence. The union appealed for support from the LaFollette

Committee to expose Bender's antiunion and criminal background. But stung by anticommunist accusations, the committee was already expecting to fold up because of congressional funding cutbacks, making it unavailable as a means of bringing pressure on the company. Logsdon wrote dejectedly that even the federal conciliator was "hesitant in doing anything" to counter Servel's power. Community supporters were silenced. While the Church League for Industrial Democracy revealed startling findings of its investigation of Servel and the city's antiunion community actions, the local press did not report them. The NLRB finally handed down its decision from a year-old case on March 27, revealing and condemning Servel's interference with union organization, but by then the strike was already lost.[109]

"This is the worst mess that it has ever been my misfortune to be around," Logsdon reflected. He noted that the intense shop floor militancy of Servel workers and the fledgling support from community groups and the UAW were not enough to overcome Servel's community control.[110] Sentner admitted that "I can say personally that I underestimated the forces of reaction that were in command of the company and overestimated our forces and the auxiliary forces."[111]

The Servel campaign exposing Sentner's political affiliations had been effective. Just as at Maytag, key activists trusted Sentner and dismissed the bogeyman charges regarding his affiliations. But in light of the events involving Maytag, Sentner had planned to remain out of sight in order to avoid attacks. Logsdon had called on him to come to Evansville in the middle of the strike's declining fortunes. Sentner concluded that "it was certainly not good for our organization in this territory that I had to stick my neck out to get our heads chopped off on the red issue."[112]

The Maytag and Servel campaigns were emblematic of how the union tide was rolled back in the wake of political and economic retrenchment. The waning of the progressive instruments of the New Deal such as the LaFollette Committee brought the union movement into a defensive position. Bender's ability to be more open in Servel showed how forces of reaction came forward at the first opportunity. This was a critical factor, much more so than the degree of workers' class-consciousness, in thwarting the union insurgency. Without the political power to counter the forces of repression, the Left was unable to present alternatives to the CIO's lackluster fortunes.

District 8's attempt to face down the employer backlash brought better results in St. Louis, where the union survived through shop floor and community struggles. However, even there the struggle brought mixed results, and the CIO began to turn against its left wing.

St. Louis Layoff and Dues Campaign

By late 1937 District 8 had turned the layoff crisis in St. Louis, which Sentner wrote had "wrecked us morally and financially," into a spirited mobilization of

St. Louis union workers in a fight for relief and WPA jobs for union members. The campaign owed much to the experience of the nut pickers four years earlier. This community activity gave the union strength in the midst of layoffs. Many of the young workers who had engaged in the Emerson sit-down were those laid off, and the union sought to keep those activists in the fold as well as to support all workers and build allegiance to the union.[113] Women members were prominent among the key activists who organized Wagner Electric's "picket for relief" at the St. Louis County courts, where workers advocated the thirty-hour work week.[114]

Local 1108 at Century Electric produced the most impressive results of this campaign. Henry Fiering and the shop "shock brigade" set up a "roving committee" at the plant to maintain union affairs there after all officers were laid off. Local 1108 campaigned for relief and WPA jobs and established a gas, electric, and rent committee, which prevented evictions and utility cutoffs.[115] When workers found relief officials unresponsive, the shock brigade occupied the main relief office, demanding a meeting with the director. Fiering described the encounter:

> I remember it well, the director of relief on one end of this long table, me on the other end, and a large group of workers in between. He looked like he thought we might tear the place apart if we didn't get what we wanted. . . . And we said we don't want any of our people to suffer anything—coal, food or anything. . . . So the upshot of it was that he guaranteed that every worker from Century no matter what would be guaranteed food, coal, shelter for the duration of the recession. And if anything happened, [if] somebody was wronged, he said, "Call me up." . . . Every one of the Century workers who needed anything at all never suffered a thing as they had in prior years. It was a complete reversal of the experience they had seen during . . . [the] Depression.[116]

For almost two years Local 1108 placed seven hundred members on the local relief and WPA agencies. By February 1938, 95 percent of District 8's unemployed members had been placed on relief or WPA jobs. Fiering claimed that District 8's example became a model for the local CIO.[117]

Activists had sought to sustain the UE with public funds in order to counter the employers' strategies of using economic downturns to destroy the union. Indeed, St. Louis employers, sensing the opportunity and with a push by NMTA managers from St. Louis and Evansville, had organized under the Associated Industries, which emphasized that "industrial relations has now become a community problem." In early 1938, the group heard from Servel's Charles Ruthenberg on how employers could prevent "infection" of unions by organizing on a community basis. Century vice president R. J. Russell joined in, echoing NMTA officials' long-held wisdom that "industrial unrest" was like a "disease which spreads from one plant to another." In January 1938, UE activists discovered that Century Electric and other antiunion employers were subsidizing a Cooperative Employment Council (CEC), whose purpose, Sentner charged, was "to make loyal workers out of the unemployed" and to counter the union's unemployment activities. Unemployed movement activists, acting now as a committee of the CIO, attended the meetings and exposed the CEC's funding to those who attended. By late spring 1938, the group had collapsed after the union got the LaFollette Committee to publicize its findings.[118]

Sentner wrote to the national office that UE unemployment activities "smacked them [employers] all between the eyes." Century managers, for instance, "had hoped to some degree that they would have by this time gotten inner control of the organization and . . . soften[ed] the whole tune of the union; they had also depended upon their mass layoffs to undermine the prestige and morale of the organization. The mass layoffs, etc., prior to the successful struggles for WPA did have that effect. Century was surprised we could give them a solid licking."[119]

District 8's activists sought to make the CIO the base for broader movement activity on behalf of all the unemployed. In November 1937 they launched the CIO campaign to force city and state officials to expand relief budgets and establish more WPA jobs. District 8 threatened a statewide boycott of sales tax payments until relief was given. Sentner organized the first citywide mass meeting for relief under the CIO, and Logsdon chaired the local CIO unemployed effort.[120] By early 1938 the CIO was beginning to lead a campaign for more relief and for the removal of restrictions that discriminated against needy St. Louisans. It demanded the removal of eight "stringent rules"—such as refusal of aid and WPA jobs to women and people over age seventy and the one-year residency requirement—all of which were based on employer influence emanating from the 1920s Community Fund days. This movement won the removal of some of these rules, the release of more funds, and the reduction in delays for obtaining relief.[121]

But a more sustained coalition for building unemployed activities among CIO unions was elusive. The Industrial Union Council (IUC), the central CIO body, refused to integrate its activities with the Workers' Alliance, the national unemployment organization, because St. Louis CIO leaders suspected that unemployment activity would give more leverage to the Left and were already discouraging involvement with the Workers' Alliance because of the prominence of CP activists. Nevertheless, the UE continued to lead the CIO efforts to sustain and increase relief allocations from state and city governments.[122]

These struggles also indicated that the independents had clearly "not reconciled themselves to collective bargaining."[123] By early 1939, the St. Louis locals of District 8 had faced more than a year of chronic unemployment. Nationally, appliance sales dropped 27 percent in 1938. St. Louis's electrical industry, as motor suppliers to smaller producers of appliances and as producers themselves, was affected even more seriously than eastern companies. In the mid-1930s, most refrigerator manufacturers switched to hermetically sealed motors, which required a clean environment to produce. St. Louis's dirty, dusty build-ings were unsuited to this. More than 50 percent of the electrical workers in St. Louis UE shops were laid off from their jobs in 1938; the remainder worked only part-time. In late 1938, three-fourths of Emerson's employees were still laid off, and only one hundred were employed full-time, the same as 1932.[124]

The struggles over relief and WPA jobs were no panacea, and by early 1939, as business began to slowly pick up, the union needed to rebuild the local.[125] With the more conservative political climate and the decline of New Deal fortunes, the union's ability to exercise shop floor power was put to new tests, especially given the loss of key activists who had moved on to other jobs. For example, Emerson worker Orvil Heflin, one of the many young workers who had placed so much hope in the union insurgency and had been part of the leftist coalition, had decided that he "couldn't afford to stay at Emerson" despite his allegiance to the union. On the other hand, a seniority system kept many of the longer-term workers employed; many of these were less militant and less favorable to the dis-trict's leftist leadership.[126]

As laid-off workers returned, they found that the companies had "started the introduction of new machinery and production methods." As production changed, new job categories were established, often with lower piece rates or incentive earnings. Johnston Tin-Foil workers, who defied the economic down-turn to win a four-month strike in mid-1938, found that the strike gains were being eroded by a speedup system. Similarly, while Wagner Electric's economic fortunes soared when it won contracts as a major supplier of brakes and starters for Ford automobiles, workers there also complained of intense speedup.[127]

The district leadership worried that the low level of dues payments exposed the union's weakness to the company. Stewards complained that foremen harassed workers who regularly paid dues. Even at Century, only ninety-two workers paid dues in December 1938. Century managers sought "to discourage dues payments and to lower the spirit of the members" as workers returned to the shop.[128] Dues were highest at Wagner, where the union was weakest simply because employment was steadier, but even there, on average only about one-third of the workers made dues payments every month. Wagner managers rewarded those not in the union. One activist noted that "colored people and the girls in the plant" were not yet committed to the union and suggested that the union needed to address this problem.[129]

The district's activists approached the problems of dues collection through a community campaign and included picketing at nonunion workers' homes. Century activists started to picket the homes of workers who refused to pay dues or join the union, especially those who were "key bastards" or bosses' favorites in the shop. Fiering noted that in some working-class areas of St. Louis, the "feeling of unionism was so strong [that] people who weren't members used to masquerade as union members to neighbors." A leaflet distributed in one neighborhood appealed to workers on the grounds that Century helped set the wage standards for all. The leaflet called on the residents to urge their neighbors to join the union and argued that a nonunion worker was "UNAMERICAN and a disgrace to your community." The NMTA and the St. Louis Chamber of Commerce brought legal action to prevent the picketing, and many activists were arrested.[130]

But the drive was successful. Fiering recalled that "one guy came out with his mother and was pleading with us 'Please go away—I'll join the union, please go away!' And he was a dirty rotten skunk in the shop, you know." By March 1939 only eight workers were still refusing to pay dues, and, Fiering remembered, "the spirit" in the plant had risen "100%."[131] Emerson Local 1102 also saw a similar rise. In cases where workers were not antiunion, the locals hosted home visits to find out why workers were not paying dues, try to gain the allegiance of spouses, and inquire into family circumstances. Lloyd Austin was appalled by the poverty he witnessed among some of his fellow workers during these visits: "One guy and his family lived in a shack, and I almost felt guilty to ask him for dues after that."[132] At Wagner, the home visit campaign enabled workers to avoid the coercive presence of company deputies who were "causing fear among those still unsigned" and to develop a deeper understanding of the particular concerns of African American and women workers. It helped the local to reenergize its steward system, which resulted in higher piece rates for more than eight hundred workers.[133]

During the course of this drive, District 8 made a dues checkoff a key part of the 1939 round of contract negotiations. Activists agreed that a dues checkoff would force the employers to finally accept the union rather than continually fight it. Sentner also was concerned that the district's capacity to organize would continue to be handicapped by inconsistent dues collection.[134] The drive for the checkoff energized and inspired the most militant activists in ways that confound some perceptions about the relationship between the checkoff and militancy.[135] The focus for the dues checkoff was initially at Century, where militancy was at its highest level. But unexpected overtures came from Emerson's new head, Stuart Symington, who became president of Emerson in fall 1938 and who sought to change the contentious relationship between the company and the union. The end result of that process would have significant repercussions for the district's Left as they sought to balance militancy and the carrot of cooperation to save the industry.

Stuart Symington and the Perils of Cooperation

Symington came to Emerson because of the company's deepening financial crisis. Seeking an infusion of capital for the company, Emerson's board made a stock offering just after the sit-down. This was a complete failure, but it allowed the stock underwriter, David Van Alstyne, significant leverage in the company.[136] Van Alstyne was able to name a new president, and in the summer of 1938, he called upon Stuart Symington to take the Emerson job.[137]

Symington was only thirty-seven years old when he came to Emerson, but he had already been head of six companies and had gained a reputation as "a rehabilitator of run-down or distressed companies." Symington was from a wealthy, socially prominent Baltimore family whose access to capital had allowed him to set up and acquire small businesses. Symington used his and his family's social contacts to gain contracts for these businesses; he used efficiency experts to revive older businesses and then sold them to competitors after they became viable. When Symington later built a political career, he would tout his belief in antitrust, but his stance was that of an interloper who shook up market arrangements in an opportunistic fashion, enough to produce a buyout offer. The game was small-time but personally lucrative.

One of Symington's businesses made radio loudspeakers. The 1929 crash and the switch to radio sets with built-in speakers seemed to doom the venture, so the family merged the business with Colonial Radio, which manufactured radios for Sears-Roebuck. When Colonial was failing in the summer of 1932, Symington appealed to Robert Wood of Sears to keep the company afloat in exchange for a majority interest in the company. With Wood's financial backing, Symington fought Dave Sarnoff of RCA, who sued Colonial for violating license agreements. Colonial countersued RCA, AT&T, and IT&T for millions and won the right to license radios. Then in 1934, Symington sold Colonial to Sylvania, the country's third largest radio manufacturer, for a tidy profit.[138]

In 1935 Symington took on the presidency of Rustless Iron and Steel Company of Baltimore, an old independent company, and got markets for the company through his uncles' contacts. In 1938 he sold it at a substantial profit to a much larger concern, American Rolling Mill.

Behind his success were his personal connections, an unabashed level of self-promotion, a dynamic salesman's demeanor (later it would gain for him the label "Mr. Charm, of Washington"), and, at least as important, an engineering team geared toward implementing efficiency regimes that would make smaller companies competitive with larger ones. In both Colonial and Rustless, Symington had employed Trundle Associates, a management-engineering firm. Symington sold Trundle's operational methods to workers. Trundle had "wide connections in the business world," among them the executives at Dillon Read, a substantial Wall Street firm whose executive, James Forrestal, had taught Van Alstyne the brokerage business. Van Alstyne turned to Forrestal for advice in the Emerson crisis, and this in turn led him to Symington and Trundle.

Thus, as a result of family and business adventures, Symington had become part of a developing network of efficiency experts and investment bankers and brokers. This group was among the small but important sector of business and banking that had friendly ties to the Democratic Party, largely because of

Roosevelt's favorable stance on global trade issues. During World War II, these connections would prove extremely valuable to Symington and Emerson because this sector of business ran the government defense establishment. Of course, all of this was not foreseen when Symington took his position, and Symington was not even a Democrat at the time. But Symington was also not part of the NMTA crowd. The circles in which Symington traveled, as well as his interloper status in the St. Louis business community, influenced his demeanor toward labor and the economic crisis at Emerson.[139]

When he came to Emerson in September 1938, Symington replaced some of the old managers and convinced the board of directors to pay a substantial fee to Trundle Associates for an engineering study. Symington saw Emerson as a stodgy old company caught in a "vicious cycle of low volume and high costs," a company that needed to break out of a dependence on fans. General Wood reportedly handed the Sears catalog to Symington and asked him to choose something Emerson could make. Soon the company had an order for fractional horsepower motors for Cold Spot and Speed Queen appliances, the first of many orders. Symington found ways of getting bank loans from New York to St. Louis to meet the payroll during the summer months of 1939, as the company remained in financial crisis.[140]

Symington later gained recognition for his "skill at labor relations"—a reputation he vigorously inflated when he ran for U.S. senator—and gained folklore status in the 1980s when he was compared to the notorious antiunion regime at Emerson under Charles Knight.[141] The real story has more to do with Symington's interloper status and with the legitimacy crisis for the union and for Sentner in the context of the sharp turn by the national CIO against the Left. In fact, Symington did not break with the past when he came to Emerson. During contract negotiations in fall 1938, the new management stood firm on critical union issues. For example, the company refused the union's request to extend seniority to account for longer than expected layoffs, threatened that any worker paying dues on company premises would be liable to discharge, and followed the old management's effort to weaken the arbitration clause. Given the company's weak economic position, workers settled for minor wage changes, seniority extension, and a somewhat weakened arbitration clause but also a guarantee from the new management that there would be no reduction in wages.[142]

Symington did make overtures to the union that other St. Louis managers would have eschewed. Century and Wagner management looked at control of their plants for the long term and viewed their obligations to maintain a united community front as sacrosanct. But Symington's formative experience with unions at Colonial Radio, where James Carey had been the key negotiator, convinced him that a union could be a moderating force. In fact, it is likely that Symington "thought that his friendship with Carey provided some sort of insurance" against any attempt by the Local 1102 to reject his designs for Emerson. Still, Symington recognized that the low wage structure at Emerson was a card that could trump the "big boys."[143]

In early February 1939, Symington sought the union's cooperation with Trundle engineers' new production methods. After checking with Carey about Sentner, Symington told Sentner of his plans. GE and Westinghouse were engaging in a price war on motors, upsetting the old arrangements in the industry. He claimed that this put the company's wages under pressure but also gave them a potential to "upset the apple cart in regard to prices unless GE and Westinghouse lets them in on a part of the output" and was using the financial clout of ties to the "Sears-Roebuck crowd" to ensure that the "big boys" would listen and grant more of the market. Symington was also trying to consolidate mergers with Century in order to make the area into a larger player in the industry. Symington indicated that if his plans were realized, St. Louis workers would have more steady employment.[144]

Sentner wrote to the national office that the union could "drive a hard bargain" to secure stability and recognition in an industry that had not yet come to terms with the union, using Symington's offer as an "avenue to break thru the St. Louis employers." Symington assured Sentner that he would try to persuade other managers to grant a union shop if the union would cooperate on the production changes.[145] In early February, Symington agreed that a union committee could visit around the plant during off periods to solicit dues and membership, "a distinct concession as the contract strictly forb[ade] this." Then, in mid-February, Symington agreed that "all piece work rates now w[ould] only be put into effect after agreement with the union." The union placed two representatives in the time study department to oversee this agreement.[146]

The district sought to establish the ground rules for cooperation with Emerson and other employers on production issues. Officers of St. Louis locals at a special meeting pledged cooperation in exchange for a union shop, a larger role in the industry, and a commitment that wages would not be reduced for any group of workers and that cooperation would not mean a speedup for workers. Pointing out that St. Louis companies had been using "new machinery and production methods" to reduce wages, they argued that wages "should be increased in proportion to the increased production."[147] After workers found that some jobs were targeted for wage reductions by the Trundle engineers, they refused to agree to the new pay system. Symington angrily accused Sentner and the union of failing to understand their position and of defending a confusing old pay system that the union itself condemned. Sentner responded that the issue was Trundle's attempt to reduce wages and reminded him that he had not yet granted the checkoff, which would help to "clear away the vestiges of fear and uncertainty that ha[ve] prevailed heretofore" between Emerson and workers.[148]

Sentner continued to pursue the proposal, convinced of Symington's pledge that no employee would "suffer in weekly earnings because of change in materials, methods, [or] time" and "that no greater effort [would] be required in working under a change of materials, methods or time than under the present method."[149] More than eight hundred activists attending a special meeting agreed with Sentner to "make it clear that we intend to participate in the increased benefits that may be derived from the joint and cooperative efforts of management and union" without speedup.[150] The district brought in James Carey in late March to "fill [the independents' management] with the union shop idea" through this pledge of cooperation and to reduce the still prevalent tensions over negotiations with a Communist. Using Carey's assurance about how Sentner "stood in the eyes of the International," Symington sought to persuade Century and Wagner's management to join Emerson in a voluntary checkoff with the union but was "flatly refused." Symington related to Sentner that he told the other companies to "go to hell" and that he was "ready and w[ould] put the deal before the Board of Directors of Emerson in May with his O.K. for adoption."[151]

Symington's stance on the issue encouraged Century workers, who were "stripped for some kind of action," as Century had refused to give any ground in contract negotiations, especially on a major issue regarding the minimum wage. According to Sentner, "when we announced that Emerson was ready to go along on an improved recognition clause [and] voluntary check off, the meeting went wild." After all but twenty workers voted to strike, the negotiators found that Century management began to "give ground" and agreed to raise the minimum wage to thirty-eight cents.[152] Century's "shock troops" still wanted to strike to bring the local up to forty cents minimum, the district's immediate goal. Clearly influenced by the overtures from Symington and convinced that Century would wage the same kind of battle Maytag had, Sentner successfully urged settlement.[153]

Sentner, acknowledging qualms about having "to cooperate in production questions, new machinery, increased speed of operation, etc.," said that he was willing to go along in order "to make hay while the sun shines for the consolidation of the union and attempt to enter into a different form of relations than heretofore of the dog eat dog variety. On this if necessary to go along in production, at the same time thru the consolidation of the organization lay the guarantees for our proper share of the take, and for our protection against abuses" such as speedup and pay cuts.[154]

Symington clearly wanted to use the checkoff as a carrot to reduce shop floor conflict. When he found Sentner an unwilling ally on this score, he refused to grant it. On the shop floor, contention over the meaning of union-management cooperation continued. Symington had agreed to make new pay rates a subject of "mutual agreement" with the union, but workers continued to experience downward pressure on piece rates. Logsdon helped Local 1102 organize around these issues in preparation for new contract negotiations. In June 1939 the local announced that it had never agreed that improved efficiency would be "taken out of the employes' pocketbook, or sweated out of them by increased effort or speed up. . . . We are anxious to have the company demonstrate the reality of their plea for harmony by meeting this issue in a realistic way."[155] Logsdon complained that "considerable chiseling" continued with the new pay system. Further, responding to his organizing, "the company has gone back to their old policy of calling in members individually and explain[ing] their timing to them in violation of their agreement to call in the chief steward on such occasions. It is apparent that the company is determined to readjust rates which are too high to suit them, in spite of the agreement."[156]

Logsdon soon concluded that "the new management differs from the old only in that they try to soft soap the local people while putting cuts into effect, while the old management went about it openly."[157] Moreover, in contract bargaining, Symington, although friendly, refused to consider subjecting the issue of piece rates to arbitration. Logsdon complained that while Symington had "tamed down" the foremen, it was "impossible to pin him down on the principle that net earnings shall be maintained when any change in timing is made" or operations were changed. Ironically, Wagner and Century had agreed to that principle, and stewards used arbitration to hold them to it. Logsdon concluded that Symington wanted to "stall along until the next agreement when he can use this as a basis for requesting our acceptance of this practice."[158]

By mid-July 1939, Local 1102, having refused to budge on these issues, had won a joint union-management committee to deal with future wage rate changes and had gained access to company time studies. In a special resolution in August 1939, Local 1102 declared that the company was "promoting an old tactic of speed-up and lower wages concealed behind the rhetoric of cooperation."[159] As the union authorized a strike and continued to contest issues on the shop floor, the company again conceded some points. Nevertheless, after September 1 negotiations stalled.[160]

Sentner had misjudged Symington in his attempt to "break through" the hard line of the St. Louis independents and began to "wonder if we would have been better off it we would have struck Century." As it fell out of reach, the checkoff issue grated at Sentner, who sought organizing funds and realized that there would be "no major changes as far as recognition is concerned, and of course this is really our big question in St. Louis if stability of organization is to be achieved. . . . [I]t means another year fighting for dues. This question is becoming most acute. Our people, we find, are tiring of this constant fight both against the bosses and the people who haven't as yet been convinced of unionism and don't shoulder their financial obligations properly."[161]

In October, with Emerson contract negotiations still stalled, the union learned that Emerson was considering an offer to move its plant to Evansville, Indiana, whose Chamber of Commerce offered one hundred thousand dollars toward a modern facility.[162] Emerson's official history acknowledged that Symington designed the threat to demonstrate to workers that he "could wield the stick as well as show the carrot." Symington felt that workers had read his offer of the dues checkoff and cooperation as a sign of weakness. Years later he said that "he never had intended to move," but he wanted workers to understand that "Emerson's interests had to come first—before ties to a particular city."[163] Symington may have machinated the Evansville offer through his Sears connections. Sears had brought Emerson the contracts for hermetically sealed refrigerator motors, which required new facilities. General Wood was vehemently antiunion and had connections not only with Servel (where he sat on the board) but also with companies that would combine to form Whirlpool and produce refrigerators for Sears in Evansville. It may well be that Wood helped Symington set up the inducement in order to impart a lesson to Emerson workers or that Wood urged Symington to consider seriously the possibility of locating in Evansville, since it had such influence there. Or perhaps this was an NMTA-Ruthenberg overture, a gesture to bring Symington into the fold of the proper community-based labor relations policy.

In any case, the threat worked. Local 1102 members quickly approved a contract that retained a thirty-eight-cent minimum rate, though subfractional motors employees reached that only after eight months of employment. On the crucial issue of timings and pay plans, the company retained control, although if a worker was dissatisfied, a recheck of the times could be made with the oversight of a steward. However, the company did agree to the principle that base rates and day rates then in effect would remain the standard.[164] The contract was not a reversal for the union, but neither was it much of an advance.

Local 1102 took Emerson's threat to move seriously, as runaway shops were not new to District 8. Indeed, the St. Louis shoe industry had made inducements such as Evansville's very familiar by the 1920s. When Superior Electric workers organized in 1937, the company threatened to move to Centralia, Illinois, which offered the company sixty thousand dollars to move in the midst of a strike. The NLRB agreed to the union's unfair labor practice charge, and this prevented the move. But in early 1938 Superior moved when Cape Girardeau, Missouri, financed the move.[165] Workers at Baldor Electric won a strong contract in 1937, but in early 1939 the company refused to bargain and began moving one of its departments to Greenville, Illinois. The union filed suit in St. Louis Circuit Court for an injunction to prevent the company from moving. That "forestalled" the company's plans, Sentner reported, "but the Company is still attempting to hold this over the heads of the employees."[166] Baldor UE Local 1107 workers struck in September 1939, just prior to Emerson's threat to move. Throughout the fall, Baldor workers put up a fiery battle that included mass arrests. Only two union members crossed the picket lines, but the company secured other workers, some though the AFL, and by December the strike was clearly lost and the local decimated. Baldor remained in the city, however.[167]

The response to the Emerson threat to move cannot be fully understood outside this context or without looking at the legitimacy crisis experienced by the Left and in particular by Sentner beginning in the fall of 1939, with the escalation of anticommunism nationally and within the CIO.

The Crisis of the Left

At the national level, anticommunism was set in motion by antilabor elements and by the international events that depleted the willingness of many to overlook the CP's association with the Soviet Union. Antilabor Congressman Martin Dies established the House Un-American Activities Committee (HUAC) in late 1938. Over the course of the next year, it suggested that the NLRB and the LaFollette Committee harbored or catered to leftists. The committee was supported by key AFL officials who hoped to exploit charges that the CIO was riddled with Communists. Then, in August 1939, the Nazi-Soviet Pact provoked bitter condemnations by anticommunists and liberals. When the Soviet Union invaded Poland, Finland, and the Baltic states, the fission widened as the CP quickly adhered to the new Soviet line and began to condemn any effort to involve the United States in what they now called an imperialist war. National CIO leaders John L. Lewis and Philip Murray were anxious to avoid weakening the CIO by preventing an internal split. At the same time, together with Sidney Hillman, they were determined to limit the influence of Communists inside the CIO. This commitment escalated in late 1939 when, for instance, former Socialist Adolph Germer was sent by the CIO leadership to Washington to weed out Communists, through less than democratic means, from their elected positions in the International Woodworkers of America.[168]

The St. Louis CIO, through 1938, defended Communists' right to participate and hold positions. John Doherty, the Lewis-appointed St. Louis CIO district director, had originally hired Sentner, Shaw, and Fiering for the steel drive. When questioned about Communists in the movement's ranks during the 1937 strikes, Doherty set the tone by responding, "We are not interested in the private affiliations of men active in our movements."[169] In early 1938 the St. Louis IUC responded to the issue again: "The cry of radicalism often has been raised against the CIO. That cry is now generally accepted as ridiculous. It is the CIO's fight for decent distribution of mass purchasing power that fends off radicalism; it is precisely industry's manipulations which result in mass impoverishment, that encourages radicalism. We do not fear radicalism in this country. We most decidedly do fear the drift of industrialists toward Fascism."[170] Though dissent was brewing, it was not yet in the open.

In late 1938, HUAC's first witness, John Frey of the AFL Metal Trades Department, accused the St. Louis CIO of being dominated by Communists and cited the Maytag strike as a consequence of this. Frey's accusations cut such a wide swath (he included Doherty on the list) that the St. Louis CIO easily dismissed them. Doherty averred, "I am not a communist and I am not a red-baiter."[171] District 8 responded to publicity around Fred Bender's announcement during the Maytag strike that Sentner, Fiering, and Manewitz were party members, especially the argument that the latter two were placed to further the party's agenda. Logsdon, in response, pointed to the democratic structure of the UE, noting that Fiering had been reelected to financial secretary by a large majority of twelve hundred votes, and argued that it was a civil right for CP members to be in the union: "It makes no difference (what their political beliefs are), because the constitution of the union, which I assisted in drafting, states that no worker shall be barred because of either his religious or political beliefs. I have come to know the political beliefs of a vast number of our officers, and I can state of my own knowledge they are not Communists."[172]

As the CIO movement faced defeats and decline in the wake of the 1937–38 recession, a right-wing faction coalesced in the St. Louis CIO. The motivations were various, much of it principled opposition to communism, but other factors drove the movement. Local UAW delegates who were embittered about the role of Communists in elevating racial justice issues not only in the UAW but also in the CIO council led the faction. This faction also blamed Communists for the 1938 defeat of the CIO's candidate for Congress, A. J. Pickett, to a right-winger who launched an anticommunist campaign.[173] A slate of candidates opposed to Communists was successful. The rift became open when the IUC executive board refused to sanction the May Day observance as a CIO event, with the explanation that the "feeling of some locals [is] that the day's meaning to labor ha[s] been obscured by radical celebrations abroad."[174] As plans were launched for Labor Day events, the local CIO allowed the Veterans of Foreign Wars and the American Legion to take part but denied admission to the Workers' Alliance.[175]

The CIO's leftist faction organized to counter this right-wing turn. Bob Logsdon opposed incumbent IUC secretary/organizer Luther Slinkard, an auto worker who had led much of the opposition to the Left but whose performance in this important position was criticized by delegates. In late August, Logsdon was confident that he would win the October 1939 election.[176]

But the Nazi-Soviet Pact and the subsequent invasions reversed that prospect. In late September, right-wing forces in a meeting preceding the elections passed a resolution condemning all "isms," arguing that the issue had "taken its toll." "Some have actually begun to believe we are a bunch of Communists," complained Joe Appelbaum, a Gas Workers Union official.[177] Sentner acknowledged in the meeting that the "overwhelming majority" of workers were "against fascism, Nazism, socialism, and communism," but they were against each for "different reasons," so it was wrong "to lump the so-called isms together and say we're agin it, . . . like an ostrich hiding its head in the sand and refusing to exam-

ine what makes the sand storm."[178] Appelbaum demanded a roll-call vote. Sentner, realizing that the resolution would pass anyway, asked that it be adopted
unanimously in order to prevent targeting leftist supporters.[179] At the next
meeting, the entire slate of right-wing candidates was elected.[180]

The resolution coincided with the start of Sentner's criminal syndicalism trial
in Iowa. Since September 1938, attorney John Connolly had tried to get Sentner's
and the other cases dismissed. The Iowa Supreme Court refused, and the trial
was also moved to rural, conservative Montezuma, Iowa. Sentner felt that the resolution would make it look "as though my own union repudiated me when I go
on trial Monday," and he complained to Matles that "the heat is on and how I like
it—Of course it's no joke when already they prepare the stage in Iowa with a bas-
tardly resolution in the St. Louis Industrial Union Council. This is a sign of the
times and I think we can look for them to throw the book at me up in Iowa."[181]

But Sentner felt it important to bring the issue of "reds" in the labor movement into focus. The city editor of the *St. Louis Post-Dispatch* had told Sentner
that he viewed the case as "a test trial against reds in the labor movement." Sentner thought that the criminal syndicalism trial was designed as "the opening
gun for such red baiting that hasn't been seen in a long time," the leverage, he
wrote to Matles, for "a general attack on our union" and all its officers. That
Carey and other noncommunists were prosecuted was fortuitous, and his case
could be used to combat "red hunt attacks against leaders of labor."[182]

Sentner accurately predicted that it would take the Montezuma jury less than
twenty minutes to find him guilty of advocating criminal syndicalism, which
carried a maximum penalty of ten years in prison and a five thousand-dollar
fine. During the trial, the prosecutors used Sentner's Maytag military commission testimony in which he had acknowledged his membership and had argued
that ownership of the Maytag plant by the workers "would be a good thing."
Connolly said that jurors felt "that they were viewing some monstrosity." The
case was appealed to the Iowa Supreme Court.[183]

Upon Sentner's return to St. Louis from Iowa, he was arrested in an obvious
setup between the Red Squad of the St. Louis Police Department and company
officials of Baldor Electric, who called him there on the pretense of conducting
negotiations.[184] The Red Squad, established in the early 1930s to infiltrate Communist and Socialist organizations, was now targeting Left-led unions in St.
Louis as well, providing strategic service to employers in their struggles; it was a
significant reversal of the brief entente between unions and police that had
developed during the 1937 sit-down. "It seems that this attack against us will
never end. The heat is really on," Sentner wrote, "and aimed at our organization
here as the focal point, with reaction knowing that if they can get us then they
will be able to move in on all fronts with ease."[185]

Sentner and Connolly hoped that CIO leaders would view the conviction of
a labor leader for his conduct during a strike as an attack on the entire CIO

movement. Sentner wired Matles that he and Connolly viewed it as imperative that the national CIO, meeting in San Francisco in mid-October, spearhead "the uniting of labor behind the right of political affiliation." After outlining a potential program of action in consultation with Connolly and UE secretary-treasurer Julius Emspak, Sentner proclaimed: "goddamn it this is the time to make hay and I think that the CIO Convention should in no uncertain terms lead off with a powerful right cross to the jaw of Criminal Syndicalism."[186]

The convention did pass a strongly worded resolution condemning criminal syndicalism, stressing that the real target of the case was not William Sentner but the "right of collective bargaining, the right of self-organization," and pledged "full support" to the UE. Don Harris of the Iowa CIO, who by this time was almost certainly a party member, spoke for the resolution, acknowledging that Sentner was a Communist but that noncommunists such as Hollis Hall, vice president of Local 1116, were due to be prosecuted under the statute and that the law could be invoked in any labor dispute. James Carey rendered a dramatic account of the prejudiced motivations of the prosecutor and judges during the Maytag strike.[187]

On October 18, Matles wrote to Sentner that the convention had passed the resolution unanimously. But he also indicated that the UE and the CIO had reached the limits of their support for an open Communist:

> The present attacks on the labor movement, and especially on the CIO unions, are assuming serious proportions, and I do not have to tell you that our organization is carrying its share of this attack. The fact that during the trial in Iowa you stated that you are a member of the Communist Party has in no way changed our efforts and the efforts of the entire membership in defending you and the other local officers and members in Newton, Iowa. Brothers Carey, Emspak and I discussed on several occasions the difficulties our organization is confronted with in view of your holding membership in the Communist Party, and after due consideration I want to take the liberty of suggesting that you seriously consider the advisability of your resigning from the Communist Party. I am sure that if you give this matter serious consideration you will agree, as a loyal member of our union, that the interests of our organization and of the many thousands of its members would be better served by such action on your part.[188]

Matles suggested that they discuss the matter further in December at the UE Executive Board meeting.

Matles's letter raises all sorts of interesting questions and insights for those familiar with the UE. There is little doubt of Matles's and Emspak's sympathy with, if not membership in, the CP at the time Matles wrote the letter. But they had denied their membership when pressured by the Dies Committee and had even published their denial in the *UE News* on October 7.[189] While the CP had had a policy that favored openness most party members thought it prudent as part of the national CIO coalition to hide their membership, and almost all had chosen the route of secret association. Now, apparently, Matles was asking that Sentner follow their path, and both had apparently commiserated with James Carey, whom they viewed with some derision, over the problems of dealing with Communists in the labor movement. The letter, viewed from this perspective, reveals what a jumble of poses and twists party secrecy and anticommunism in the labor movement promoted.

The pressure on Sentner was related to the CIO national leadership's changing stance. At the same convention that expressed support for Sentner, John L. Lewis and the top leadership of the CIO gave notice that the CIO-Left alliance was on shaky ground. Lewis kept resolutions regarding subversives and "isms" (such as one submitted by the St. Louis CIO) off the convention floor. But after the convention was over, Lewis, speaking to the executive board, "warned Communists not to press their luck" in the organization. "I don't want our organization to waste time and energy in red-baiting," though he added that "if I were a young Communist looking for a future in the labor movement, I would not look for that in the CIO." Lewis demoted party member Harry Bridges from West Coast director to California director. He also abolished the post of national director of the CIO, held by John Brophy, who had "shied away from purges." The CIO executive board passed a resolution opposing "subversive movements aimed against our nation and government, or the basic free and democratic institutions upon which our Republic has been founded."[190]

Ironically, a campaign in Iowa and St. Louis was already demonstrating that combating red-baiting from a civil rights stance might have been effective. District 8 initiated a Civil Rights Committee in Iowa and St. Louis, beginning with a pamphlet that set out the facts of the case and its context in the Maytag events. Iowa activists developed a coalition between the AFL and the CIO unions, aided by John Connolly, who helped by "swinging the AFL in line on the question." John C. Lewis, head of the Iowa CIO, actively campaigned with Iowa AFL president Al Couch, who had much respect for Sentner. Teamsters Local 90, whose solidarity in the Maytag strike had been so dramatic, took part. The AFL's *Des Moines Federationist* reprinted the Civil Rights Commission's pamphlet.[191]

Iowa AFL contacts, on Sentner's request, encouraged Missouri affiliates to join in the campaign. The St. Louis CIO also came around, condemning Sentner's prosecution for a "crime [that] . . . consisted of advocating industrial reform" and argued that he was "found guilty because those in control of industry and those in high places in Iowa sought to break the spirit of organized labor."[192] The St. Louis *Union Labor Advocate,* an AFL paper, declared that the case was reminiscent of the "mad orgy" of the Palmer raids after World War I and that labor needed to unite around Civil Rights. The St. Louis Civil Rights Committee included the Urban League director, the American Civil Liberties Union (ACLU) director, and leaders of the largest CIO unions as well as a significant number of AFL officials. The committee established a speakers' bureau that included "a contingent of rank and filers." The fact that the St. Louis Police Red Squad had conducted raids on the homes of Baldor Electric strikers and UE officials (Sentner and Fiering) in late October fueled support for the committee, as did supportive editorials in the *Post-Dispatch* and *Star-Times*. Sentner wrote to Matles in early November: "We have been able to turn the case from an attack against Bill Sentner, the Communist, to the defense of civil rights."[193]

Sentner concluded that rather than fight to dismiss the criminal syndicalism cases, the UE should have used them as a coalition-building tool to bring the issues out in the open through "a mass defense campaign . . . which is the only thing . . . that will mean anything whatsoever, especially in view of the changed situation due to the war." Sentner outlined for Matles a potential campaign, beginning with funds from the national CIO and then through locals, to "make the CIO resolution [on criminal syndicalism] do something."[194] But Matles responded that Sentner did not understand the changes at the national CIO: "I can tell you to forget about it because you won't be able to get it."[195] Sentner was left to imagine the possibilities if the Nazi-Soviet Pact had not been an issue.

After the December UE executive board meeting, where the issue of Sentner's affiliation was again apparently discussed, Sentner wrote to Matles that he had resigned from the party. "My decision on this matter was prompted by the realization that my undivided attention and service could be best spent in serving the thousands of members of our Union and the CIO." Soon thereafter, the civil rights campaign was slowed. The legal case against Hollis Hall and Carey was dismissed, and Sentner's case awaited hearing before the Iowa Supreme Court.[196]

Why did Sentner resign from the party after having already paid such a high price? One possible explanation is to take Sentner's words to Matles at face value. Between November and December, Sentner may have decided that his open membership in the party was too great a liability to the national union. It is also possible that he resigned because the CP, acting through Matles and Emspak, directly or indirectly ordered him to do so. The top party leadership since 1938 had abandoned open advocacy for socialism as part of the Popular Front and now sought to accommodate John L. Lewis because he shared their antiwar line. Further, the party's fear of repression was so severe that by December 1939 some party officials, including Henry Fiering's wife Clara Warnick, had gone underground. Another possible explanation is that Sentner felt his membership was harming his wife's citizenship application, which was rejected in late 1939. Finally, it is also possible that Sentner found resignation more agreeable because of the Nazi-Soviet Pact. He was irritated when Maytag officials tried to bait him about the pact during attempted negotiations. No clear record exists of his stance on the pact at the time of his resignation (which in itself is significant evidence regarding his desire to keep the issue from dividing workers). There is evidence that Sentner and Logsdon encouraged locals to condemn Naziism and to call for a trade embargo.[197]

In any case, Sentner's resignation was somewhat "incomplete." On the one hand, according to reports from the Federal Bureau of Investigation (FBI), which conducted regular surveillance of the party in conjunction with U.S. Army Military Intelligence spies, Sentner had no further open association with the party until 1942. He did not attend conventions or local party meetings. For instance, an August 1941 FBI report noted that neither he nor his wife Toni had been active in the CP or even around St. Louis party headquarters.[198] When arrested in mid-1940 during a strike, Sentner denied being a member of the CP.[199] In the late 1940 appeal of his criminal syndicalism case before the Iowa Supreme Court, his attorneys argued that he "had long since resigned as a member of that party."[200] On the other hand, Sentner was still widely considered a "red" by the membership. Even Logsdon did not recall his resignation years later and only recalled that he continued to discuss socialism openly especially to the local leaders who were open to it. The May 1940 letter that initiated Sentner's FBI file asked the agency to investigate Sentner because he "brags about his communistic beliefs."[201] Further, in late 1941, as discussed later in this chapter, he was opposed for district president mainly for his "political affiliations." Clearly, the formal break with the CP in 1940 and 1941 did not alter Sentner's views on the need for a working-class party or his belief in open advocacy of socialism.

Through this "resignation," Sentner, riveted from all sides on trade union and leftist issues, sought the means to legitimize himself in a way that allowed him to continue in a leadership position and voice his socialist beliefs but deny his membership when it was expedient. For the next two years, he would explore the fit of such duplicity. By 1942 he would reject it.[202]

It was in this context that Sentner's efforts to legitimize his role in the labor movement became awkwardly tied to Stuart Symington and the Emerson situation. On October 18, 1939, in the aftermath of the Iowa trial decision and only a week after the union learned of the company's threat to move to Evansville, Symington telegrammed James Carey that he "would be glad to give whatever help I can" to Sentner.[203] The timing of Symington's telegram, which came on the same day that Matles asked Sentner to leave the party, suggests that it may have contributed to the officers' pressure on Sentner to resign. Symington's motivations may have been partly noble, but he no doubt also saw Sentner's problems as an opportunity to tame a recalcitrant workforce.[204]

The Community Campaign to Save Emerson

By the time of Sentner's political crisis, Symington had softened his position on the union recognition issue and on moving the plant. The union had, after all, signed the new contract. He began tentative arrangements to implement a voluntary checkoff (workers who signed authorization cards could have their dues deducted). In early December he hinted that if certain conditions were met, he would not move the plant out of St. Louis. Logsdon reported that the company really wanted to move to a site in St. Louis County where it could rationalize its production and design a building that was conducive to producing hermetically sealed motors.

Symington now sought to use the threat of moving to extract funds from St. Louis to match the Evansville offer. He had already been rebuffed by the St. Louis Chamber of Commerce. Symington "hint[ed]" that the company would remain if workers were to "buy enough common stock over a period of time, through weekly payments, to make up approximately $100,000.00 in moving expenses." Logsdon was concerned that most of the local's executive board favored the plan because of the "close attachment" to Emerson by older employees who were influential. The foremen were "subtly leading this" initiative. Earl White and Eustius Brendle, two conservative officers now wary of the Left, were "going to insist on bringing it back up, sooner or later, and would rather kick back than have the firm move."[205] Even while Logsdon chafed at the idea, Symington, after meeting with Sentner, Matles, and Carey in New York, noting that another city had offered them money to move, agreed not to move if the union helped them get the money. It is likely that Symington's offer was conditional on Sentner's withdrawal from the party.[206]

Even as he helped to launch the effort by Local 1102, Sentner condemned the threatened move to Evansville, calling it "a competition of bartering hardships and sufferings—a competition which at best merely relieves unemployment, hunger and human suffering, of one community at the expense of another."[207] Nevertheless, he campaigned vigorously, as did the local, organizing a speaker's bureau of workers to solicit community and business groups for support, from bridge clubs to American Legion posts, which generated resolutions calling for the company to remain. Members' children distributed flyers against the move at meetings. Union committees met with the mayor, the Board of Aldermen, Governor Stark, and St. Louis congressmen. They visited groups such as the Real Estate Exchange and especially the Chamber of Commerce.[208] In January, Sentner wrote that the campaign had a positive effect, allowing the union "to come out of the deal with much credit."[209]

This community campaign revealed a degree of public relations duplicity between Symington and Sentner (and the union local leadership). Both the union and the company now suggested that the relations were "excellent . . . for the third successive year." No doubt many workers found such descriptions hard to recognize.[210] It was as if both Sentner and Symington were rewriting a script of the history, each for his own purposes. It is likely that the Left lost some support among workers who recognized the charade. Choosing to ally with the right wing in the local over this issue may have seemed expedient, but it reinforced a conservative leadership.

St. Louis business chafed at the idea that a major city would have to give inducements to stay and refused any subsidy. The union then proposed an employees' loan of $140,000 based on monthly payroll deductions over fourteen months, just before the board of directors was due to vote on the Evansville offer. In return, Emerson was obligated to build on a local factory site where it would remain for ten years and to create at least 160 new jobs in 1940. The company was obliged to return 80 percent of the loan to workers by hiring them to do most of the moving and to institute employee profit sharing when profits exceeded a certain amount. Workers approved the loan at a meeting.[211]

The Emerson board voted to remain in the St. Louis area and announced plans to build on a new location in St. Louis County. Symington declined the workers' offer of a loan but nevertheless announced a new profit-sharing plan, suggested by Sentner, that was prorated according to length of service.[212] Symington wrote to Carey that "you were confident we would find Sentner cooperative in attempting to improve the unfortunate management-employee relationship prevalent in this company," and he told Carey that he was not disappointed.[213] Publicly, Symington suggested that the vote signaled a new era of labor-management cooperation. Sentner and Local 1102 presented their gesture of cooperation on different terms. In a pamphlet widely distributed throughout St. Louis, the local called for "outlaw[ing] runaway shops" and "inducements that lure industry from one community to another. . . . It is a traffic in hardship and suffering almost as bad as the old slave trade." Nevertheless, it suggested that the union's role in keeping the company in St. Louis should help "organized workers being accepted as an integral and vital part of the community life of St. Louis." Sentner portrayed the union's role as building workers' capacity for executive decision-making. "Workers, if they expect a voice in the management of industry—industrial democracy—must be willing to help solve the problems of management," he said in an interview with the *Des Moines Register,* adding that "anything which strengthens organized labor paves the way to an industrial democracy that is complete—some form of socialism."[214]

Sentner recognized that Symington expected him to help contain shop floor dissent and thus welcomed evidence that Emerson workers still chafed at cooperation. While the loan proposal passed by 360 to 290 votes, 100 members walked out of the meeting before the vote was taken, and 350 refused to vote.[215] Sentner reported that "the meeting was healthy and full of fire—which also was alright as far as I was concerned. The 'no' vote in my opinion places us in a better bargaining position with the Company—as it is an object lesson on 'the fact that the people in the plant still have much against the company' and the top people in management can't expect us to give them any blank checks—and they'll have to work with us."[216]

Sentner viewed his position vis-à-vis Symington and the campaign to save Emerson as part of a longer effort to change the political economy of control

that had existed in the industry locally and nationally. Symington's new determination to build a reputation as a fair employer could be useful to the union's
strategy of breaking corporate unity on labor issues at the local level. Indeed,
over the next several years Symington supplied the local and national UE with
insider information on the industry and other companies, including Century
and Servel, that proved useful in organizing and negotiations.[217]

Years later, Logsdon suggested that Sentner had sought to use Symington in
much the same way that Symington sought to use Sentner and that it was not
clear at the time who would benefit most from the relationship. Unlike Carey
and evidently Emspak, Sentner was not ready to relinquish the goal of challenging management rights in pursuit of legitimacy. For instance, when shop steward Charles Anderson, part of Emerson's embattled leftist caucus, asked Emspak
in May 1940 to aid the union in its quest to force Emerson to replace a piecework
operation with another kind of pay system, Emspak warned that "it is the function of management to run the plant."[218] Sentner in contrast encouraged this
type of challenge, though he had effectively consented to avoid this as an immediate focus at Emerson. One cannot avoid the conclusion that the immediate
interests of workers in Local 1102 were to some degree sacrificed in the determination to gain legitimacy for the union and for Sentner, and certainly the Left
never regained the ground it had in the local. When Thomas Knowles was hired
at Emerson in 1940, he noted that the right-wing leadership who took hold after
the moving campaign was "lackadaisical" about enforcement of the contract on
the shop floor. UE local autonomy prevented intervention by Sentner except
when welcomed by local leadership. Later Sentner tried to get Logsdon back
into the plant to organize a leftist caucus and sought to recruit militant workers
such as Knowles to join the party or work with him to build the local. But by
that time, the right was more powerful than in 1940.[219]

The cloak of legitimacy enabled the UE Left to fight more effectively and
openly to organize workers to challenge management's rights and the political
economy of control. Simultaneously with the moving campaign, the UE locals
started organized meetings of St. Louis CIO shop stewards to "halt speed ups"
and sparked the idea among CIO shop stewards that the CIO could work to
"bring more of the share of profits to workers" and bring about "a new status in
production for organized labor."[220]

More immediately, the outcome of matters at Emerson proved invaluable in
a looming battle when Century Electric struck for the third time since 1934, a
strike that lasted more than four months, tested the union's strategies, and indicated growing factionalism in the CIO.

The 1940 Century Electric Strike

Workers at Century Electric struck over a long list of demands and grievances
but, above all, because Century management had not accepted the union. When

Henry Fiering left the local to become a national UE organizer, management tried to "wear down" workers by attempting to keep stewards from policing the contract. But workers were ready for a showdown by March 1940 because they felt that they had missed their opportunity the year before, and some had called Sentner a "sell-out artist" for resisting the strike. Workers were determined to raise the minimum rate at their plant to forty cents an hour and to adjust other rates to ensure fairness. When the company refused to move on those issues, the union voted to strike in early June of 1940. Now, as Logsdon put it, "it is them [Century] or us." Century saw the strike as an opportunity to eliminate the union.[221]

The strike elevated the art of the community-based struggles and showed how much more clearly community support could be tapped, even in the face of little CIO support. Workers organized mass picket lines with children sometimes at the head and women in the lead. It sought to organize office workers and foremen and made significant headway, though it ultimately failed. Workers distributed sixty thousand leaflets by the seventh week of the strike, leaflets that linked the strike to a larger battle for a higher St. Louis standard of living.[222] The strike support was extraordinarily well organized, reminiscent of the Emerson sitdown. The *UE News* suggested that the wealthy could "learn something" from the ability of Century's workers to "organize, manage, and administrate" by making "a study of the Century strike." Sentner and William Chambers, the district's new education director, organized a committee of "prominent citizens" in support of the strike. The St. Louis League of Women Shoppers concluded in a lengthy report that the company "has failed to meet [the union] half-way."[223]

By the seventh week of the strike, as Century began to recruit scabs from Arkansas and southeastern Missouri, strikers, some of whom had taken that same step over the picket lines seventeen years earlier, set up mass picket lines to prevent it. They met the full force of the St. Louis police, who had retreated from the 1937 stance of neutrality. Logsdon alleged that "the police are more viciously opposed to us in this strike than in any St. Louis strike to date." By late July, police action resulted in restrictions from the main worker entrance and refusal to allow handbill distribution around the plant.[224] Police frequently arrested picketers, often at night so that they could be held overnight. They severely beat and wounded one striker, injured women picketers, and allowed scabs to beat workers "around the head with hammers" without interference. Scabs flourishing weapons were not arrested. When Sentner protested the police practice of directing scabs to Century's employment office, he was arrested "for investigation."[225] The union alleged that the kind of actions engaged in by the police contributed to the death of one of the strikers, Oscar Buckley, who was stabbed to death by a scab who lunged at him after Buckley called him a "scab herder."[226]

Community support for the strikers curbed the police. The union called on Mayor Dickmann and Missouri's governor to "save the reputation of our city" by appointing a "committee of representative St. Louis citizens" to investigate police action.[227] Meanwhile, the union's "citizens committee," composed of leading ministers, lawyers, doctors, and a banker member of the local ACLU, put pressure on the company to negotiate and on the police to cease its grossly biased tactics against union members. While Century, as Logsdon put it, "does not seem to care too much what anyone thinks about them," the committee's pressure affected the police.[228] By August, picketing at all entrances and leaflet distribution resumed with fewer arrests.[229]

What Logsdon described as CIO officials' "complete lack of unity" contributed to the problems during the strike. Logsdon claimed that the "strike [wa]s supported by the rank and file of the CIO, even if not so much by the leaders of some of the local unions who yearn for peace and quiet."[230] Local UAW officials tried to dissuade delegates attending the national UAW convention from massing on the lines. (At one point, two thousand delegates surrounded Century.)[231] UAW and steelworkers' union officials in the CIO "prefer to associate with city officials and police officials than with us," Logsdon commented. In early September, CIO district director John Doherty, apparently at the direction of national CIO leader Van Bittner, arranged a meeting with Century officers in Chicago to settle the strike. James Carey, who was beginning to lead a faction opposed to CP influence in the UE, was asked to attend, but Logsdon averred that he "was too smart to be the goat in this case." When negotiations collapsed Doherty confessed to Logsdon, who wrote that "Doherty is badly scared at what is happening to the CIO unions in St. Louis and does not know what the hell to do."[232]

Century workers maintained their resolve even as the company refused to budge. The continued expressions of support by community groups were key. Editorials in leading St. Louis newspapers condemned Century and supported the UE, reminding readers that the union had saved the Emerson plant and was an organization "closely interwoven in the business life of the community." The union continued to call on the mayor and the governor to appoint a citizens' group to investigate the issues, while Century refused arbitration and conciliation.[233] Century's intransigence began to take its toll by mid-September, as trouble with police resumed. With picket line harassment and an injunction restricting pickets to seventy-two, enough scabs got through to resume some production. Logsdon claimed that the company used "a cute trick of sending out bums with bricks and throwing them through windows indiscriminately with threats signed CIO attached by them," a tactic reminiscent of Servel and likely a ploy of the NMTA crowd. The citizens' committee issued an "open statement to the press condemning the company," steeling workers' resolve. The community support was essential to again coaxing Mayor Dickmann into the fray. He called on Century to settle and offered to help negotiate. The company seemed unmoved.[234]

Then, as the strike entered its fifth month, Sentner, in Logsdon's words, "really pulled one out of his hat." Sentner sent the union attorney to find any state statutes that the union could employ, and he found "an old Missouri law to let us into the company books for a complete look at the records." The threat to "open the books" brought an immediate reversal and resulted in a quick victory for the union. Workers won the forty-cent minimum as well as most of their other demands, while minor issues were placed in arbitration.[235]

The UE had prevailed through a community campaign in a bitter battle with the most obstinately antiunion company in St. Louis. Despite the downturn in union fortunes, Century had been unable to draw effectively on political and economic resources that had formerly allowed it to utilize the labor market to suit its purposes. Logsdon couldn't help but revel: "The most completely beautiful feature about this is . . . to be able to see the expression on the face of Doherty and the other skunks" when they learned of the victory, especially when they had neglected to ignite a community campaign for a steelworkers' strike that was "just about gone with the wind."[236]

Survival of the Left

Logsdon's bitterness was the result of the Century strike and more. In September 1940, the local and state CIO's right wing moved decidedly against the Left. The St. Louis IUC set up more stringent bars against "supporters of foreign 'isms,'" warning that any delegate challenged by a majority "will be required to furnish a sworn affidavit" denying membership in an "ism" group. A few days later the Missouri IUC passed a similar resolution prohibiting officers of member unions from membership in a Nazi, communist, or fascist organization.[237] More aggravating was the CIO's efforts to support internal opponents of the District 8 Left. In the late September election, Sentner, on instructions from the St. Louis district UE council, nominated Thomas Barry for president of the St. Louis IUC. In response, the Right nominated George Apel, right-wing president of UE Local 1104 (Wagner), who won the CIO election.[238]

But the right-wing activists made missteps. Apel earned the enmity of a large section of Wagner workers, especially women who had been "particularly left out," for neglecting grievances. Then, by early January, Sentner excitedly wrote to Matles, "We have the good[s] on George Apel." Apel had gone to the police station "and spilled his guts to Dies Committee finks, two dicks and one F.B.I. guy—labelling a bunch of good guys in the CIO movement here as reds. Watch the smoke." Apel and Luther Slinkard of the UAW painted too many with the brush of Communist affiliation, and for all but the most reactionary they had committed a cardinal sin against the CIO by working with Dies, "the father of all anti-labor bills." By March, the Left claimed to have evidence revealing that Apel was always an anti-union spy. Apel vanished from the local, taking a job with the Department of Labor. Workers who complained that under Apel the "local union had more or less the status of a company union" now sought to rebuild the union.[239]

More good news came in June, when the Iowa Supreme Court reversed Sentner's criminal syndicalism conviction, noting that Sentner's membership in the CP was inadmissible because there was no evidence that the party advocated the violent overthrow of the United States or the industrial system and indirectly suggested that a local labor dispute should not come under the purview of the criminal syndicalism laws. By the time of the 1941 Missouri CIO convention, support for the inclusion of radicals regained approval.[240]

Sentner also routed a challenge to his leadership of the district led by James Click of Local 1102. Click, a former Socialist Party member (though not a pacifist), organized the campaign after Sentner, like many other CP members, expressed support for U.S. intervention after Germany invaded the Soviet Union. Click allied with Local 1102 executive board member Ernie Stuebinger, Catholics, and other conservatives. Sentner observed that the "boys who nominated Stuebinger" had become aligned with America First, the isolationist group chaired by Sears CEO Robert Wood but popularized by St. Louisan Charles Lindbergh, whose association lent the group a strong anti-Semitic tinge. Sentner won the election by a three-to-one ratio, though Local 1102 cast most of their votes for Stuebinger, a harbinger of the future role of that local as the base of the anticommunist movement in the district.[241]

District 8's Left had survived employers' community-based strategies, countersubversive networks, repressive mechanisms, and arguments that labeled radicals as "outside" and "violent" influences in their community. These were all strategies that radicals of previous generations would have recognized. The attempt to use agents such as Bender, members of the American Legion, and "finks" such as Apel as well as ministers and other community allies was not a new phenomenon but rather was tied to a long tradition deployed by the electrical independents. The period marked the emergence of a populist language in an effort to resist unionization. This language suggested that social reform was the work of "outsider" radicals whose aims could wreck communities and who were the agents of a federal elite. And even a Democratic governor would agree with that when challenged by the Right.[242]

The heady expectations of rapid change based on a workers' movement were over. The CP's ties to the Soviet Union made the Left that chose to defend those associations and call for acceptance of CP members very vulnerable, showing how international developments could present problems for carefully built local coalitions and making it clear that anticommunism lurked as an effective weapon for labeling unions as part of a totalitarian fifth column, even when District 8's fight was for more democratic structures.

It is worthwhile to point out, given the common suggestion that the CP's changed line on foreign policy in this period affected trade union behavior, that Sentner's position regarding Emerson was influenced by other factors. In many respects, the district Left was confronting some of the same problems experienced by Amalgamated Clothing Workers union radicals in a previous era who also had to deal with marginal employers in the garment industry. This experience led Sidney Hillman to abandon his socialist dreams and move in the conservative direction of coalition with the New Deal elite, which in turn affected the possibilities for CIO movement in the 1930s and 1940s. Clearly, though, Sentner was not preparing for that path however much the CP policy had caused him to participate in renouncing support for the Farmer-Labor party, which very possibly caused Kraschel to kill the Maytag union insurgency. Part of what kept Sentner from going down the path to respectability was his continued advocacy of socialism, whether or not he was openly in the party. The campaigns of this period also showed that the Left in District 8 had not lost sight of its broader goals for developing activists for a long-term struggle.[243]

In searching for an alternative to capitulation from the top echelons of the CIO, District 8's Left had continued to develop its community coalition basis of struggle. By 1940, Logsdon was already very critical of what he called the "flying squadron" CIO approach and blitz campaigns that did not take into account the political economy of the city. Logsdon felt that the lessons of this period were that organizers needed to entrench themselves in the community if they hoped to create a movement. Layers of experience, both in victory and in failure, would reinforce this insight.[244] As World War II and the international coalition between the United States and the Soviet Union muted anticommunism, the community organizing strategies of the Left developed into a means to build a challenge to employer power.

William Sentner with his Missouri Meerschaum pipe, early 1930s. Sentner's experiences in the interracial unemployed and union movement of the early 1930s inspired a vision of Unionism that he and others carried forward into the CIO. Sentner was the model for the man leading the unemployed march under the Eads Bridge in the "We Demand" painting by St. Louis housepainter-turned-artist Joe Jones (*cover*). Sentner had gone to grade school with Jones. Courtesy of William Sentner Jr.

The community-based unemployed movement of the early 1930s made the sit-down tactic familiar to St. Louis workers. In April 1936 the unemployed took over the city's Aldermanic Chambers, refusing to leave until fifteen thousand families were guaranteed assistance. These struggles created alternative networks among workers, outside the AFL. Photo courtesy of the *St. Louis Post-Dispatch*.

A festive atmosphere took hold while male workers occupied the Emerson Electric factory on Washington Avenue in St. Louis in 1937. Emerson and the electrical independents in St. Louis had used a community-based strategy in the early twentieth century to keep unions out of their plants. The Emerson strike challenged the low wages of the entire region. It established the Left as a force in the St. Louis CIO and was the basis for the formation of UE District 8. Outside the plant, an array of community supporters joined the picket line, and an interracial group of members and supporters occupied the St. Louis relief offices to force the St. Louis welfare system to support the strikers. Top photo courtesy of *St. Louis Post-Dispatch*. Bottom photo used with permission of Western Historical Manuscripts Collection, University of Missouri–St. Louis.

At the height of the Maytag plant strike in Newton, Iowa, in 1938, an all-women picket line circled in front of the plant. The Maytag strike was District 8's attempt to use its strong community-based unionism to stymie the efforts of employers to roll back the momentum of the CIO. Workers engaged in a sit-down to counter Maytag's violations of labor law and cast their struggle as one of "human rights over property rights." Reprinted with permission from the *Des Moines Tribune.*

From the roof of the Maytag Company plant, National Guardsmen, armed with hand grenades, tear gas, and rifles, keep watch over the street below at the moment workers were forced to return "under compulsion of military force." The union ended the strike after the governor's declaration that the military would reopen the plant because workers were influenced by "outside agitators." Maytag workers claimed that the main outsiders were the company's agents and lawyers. Reprinted with permission from the *Des Moines Tribune.*

William Sentner addresses a group of laid-off Small Arms Plant workers in St. Louis. District 8 argued for community-based planning for full employment to ensure that African Americans and women would not be repositioned to the lower rung of the economy at the end of the war. But as the war wound down, the Small Arms Plant became the base for a right-wing faction that helped to build an anticommunist coalition in the district. Reprinted with permission from the United Electrical Workers/Labor Collections, University of Pittsburgh.

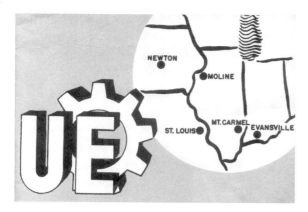

The United Electrical Workers District 8 region, 1946. District 8's territory covered
much of the electrical industry "independents" who were intransigently antiunion and
fought labor rights on the periphery of the industry. They were shaped by the policies
of the National Metal Trades Association, which adhered to a policy of fighting unionization with a collective policy that used spies, propaganda, and labeling unions as subversive. Courtesy of the Lloyd Austin Collection, Western Historical Manuscripts
Collection, University of Missouri–St. Louis.

Evansville Local 813 members picket Seeger, 1948. By the postwar era, many District 8
activists viewed the union as a force for social transformation and a contest over corporate control of their community. Evansville's Local 813 argued that the struggle for a living
wage would raise Evansville up from "southern" wage standards. Reprinted with permission from the United Electrical Workers/Labor Collections, University of Pittsburgh.

State police, 140-strong, formed a corridor two blocks long
"to prevent mass picketing" during the Bucyrus-Erie strike,
Evansville, Indiana, August 1948. This was a pivotal event in the
district's history, an effort to establish the community-based
strategy for industry wage patterns. N. R. Knox, head of
Bucyrus-Erie, announced that the company would not negotiate with the UE because "it was dominated by Communists."
Congressman Edward Mitchell aided the company by calling
hearings to investigate Communist influence in the strike.
Reprinted with permission from the Labor History Collection,
Archives and Special Collections, University of Southern Indiana, Evansville.

Robert Logsdon, vice president of District 8, and Liz Moore, District 8 organizer early 1950s. By 1946, Sentner claimed that District 8 had trained more organizers for the United Electrical Workers than any other district. The district's model of community mobilization was influential on the national organization as well. Reprinted with permission from the United Electrical Workers/Labor Collections, University of Pittsburgh.

In 1952, these women picketers at Eagle Signal in Moline, Illinois, were recovering from an attack by a company foreman. Meanwhile, District 8 president William Sentner was arrested and charged with conspiracy to advocate the overthrow of the U.S. government under the Smith Act on his way to negotiations. "The charge is ridiculous," Sentner said. "They are going stark mad in Washington when they do this kind of stuff. The only thing I have conspired in is to keep the Eagle Signal Corporation from installing an incentive system at the plant." Reprinted with permission from the United Electrical Workers/Labor Collections, University of Pittsburgh.

Additional photos available at www.radicalunion.niu.edu.

CHAPTER 5

World War Two and "Civic" Unionism

Wartime developments, especially the alliance between the Soviet Union and the United States to defeat the Axis powers, curbed anticommunism in the Congress of Industrial Organiztions (CIO) and in the communities where District 8 organized. During World War II, District 8, drawing on an organizing cadre that had developed from the struggles of the 1930s, significantly enlarged its membership base—up to a peak of fifty thousand workers represented in contract negotiations—and its influence.

The patriotic ideology of wartime, however, constricted the range of options open to workers and unions. Most especially, workers lost the right to strike. Class politics were quieted by a wartime "politics of sacrifice" that masked the enhanced leverage of business and wealth.[1] But despite the constraints of wartime patriotic cooperation, District 8 sought to find ways to build workers' power.[2]

Logsdon outlined the district leadership's position to the national office early in the war:

> Our union, and the nation, is committed to a fight for democracy and against fascism. There can now be no fundamental differences on that score. The important thing is that we must not lose sight of or neglect in the smallest measure the defense of democracy here—and that means an all out fight for the maintenance of the rights of our union and our membership. . . . We cannot surrender to any attack by either the administration or those who are to the right of Roosevelt. We can be of value in the fight of the peoples who are fighting for democracy in exactly that measure that we are successful in fighting for democracy and for our union in the United States. There can be no separation of objectives in fighting for the rights of a UE [United Electrical, Radio and Machine Workers Union of America] member in his shop and the conditions under which he works, and of that of the armies who fight the physical battles.[3]

While they endorsed the no-strike pledge and the commitment to all-out production for the war effort, the leftist leadership did not ignore shop floor concerns of workers. They sought to use government bodies such as the National War Labor Board (NWLB) as a lever to expand workers' rights and challenge community rates. More importantly, the Left sought to build grass-roots "civic" campaigns for an expanded role for workers in determining the shape of the political economy during the war and in the postwar period. These campaigns challenged the assumptions and prerogatives of managerial capitalism. They also sought to more fully integrate racial and gender concerns into their union and into a critique of the political economy.

The Wartime Political Economy and District 8's
Community-Based Strategy for the Murray Plan

By 1941 the Roosevelt administration had, as one scholar puts it, allowed the defense mobilization apparatus to be "rapidly converted" into "a branch of corporate America."[4] Large corporate interests guided defense production allocation, resulting in a private planning system and the intense concentration of defense contracts. Two-thirds of all wartime defense contracts were awarded to one hundred of the largest corporations. Major employers such as General Electric (GE) and Westinghouse were given cost plus profit contracts. Those corporations could subcontract to whomever they wished. They reaped the most benefits of huge modern government-built plants. In the metal industries, the war mobilization promised unprecedented rewards, as the Defense Plant Corporation "underwrote virtually the entire machine tool production in the country."[5]

National CIO leaders offered an alternative to the corporate-dominated defense mobilization, an alternative that proposed an equal rather than a subordinate role for labor in exchange for labor's cooperation. They proposed the Industry Council Plan (ICP), commonly referred to as the Murray Plan after its titular author, Phillip Murray, the new CIO president. The Murray Plan called for organizing industry councils, composed of representatives of government, labor, and management, to coordinate the nation's wartime production needs and labor supply. The councils would have the power to allocate natural resources, distribute orders for production, and direct manpower in a rational way, ensuring that human issues such as labor supply, unemployment levels, or housing availability were considered in contract allocation and that small business would receive a share of the contracts. Criticizing the slowness of conversion, the ICP advocates argued that planning that included labor could be more efficient and cost-effective for the nation than corporate-dominated mobilization. As Nelson Lichtenstein has summarized it, the Murray Plan was an attempt to "direct the collectivist tendencies of a publicly-financed war mobilization in more progressive, and pro-labor directions."[6] The most publicized attempt to implement a Murray Plan was Walter Reuther's "500 planes a day" proposal for the automobile industry. Reuther, director of the United Automobile Workers (UAW) General Motors Department, recommended utilizing a tri-partite board that would direct the conversion of Detroit auto factories into air-plane production. The plan was met with relentless opposition by the industry and was rejected by the Roosevelt administration.[7]

Even as some CIO officials grew increasingly frustrated with labor's subordinate role in the wartime agencies, they were unable or unwilling to mobilize workers in support of the Murray Plan. Divided on issues of war preparations, CIO officials did little more than make appeals to sympathetic liberals in federal government echelons. The CIO's representative in the government war mobilization apparatus, Sidney Hillman, refused to advocate the ICP.[8]

Meanwhile the CIO and Hillman cut the UE out of any attempts to gain entrance and leverage within wartime agencies or advocacy of the Murray Plan. In July 1940, James Matles complained to John L. Lewis that Hillman refused to appoint UE members to positions within the wartime agencies despite the UE's record of "cooperating with industry and government . . . in the present defense program." Hillman denied the UE any voice because "our organization is tinged with 'red' [and] our organization doesn't find it advisable to 'square ourselves politically.'"[9] Yet even after the UE "squared itself" with the CIO officialdom by endorsing the war effort, it remained ostracized from the inner circles that planned the CIO's approach to the war effort.[10]

Yet it is not quite accurate to conclude, as has a leading scholar, that the Murray Plan and the Reuther plans for the auto industry "represented the only serious attempt to institutionalize labor participation and some meaningful measure of control over the operation of the economy."[11] District 8 developed a community-based approach to promote labor's inclusion in wartime planning. Sentner viewed mobilization for the war as an opportunity that might allow U.S. labor to move toward the more politicized direction of the British Labor Party.[12] He hoped that wartime exigencies, which disrupted the existing political economy of the cities, might provide opportunities for labor to help define labor market conditions and production issues. The Left used the Murray Plan as a platform to legitimize the pursuit of such a program.

Corporate control of planning, along with restrictions of consumer goods production, threatened not only to entrench corporate control and concentration but also to devastate communities that won no major defense contracts.[13] By summer 1941, workers in District 8's region, employed mostly by small manufacturers, were especially threatened by the pending curtailment of production. This was particularly the case in Evansville, where District 8 was resuming its aborted organizing drive.[14]

When layoffs began in mid-August 1941, UE Evansville lead organizer James Payne, stationed in Evansville for months, began a campaign designed to save the organizing drive and join the national debate over labor's participation in wartime planning. Payne, who was originally from St. Louis's Johnston-Tinfoil

Plant and who had joined the Communist Party (CP), led a core group of union supporters in a campaign titled "Prevent Evansville from Becoming a Ghost Town."[15] District 8's tentative proposal called upon union and civic and business leaders to request the establishment of a federal program that would "be administered through joint and bona fide union-management-government cooperation" at the local level. It would ensure that before reductions in the production of consumer goods were instituted, government must give enough primary war contracts and subcontracts to "take up the slack" of unemployment caused in cities such as Evansville. It also proposed that laid-off workers would get "first claim on jobs with other companies in the community," while excessive overtime would be eliminated until unemployment was reduced.[16]

The UE organizing committee urged Evansville's Mayor William Dress to convene a midwestern meeting of community labor and industry representatives to take the needed steps to save Evansville's jobs in the refrigeration industry. They collected thousands of petitions supporting the idea and found enthusiastic response from workers, merchants, and community groups, and they reported this to congressional representatives.[17]

In mid-September, in response to this campaign, Mayor Dress organized a Midwest conference on priorities in Chicago. Dress asked five hundred mayors of cities with populations under a quarter of a million in eleven midwestern states to appoint delegations of "city officials, labor leaders, managers of industry and other civic leaders to the conference."[18] Fifteen hundred delegates representing hundreds of cities in the states of Kansas, Michigan, Missouri, Iowa, Oklahoma, Minnesota, Wisconsin, Indiana, Illinois, Nebraska, and Ohio convened in Chicago on September 12. Only eighty delegates were labor representatives, and fifty-four of them were from thirty different UE plants. The others were mainly UAW workers from Indiana, Michigan, Illinois, and Wisconsin. Sentner reported that the "best representation came from cities where labor called upon the respective mayors." Moreover, Sentner stated, "as the conference got under way it was apparent that they [the delegates] were depending on the labor people to help steer the meeting. Before it was over, labor was not only steering it, but was giving it tone and direction." The major American Federation of Labor (AFL) representative at the conference was Al Couch of Iowa, an ally of UE representatives during the Maytag strike and criminal syndicalism trial. James Carey presented the working program drawn up by the UE. "With the practical proof of labor's ability vividly before them," Sentner told a District 8 gathering, "the delegates freely accorded to labor its right to participate."[19]

The results of the conference were an impressive victory for what Sentner called District 8's grassroots approach to gaining a voice for labor in the wartime economy. The conference program endorsed "equal participation of management and labor in determining a proper and adequate retraining program and allocation of primary and sub-contracts." It endorsed the aim of keeping maximum local employment and urged "all possible steps be taken to avoid serious dislocations in non-defense industries."[20] Sentner was one of two labor representatives on a committee of seven elected to draw up a more comprehensive program of action and steer the program. That committee then elected Sentner to serve as one of the two Washington representatives of the Chicago "confab," as it came to be known. Sentner soon found himself with an Office of Production Management position that was equal to the industry representative (and a distinct difference from the status of generally subordinate labor advisory boards to which labor was relegated). Logsdon remarked that the industry representative was "considerably in awe of Sentner."[21]

This must have been a satisfying rejoinder to Sidney Hillman's exclusion of the UE. Sentner told district delegates to an unemployment conference that "while the top echelon in Washington had impugned the Murray Plan as unworkable, derided it as socialistic, or simply dismissed it without consideration, the Chicago conference participants seemed to have no problem in gaining (the support of) small business and those left outside the contract allocations crowd." Certainly, as Sentner recognized, this was in part because small business was using labor to "suck up to FDR" to get war contracts. Nevertheless, labor's role opened avenues for inclusion in the community and national planning, a goal consistent with curtailing business control of the economy and the labor market.[22] Was it possible that those small businesses that had been on the front lines of antiunionism could now be a vehicle to expand workers' power? Could a mobilized CIO membership position itself as the savior of communities?

By early October, District 8 leaders were convinced that the approach used in Evansville could be a model for the CIO. Already UE organizers were using it "with great and promising results" in Newton, Iowa, and in Dayton, Ohio, where District 8 organizers assisted an organizing drive. In Mansfield, Ohio, Dick Niebur, an organizer who had come out of the Maytag plant and was now also a CP member, organized a priorities conference that, as Sentner wittily put it, "secured his niche in the Holy Trinity of Mansfield Patron Saints for having come to the assistance of their city in its darkest hours."[23]

As a result of all "the hell we've raised in Evansville and Iowa," Evansville and Newton were named as "test towns" for "an experiment for community-based solving of unemployment and dislocations caused by [war] priorities." These Priorities Unemployment Plan areas attempted to coordinate the transition from consumer goods production to defense contracts on the community level. Sentner's proposals for "worker training on the job" were eventually incorporated into the experiment.[24] Under these plans, companies would keep workers employed and provide training to upgrade workers' skills in the transition to war work, in part through the use of unemployment insurance funds.[25]

Sentner suggested that community-based campaigns for the Murray Plan, developed through regional conferences of labor organizers developing strategies on unemployment, could be the basis of "labor unity and its results on National Defense efforts." He suggested regional conferences of labor organizers to develop strategies on unemployment. In testimony before the Tolan Committee hearings, Sentner called for the organization of community-based labor-industry-government councils. Logsdon told of continuing agitation and success in drumming up support for the Murray Plan in Evansville, Newton, and Dayton and argued that these examples held the key "to a nationwide" way to deal with the issues.[26]

But prospects of using the UE's model in the CIO were dimmed not only by hostility from Hillman but also by the capitulation of even the strongest Murray Plan supporters in the national CIO. Lyle Dowling of the UE national office wrote glumly to Sentner in late October that at a CIO war priorities meeting, there was much complaining about the CIO's somnolence regarding wartime government labor representation, especially by UAW representatives and even by groups under Hillman's influence. While the CIO was due to have a conference on the issues of priorities unemployment, James Carey, secretary of the CIO, and Allen Haywood, organizational director of the CIO, "made it clear that the conference would not be permitted to take any action." The position of the Murray Plan in the CIO was in decline: "The great little Murray-Plan boys (James B. [Carey], [Alan] Haywood, etc) are losing interest in the CIO industry council plan. They now represent it as a desirable, but utopian thing." Besides, Dowling concluded, "so far as being a labor organization with the old punch, the CIO is losing it."[27]

Pearl Harbor dealt a more serious blow to the potential for District 8's strategy. The sudden expansion of wartime contracts and subcontracting after Pearl Harbor alleviated some of the dire predictions of decline of smaller industrial cities. Already by January of 1942, Sentner reported that Evansville's Mayor Dress "is seeking to junk the Emergency Conference" on the grounds that it "had outlived its usefulness." Moreover, among workers there was "a slowing down of interest in this—one hell of a thing to get our people excited about" in a flush job market, Sentner remarked. Sentner retained an office in the new War Production Board (WPB) operated by Donald Nelson, a factor that proved of some value to the UE in gaining a few appointments to government posts, since Hillman "still has us on the s—— list," refusing to allow UE representatives on any wartime boards over which he had control.[28] Throughout the war, Sentner continued to complain that Hillman appointed "dullards" to government agencies, people Sentner felt were "used as a barrier against labor's full participation directly in every branch of the WPB." Yet he and others recognized that contesting this meant "taking on" the top CIO apparatus, an unpromising prospect.[29]

The UE's campaign helped to mitigate some attacks on the union in the Evansville organizing drive.[30] Sunbeam and its company union launched a red-baiting diatribe against Sentner and District 8 in September 1941, utilizing James

Carey's well-reported remarks about CP control of the UE to great effect (Carey's reports were issued in the aftermath of his loss to Albert Fitzgerald in the union's hotly contested national presidential election and in response to the union's stance on foreign policy after the Nazi-Soviet Pact).[31] Yet at the same time, the *Evansville Courier* was covering Sentner's participation in the committee of the Chicago conference, which the *Courier* endorsed. Sentner even won the grudging admiration of the paper's editor, who had done his best to label the 1938 union organizing campaign a "red" invasion.[32] Nevertheless, the union was trounced in the Sunbeam National Labor Relations Board election. The company gained leverage from layoffs and threats of a complete plant shutdown if the union won.[33]

But as the Priorities Unemployment Plan policies Sentner had helped to design went into effect, the UE star rose amongst Sunbeam workers. In August 1942, the UE won solidly in the Sunbeam plant, finally giving a base for the UE in Evansville. Sentner suggested that the UE won because "every issue that arose in the city affecting the welfare of the Sunbeam workers received the attention of the local." Because of UE's efforts, "every manufacturer in Evansville now sponsor[ed] such training courses for which workers receive[d] training rates." Workers credited the UE with helping to make Evansville a "thriving" city.[34]

But Sentner's hope that recalcitrant antiunionism might be curbed by the union's role in gaining defense contracts proved to be overly optimistic. In Newton, despite the Priorities Unemployment Plan, it took an NWLB decision in early 1942 to force Maytag to negotiate a contract. Similarly, Sentner's declaration late in 1941 that the amount of defense work for local companies "will depend greatly upon their relations with our Union" was not borne out. The successful organizing drives in cities such as Evansville, Newton, Moline (in Illinois), Ft. Smith (in Arkansas), and St. Louis were much more dependent on crusading organizing drives rather than on any noticeable waning of antiunionism among employers. To list just one example, the years-long drives for organization in Servel ended in a major victory only in 1946, confirming that the war period did not easily deliver new groups of workers to the district.[35]

Though District 8 succeeded in broadening its geographical base during the war period, the largest expansion of the district was in St. Louis, which was transformed into a major defense supply center. St. Louis business positioned itself early to take advantage of wartime allocation mechanisms. The Chamber of Commerce organized a private planning mechanism to produce subcontracts to St. Louis's mostly small- and medium-sized businesses, "giving St. Louis at least a six-month jump on other cities." In addition, organized business groups began a "training within industry" program in cooperation with vocational schools. By the end of the war, 75 percent of St. Louis manufacturers had defense contracts, while the national average was 50 percent. St. Louis's base in aircraft and artillery and machinery attracted some major contracts that were

placed either through existing companies or through privately managed gov-
ernment-owned plants. Twelve major defense plants eventually brought a
wartime boom to the St. Louis area. Aircraft were built at Curtiss-Wright. The
nation's largest high-explosives plant was built in Weldon Spring. U.S. Cartridge, a small arms ordnance plant in northern St. Louis, under the management of Western Cartridge (Olin) officials, broke ground in March 1941 and
began production seven months later. It eventually became the largest plant of
its type in the world, employing more than thirty-five thousand people by
August 1943.[36] The Small Arms Plant, as it was commonly known, became the
focus of District 8's organizing drive in St. Louis.

Among St. Louis companies, Emerson Electric stood out as the most transformed by the war. Symington's connections to James Forrestal (who had recommended Symington to Van Alstyne, Emerson's underwriter in the 1937 crisis)
and others in the wartime administrative echelons proved decisive in making
Emerson one of the area's primary defense contractors. Symington used his
connections to position Emerson as a major airplane gun turret producer. By
early 1941, Van Alstyne sent Symington to Detroit to negotiate with Preston
Tucker (the inventor who later gained fame for his unique automobile designs),
who lacked financing for his newly created turret designs. Instead of negotiating
with Tucker, Symington lured away Tucker's engineers. The government paid
for the construction of a seven hundred thousand-square foot plant for Emerson, "one of the largest metal-working facilities in the nation," that employed
nearly ten thousand workers at its peak.[37] Emerson's transformation made
Symington an even more important local player in St. Louis.

These significant boosts to the St. Louis corporate economy did not, however,
elevate labor's position in crucial decisions affecting workers. The exclusion of
St. Louis labor from wartime economic planning, District 8 argued, compounded the difficulties that workers confronted in the war boom. U.S. Cartridge, for example, started to recruit from outside St. Louis rather than recruit
local workers, in particular still-unemployed black workers. Housing problems
multiplied as workers drawn to St. Louis were forced to live in mobile home
parks, reside with relatives, or cram into St. Louis's dilapidated rooming houses.
Throughout the war, bottlenecks caused by uncoordinated or self-interested
resource allocation resulted in layoffs and consequent uncertainty that made
organizational progress slow. For instance, in September 1942, just as the Small
Arms Plant had escalated its employment levels past twenty thousand, three
thousand workers were laid off because the WPB decided to divert more copper
to "other munitions channels." Sentner telegrammed Nelson that the bottlenecks were due to business control of the WPB: "If there isn't copper enough to
operate this huge plant at 100% of capacity then the empty buildings and thousands of laid off workers are monuments to the dead wood, the misfits and
those who think in terms of competitive business habits and business as usual

who have been infesting the ranks of the so-called dollar-a-year-men."[38] Such biting comments, repeated in conventions and reported in local newspapers, were common discourse from Sentner and Logsdon throughout the war and challenged the notion of an inherent right of management to control the wartime apparatus.

Such rhetorical flourishes underscored the absence of a concerted CIO campaign to maintain its power during wartime. With no CIO program for implementing the Murray Plan and in the context of the no-strike pledge and the pledge to increase production for the war, District 8's leadership faced the frustrating search for ways to keep alive the challenge to management power and to uphold their pledge to maintain shop floor rights for workers. In late 1941, Sentner wrote bitterly that "I personally believe that the forces around Roosevelt and to some degree Roosevelt himself, are consciously going into the direction of the French ruling class who embraced Fascism rather than turn France over to the people of France."[39]

The CIO's inability to aggressively shape the national context of labor relations led District 8's Left to reconsider its role strategically. The lack of attention to political education of their membership worried Logsdon, who noted that the Left and the CIO confronted a "lag between the economic understanding of our membership" and their grasp of the legislative and political initiatives labor must undertake.[40] Workers who recognized the great gulf that separated their interests from management on the shop floor needed to be better educated about the political context that meant so much for labor's ability to make gains. The easing of attacks and the steady dues receipts raised the possibility that the Left could influence the CIO's direction. But the job of politicizing workers could only be undertaken after organizing them.

Strategic Organizing and a New Critique of the Political Economy

District 8's decision to pour a substantial amount of resources into organizing the St. Louis U.S. Cartridge Small Arms Plant was undertaken not only to expand its numbers but in order to place itself in a position to influence the new working class in formation during wartime and to establish new wage rates. Western Cartridge (Olin Industries), one of the most antiunion companies in the St. Louis area, ran the facility and recruited workers from rural areas, especially from Arkansas and other areas south of St. Louis. Many of these workers had never been members of a union. "They come from farming to dishwashing. . . . [W]e are certainly doing much to promote labor's cause among the influx of rural people," Logsdon reported. District 8 reckoned that these workers' initiation through the UE would help to define their understanding of unionism. Further, as representatives of workers who stood to lose their jobs at the conclusion of the war, this also allowed District 8 to be strategically situated to continue its push for wartime and postwar planning that included labor. Finally, organizing the Small Arms Plant resulted in a substantial new influx of blacks and women into the district's membership (after the company responded to union and community protest over their refusal to hire blacks) and gave leverage to the Left's ability to maneuver on issues of broad concern to these groups. These concerns were clearly a factor in the district's decision to organize this huge company.[41]

The district's commitment to racial justice issues during World War II is especially notable given scholars' suggestions that the UE Left made only rhetorical gestures toward racial equality, with one historian concluding that this illustrates a "serious inconsistency" on racial issues among CP-influenced unions.[42] A fair assessment of the role of District 8's Left in the promotion of racial justice issues during World War II challenges this view. Black workers never composed more than 10 percent of the district's membership, but World War II opened an opportunity for the Left to bring race issues into the center of a confrontation with the area's political economy based on racial and social division.

The Left in District 8 was already defined in part by its commitment to racial justice within the plants, with a core of workers constituting a resource upon which the union's leftist leadership could draw for organizing campaigns and leadership in the district on this issue.[43] This was despite the fact that the industry in St. Louis and elsewhere in the district was largely white and had become more so during the 1930s. By the time of the 1937 UE drive in St. Louis, black workers composed only around 5 percent of the local industry. They held jobs as porters, in foundry work, and as material handlers, jobs traditionally available to African Americans in St. Louis. Local autonomy and the necessity of concentrating on keeping the union together at all in the wake of the 1937–38 recession held back attention to this issue. In October 1937, Sentner reported to an Urban League liaison that "we still have much to do to educate the white members regarding discrimination in social life, etc," but he remained optimistic about prospects for building interracial solidarity.[44] By mid-1938 Sentner seemed less encouraged about those prospects. He told Lester Granger of the national Urban League that "I believe that the slowness of the task of convincing our white membership of the rights of our Negro members to production jobs hampers a more rapid progress in the direction of actively bringing ALL NEGROES in our industry into the union."[45]

At Wagner Electric, where the largest number of African American workers was concentrated (around 175 out of a workforce of 2,500), the district's leftist leadership supported black workers' attempts at self-organization. Orville Leach and Zollie Carpenter, elected to the executive board, invited Sentner to a meeting where the issue of low black membership was discussed. "He asked us, 'What are you doing to correct the situation?' We said, 'We're asking you!'" Sentner advised putting the issue of appointing two African Americans to the executive board; the proposal passed, although "two guys we knew we couldn't convince . . . walked out." One of the new board members was Lee Henry, a dynamic black worker discussed in chapter 4, who helped to integrate the local's social and sports events, a process that took years. Monthly meetings of the "Wagner Scouts" began in early 1940 in order to organize Wagner's black workers into a force within the local. By 1942, Henry organized 99 percent of the 350 black workers at Wagner Electric into joining the UE and achieved the beginnings of an organized black caucus in the district.[46]

Other evidence of progress was the development in the district of key groups of white workers with a serious commitment to these goals. The presence of key actors such as Henry who took center stage in challenging whites and blacks to make industrial unionism meaningful to African Americans and who promoted racial awareness did much to break through stereotypes and prejudices. The district's educational apparatus continued to stress these issues despite their unpopularity among some white workers.[47]

The war period's emphasis on patriotic unity enabled the district's Left to press the "CIO policy" on racial equality. At the turret plant white workers reacted negatively when Symington honored his pledge to hire more black workers and to upgrade them to semiskilled positions. In June 1941, Emerson introduced a segregated unit for black workers; white workers, led by local president "Pop" Schliemann, the IAM stalwart in the UE, organized against it, leading to a sit-down against the hiring and promotion of blacks, and voted (in a meeting attended by one hundred members) to bar blacks from the plant. Years later, Marian Barry recalled her horrified reaction, because interaction on the shop floor and within the leadership of the union had led her to recognize that the black workers at the downtown plant "were the finest men you could ever meet." Her husband Tom "got so mad" about the vote that "he flew all over" and within two weeks succeeded in organizing the effort to reverse the decision, in a meeting attended by huge numbers of workers. In other cases, district and local officials threatened the jobs of white workers who would not budge on these issues.[48]

It was within this context that the district Left designed an organizing campaign at the Small Arms Plant that placed them in a strategic position to influence the district's own membership, the CIO, and the larger community on issues of racial justice. Western Cartridge management reproduced the social structure that Olin had adhered to for generations: they had not hired one black worker in its established East Alton, Illinois, plant across the Mississippi. But as a government contract plant, it succumbed to pressure and pledged to hire black workers. By the time the UE organizing drive was under way, however, the company had hired only six hundred blacks (in the traditional positions of porters and common laborers) out of twenty-one thousand total workers.[49]

Despite the initial low number of African Americans employed at the plant, Sentner designed the UE's organizing campaign to include a special "Negro committee" that would address the special concerns of black workers and create liaisons with black community groups. The UE added Lee Henry as the first black organizer in the national union. Otto Maschoff, originally from Century Electric, and Betty Raab, a white woman who was brought into the drive early on (women would eventually comprise the majority of workers at the plant), also shared these commitments. Raab had established prounion sentiments from her husband's experiences as a brewery worker, but her identity with the Left developed in the course of the organizing drive and from her perception that the union would be a "wave of change."[50]

Many of the 600 or so black workers at U.S. Cartridge had become members by April 1942. On their behalf, Sentner complained to WPB officials that black workers had not been hired for production work and pressed these government officials to force U.S. Cartridge and other employers to begin the process, pointing to a "growing and deep resentment" by blacks at the plant.[51] This resentment was acted upon in June 1942 when 150 of 600 black porters were laid off even while the company continued to hire as many as 1,000 new production workers per week.[52] UE Local 825 called for a government investigation of what Sentner called "brazen acts of race discrimination."[53] But it was black workers in the plant and their community allies who forced U.S. Cartridge to act. The firings activated the St. Louis branch of the March on Washington Movement (MOWM) when some of the fired workers, including Small Arms worker and CP member Hershel Walker, attended meetings of the group and called for a march on the local plant. More than 200 African Americans marched on the factory on June 20, 1942, many walking more than five miles to get there.[54] This march and continued pressure from the union forced U.S. Cartridge to finally make good on its pledge to hire blacks as production workers.[55]

However, U.S. Cartridge established a Jim Crow production setup, using a segregated building for black workers. By mid-1943, black workers' numbers increased to thirty-six hundred (a majority of them women) out of thirty-four thousand workers; black workers could advance to every skilled position in that unit, and their training and wages were the same as whites. The company claimed that "various Negro organizations had approved this arrangement," and indeed, only the MOWM and the UE vigorously protested the segregated situation.[56] U.S. Cartridge's policy became the model, as the St. Louis Chamber of Commerce advocated "complete separation," "careful screening," "special arrangements," and "special shifts" for African Americans. Sentner claimed that the policies were designed to keep in place racial divisions that they had used effectively over the years to divide the St. Louis working class and that in effect it was "an instrument of anti-labor employers to bust unions and maintain low wages."[57] He argued that "in peace time such a policy is detrimental to the living standards of American workers" and is "a blot on the Declaration of Independence and the Constitution of the United States, and the pages of history devoted to the great American traditions of democracy and equal opportunity." During a "desperate war against Fascists whose own systems are based upon discrimination against minorities," such "policies by employers come close to treason."[58]

Local 825's policy of plantwide seniority and integration during the organizing drive risked loss of white workers' votes against rival AFL unions. Just before the union election in May 1943, in what Local 825 saw as an attempt to take advantage of racial divisions, the company moved black workers into a white section of the plant. Around thirty white workers struck in response, and the company withdrew the black workers. In June when some white supervisors were brought into the black unit, black workers struck until the company pledged that it would promote only blacks into supervisory positions. The company used these incidents to forestall integration, even after Local 825, which won the union election by a close margin in May 1943, pledged to enforce integration among white workers.[59]

Otto Maschoff and Betty Raab, key organizers for the union drive, became president and secretary, respectively, of the local and led attempts to break down racial divisions among workers. Maschoff's and Raab's commitment to this issue deepened over the course of the organizing drive and in the face of the intransigence of U.S. Cartridge. Their commitment was evident in their efforts to heighten the understanding of white members for the need to break down social barriers to black participation in the union. Betty Raab negotiated at-large delegate positions so that black workers could have representation at the National UE Convention. Local 825's social events were integrated. Lou Kimmel set up integrated baseball teams and other sports activities. Raab recalled how she and other white women contested racial norms by dancing with black fellow workers at Local 825 dances.[60]

Local 825's first contract included a plantwide seniority system and prohibited discrimination against black workers. However, it made no mention of the segregated unit, and initially the union also made little effort to actively challenge the segregated setup.[61] The company's promise to keep 10 percent of black workers employed (their proportion of the general workforce population in St. Louis) in the segregated unit appealed to many black workers, and others preferred black supervisors. When a series of layoffs was announced in November 1943, the union found that its established seniority clause was "impossible to enforce" because of the segregated unit. When it became apparent that black workers would have fared far better under the plantwide seniority clause, and when the company began recruiting new hires without attention to the seniority clause, the union garnered support from white and black workers to protest the actions. After an intense education campaign among the membership, the union adopted a resolution demanding that the company "cease its discrimination in the re-employment of laid-off Negroes" and called for reemployment of all black and white workers before any new hires were made. The issue led to an organized faction against the Left, a subject that will be discussed in chapter 6.[62]

The UE's base among black Small Arms workers generated pressure on issues of hiring and integration of black workers into better jobs in other locals. In May 1943, the district held a special "Conference on Negro Problems" attended by black and white representatives from each plant. After a series of panel discussions, the conference urged all locals to push for Fair Employment Practices Committee hearings in St. Louis. Delegates called on all constituent unions to negotiate clauses guaranteeing the training and upgrading of workers "regardless of race, color, or creed" and to establish permanent committees within the district's locals. This provided a structure through which black workers could express their rights and demands that locals live up to "CIO policy" on race issues.[63]

Ongoing resistance among a segment of the white membership as well as employers slowed progress and often caused it to be measured in such things as the addition of more black workers to local union executive boards, the integration of cafeterias (such as at Emerson Electric, where a black band entertained during lunch hours, though black members still held separate dances), and the action against white workers who caused work stoppages over the hiring or upgrading of blacks in heretofore exclusively white jobs.[64] At Emerson Electric a Committee on Interracial Equality was organized under the leadership of key black activists who pressed for more skilled and semiskilled production jobs. By-mid 1943, 125 of Emerson's 425 black workers were on production jobs.[65] By 1944, union efforts at Century Electric finally placed the first blacks on non-foundry production jobs and pressured the company "to discharge a white man who caused a work stoppage in an attempt to force the company to provide separate toilet facilities for the Negroes." By May 1945, Logsdon noted that Century's foundry was "one of the very few plants in St. Louis where [there was] complete integration."[66] Perhaps the most notable educational effort succeeded in Local 810, an amalgamated local of sixteen small electrical shops in the St. Louis area. The leadership of that local pushed successfully among its white membership for the hiring of black men and women and thus, noted the Urban League, "set a precedent for placing Negro employees . . . where they have not been hired heretofore."[67]

Winning the U.S. Cartridge plant made the UE in St. Louis, with forty-one thousand members, the largest affiliate of the St. Louis CIO (having more than twice as many members as the rest of the local CIO combined).[68] This allowed the UE to have more influence within the CIO and the community. Bob Logsdon was elected president of the St. Louis Industrial Union Council. From that position he condemned the Jim Crow policies of local business and government. When the UE attempted to enter two integrated baseball teams into the city's municipal baseball league and were refused, Logsdon ignited protest from the entire CIO as well.[69]

District 8 was the key to the formation of the St. Louis Interracial Labor Victory Council, which brought together around seventy-five delegates of the CIO, the AFL, and other unions and was led by Herman Webb, chief shop steward of the segregated unit of U.S. Cartridge. The council pledged to "destroy segregation and discriminatory practices" in St. Louis industry.[70] Further, the UE was the impetus behind the CIO's successful call for a city-based Race Relations Commission to deal with racial tensions and employment and community segregation issues in St. Louis.[71] This varied activity led the *St. Louis American,* the city's black newspaper, to say that the UE was at the "forefront" of organizations pledged to the fight to end discrimination against blacks.[72] When St. Louis author Fannie Cook wrote the novel *Mrs. Palmer's Honey,* about the struggle for racial equality by African Americans during the war, she drew upon the experiences of the workers and radicals she had met in the UE, especially when she served a frustrating term with the St. Louis Race Relations Commission. The novel followed a black maid, Honey, who went to work at a Small Arms plant and became a committed union activist. Through that experience, Honey viewed the CIO as the base for a new freedom movement, a prospect shared by activists such as Hershel Walker, who noted the presence of a number of nut pickers he had helped to organize in 1933 among the Small Arms workers who became involved in the union.[73]

Similar moves to bring gender issues into focus were made during the war, as the percentage of women represented in the district grew from under 20 percent to slightly more than 40 percent.[74] Before the war, the Left sought the inclusion of women in strike committees and emphasized raising wage rates for those on the bottom of the rate structure in an effort to remediate women's traditionally low rates of earnings. The Wagner local, which had the greatest percentage of women before the war, had won maternity leave provisions in the contract in 1939. Sentner was part of a coalition within the national UE that had pushed the national UE to hire women organizers. In 1939, District 8 locals proposed resolutions making this official policy at the national convention. Speaking for the resolutions, Sentner urged delegates to overrule the resolutions committee that recommended nonconcurrence, suggesting that it was a "feeling of overlordship" by men that caused them to "deny women opportunities in the organization," but the resolutions were voted down.[75] During the war period, as organizing campaigns were renewed, the district leadership recruited at least a dozen women organizers either for its own drives or to the national UE, objecting when the international paid them less than men.[76] During the war period, the district leadership continued its alliance with women in the national UE who raised the issue of gender discrimination in the national union to shape policies, constituting what scholar Ruth Milkman has called "UE's breadth of vision."[77]

The union's drive at the Small Arms plant articulated a broad vision for women's involvement in the union's affairs and their challenge to the political economy that assumed women's subordinate economic role. The drive was designed with women organizers and a special women's committee, ensuring that women would have a structure through which their issues could be addressed. Local 825 campaigned on a platform of equal pay for equal work but soon moved beyond that to challenge the entire pay structure and job allocation in the plant.[78] The local was able to implement some of these goals in its first contract, including the elimination of "special jobs for women" and the "women's rate" of pay. By late 1943, the local had established the right of women to qualify for any job, including the coveted training as machine adjusters, a job formerly held only by men.[79] Local 825 made the establishment of "day nurseries" part of their organizing drive and, in concert with District 8 and CIO leadership, successfully pushed the St. Louis Community Chest to establish child care facilities. Betty Raab proudly recalled that "we were advocating issues that had never been discussed before." Speaking of her feelings about being at the "forefront" of the labor movement and St. Louis progressivism on race and gender, she remarked that the war years "were the best time of my life,"[80] years where there was "hope for real change."[81]

The attempt to bridge workplace and community concerns about women's issues resulted in the district's establishment of a Women's Bureau division in St. Louis and the calling of a special one-week convention on "women in industry." The women's group organized within the national UE selected St. Louis as a "good spot" to host such a convention because of Local 825's work and its "complex problems" relating to the intersection of gender and racial issues given the presence of so many black women. While disappointed with the level of cooperation by the local unions, the district had made significant strides by the end of the war in placing women's issues as central to its concerns.[82]

During the war period, district leaders began to articulate a critique of the wartime political economy and its portents for the postwar economy, increasingly making racial and gender issues more central to its organizational identity and agenda. Logsdon and Sentner continually suggested that the "failure by industry to make full use of women and Negroes in the war effort" was an indication not only of ineptitude but also of the undemocratic spirit that guided mobilization. They called for plans to fully "integrate women and Negroes into plants" and not just "squeeze them into certain jobs." The two men argued that "the failure to train blacks and women [caused] the worst slowdown in production," hampering the war effort and preventing true national unity.[83]

Challenging the Community Wage and Management Rights

Even as they condemned the control of the wartime economy by business interests, District 8 sought to use government agencies, in particular the NWLB, to gain leverage for workers. While district leaders disparaged the NWLB's Little Steel Formula, which held workers' wages to 15 percent above the amount they earned in 1941, they found that there were enough "loopholes and special dis-

pensations" to allow them to gain significant pay increases and to challenge the
wage structures of the companies with which they bargained. James Matles
claimed that these were a quiet political victory won by UE and CIO representatives.[84] The aim, as Sentner explained it to a meeting of the Missouri CIO, was
to use these loopholes to shape the wage structure of the community in a more
egalitarian fashion. The NWLB could be used to "up the bottom people—the
people most in need"—and thus "affect the whole wage structure in this area."
Using the lever of the state in this fashion was "an inroad into managerial
power." The NWLB, Sentner argued, "has shattered the so-called management
prerogative . . . that has sort of had a hold on us since we won our rights under
the NLRA."[85]

District 8 "cooked up," as Robert Logsdon put it, various means to increase
workers' wages. They used Labor Department or their own surveys to prove the
existence of interplant or intraplant "inequalities" or "substandard rates." Proving that Wagner Electric paid more in one department than did Emerson Electric and vice versa could raise the wages of entire departments and then the
entire wage structure of a company. The district's success was in part due to the
fact that NWLB District 7, which heard most of District 8's cases, was relatively
generous in allowing increases, granting them in 68 percent of cases, overriding
the recommendations of the director of wage stabilization. (This record
prompted the NWLB to investigate the region in 1944.) District 8 prized its success in raising the rates of workers on the bottom of the pay scale. The lowest
hourly rates at Emerson went from forty cents in 1940 to sixty-five cents at the
electrical division and seventy cents at the turret division in 1944. Local 825
established a seventy-two-cent minimum at the Small Arms Plant.[86]

Raising the low rates by more than 60 percent when average urban wage rates
and the cost of living rose by 33 percent constituted a significant advance for
workers.[87] This strategy of "carrying on a consistent campaign to elevate the
wage scales" of the small plants "in keeping with those wages paid in the larger
plants" was gradually recognized by management itself, which feared the type of
control that labor might forge out of the wartime exigencies and also what it
portended for the postwar period.[88]

Managers objected that "granting substantial increases on certain jobs . . . disturb[ed] the whole rate structure" and worried that any "substantial increase in
the minimum [rate] would necessitate an upward revision of the entire rate
structure," including incentive rates. Managers in particular worried that pay
increases for production workers would "originate a request for an increase in
the rates of office workers." A frustrated Emerson manager remarked that "collective bargaining was no longer practiced in the negotiating of contracts"
because "the Union was taking every advantage in calling in Government agencies to assist in reaching a mutual agreement or otherwise certifying the case to
the War Labor Board for their decision."[89]

The district brought cases not only to contest wage structures but also to give substantive procedural means through which workers' voices could be heard on the job. Local 1108's case against Century Electric resulted in an entire restructuring of wages and an increase of three hundred thousand dollars for the two thousand workers employed there, a victory that had the company "squealing like a stuck pig," according to Sentner. The case also resulted in a checkoff and "complete arbitration of issues," demands that had been unattainable even with the long strike of 1940. To Logsdon, it was a clear victory of a long battle to force recognition of the union's right to exist. Logsdon anticipated that the settling of the "bread and butter question and the proper relationship with the company" meant that the union could "now get something done on the other phases of activity."[90]

District 8 also sought and often achieved protections against "abuses" of the incentive system, ensuring that workers' piece prices would not decrease as output rose or when operations changed.[91] Sentner complained to the CIO's John Brophy, when Brophy agreed in a South Carolina NWLB ruling to allow a wage reduction when new machinery was installed. "It seems to me," Sentner argued, "that this is an important decision which in fact agrees with industry that they may reduce the earnings of workers through the introduction of new machinery or the rationalization of operations."[92] Moreover, although the district agreed with the national UE's policy to promote incentive pay systems, which increased pay with increased production when sufficient protections against abuse could be guaranteed, it was not viewed as a panacea or the only option. For example, Local 810 (an amalgamated local of small shops whose leadership identified with the district Left) was able to eliminate incentive pay during the war.[93] Moreover, the district supported attempts to enable the union to have a determining voice in the type of "pay plans" that management could implement.

Despite its commitment for increased war production, the district publicized efficient wartime production without worker speedup from labor-management committees. Wagner workers showed that by slowing down machine speed, there was less waste; Local 825 demonstrated that having workers operate fewer machines brought better quality production. This was part of the district's ongoing campaign to argue that labor could run the war effort more efficiently if allowed a role in production.[94]

Emerson's Stuart Symington feared and slowly began to resent the erosion of management rights, even as he furthered his reputation as a liberal committed to the extension of labor rights during the war. Some have used the brief fame accorded Sentner and Symington by the remarkable *Fortune* magazine portrayal titled "The Yaleman and the Communist" as confirmation of the Communist support for a labor-management truce during the war.[95] A closer look at the relationship between the union and the company during the war reveals a far more complicated story.

Symington, overseeing the transformation of Emerson to a major St. Louis war contractor employing ten thousand workers, wanted the union to serve the production purposes of the corporation. In exchange for more solid recognition (a union recognition clause, not a closed shop as *Fortune* averred), he asked that the local contribute to "labor morale." Symington thought that a "strong union" would prevent wildcat strikes and reduce militancy. He continued to expect that rising earnings would bring about a contented workforce that identified with the company.[96] Indeed, according to one worker who entered the turret plant early in the war, Symington had little about which to complain. The combination of the entry of many people with little union experience and the rather tepid local leadership made the union, in his estimation, rather weak.[97]

District 8's leadership viewed Symington strategically as well. Symington's rising stature in the local power structure made his endorsement of the union seem extremely significant, as the *Fortune* article acknowledged. It is almost certain that it was through Symington that Sentner was invited to be part of what was dubbed the "Serious Thinkers Club," a group of leading industrialists, clergy, and attorneys whose stated mission was to discuss what "kind of a world they would like to see come out of this mess"—meaning the war—with the idea being "to exert considerable influence in the community." The correspondence of that group suggests that Sentner was quite candid about his politics and his advocacy of postwar planning. The first meeting of the group was a debate on "labor union practice and control" in which Sentner debated antiunion Monsanto Corporation's chief, Edgar Queeny. These exchanges were extraordinary. Sentner's goal was to convince St. Louis businessmen that labor's inclusion in community-based planning as part of a national program was the only way to ensure postwar prosperity. That goal was not entirely naive. Bishop William Scarlett, the convener of the group (and the chair of the Social Justice Commission that intervened during the nut pickers' strike ten years earlier), summarizing the early meetings, reported that the group had "agreed that as in the present crisis for the sake of the war effort, industry had accepted certain central controls of profits, prices, etc., so also after the war, for the sake of the general welfare and in order to prevent another plunge into wide-spread unemployment, industry would continue to accept whatever central controls might prove to be necessary."[98] At another point, Queeny wrote to William McClelland of the St. Louis Committee for Economic Development (CED) about Sentner's ideas: "We are at opposite poles, but [there is a] great broad field where [our] interests are identical. . . . It seems to me that if we are going to have private enterprise, somebody is going to have to do some planning for government so that it can re-establish conditions under which private enterprise can again furnish full employment."[99]

Sentner initially anticipated that Emerson's labor-management committee might provide the seeds for broaching key issues of management rights. In direct contradiction of WPB head Donald Nelson's injunction that labor-management committees should not be used to "insert labor into production decisions," Sentner told District 8 members that they should try to use the committees to implement "joint management labor responsibility for production planning, down below in the plants. . . . Heretofore, it was considered the prerogative of management to assume full responsibility for the handling of matters pertaining to production planning, machine use, etc." Because this was a "people's war," Sentner urged, "it is right at this time to have labor participate in the field of production which up until now was a sole prerogative of plant management." He also suggested that while workers should be "determined to increase production," that did "not necessarily mean speed up" and urged that only the "best union members" be representatives of the committees.[100]

When Sentner observed the actual functioning of the Emerson labor-management committees, he intervened to ensure that the committees would not be reduced to a management tool. He wanted Emerson workers to avoid the pitfalls that befell other such committees across the country by preventing suggestions from going directly to management. Instead, "the question of labor-management cooperation, and especially as it is related to production, should be made the property of the union membership before it becomes the property of the Labor-Management committee."[101] However, by 1943 it was clear that management was refusing to allow workers to have any true voice in production decisions.

Contrary to the *Fortune* magazine depiction of support for collaboration and harmony between labor and management, Logsdon and Sentner worried about the drift of Emerson's Local 1102 toward complacency in the midst of the entry of thousands of new workers into the company. In June of 1942, those concerns were serious enough to prompt them to agree that Logsdon should go back to work at Emerson to attempt to influence the local. Logsdon wrote that "as you probably know, I do not have too much faith in Symington, but at this time we are travelling parallel roads. How long that will continue will depend upon the course of the war." However, he observed, "it seems to me that too much dependence is placed upon Symington by the local union now and not enough upon building their own understanding and strength."[102]

Logsdon probably hoped to rebuild a viable Left within the local. However, though given approval by the national UE for a leave of absence to go back to Emerson, he never did. It is probable that James Click or other Local 1102 leaders sensed interference and objected.[103] Throughout the war, however, Logsdon complained that the local leadership concentrated too much on "social functions" and not enough on educating and expanding the strength of the local.[104] As Logsdon noted, James Click and the section of the local leadership that was relatively progressive (they had led the effort to repeal the original vote to exclude black workers) did not want to work with the district and local Left because it was "afraid of tints and hues," that is, of being associated with being "red."[105] The rest of the local leadership was more conservative and was quite taken with Symington. In fact, a close reading of the *Fortune* article shows that Sentner never claimed a special eagerness to cooperate on Symington's terms. Indeed, his only favorable quotation toward Symington was that "we said we'd take him for every penny we could, right down to the half cent. And he said he'd cut us in. He did. He carried through." On the other hand, Eustius Brendle, president of the local, called Symington "the greatest guy in town," while executive board member Ernest Stuebinger (Sentner's opponent in the district election of 1941) "emphatically" remarked, "He's tops."[106]

It is possible that Sentner's decision to tell the *Fortune* reporter about his membership in the CP was also a signal that Sentner was not ready to concede fundamental principles for a degree of respectability or legitimacy. The *Fortune* article was a vanity piece orchestrated by Symington, in order to earn him a reputation among the Dillon Read financial operatives in government. Instead, Sentner's revelations about his party membership became a major focus of the article and clearly annoyed Symington. Symington and Bishop Scarlett frantically tried to get Sentner to retract his admission before publication. Symington felt betrayed because, according to Scarlett, he had "carried the torch" for Sentner "and Sentner had let him down." The question of why Sentner chose to become a more open Communist again, when he could probably have remained hidden, will be dealt with more fully in chapter 6.[107]

By 1943, even as the article in *Fortune* proclaimed harmony between the union and the company, Symington was already privately worried about growing encroachments on management rights. What had happened? The answer lies in two primary factors: the growing sector of workers who challenged Local 1102's leadership to be more aggressive and the district's policy to use the NWLB to enhance workers' rights and to challenge the labor market.

While Emerson's conversion to major wartime contractor eased the work pace at the company and made Symington more amenable to increased wages, problems continued. For example, lax steward enforcement had created systems of foreman favoritism. By 1943, a significant faction of new Emerson workers sought a more aggressive stance. Rather than confirming Symington's prediction of worker quiescence as the outcome of a strong recognition clause, workers' demands grew. In just one example, a group of fifty women transferred from Emerson's electrical division demanded that they should not be limited to a three-week time period in which to learn their new jobs. "They thought they should be able to take as long as it took to learn the job," and they knew "Sentner supported them," recalled shop steward Thomas Knowles. Meanwhile, Emerson's management constantly worried about what their wartime behavior would mean for the postwar period. As Knowles put it, "they were so afraid those costs would carry over after the war . . . they were afraid they couldn't reduce them." On the other hand, workers could see the wartime profiteering in the plant in plain view. With this in mind, Knowles, for instance, "patrolled that plant, asking [workers] for grievances" and "cutting down" foreman power.[108]

As management began to rein in workers' new assertiveness, serious tensions arose. In May 1943, accumulating grievances resulted in a short wildcat strike that began over the dismissal of workers for smoking in a restricted area. In late 1943, district leadership sought to write contractual provisions that would allay some of the complaints and problems. In particular, they wanted to insert rights for joint determination of pay plans, departmental transfers, and apprenticeships in skilled work. This was an extension of the district's broader efforts to take these issues before the NWLB, where they might encroach on issues formerly considered to be management prerogatives.[109]

Symington objected that establishment of pay plans and transfers was "a function of Management. . . . To agree to any such position being given to the officers of the Union would be passing over management control of the company to the officers of the Union." Symington reminded the union that he had been responsible for getting war contracts, and he warned that "for some time this management has been worried about the nature of many complaints which the Union, in increasing numbers, wishes to pursue to arbitration. We trust there is no effort to harass management, because such action would be against the war effort as well as the development of the company." He concluded with a veiled suggestion that the union's failure to cooperate "would result in a decline in postwar personnel of 80% to 90% of the present force."[110] Emerson offered a more enhanced management clause (workers would be asked but not be required to sign a dues checkoff when hired) in exchange for abandoning the "sharing managerial functions such as the adoption of pay plans and the determination of individual employe efficiency other than by the judgment of immediate supervisors." However, the local and Sentner instead pursued the case to the NWLB, which eventually (in 1945) ruled in favor of the union.[111] The ruling was extraordinarily significant. The UE was reclaiming a right that had been wrested from St. Louis metal trades workers at the dawn of the century.

Meanwhile, tensions continued in the plant. District 8's Left, following CP and CIO policy, opposed wildcats during the war and consequently proved unable to build a viable Left out of this discontent. Moreover, the leadership was suspicious of the faction fostering aggressiveness because some were anticommunists whose goal was to foment unrest in order to take the local into the UAW or the International Association of Machinists (IAM). Sentner and Logsdon therefore sought to bolster Click's leadership as the best "progressive" alternative available. They drew up a proposal that addressed workers' grievances just before the local elections in which Click's and the entire executive board's positions were threatened. After Click's victory, the UAW and IAM factions orchestrated some wildcat strikes over the firing of a worker. Though orchestrated, these wildcats revealed legitimate fears of impending layoffs.[112] The UAW/IAM faction called for a vote for a strike under the terms of the Smith/Connally labor legislation, but the district and Click resisted. Click and the local leadership asked the district to take over the local, but Sentner refused to do so unless directed to by "a vote of the rank and file." Instead, the district helped Click write up a seven-point program to deal with grievances. It also pushed the local to fulfill its long promise to organize clerical and technical workers at Emerson.[113]

As Click and the local leadership began to be more aggressive, Symington responded harshly. In July 1944 he wrote to Click with respect to an attempt to increase pay rates on a job:

> This particular case perhaps is not so important, but the philosophy behind it—hit the company for every possible increase, regardless of efficiency, or postwar competitive position—is important. Through the policy of constantly trying to get more and more, regardless of skill, perhaps you are wrecking the future of many people; because if such activities put the company in a non-competitive position, there can be no effort to continue with the turret plant operation postwar. This would mean loss to your present union members of thousands of jobs, the result of union leadership not being able or willing to face the realities of the company's position.[114]

By November, Symington was after Click's job. Symington apparently believed that his personal popularity among workers might prompt them to oust Click. His appeal also contained serious threats if workers continued their aggressive style of unionism. In a meeting of Emerson workers, he called Click a "labor czar" and charged that "during the last eight months . . . some fundamental change in the attitude of some of the stewards, and the Chief Steward, has apparently occurred at Emerson [and] whereas the management of the company is fighting hard to maintain employment, your Chief Steward has adopted policies which, unless promptly corrected by you, will assure" loss of jobs in the postwar era. Symington claimed that the company had "lost several large orders to competition," and he was still fuming that the pay plans issue was being pursued. It is important to remember, in all of this, that St. Louis electrical workers' wages were still below the national average. Symington still had his eye on the postwar period and sought to keep the ability to use the wage advantage as leverage when the war was over.[115]

Symington's attacks on Click backfired, and the local rallied around Click. Sentner and Logsdon helped the local's leadership reply to Symington's charges by discussing the shop floor problems and explaining the basis for grievances that Symington callously dismissed. The letter concluded: "Seldom has a Company been so [ill] regarded by its employees, especially where the Company claims to have a liberal Labor policy. It has been necessary for the officers of this Union to continuously work to build up some semblance of goodwill between the Emerson Company and its employes. Your employees have no faith in your

Company, and their lack of faith is not based on any statements or misrepresentation by Union officials."[116] In the months that followed, the union successfully arbitrated cases and achieved victories in a number of grievances. Sentner personally pursued some of the cases. According to Knowles, Sentner "made Karches [Emerson's personnel manager] look like a fool" and led to Karches's dismissal.[117]

But clearly it was Click, not Sentner, whose reputation among workers benefitted from this more militant stance. Sentner was attempting to cultivate Click as an ally and leader within the brewing factionalism of the union while also cultivating Symington as an ally for postwar planning issues. While Click was developing a reputation as a militant, responsive shop floor ally of the workers, Sentner was directing his attention to the possibility of community-based postwar planning. It was this goal that caused him to continue to seek to make Symington an ally.

Postwar Community-Based Planning and the Missouri Valley Authority Campaign

The Emerson case demonstrated that as the war wound down, tension over layoffs and the shape of the postwar economy and labor market were foremost in workers' minds. District 8's members, especially those at the Small Arms Plant, experienced continual threat of layoffs and insecurity after 1943. Logsdon complained that wartime planning, which excluded labor's concerns over maldistribution of war contracts, failure to consider available manpower, and the unwillingness to make full use of women and African Americans in the war effort, held troubling implications for the postwar world. In a letter to Senator Harry Truman, Sentner wrote, "Apparently it is left to the hit-or-miss procedures of a loose labor market to see that laid off men and women are reabsorbed—a fantastically inadequate arrangement for an area like St. Louis."[118]

Postwar Planning Conferences

After 1943, District 8 sought to raise other possibilities for the postwar economy and to place workers' concerns at the center of discussions of postwar issues. Sentner argued that the postwar economy could only be just if labor had a major role in planning it. They got St. Louis mayor Alois Kaufman to establish a city-based postwar planning committee that included representatives of the CIO and AFL, suggesting that this kind of committee was the "first step in a nationwide application of the principles of community cooperation" for a new postwar world. They organized a CIO shop steward council in St. Louis to discuss the postwar economy as a base for future mobilization. In Newton, Local 1116 helped to establish a Post-War Planning Council.[119] In 1944, the district

hosted five "Community Leadership for Reconversion and Postwar Employment" conferences on postwar planning, held in Moline; Mt. Carmel, Illinois;
Newton, Iowa; Evansville, Indiana; and St. Louis. Representation was based on
two men and two women elected from each factory department. In seeking to
build a community coalition around postwar planning, district leaders invited
government, church, and civic organizations and women's and African American organizations. In addition, District 8 tried to garner business support for, or
at least diffuse their opposition to, postwar planning.[120]

At these conferences, Sentner expressed hopes for a transformed postwar
order. He suggested that a postwar world of "unemployment and chaos, human
misery and despair can and will be avoided" only by community-based planning that was part of national planning of postwar conversion and full employment. Labor and management could avoid "squaring off for the postwar battle"
only if labor was recognized fully as a part of the community. Sentner called for
planning for an economy that would create more interesting jobs and suggested
that one part of this planning would involve reducing working hours to thirty
per week.[121] "We will have a 30 hour week as a policy because when we increase
the American standard of living it does not just mean buying so much as more
time for study, development of family life, more time for recreation, physical
development of American men and women. The 30 hour week was not planned
as a cure for unemployment but as a benefit of American productive ingenuity."
Postwar planning would prevent "sliding back into the old way of trying to find
cures for ills." Sentner warned that "the boys who are now operating the super
fortresses are not going to be satisfied to come home and operate a drill press at
75 to 80 cents per hour."[122] Neither, he added, would women want to leave the
workforce. In polls of the women who attended the conferences, they expressed
a desire to stay at the plants. For example, at Mt. Carmel, all but three women in
attendance said they wanted to keep working after the war.[123]

At the St. Louis conference, Symington supported expanded workers' rights,
even though he was growing ever more concerned about what it meant in his
plant. "To go back to the days when labor was not represented by accredited leaders is unthinkable," Symington agreed, and asserted that the "power of employe
organizations must increase after the war, rather than become less. . . . [L]abor
leaders must take full responsibility along with management for the direction in
which industry moves." Labor-management committees needed to "devise new
products in terms of the needs of our markets and those of other nations," he
suggested. He noted that "what we have accomplished in war production was
done through planning. . . . [T]o dismiss all planning is an insult to all that America stands for." Symington agreed to government controls and called "free enterprise" an abstraction. He objected that "too many people say that anyone who
doesn't believe in free enterprise is a socialist and that anyone who doesn't believe
in Socialism is a 'free enterpriser.' . . . [That is a] 'lot of bunk.'"[124]

Nevertheless, outside of Symington and the president of Eagle Signal (at the Moline conference) who agreed to union checkoffs after the war, the conference indicated little business support for expansion of labor rights even though the union expressed desire for "cooperation." In a preview of future battle lines, George Smith of the St. Louis Chamber of Commerce interrupted the discussion to remind workers of the realities of capitalism: free enterprise was "not for the purpose of creating of jobs! It is not why men go into business[,] to make jobs, but for the purpose of employing capital and making a profit." Frank Meehan, representative of the putatively liberal business group the CED, noted that the CED's definition of "full employment" did not mean "that every man and woman, including those who want to loaf, would be working. We believe in a free enterprise system and probably some men and women [who] are working now will want to retire, especially women."[125]

William McClelland, president of St. Louis's leading utility, Union Electric, expressed similar views in a CED Eighth District Reserve report in August 1944. He argued against the need for the CIO-backed national legislation that would have set up an overall planning authority for the postwar era. He saw "no need to legislate" to meet future postwar needs. Sentner, charging that the CED "considers St. Louis in a vacuum" and not "in relation to the state and nation as a whole," objected to the report:

> You envisage in the postwar era a reduction in manufacturing employment of 67,000 and a shift to service employment. . . . Women and older workers make up the 64,000 who you say will theoretically leave their jobs for good. Surveys in our industry show that 80% of the women and almost all older male workers desire to work after the war. . . . The CED does not appear to be concerned that working mothers and wives of wounded veterans and young women will want to be assured jobs in the postwar period. Nor do they stop to consider the special problem involved in advancing democratic opportunities for Negroes to retain their newfound jobs. Negro citizens will not willingly leave their industrial jobs where they are earning 70 cents to a dollar an hour, to take menial jobs and domestic service at 40 and 50 cents.[126]

Sentner insisted that instead of writing women out of the postwar workforce, the CED should support nurseries and other aids to enable women to work after the war. The district continued to challenge business's limited vision of a postwar order and sought to bring forth specific alternatives to build connections between workers' concern for jobs and their broader concerns about the postwar world.

By mid-1944, rising in the context of the dramatic floods of 1944, District 8 had already become involved in a campaign to concretely promote postwar planning on a community and regional basis. The campaign for a Missouri Valley Authority (MVA), which sought to establish an agency empowered to plan for and develop the nine-state area along the Missouri River valley, raised hopes for what a unified CIO could accomplish in alliance with other groups by building community-based campaigns. It also gives a glimpse of the capacity of workers to bring "civic" concerns to their union involvement.

The Missouri Valley Authority Concept

The concept of an MVA owed much to the popularity of the Tennessee Valley Authority (TVA). By the end of World War II, the TVA enjoyed growing public support not only because it brought electrical power to the Tennessee Valley and solved navigation problems but also, according to TVA head David Lilienthal, because it was an example of "democracy on the march." Lilienthal promoted the idea of the TVA as a new decentralized regional planning approach involving the people who lived in the valley rather than as a distant federal bureaucracy. Later TVA developments and subsequent analyses of the authority raise questions about Lilienthal's claims. Nevertheless, in the 1930s and 1940s, the "TVA idea" continued to be associated with the popular notion of decentralized, democratically exercised power.[127]

Bills to establish other river-based authorities were submitted throughout the 1930s. In 1937 Roosevelt endorsed the establishment of seven other authorities. His National Resources Planning Board (NRPB) advocated the additional authorities but lacked grassroots support. As the New Deal's political fortunes began to deteriorate after 1938, the prospects for the NRPB's proposals eroded. In 1943, as World War II mobilization eclipsed concerns for New Deal planning, Congress easily dismantled the NRPB. Despite TVA's popularity, prospects for other planning authorities seemed dismal indeed.[128]

Then, in the spring of 1943 and summer of 1944, record flood waters came sweeping relentlessly through the lands bordering the lower Missouri River, especially from Sioux City down to the confluence with the Mississippi twelve miles above St. Louis. The annual run-off of melting snow in the upper valley states of Montana and North and South Dakota combined with record rains in 1944 caused damage totaling more than $110 million. From Kansas City to St. Louis, levees built by towns and farmers' districts succumbed to the muddy waters that brought sand and farmland dirt from as far away as Montana. The flood inundated thousands of acres of farmland and forced the evacuation of St. Charles, Missouri, leaving thousands homeless. In St. Louis, the flood contributed to the rising Mississippi crest. Coast Guardsmen, army engineers, and civilians held the St. Louis levee intact with thousands of sandbags.[129]

The devastation provided an opening for the U.S. Army Corps of Engineers (USACE) to expand its role in Missouri River development. USACE drew much of its support from private interests that supported improved navigation, but its main focus was deepening the Missouri River channel. Congress gave it a mandate for flood control in the 1930s.[130] Seizing the opportunity provided by the floods to expand its control over the Missouri River, USACE representative Colonel Lewis Pick, "a shrewd, ambitious bureaucrat-soldier," submitted to Congress a twelve-page, hastily drawn proposal totaling $661 million for flood control. It promised an end to floods through a series of dams and reservoirs on the Missouri and its tributaries, municipal and agricultural levels, and irrigation projects for dry upper valley states such as Montana and North and South Dakota. The plan, environmental historian Donald Worster wrote, "proposed the complete dismantling of the natural river." USACE submitted separate legislation to deepen the lower Missouri's river channel from six feet to nine feet. Because deepening the channel would require the release of additional waters from the upper valley, especially in dry spells to sustain it, USACE's twin proposals made its claims to balance flood control, navigation interests, and upper valley irrigation interests dubious. Nevertheless, the House flood control committee passed the Pick Plan in March 1944.

The Bureau of Reclamation (BR), an agency created in 1902 and mainly supported by irrigation interests in the upper valley, opposed the Pick Plan, stating that it threatened control over irrigation in the upper Missouri Valley. Charging that USACE was using the flood control plan to mask its navigation interests, the BR proposed the Sloan Plan. At an estimated cost of $1.3 billion, it promised to protect irrigation on the upper Missouri Valley. It incorporated some of the flood control features of the Pick Plan but also sought to construct eight or nine new reservoirs in the upper valley in order to furnish irrigation to dry land and hydroelectric power to rural residents. Sloan's plan excluded navigation provisions, thereby defining the major conflict over water use between the two agencies and between the upper and lower river interests. "One agency wanted to spread the river over fields," concludes Donald Worster, "while the other insisted on letting it flow in deep steady currents in order to float commercial traffic."[131]

As the Pick Plan rolled its way toward congressional approval, the *St. Louis Post-Dispatch,* in a widely disseminated editorial, called for a campaign for the creation of the MVA in order to implement a unified plan for flood control and Missouri River development. An MVA, the *St. Louis Post-Dispatch* argued, would replace the patchwork approach and bureaucratic haggling between the federal agencies (and the private interests that backed these agencies) over river issues. The *St. Louis Star-Times* also quickly backed the idea and called for a "genuine grassroots movement" up and down the valley for an MVA.[132]

Representatives of District 8 UE shop delegate conferences enthusiastically endorsed the establishment of an MVA as a means to promote postwar planning on a local and regional level. By the time of the postwar planning conferences, District 8's executive board committed one staff research job to the promotion of an MVA. District 8's leadership viewed a campaign for the MVA as a way to promote postwar planning for full employment as well as to place labor at the center of the "public interest" in the postwar period. They also argued that an MVA would mean "control, in the public interest, of the flow of waters and the erosion of land."[133]

The MVA Campaign

District 8's campaign began by outlining its comprehensive plan for the river in a pamphlet, *One River, One Plan*. In keeping with the district's stress on postwar planning for jobs, the pamphlet predicted that five hundred thousand jobs would be created within five years from projects such as dam building, irrigation, electrification, soil conservation, and reforestation. In many respects the pamphlet agreed with the dominant view expressed by USACE about control of the natural river for development or economic growth purposes. It stressed that electrification of rural areas (only 30 percent of all farms in the Missouri River basin had been electrified) through cheap public power would create a new market for electrical products of the region. Irrigation would become available to small farms, thus opening up opportunities that had mainly benefited agribusiness previously. Through postwar planning for the Missouri River valley basin, "its abundant resources ought to make for significant peace-time expansion." On the other hand, the pamphlet and press releases accompanying it stressed that only through regional, decentralized planning could the river "be harnessed for the public good" and the various concerns of the citizens in the Missouri Valley be taken into account. The pamphlet stressed that public involvement in utilization of water resources would bring overdue consideration of the "devastating effect of exploitation." Moreover, inclusion of soil and water conservation as well as reforestation were aspects left out of the Pick and Sloan plans.[134]

District 8 used *One River, One Plan* to launch a community-based grassroots campaign that it sought to keep out of the hands of technocrats who had dominated the NRPB. Naomi Ring, the district's staff researcher for the MVA (and a CP member), noted that the district had been approached by "every liberal from Washington D.C. to Canada writing us veiled suggestions that they would like to get in on paying organizational publicity jobs for this deal." The district promoted a structure that would create "one broad committee that [could] pull in as many farm, labor, industry and civic people" in order to increase the effectiveness of the campaign as well as to establish that "mass action of the citizens in the Valley" would frame the issues even after the MVA was established.[135]

District 8 staff soon found the "right" liberal engineer to help them formulate the bill. Walter Packard had been director of the New Deal's Resettlement Administration in five southwestern states. Donald Worster has suggested that Packard was a "community"-oriented type of New Dealer, committed to planning for a "cooperative commonwealth" in the United States. Packard had earned the rage of western corporate and agricultural interests in his work on the Reclamation Bureau's Central Valley Project, a central California irrigation and power program. He wrote to Sentner that "our experience with the Central Valley Project in California amply demonstrates the need for vigilance in protecting the rights of labor and the consumer, both in the setting of policy and in administration." He concluded that "it is not enough to secure an authority. It is equally important to see that the authority represents sound public policy. This can be accomplished only by a determined drive by labor, farmers, consumers and liberal elements, generally. These groups should be brought together in a concerted campaign in the public interest."[136]

The response to *One River, One Plan* was encouraging, "exceed[ing] UE's wildest dreams" among both its own members and workers in other unions, including rival AFL unions. Sentner said that the issue "caught on like no pork chops issue ever did," not only because of workers' concerns for postwar security but "also because there's hardly a union man or woman [in the district] that isn't tied either through family or tradition to the rural areas and the woes they've suffered through Old Man River." Indeed, many electrical workers and especially many defense workers were recent migrants from the rural areas of Missouri and maintained ties to their rural past. James Davis, an auto worker and secretary of the Missouri CIO, which quickly embraced the MVA proposal, was "raised within three-quarters of a mile of the Missouri River." He recounted that "I have seen the place I was raised on covered with about a foot of sand that probably came from Montana." The visionary hopes for the postwar period resonated with many industrial workers in part because of the multidimensional characteristics of working-class formation during wartime. Many of these same workers shared Sentner's enthusiasm for recreational activities such as fishing in Missouri's rural regions. They showed concern not only for jobs but for a broader enhancement of life in the postwar world.

Thus it was not only the promise of jobs that attracted workers and unions to the proposal. After all, the USACE plan also promised development and jobs. In Iowa, AFL leaders had forged unusually cordial relations with CIO unions. These AFL leaders admired and respected Sentner and helped District 8 representatives gain the cooperation of building trades unions for the proposal. The attraction of an MVA was thus tied not only to some of the same rural issues but, as Sentner noted, to a high level of enthusiasm from Iowa AFL leaders for establishing a place for labor in postwar planning. Further, USACE had traditionally bid out contracts for its projects, often resulting in undercutting the union-established prevailing wage for construction work. The MVA, its supporters argued, would follow the TVA's practice of hiring workers directly and paying the union's prevailing wages.[137]

Farmers and farm groups responded enthusiastically to the MVA campaign and took a central role in it. District 8 increased contact with farmers across the nine states, especially with the 86,000-member Missouri Farmers Association (MFA) and the 250,000-member National Farmers Union (NFU), headquartered in Montana.[138] These organizations bitterly opposed the USACE based on past experience. Writing to Sentner in summer 1944, MFA leader H. E. Klinefelter condemned the Pick Plan as an "army engineers' scheme." He charged that USACE had "all but ruined the Missouri River with their attempts to develop a 6 foot channel. Now they talk of a 9 foot channel." Klinefelter favored any plan that would "take authority away from the army engineers and give it to some independent agency that hasn't any axes to grind."[139] *The Missouri Farmer* expressed "hope that by superseding the new flood control law with an MVA, at least SOME of these monumental dams might be replaced with extensive soil conservation measures which are quite as effective as dams—if not more so—in holding back floods." In the upper valley, according to a St. Louis *Star-Times* investigation, "many small farmers, dirt farmers, [and] small town merchants" were "skeptical toward grandiose plans for irrigation," such as those proposed by the BR that had usually benefited large farmers only.[140] District 8's MVA pamphlet pledged that water resources would favor small farmers over agribusiness. In addition, the pledge of public power from water resources won over many farmers. The NFU had proposed in 1942 that the "TVA be made a pilot operation for the nation." By late August, the NFU was using *One River, One Plan* as its "tool."[141]

The coalition with farmers had a pronounced effect on the perspectives of the labor activists. Farmers and soil conservationists challenged prevailing notions of "taming the river" to control floods, stressing to the UE a preference for soil conservation and erosion control rather than dams. In August, Naomi Ring confessed to farm representatives that this was her first "encounter with river development. . . . I have come to the conclusion that more stress should have been put on irrigation, soil conservation and the general well-being of the farmers."[142] Sentner wrote to another correspondent who worried about the navigation provisions of the MVA that the "MVA would only undertake regional projects that are both feasible and benefit a maximum amount of the people in the valley; therefore, I am sure we will have no worry." Klinefelter wrote Sentner with regard to concerns about soil and flood control issues that "I do not believe we are very far apart on the subject."[143]

MVA supporters recognized that they would encounter stiff opposition from the BR and USACE but were gratified to win support from the Rural Electrification Administration (REA), a governmental agency that had promoted public power projects and cheap electricity for rural regions in the New Deal administration. The REA, however, was defunded during the war, and its staff had an obvious interest in promoting the MVA. In addition, by this time Sentner had established a friendship with REA staffer Sadelle Berger, an activist in the CIO's Federal Workers Union; by 1944 Berger had come to work for the UE and would lead the district's 1944 political campaign. Ring used Berger's and

Packard's contacts in the REA to secure staffers' support and advice. She reported to Sentner that after a meeting between herself, Packard, and the REA, the agency was willing to "go along" with the labor-farmer coalition that was developing out of the UE's efforts because of the respect they had for Packard. She added that "the fact that you and Packard are so 'close' gave them more confidence in the role labor will have to play in a MVA organization."[144]

Senator James Murray of Montana submitted MVA legislation, written by Packard, REA staff, and District 8 representatives, in August 1944. Later, Missouri representative John Cochran sponsored another version in the House.[145] Both allowed the authority two years to develop a plan that would "reconcile and harmonize" the requirements for flood control, navigation, reclamation, power, and other needs "in such a way as to secure the maximum public benefit for the region and the nation." The plan would then be submitted for congressional approval. A board of three directors who "would utilize to the fullest possible extent the advice and assistance of the people of the region, including local and state governments," would govern the MVA. MVA directors were barred from having any financial interest that would benefit from potential development. The bill gave the MVA "broad powers to sell and distribute electric power and water and to fix rates" for sale to consumers, with a preference for sale to cooperatives. The legislation barred dams not approved by the MVA. Evidence that environmental concerns were gaining ground in the conceptualizations of the MVA was apparent in a provision that gave the authority the power to "prevent pollution of the waters of the Missouri and its tributaries."[146] On September 22, Roosevelt issued a strong endorsement of the bill and called for more such proposals. Vice presidential candidate Harry Truman also wholeheartedly endorsed the legislation.[147]

That fall the grassroots campaign for the MVA began to take shape. UE delegates shepherded support for the bill through the Missouri CIO Convention, which endorsed it and organized a nine-state meeting of CIO unions to promote it. The Missouri CIO and UE representatives pushed the National CIO Convention, held in November, to make the MVA part of their "People's Program of 1944." Phillip Murray of the CIO claimed that the project should be the top congressional agenda item of the CIO.[148] Farmers' groups increased their efforts. The Cooperative League, a two million-member association advocating cheap power, and the Consumers Cooperative Association also endorsed the measure.[149]

The momentum for an MVA was strong enough to prompt what James Patton of the NFU called a "shameless, loveless, shotgun marriage" between USACE and the BR. In early November, the two agencies quickly threw together a new proposal called Pick-Sloan, which combined elements of the two plans and specifically prohibited an MVA. They divided up jurisdiction, with the BR having authority over the upper valley and USACE retaining control on all navigation and lower valley projects. As scholar Donald Spritzer has pointed out, "the new plan said nothing about how the water would be proportioned to meet conflicting needs," and while it called for hydroelectric power, the program did not include public power projects. Pick-Sloan was nothing more than "a subsidy for the privileged interests," wrote Walter Packard. There were no provisions for soil conservation or other environmental measures.[150]

After much wrangling, and fearing that Pick-Sloan might be approved with the anti-MVA provisions, MVA congressional allies worked out a compromise with Pick-Sloan backers, despite protests from grassroots supporters in farm and labor groups. Senator Murray consented to postpone the push for MVA legislation until the next Congress if the Pick-Sloan bill would take out the anti-MVA provisions in return for the promise of early hearings. Murray reasoned that because only four hundred million dollars had been appropriated (for the initial phase of Pick-Sloan), the fight for an MVA was best postponed until more momentum could support it. The Pick-Sloan Bill passed Congress in late December 1944. President Roosevelt's suggestion that Pick-Sloan should not be considered a substitute for the MVA buoyed MVA supporters.[151]

A new determination took hold among MVA advocates. *The Missouri Farmer* excoriated the Pick-Sloan plan in a scathing editorial, warning that the twenty-six proposed Missouri dams were not for flood control but to satisfy Kansas City interests who wanted to deepen the channel. The dams would "ruin approximately 900,000 acres of Missouri's best farm land, and force some 20,000 families out of their homes." The dams would "ruin" six counties and parts of five others. The proposed Table Rock Dam in Taney County would flood "most of the best land" in three counties. Parts of other counties "will be flooded while lakes of water and mud will destroy . . . some of the world's finest springs and beauty spots in Wayne, Reynolds, Shannon, Carter and Ripley counties." Chillicothe "will be located on a peninsula—an enormous lake will almost cover up Livingston County and a corner of Linn County." A dam on the Grand River meant that a fourth of Davies County "will be inundated," and dams on the Meramec River and Big River would "blight" Franklin and Jefferson counties. The editorial concluded that most Missourians in the affected areas "appear not to comprehend what has been done to them," and "the few" who understood Pick-Sloan "seem to believe that their Government 'will not do this thing to us' as one of them recently put it."[152] Warning that "it will be done" without action on the part of the citizenry, *The Missouri Farmer* predicted "that when the people living in these condemned areas of Missouri learn the full import of the new flood control law they will never return any Missouri Congressman to office who voted for it!" Upper Missouri farmers also argued that navigation interests would dominate even under this "compromise" plan.[153]

The November 1944 elections, in which the UE led the CIO efforts, contributed a significant number of new voters, and influenced the outcome, seemed to confirm for the Left the merits of political mobilization with concrete issues such as the MVA. The St. Louis CIO-PAC (political action committee), under the direction of UE staff, enrolled hundreds of supporters who in turn registered sixty thousand new voters. Charles Wright, president of Evansville's Servel local, won a congressional seat. These advances seemed to suggest that Logsdon's goal of politicizing workers was beginning to gain ground.[154]

Assessing Sentner's role in the varied activities that included the campaign for an MVA, the St. Louis office of the FBI reported that Sentner "manifests . . . a belligerent aggressive offense on behalf of labor which is designed to take the part of labor in all its controversies in the St. Louis area. Subject strenuously endeavors to inject himself, as well as the U.E., into any social problem which touches the labor field. It is estimated that the local St. Louis papers carry news stories concerning him on an average of one story or more each week."[155]

In mid-December Sentner, considering the way the MVA unified labor, farmer, and consumer groups, outlined plans for a "movement [that] should become the broadest movement developed since the days of the Populist[s]." Sentner emphasized that the "movement should be local in character but should be linked with the national program." Unions could "be the force that ties in these regional projects with the overall national program, thus prevent[ing] these projects from becoming a political football with regional trades in congress, etc." In order to move on the program, District 8 representatives persuaded their national union office to allocate a staff member to work for the establishment of a St. Louis MVA committee, a nine-state committee, and a national committee to support the MVA.[156] William Chambers, a UE and MVA staffer, emphasized to farm organization allies that UE's goal was to get "community people to take the lead rather than [having] one of the Congressmen [do so]," as some had suggested, in order to keep the campaign a grassroots drive.[157]

In January 1945, the St. Louis committee was formally established, with engineer Raymond Tucker as chair and with representatives from labor, law, veterans groups, women's groups, and church groups. Chambers and Sentner worried that the committee was "weak on industry people," who they thought were necessary to combat criticism of the MVA.[158] Under the guidance of Chambers and Sentner, the group established a speaker's bureau to expand its outreach. Over the course of the next few months, the St. Louis committee speakers went before groups such as the St. Louis Women's Chamber of Commerce, the Liberal Voters League, the St. Louis Branch of the National Association for the Advancement of Colored People (NAACP), local posts of the Veterans of Foreign Wars (VFW), the Missouri Federation of Women's Clubs, and many church groups. By spring 1945, the campaign was yielding "strong official backing from the Catholic Church." This campaign also helped to develop support among business, especially from small businesses, using the argument that by electrifying farms in the Missouri valley, industrial expansion would help many St. Louis businesses. Then, in April 1945, the St. Louis committee scored a major victory. In a referendum, the St. Louis Chamber of Commerce members voted to endorse the MVA.[159]

By early 1945, other city-based committees were organizing in the nine-state region. A new national CIO committee for an MVA laid plans for "reaching every CIO member in the nine-state region on the importance of regionally administered MVA." In addition, other state CIO federations pledged to organize for an MVA and to disseminate material on the MVA through local unions to individual CIO members.[160] Further, the seeds planted in 1944 among AFL unions were beginning to develop into a real coalition. In Kansas City, the AFL was "circulating all the building trades unions in the nine states for support" to establish a nine-state building trades MVA committee. Both the AFL and the CIO held valleywide conferences on the MVA to promote and organize for it. Finally, in spring 1945, a Friends of the Missouri Valley national committee— based in Washington, D.C., and chaired by Thurman Hill—was established and claimed that it would "coordinate efforts of state and local proponents of the MVA." While Sentner was included among the endorsers, he stressed that the impetus for the campaign should remain at the local level.[161]

As the campaign progressed, and even as the issue of jobs and development remained a primary emphasis in the arguments for an MVA, proponents sought to differentiate their proposal from Pick-Sloan by arguing that only through the MVA would concerns for the environment be taken into account. This example speech for the speakers' bureau, probably written by Sentner, stated "We are in the process of closing a three-century long epoch of planless exploitation of the human, natural, and physical resources of North America. During these three centuries, it has been assumed that untrammelled individual initiative would somehow yield the greatest long-run social progress. Now we know the error of that assumption. The practices of the past compel the immediate formulation of regional and national plans. Not to do so now may lead to disaster not many years hence." Another CIO representative suggested that the "present practice regarding rivers is to work backwards. We spend millions of dollars to buy fertilizer to replace ruined soil. We spend millions of dollars to purify river water polluted by soil. But we refuse to spend money to eliminate the conditions which would lead to soil protection and a pure flow of water."[162]

The new Murray Bill, submitted in February 1945, put more emphasis on soil conservation and promised to "restore the declining water table, protect wild game, [and] conserve water, soil, mineral and forest resources" in addition to development through energy dispersion in the upper valley. It also added to the MVA's duties the "disposal of war and defense factories to encourage industrial and business expansion," in line with the increasingly popular idea of decentralization of power. Structurally, the proposed and revised legislation added an advisory committee to be composed of representatives of labor, farmer, business, and citizens' groups, reflecting proponents' attempts to enhance the viability of public input into decentralized, regional planning.[163]

By summer 1945, the ranks of supporters of the coalition had expanded and the campaign had begun to show its effect on opinion in the nine-state area. In May, a Missouri Conference on MVA, organized by the St. Louis group, was sponsored by more than fifty organizations.[164] This meeting spurred the organization of a regional committee for an MVA, founded at a July 1945 convention and headquartered in Omaha. There, hundreds of leaders of various groups (including farmers' groups, labor groups, women's groups, the NAACP, the VFW, and others) voiced their commitment to organize a petition drive for one million signatures to win congressional support for an MVA.[165] A Gallup poll during the summer indicated that three out of every four people in the Missouri River areas favored an MVA.[166]

But the MVA's political fortunes in 1945 certainly failed to match the expectations raised by such polls. Murray expected that the bill would be sent to the agriculture committee, as he had requested and as had been the case with the TVA and similar legislation. But Vice President Truman, who had been considered an "ardent advocate" of an MVA, referred the bill to the Commerce Committee, chaired by a Senator hostile to MVA. It was the first of what many in the campaign would later view as a series of outrageous betrayals by the vice president. Since his early political career, Truman had been a close ally of the USACE and Kansas City navigation interests and in fact "was a friend of Pick's."[167] The MVA bill faced an uphill battle as it steered slowly through two hostile subcommittees, one of which was chaired by John Overton, head of an organization formed to oppose the MVA.[168]

Behind these strong congressional opponents was a growing overlapping coalition opposing the MVA, totaling thirty organizations, that began to mobilize and spend exponentially more than the ten thousand dollars that the pro-MVA forces raised for their entire campaign in 1945. Leading the opposition was the National Association of Electric Companies (NAEC), formed in the summer of 1945 and composed of 170 private power companies that undertook a richly financed campaign to influence public opinion against the MVA. They placed full-page advertisements in newspapers across the nine-state region, financed a weekly radio program, and subsidized the publication of a book attacking the TVA. (A later investigation found that the NAEC had made kickback arrangements with its suppliers to finance anti-MVA propaganda in each state.) Another new organization, the Missouri Valley Development Association, worked with power interests but also began to organize the many other groups that had a stake in keeping out an MVA. These included, for example, upper valley cattlemen, who opposed it because they feared loss of rangeland to irrigation; barge-line operators and river construction contractors, two of many groups with a financial stake in navigation; the Associated General Contractors, who opposed it because an MVA would hire workers directly instead of contracting out to private companies; and the National Reclamation Association, an upper valley group composed of power companies, railroads, chambers of commerce, and corporate ranchers who sought to maintain their entrenched position with the BR.

The Mississippi Valley Development Association (MVDA), which represented navigation interests and was headed by St. Louisan Laclan Macleay, lined up the key testimony at the congressional hearings. The MVDA was especially successful in organizing governors, state legislatures, and business groups to go on record against the MVA.[169] Finally, the MVDA set up an anti-MVA office in St. Louis specifically to target the St. Louis Chamber of Commerce. By October, it was successful in keeping the Chamber of Commerce from acting on its favorable referendum vote to support MVA. As commentators noted, that vote had been "a blow" to anti-MVA forces and had "hampered their campaign ever since. . . . When they attempt to brand MVA and its supporters as 'socialistic,' opponents lay themselves open to the retort, 'The St. Louis Chamber of Commerce voted to support MVA. Is that organization socialistic?'"[170]

Opponents were unified in their arguments against the MVA: it was unnecessary in light of the Pick-Sloan plan, it would establish a "super-government" and was a step toward "state socialism." As Sentner later put it, "All of these organizations assailed MVA as 'unAmerican' and a 'threat to private enterprise.'" Disputing MVA supporters' claims that their plan was a move away from distant government bureaucracy and would place more control in the hands of the citizens of the valley, the opposition groups suggested that the MVA advisory board would interfere with state governments' ability to control the waters of their state and thus their own destiny. Anti-MVA pamphlets with titles such as "Totalitarianism on the March" suggested that sinister forces were involved in the MVA campaign. The MVDA called for an investigation of the pro-MVA campaign, accusing it of "unAmerican activities."[171]

Opponents also charged that most of the pro-MVA advocates at the congressional hearings were "unqualified" to testify on river problems. James Davis, head of the CIO nine-state committee, chafed at this allegation. He retorted that he had "seen with his own eyes" the "mistakes made by army engineers" whose experts had "ruined the farm owned by his family in the Missouri bottomlands." Davis stated that he had "worked for the Army Engineers when they threw the dikes up on the Missouri River. . . . I have seen, in the last four years, land worth $200 an acre covered over with willows and sand because of certain dikes in there, when the floods came. No one up there had any way of knowing which way they were going to channel the river. My experience has been very practical, something I could see." Davis criticized Pick-Sloan for ignoring "any attempt to integrate soil conservation, erosion control, community development or cheap power," as called for by the citizenry. He also noted that Murray's bill at least provided a role for "the farmer, the business man, and labor," and "reaches all walks of life." Davis's statement suggested that the field of vision of the program was extending to a critique of the Progressive-era "cult of the expert" in government agencies. The theme of the MVA was that ordinary people should have a say in the construction of the space they inhabited.[172]

By the fall, when it was clear that the MVA bill was being picked apart in committee hearings, Murray asked that further hearings be postponed. Meanwhile, Sentner and other activists outlined the longer-term political fight that would have to be waged, state by state, around the issue. Sentner reflected cogently on the entrenched opposition, but he remained focused on the growth of the coalition that had come together over the issue. The campaign for the MVA, he noted, "has united progressive forces . . . as they have never been united before"; had been the catalyst for the organization of citizens' groups in various cities, including St. Louis; and had united farm and labor groups in a way that no other issue had been able to do. "Farmers Union and MFA leaders addressed Labor Day picnics and are speaking at the state conventions of labor organizations this fall," while groups such as the Catholic Rural Life Conference, among the most progressive forces in the Catholic Church, had become energized over the issue. The "movement has grown . . . and no longer can be considered as a simple movement in support of a piece of legislation. It is and must be considered as a major political movement with all of the elements of populism which is so native to our section of the country. . . . This movement[,] if given proper support and guidance, can go out in the 1946 election campaign and make a major contribution to the election of progressive members of the U.S. Congress and Senate."[173]

Sentner's vision of a unified grassroots campaign was stymied by the myriad problems and divisions in postwar-era labor politics, the subject of chapter 6. After 1945, the CIO on a national and local level found itself in a contest in which business sought to reassert its power over workers at the same time that anticommunist drives severely divided the labor movement. The MVA proposal continued to garner significant popular support in the postwar era, at least through 1948. The CIO continued to support the proposal, but Philip Murray and John Brophy excluded Sentner from representation on the MVA committees and centralized the campaign from its Washington, D.C., offices, appointing lackluster bureaucrats to organize it.[174] This was certainly not the locally based campaign that Sentner was sure was the key to success. While publicly calling for planning in the postwar era, the CIO seemed unable to mount the serious campaign for it in the face of the rebounding postwar economy, which disproved the predictions of a return to Depression-era conditions. Pent-up consumer demand boosted the economy until late 1948, when a severe recession set in. Then, with the onset of the Cold War and of the hot war in Korea, defense spending surreptitiously crept in as a jobs program that both the CIO and conservatives could accept. In St. Louis, Emerson Electric was just one of many businesses that benefited from these developments. It was a new kind of planning that replaced the visions of participatory planning articulated during the war. The MVA reemerged and seemed to have good prospects in 1948, when more floods devastated the Missouri and Mississippi valleys. Yet by this time, the grassroots campaign had little chance of getting off the ground because the CIO was torn apart by the Cold War anticommunist campaigns. While the CIO gave lip service to the need for the legislation, it kept a tight rein on leftist participation and directed the campaign from Washington, D.C.[175]

One analyst has suggested that the "debate over valley authorities was one of the few wide-ranging explorations into the structure of the American economy," an "inquiry into large issues . . . of political economy."[176] For District 8's Left, it was an attempt to engage in a type of political discourse that drew on workers' own hopes for a better postwar world. The interaction between the labor movement and progressive farm groups and conservationists had moved labor from a developmental perspective and toward a prefigurative environmentalist approach to floods. It is well to remember that the community-based grassroots strategies developed with the encouragement of the Left, which sought to engage workers in support of extraordinarily visionary programs in economic, environmental, and democratic reform. Nevertheless, the structure of the CIO and labor politics in the postwar era ensured that these lofty ideas lacked a community-based grassroots campaign that could have brought them to the center of political action as well as discourse. Moreover, the die cast between labor and the Democratic Party was clearly a factor in killing the proposal, as Truman could play politics with the MVA and bear no consequences for the betrayal. One has to wonder whether even a small Farmer-Labor party in Iowa such as Sentner and the CP abandoned would have propelled this politics forward. By 1948, Sentner and the CP would agree that a third party was an absolute necessity. But by then the possibilities for coalition based on alternative politics was over.[177]

In the middle of the war, Sentner seemed sanguine about the prospects for the Left's influence on the CIO's postwar agenda. "We can be proud that the CIO has made our community action program its own, that where we get in and pitch, we more than get full support for this program by the leaders and membership of other CIO unions." James Matles, writing to Sentner, credited District 8's community campaigns with helping the entire UE formulate their agenda: "[I] feel that the development of such a program on a national scale should put our outfit out in the front not only as far as the labor movement is concerned but even as far as the nation is concerned." In late 1945, Sentner also boasted to district shop stewards that the national UE was taking cues from the community campaigns that had developed from District 8 and was calling for advice for its showdown with GE in the great 1945–46 strike. That District 8 organizer Vic Pasche was sent to that campaign was a signal that the UE was thinking seriously about how to develop further its community-based campaigns, which might help to redefine unionism and civic life in the postwar period. Lisa Kannenberg has noted that this marked a shift toward an approach that incorporated women and civic concerns in a way that differentiated Schenectady's UE from the rest of the local CIO there.

District 8 activists were also gaining insights from its encounter with the farmers' movement during the war. After attending a convention of the Farmers' Union, Logsdon expressed that the UE should learn from that organization, especially how they achieved a high degree of activism among women. The percentage of women attending the convention was "far higher," and they took a "more active part" than in any union convention he had observed, in part because of the influence of the women's auxiliaries. To develop the union as a force to build worker power, they would need to think about how to get the UE women's auxiliaries more "fully integrated into the UE and to further develop their women activists."[178]

By the time Logsdon wrote this, the district Left was already engaged in a rearguard battle that robbed the union of the energy to fully pursue these ideas. Anticommunism came to redefine civic life in the postwar era in a way that destroyed the vision of union-based community coalitions and reinforced a fratricidal war that allowed capital to exert newfound power in the community and the nation.

CHAPTER 6

"To Be Full-Fledged Citizens of This Union"
Contesting Anticommunism, 1945–50

The goal of organizing and mobilizing workers through community campaigns, politicizing workers, and addressing corporate control of the political economy was subsumed by the intense factionalism that gripped the district in the years after World War II. During this time, Sentner's membership in the Communist Party (CP) became the focus of a campaign that charged him with being a Communist "strongman" who controlled the district as part of the "international Communist conspiracy."[1]

In combating this campaign, the Left tried to suggest that the right to association was enmeshed with the struggle for human rights and the extension of worker power. They tried to direct workers' attention to the class-based assault on unions in the postwar period. Indeed, District 8's "militant minority" continued to recruit workers new to the union during and immediately after the war to endorse the idea of challenging managerial control through a vigorous defense of shop floor and community campaigns that had come to define the district. District 8 advocated aggressive policing and expansion of shop floor rights, directing stewards to search for shopwide grievances that ultimately allowed workers greater direction over their jobs. The Left still argued that arbitration, used effectively, could expand workers' rights, while District 8 employers continued to vigorously oppose arbitration. As the district set its agenda in the immediate postwar period, it also looked to expand its regional influence by solid community-based organizing campaigns on its southern periphery. In addition, it sought to establish pattern agreements in the industry, but these were patterns that did not substitute local power with national officialdom. Instead, it sought to enhance worker power and to prevent corporations from whipsawing and decentralization strategies with a creative reliance on its strongest local link, a rank-and-file pattern bargaining that harkened back to the early-twentieth-century battles between the National Metal Trades Association (NMTA) and the Federated Metal Trades Council of St. Louis and Vicinity. The Left sought to use its strengths in one area, community-based mobilizations, and communications across union and shop boundaries to strengthen pattern bargaining in a way that put employers on the defensive about low wages and reduced rights. These efforts, which differentiated District 8 from the rest of the Congress of Industrial Organizations (CIO), climaxed in the heated battle to get a contract at Bucyrus-Erie (B-E) and puts the use of the anticommunist issue and employers' role in combating the Left in a larger context of the political economy of control.

With this issue, as with others, postwar struggles in District 8 reveal clear distinctions related to ideology and alliances. Certainly most workers found Sentner's ties to the CP objectionable. And it is important to emphasize that the grassroots internal UE movement in opposition to the Left was initiated within the union movement, not orchestrated by employers. But in District 8, employers and very reactionary forces were part of the equation that challenged the Left. The coalition that opposed the Left in the district sought to make association the key issue and argued for the elimination of any leader who had supported Sentner. They chose to ally even with reactionary forces in the community, including racists and antiunion employer forces. They parlayed the countersubversive tradition that some coalition members had revived in the 1930s and for which they seemed to be awaiting the next opportunity, an opportunity that rang out in the context of an international Cold War. This coalition sought to polarize the membership over the issue of communism and suggested that the Left was an outside influence and outside the bounds of sound trade unionism. Nevertheless, governmental and corporate elements contributed most of the leverage for the elimination of the social unionism that had defined District 8.

Origins of the Anticommunist Drive

Sentner's open declaration of his membership in the CP in the 1943 *Fortune* magazine interview made him an ideal target for attacks on District 8 in the postwar period. Whereas the charges against the United Electrical, Radio and Machine Workers Union of America (UE) nationally and within other districts were often unsubstantiated allegations, there was no room for doubt in District 8; the head of the district was a Communist.

Why did Sentner choose to reverse his 1940 formal resignation from the party? Clearly, he held serious reservations about secrecy, even though he had used his formal resignation when expedient. For example, when Servel's attorneys refused to participate in the 1941 National Labor Relations Board (NLRB) hearings on the grounds that Sentner was a Communist, Sentner shouted back, "That's a lie!" Later that day he calmly argued that his politics were not relevant to the question of union recognition.[2] Sentner believed that secrecy fueled conceptions of "conspiracy" about the party that he believed were wrongheaded, both for the party's sake and for the sake of the trade union movement.

Following Sentner's 1941 victory for district president against the anticommunist candidate, both Sentner and Logsdon agreed that secrecy was a bad policy. Logsdon, in a letter to the national UE stressing the importance of trying to build workers' understanding of the connections between shop floor issues and larger political issues, concluded: "One final factor—the Red question. It is time for us to quit any quibbling on this. We may as well face it now as later. The Dies Committee had a big splurge in the *Chicago Tribune* naming several UE leaders as Communists, and I do not think that a single one of our members got excited."[3]

Sentner thought that CP trade unionists had to connect their politics more openly to a rejection of capitalist power and a vision of democratic worker control. He felt that workers and their allies would accept their right to be members if the issue was presented as a civil liberties right to expression. As Toni Sentner later emphasized, "the basis of his work in the trade union movement was his belief in the socialist system, that each should have a job regardless of race, color, creed; each should have a home; each should have enough to eat; [as well as a] right to good education, right to expression, a right to one's beliefs and religion." Sentner felt that these goals were nothing that he should be ashamed of or have to hide. "So, for [some to say] I accept you as a leader, you're doing okay for me in the trade union movement, [but I don't want you to express your politics]—that wouldn't work! Because that's what he believed in. And that's why he became active in the labor movement."[4] Morris Levin, a district attorney, suggested that integrity played a role: "He was a man of principle" who "always held his head high about his politics."[5]

Sentner believed that open affiliation was the only way to allow workers to draw connections between their own desires and alternative ideologies. During the war, as Sentner observed workers' enthusiasm for participation in postwar planning that sought solutions outside the capitalist market, he became more and more convinced that "people like Communism when they are not aware that is what they are getting." He concluded before a CP meeting that workers "are getting something for nothing," that an openly socialist alternative needed to be part of the postwar agenda. Repression of earlier socialist and radical movements had robbed workers of their own ideological legacy. Sentner argued that the CP was the inheritor of a long radical tradition going back to the abolitionists but that from the base in the trade union movement, and with open advocacy, the ideology to which the CP was heir could be legitimated. At the 1945 UE District 8 Convention, Sentner remarked wittily to the delegates: "[One] brother told me that Communists are clever. They do things that you are in favor of." He agreed and urged workers to see that the concepts of socialism were in sync with their own democratic hopes for the future.[6] Sentner believed that Communists would continue to revive a radical legacy only if democratic ideas that challenged capitalism but were part of a socialist alternative were actually presented to workers.[7] In an exchange with District 8 convention delegates in 1946, he argued that the CP was simply another political party, like the Republican or the Democratic Party, thereby linking the party to democratic traditions. Suggestions that the CP was an agent of a foreign power ("a lie") were designed to prevent workers from examining the party's ideas seriously.[8]

Those who knew him well never doubted Sentner's strong personal commitment to democracy in theory and in practice. In an early 1939 speech, probably given at a St. Louis CP meeting, Sentner claimed:

> Communists make their program known—they do not fly under false colors—they openly state they feel that socialism, the highest form of democracy[,] is the only solution to the economic and political ills of our nation ... and that this will be achieved when and only when the vast majority of the American people want socialism. I am a member of the CP. My office in my union is an elective post. . . . When the time comes that I no longer serve the best interest of the membership of my union, I am sure that they will exercise their democratic prerogative and elect someone else.[9]

In this example, Sentner tied his vision of socialism and the CP to familiar trade union–based democratic structures that were understandable in U.S. experience, not modeled on Soviet Union structures. Throughout the campaigns that centered on his membership, Sentner pointed to the democratic structures he had sought to create in the trade union movement as the model for his own vision of socialism.

No matter how truly democratic his vision of socialism was, Sentner could not single-handedly overcome the party's many liabilities, among them workers' belief that regardless of whether it was a conspiracy there was indeed something "foreign" about it and that its leadership did march lockstep to the Soviet Union line on foreign policy. By acknowledging openly that he was a Communist, Sentner accepted a heavy burden indeed, not the least because, as he occasionally acknowledged, the party did not live up to his idealized portrayal of it. The *Fortune* article described Sentner as a "Communist proud of his political beliefs" whose trade unionism was not controlled by party interference and who "doesn't talk party jargon." Sentner declared that "the C.P. never ran Bill Sentner. . . . No one fools around with what I believe and I don't fool around with what they believe."[10]

It would be misleading, however, to suggest that Sentner was just a trade unionist who borrowed from party doctrine to suit his own purposes. Sentner continued to hope that the party would be the agent that would move American workers toward a socialist future. He thought it essential that the party determine the "correct line" for the direction of the labor movement just as it had in the concentration policy that had directed activists toward organizing Emerson years before. For this reason, Sentner had doubts about the party line during

World War II. In early 1945, he upbraided those CP unionists whose solution to the party's position was to "run away from strikes" rather than offer solutions. He refused to join Herbert Benjamin, the new head of the Missouri CP, in condemning the union involved in the most heated labor conflict of the St. Louis war period, the transit strike of 1944. Though he supported party leader Earl Browder on many points, he obviously did not agree with the party line that the "struggle for socialism should be shelved for the foreseeable future." According to a Federal Bureau of Investigation (FBI) informant, Sentner emphasized in a CP meeting that "after the war has been won, then comes the fight for socialism and this will not be possible without a fight."[11] (This line, if indeed reliable, was probably intended to contest party policy but was later used in a distorted way in his Smith Act trial to persuade a jury that he was referring to violent overthrow of the government.)

Sentner, like many in the party, was jolted by the criticism of CP chair Earl Browder by French Communist leader Jacques Duclos, who charged that the American CP had engaged in "class-collaboration" during the war.[12] This burst the dams of Sentner's qualms about party direction. In June 1945 Sentner wrote to William Foster and to the CP's National Committee and suggested that the problem with the party's wartime line was that it had not been based on American workers' experiences during the war. Sentner complained that the party's advice to trade unionists had caused them to be easy prey to anticommunist "opportunists" such as Walter Reuther. Citing District 8's own postwar conferences, in which only a handful of businessmen supported extending "workers' democratic rights in the postwar," he complained that the party had done little that was constructive in battling American industry's "ideological influences over the working class." He concluded that party leaders were out of touch with the American working class. The attempt to suppress criticism within the party "reflects a lack of confidence in the working people and must be cut out" of the CP's work. In addition, "members of the National Committee responsible for creating this kind of undemocratic non-Communist atmosphere, which prevents the fullest discussion of policy questions, have no place in the leadership of our Communist movement." Finally, the party needed to "cut out the cancer of isolation from the main stream of the American labor movement" and "promote and develop within our leading committees, local trade union leaders, shop stewards and rank and file workers from the unions and the shop." Only when "a majority of our leading committees from top to bottom are composed of workers actively associated with the mainstream of American labor [will the party be] capable of understanding and solving realistically the complex problems that confront America and its toiling millions."[13]

Sentner attempted to convey his views on the floor of the national CP convention in late July 1945, though he was not an official delegate. One of Sentner's supporters regretted that the "criticism did not go over so hot." Nevertheless,

Sentner was probably encouraged by the party's new commitment to recruit and promote industrial workers to leading positions.[14] In any case, his enthusiasm for the party did not dampen after this point, though his independent position apparently caused the party hierarchy to be suspicious of him. The cruelest irony, one indicative of the tangled history of the CP, is that during part of the time that Sentner was defending his right to his political beliefs before District 8's membership, he was "suspended" from the CP because of "doubt as to his loyalty to the organization," a fact he learned only years later.[15]

More ironic still was the fact that Sentner's attempt to prod the CP toward more democracy and contact with workers fueled the anticommunist campaign in District 8. The district's anticommunist faction cited Sentner's criticisms, printed in the letters section of the *Daily Worker* in mid-July 1945, as evidence of the party's effort to influence and control workers.[16]

Logsdon recalled that Sentner's rhetoric on labor-management issues did appear to shift in correspondence with the Duclos letter. An "embarrassing" episode was still etched in his mind years later. He had agreed to let Sentner speak before a St. Louis CIO council meeting on issues of wartime reconversion and labor-management cooperation. Logsdon was taken aback by Sentner's bellicose rhetoric during the speech. That night, he claimed, he found out about the Duclos letter and was seething with anger. "I gave it to him!" he exclaimed. "I told him he was marching this way and that and was doing it right in front of everybody. He tried to claim he wasn't, that [this] was the way he felt." This exchange speaks to the degree of open dialogue on party positions in district leadership that resulted from Sentner's open position. Sentner was in constant negotiation about the validity and applicability of CP policy toward union affairs. Logsdon regretted that incidents such as this cast a pall of suspicion over Sentner among some of the shop stewards, because in practice Sentner never imposed CP policy but would usually toss out an idea that was from the CP "line" to "maybe a half-dozen of us. . . . You see, if there were things that he couldn't even convince us of, we told him, 'Don't take it up.' He'd boil sometimes, but he wouldn't. He listened to us." But while the policy was negotiated with members and they might support socialist statements on the part of their district president, they were not willing to defend the CP and its many liabilities forever.[17]

Sentner vastly underestimated the potential for an anticommunist drive in the postwar period. In 1942, when Eustius Brendle, president of Local 1102, nominated Sentner for president of the district, Sentner viewed this as a turning point.[18] According to Logsdon, wartime politics and alliances caused Sentner to declare that there "would be no red-baiting after the war." Logsdon "just laughed" in response, recognizing it as a product of Sentner's optimistic personality. When Bishop William Scarlett learned that Sentner's party membership would be revealed in the *Fortune* article, he urged the reporter to warn Sentner that this would have serious repercussions for his position as a labor leader. Sentner brushed off such warnings, happily distributing copies of the *Fortune* article to many associates.[19] The publicity of the article brought a visit from the FBI, which forced him to attest to his affiliation and then compelled him to resign from the National War Labor Board.[20]

The key figure in the district's anticommunist coalition was James Click, Emerson's chief shop steward, who led the 1941 campaign against Sentner. Click, twenty-eight years old in 1945 when he began the drive, came of age during the Depression and had considered himself "something of a socialist" in the 1930s. His father was what he called "a belly socialist" who brought his family to St. Louis in 1925 from Tennessee when farming was no longer viable, got a job on the railroad, and ran for Missouri state representative on the Socialist Party (SP) ticket in the early years of the Great Depression. Click attributed the origins of his antipathy to the CP to his childhood memories, when he had observed Communists heckling his father's soapbox speeches. "I had a wee bit of bitterness about them before I even met those in the UE." He went on to state, "But then the flip-flops! The flip-flops in policy in the leadership of the District, whenever there was a change in the world situation." Sentner's stance on the war, he knew, had been clearly influenced by fealty to the Soviet Union.[21] Click had determined to contest Sentner long before the party's change of line in mid-1945, in an alliance with new forces emerging in the district.[22]

Click was not a very compelling figure and relied on the saliency of the Communist issue to challenge Sentner.[23] Even his champion, the *St. Louis Globe-Democrat,* in a 1951 feature article titled "Meet the Fellow Who Whipped Bill Sentner," noted that friends called him a "cold potato" and "a man you have to know for a long time to really like."[24] Thomas Knowles, an Emerson shop steward whom Sentner tried to recruit to the party, argued that without the Communist issue, Click would never have vied for district president: "he seemed like an egghead rather than a union leader." When Knowles started work at Emerson in 1941, he considered Click part of Local 1102's old guard leadership at Emerson, "useless" as far as enforcing a "beautiful contract" whose shop steward and grievance provisions could have gained more workers' rights. But he added that Click began to get more aggressive and ended the war with a good reputation of service to the workers, though not a reputation for militancy.[25]

According to Lloyd Austin, shop steward at Emerson's downtown electrical plant, the anticommunist drive originated at Emerson when Click decided to abandon the Left and in the context of shop floor and contract troubles. Click, Austin argued, decided to use the anticommunist issue to unify the local behind his leadership:

> Click told me he was concerned about some of the people who were coming into the union during the war. [He] saw [that] they were opportunistic. Many of these people were flexing their muscle [in the wildcats, for example,] to

advance themselves, but they didn't have the kind of union-consciousness, the spirit of one for all and all for one. A lot of these guys came to get these defense jobs just to get out of the service; these were the ones that became our union leaders [after the war]! They wanted shop stewards jobs because shop stewards had top seniority, and they wouldn't lose their jobs after the war.[26]

The Emerson wartime wildcats, Austin and Knowles made clear, were organized by a faction of former United Automobile Workers (UAW) and International Association of Machinists skilled trades workers who aimed to use strife to take Emerson workers into one of these unions. Knowles, who was involved with the group for a while, said that "they were just trying to stir up something so they could hold an election and take the local out of the UE." Austin claimed that "Click was really worried about the in-fighting and about their motivations but wasn't enough of a leader to bring everybody all together." Sentner tried to bring all factions together on a "constructive" program, "but Click was too afraid of getting together with Sentner, for fear of being red-baited" by other factions. Austin and others on the Left tried to get an education program for new workers without union experience. Click expressed support for the Left privately and, according to Austin, assured him: "Don't worry, Lloyd, these people will be gone after the war, and we'll be in charge." But then Click "left me and people like Bob Heim [a shop steward close to Sentner] out in the cold. He thought it would label him.... Then come[s] the end of the war, and we found he had gone to the other side. When he saw they [the new group] were getting too strong, he went on their side, and he used anticommunism [to unify their group.] He double-crossed us."[27] The leftists in the local who had backed Click on Sentner's and Logsdon's advice became an increasingly isolated group whose strongest adherents felt under siege as they were targeted for their support of Sentner.

Sentner and Logsdon had tried to work with Click because he held relatively "progressive views" on race issues and adhered to "CIO policy" regarding wildcats during the war, a policy also pushed by the CP. They had supported him and had abandoned efforts to send Logsdon into the local to rebuild the leftist presence. Sentner might have calculated that he could keep the conservative forces at bay because Symington, whom the conservatives trusted, gave him legitimacy. In July 1945, Symington, realizing that the good times of cost plus profits were over, left Emerson, becoming head of the Truman administration's Surplus Property Board, and that source of legitimacy was gone. Logsdon recognized that the Left had miscalculated about the Emerson local and about Click, the source of the anticommunist drive.[28] Logsdon still held raw feelings years later, lambasting Click as a "plain, out and out opportunist" who "used" the anticommunism issue to advance himself. Logsdon charged that Click, worried about "tints and hues" of his own association with socialism, was forced to "out-red-bait the red-baiters.... Truthfully, I don't think he could stand to take the heat. Heat got hot in the kitchen. The red-baiting got hot. He didn't want to get tarred. He wanted to get ahead. So, he could serve two purposes. He could get away from [being] red-bait[ed], and he could get a better job."[29]

Click and the anticommunist faction made no differentiation between those who were Communists and those who supported the right of Communists to be part of the trade union movement, asserting that anyone who supported Sentner was a Communist or a dupe. Years later, Click still held that position: "Logsdon swore . . . that he had never been a member of the Communist Party. . . . I used to say to him, 'That's the only thing that says you're not, because all your actions say you are!' I said, 'You look like one, you talk like one, you act like one. So whether you say you are one or not doesn't make any difference to me.'" Click regarded Communist influence as evil, compelled by forces more powerful than ideology. Sentner's refusal to give up the party even when it might have saved his union position was explained by that hold: "once in the party, they have a grip on you, and you never leave." Only those who were expelled or who openly renounced the party and revealed information about it had really left the party (the same position Joseph McCarthy adhered to). Sentner's motivation, he argued, was like "all of those in the Communist Party. . . . Their primary purpose was not to organize the union. It was to get members of the CP."[30]

"We were against the whole concept of Communism in the labor movement and in the United States," insisted William Drohan. Drohan and John Burns, both young skilled trades workers and later union officials at Emerson, labeled themselves the "brains trust" behind the anticommunist campaign and took over especially the publication of the local's newspaper to have a base to attack the Left. Drohan felt that the goals of the union movement were "perverted" by the association with communism. Burns considered Sentner's public appearances at meetings that supported Soviet-American friendship evidence of "treasonous" behavior that made Burns "ashamed." Eugene Paul, another young skilled worker at Emerson Electric who was part of this faction, called Sentner a "madman" for being a Communist and blamed him for the derision Paul endured from his neighbors: "'Oh, you're part of that Communist union,' they would say."[31] Sentner's identification as a Communist in St. Louis newspapers angered some of the union members. When Sentner was identified as president of UE District 8 at CP events during and after the war or after the *Fortune* article was relayed in condensed form in the *Post-Dispatch*, they felt personally violated. In July 1945, a *Business Week* article identified the Emerson local as being CP-dominated. Local 1102 demanded a retraction.[32]

Click reflected: "There were an awful lot of us whose primary ideology was the union and not something else. Who were politically active but not to the point of being a slave to somebody's thoughts." That reasoning led Click to contend that ideology had no legitimate role in the union, a point that undermined support for the socialist viewpoint as well. Nevertheless, the SP arranged meetings in mid-1945 and in 1946 with UAW figures and others to plan for the factional battle in the UE, and these contacts encouraged the fight and proved vital later on for building a national movement.[33]

Click, who described himself as someone "without a religion," recognized the value of the anticommunist stance of the Catholic Church. As Steve Rosswurm has shown, beginning in 1944 and 1945 "Catholic laborites waged a relentless war against CIO Communists and those who worked with them," and these activists played a significant role in the postwar drive. Click acknowledged the valuable assistance of Father Leo Brown, a Jesuit priest who established the St. Louis Labor College at St. Louis University in 1943. Brown, who had become an arbitrator during the war, taught courses to union and management representatives "so that he might affect their thinking" and contest the influence of the CP that he viewed as damaging to the union movement and to "harmonious" relations. Courses on world communism labeled Communists in the labor movement as part of a worldwide conspiracy.[34] Burns proudly stated that he and Drohan were part of an "Irish Catholic gang" assisted by Father Brown to rid the union of Communists. Burns credited Brown with "schooling" them to "beat the Commies." "We were closely allied with him," Drohan recalled. "We used to sneak up the alley to St. Louis University from our union offices on West Pine to Father Leo Brown. We said we wanted an education" on how to wrest power from the Left. Brown taught them practical skills that he claimed were the "Commie methods" of controlling unions, including manipulation of parliamentary procedure to get membership approval for resolutions. Tactics such as building support within a membership meeting by strategic placement of advocates (a diamond shape) seemed to Burns deliciously devious and effective.[35] Of course, it oversimplified the complicated support for the Left in the district. In fact, had the Left been built on such a simplistic basis, it would never have survived to that point.

In building this movement, Click knew that he was allying with forces that were reactionary. Click clearly had some qualms about where such involvement might lead: "Some of us in the anticommunist drive used to jokingly refer to the red international and the black international." Their alliance with a "black international" was something that they sought to cover. It is clear, however, that Click and his supporters became convinced with each defeat that drastic measures were justified in breaking Sentner's hold on the union structure, allying not only with reactionary religious forces but also with racists and employers.[36]

Anticommunism gave a respectable cover for racist sentiment and opportunism in some cases. In mid-1945, Click's faction formed a coalition with the right wing of Small Arms Local 825 (U.S. Cartridge), which had the largest bloc of votes in the district despite severe cutbacks and layoffs at U.S. Cartridge. In Local 825, the leftist leadership had been identified with the position of plantwide integration of blacks and with "integration of Negroes into the life of the local." Though much progress had been made by 1944, Logsdon worried that "until all of the officers of this local take a firm position, this issue will continue to be a thorn in the side of everyone connected with the local union."[37] Instead, as periodic layoffs heightened insecurity, some officers used red-baiting together with race-baiting to produce a countermovement among a segment of white workers opposed to the Left's agenda. "There is a group within the plant," Logsdon reported in January 1944, "whose only objective is to disrupt and seize control of the local at election time next June." In June, this group elected a few more members to the executive board. By August, when union officer Betty Raab ceded her delegate spot to ensure black representation, she was "severely criticized" as a dupe of Sentner.[38]

Then in December 1944, as mass layoffs threatened, the local was "split wide open over the issue of employing Negroes." In a membership meeting, the Left moved to reaffirm the union's position on the integration of black workers by specifying that they should be "allowed to work in a non-segregated sense in the Packing and Shipping Departments of the Company." The meeting voted to support the proposal, but a small faction succeeded in getting the membership to reconsider and reverse its affirmation. After an acrimonious debate, Raab and Otto Maschoff resigned their positions as secretary and president of the local in protest, thereby ceding control of the local. "There is growing hostility between white and Negro workers in the plant," Logsdon reported in May 1945, "fermented [*sic*] by the position of the majority of the Executive Board of the local union."[39] Logsdon derisively noted that the officers of the local were "bitterly anti-Negro, anti-red and anti-national office. . . . [T]hey got their jobs by appealing to the prejudices of the workers and faithfully follow that line now."[40]

The local's officers eyed its substantial treasury as their personal severance package and the means through which they could campaign full-time against the district Left. "The Local office is overstaffed, but resolutely determined to do nothing about it," Logsdon complained. The officers, Maschoff protested, declared that a vote to continue to pay their salaries for six months after the plant closed "passed even though the majority of the people present clearly voted no on a voice vote and then the chair adjourned [the meeting] to prevent a standing vote of those present." Under the UE national constitution, if a local disbanded, the treasury reverted to the national office. Harvey Smith, a Local 825 executive board member, remembered that when Logsdon asked him if there would be any treasury left, he gleefully replied, "not if we can help it!" Meanwhile, Smith and other officers strategized with Local 1102's faction to gain control of the district in the next election.[41]

An opportunity for the right-wing coalition emerged in summer 1945, when District 8 won an agreement with the state Unemployment Compensation Commission through which workers could refuse to take a job at less than 90 percent of their previous hourly earnings. The district set up a center to process veterans, using representatives from each local. Logsdon complained that "a horrible mess ensued" when the center became the venue for attacks by right-wing forces. Local 825 "hired a former AFL [American Federation of Labor] waitress-organizer who led in the fight against Negroes at Small Arms" as their representative to the center. Harvey Smith remembered that it was there that James Click suggested that Smith should get a job at Wagner Electric in order to plant an anticommunist activist in the local, where the Right was weak.[42]

Framing the Debate

The official opening salvo by the anticommunist campaign was a resolution to eliminate District 8's direct election of officers, a wondrously ironic fact given that the whole campaign in the public eye was to suggest that the CP control mimicked Soviet totalitarianism. At the national level, the UE anticommunist forces fought for a referendum election for officers, suggesting that the CP exerted control through convention elections. District 8 was the only UE district with a direct member referendum election. In the August 1945 district council meeting, Click argued that the district should follow other UE districts and use an annual district convention delegate vote. The resolution was intended to give a quick victory to the anticommunists based on the combination of Local 1102 and Local 825 votes. A resolution embodying the demand for rescinding the referendum lost by a close vote of 130–113. Sentner felt that the resolution might pass at the October district convention.[43]

But Click's faction never reintroduced it. Or it might have seemed incongruous to charge Sentner with stifling the "democratic forces in our union" through "Communist control" while asking for less direct democracy in the union. Perhaps because some of Local 825's delegates were rejected, they may have realized they did not have votes needed. Those charges, including the assertion that staff had to promise loyalty to the CP line whether or not they were members, dominated the convention's opening session.[44]

Click's faction sought to admit Local 825's delegates despite evidence that some had not been democratically elected. Debate over the issue was rancorous, with Click implying that the constitutional issue was a cover for political motives to keep out Local 825's right-wing delegates. But evidence of irregularities in voting in Local 825 was stark. Click argued that the district "should not be bound too much by the constitution" and should seat the delegates anyway. Others in the anticommunist camp suggested that "a constitution has to be stretched a little bit for the benefit of all members and not a few." The convention refused to seat the delegates, thereby considerably reducing the voting bloc for the anticommunists.[45]

In response to Click's resolution, Logsdon and Sentner established key themes at the convention to counter anticommunism: first, that the UE was not controlled by the CP; second, that the union should confirm the right of Communists to be a part of the union movement; and third, that red-baiting led to divisions that aided employers and obstructed the union's efforts to gain power. Logsdon condemned the anticommunist leaflet as "a lie! . . . Nobody has attacked me as a Red. I'd like to see it. I believe in our constitution." Scoffing at the suggestion that the district organizers might be Communists, he reminded delegates that "this union was founded on the notion that anybody working for a living whether red, black or white, Catholic, Protestant or Jew, Communist, Democrat or Republican or anyone else had a right to membership. . . . The day that fails, that is the day this Union moves down hill. That is the beginning of all forms of discrimination, not only of the Reds, but the Negroes, the women, in some shops religious persecution. . . . The people who wrote this are afraid of American democracy. This is a country of free expression, of certain basic rights, a country that grew up with certain traditions. This approach means abandoning that."[46]

Sentner asked delegates to recall their direct "experiences with me," which would show that "I don't take orders from anybody, except the desires of the membership of our Union." Reminding them of "the reputation and respect" the union had among employers—"They may not like us. We don't expect them to. Sometimes we bludgeon them, we black ball them, they don't forget it; but they have respect"—and "among our friends," he warned that the movement afoot would do serious damage to unity and to community respect necessary to make further advances for the membership. Sentner recounted a list of district staff, showing that most had come out of the shop ("the policy of this Union") and most were not "red." He reminded Click of the times he had asked him for suggestions for union positions and of the three times since 1940 he had asked him to join the staff.[47]

Sentner refuted the charge that he had a hidden agenda: "You know that I am a member of the Communist Party. I think I must decide that for myself, my own politics, if I believe in socialism and I believe in it, deeply, and I think the Communist Party is an organization by which we can advance the interests of the people of this country toward the direction of accepting Socialism, when the people decide they want to. I believe that sooner or later the people of this country are going to have to nationalize the banks. I believe the government has to take over the natural resources." He added that "I don't believe the people in the US are ready for socialism" and that it would not serve his aims to impose his views on anyone.[48]

Challenging the "implication" of the leaflet's charge that "democratic forces" were "submerged" by the Communists, Sentner contended that "no union in the U.S.A. enjoys more democracy within their organization" than the UE. He derided the notion that he and Logsdon were "trying to take over any Local Union," adding "why should we." (Later, Sentner issued an "open letter" to Click reminding him that Sentner "refused to seize control" of Local 1102 when Click had requested it during World War II wildcats.) While admitting to "mistakes" in the past, Sentner said that "I challenge anybody to say we haven't done a job on behalf of our membership" and asked delegates to "judge me and my work in the labor movement on what I am doing," to keep an "open mind." He went on to say, "I hope that each of you will take the issue with me and make your membership articulate so we will have this democracy that you talk about. Don't jam it down and say there are 10 guys in this plant. . . . Anything they say is no good because they are Reds. . . . Look at his opinions. . . . As far as I am concerned when you want to talk Communism with me, I'll talk all night with you, if I can stand it. But not until we finish this strike or this contract."[49]

When the voting concluded in late October, Sentner and William Cuthbert (of the Maytag local) won the contest by a margin of nearly three to one. Only Emerson Local 1102 and Century Local 1108 voted overwhelmingly for Click and Lenhardt. Small Arms Local 825 and Wagner Local 1104, the other two large locals in St. Louis, gave a majority vote to Sentner, as did all but one other local.[50] While a group of black workers signed and distributed a leaflet titled "William Sentner, the Man Who Fights for the Rights of the Negro People," Click's faction went to Mt. Carmel, Illinois, and predicted that the Communist leaders of the district "were going to send our Negro people down" to take the jobs of white workers.[51] By the time of the next district convention in March 1946, there were significantly less support for Click's faction among the delegates and a significant internal momentum against the anticommunist faction. Local 825 was dissolved amidst more specific revelations of financial malfeasance and race-baiting. With the plant shut down, it would no longer provide any base for Click's faction, which in any case was further diminished by the Servel election victory in Evansville.[52]

The 1946 Servel Victory: Community-Based Unionism Boosts the Left

Recall that in Evansville, Servel had been the major bulwark against unionism. Since 1937, District 8 had attempted to organize plants in the city, some with disastrous results such as the 1939 strike against Servel discussed in chapter 3. District 8's first major breakthrough in Evansville came when it organized Sunbeam (now Seeger), Faultless, and some other smaller shops. But by 1944, Local 813, the amalgamated UE local in Evansville (replacing the original Local 1002), gained its first toehold in Servel, by isolating strong points of unionism in the plant: foundry, powerhouse, and electricians. But in plantwide elections in late 1944, despite an impressive effort at organizing, Servel workers voted against the union. Still, the UE remained committed to the area, building contacts and presence in the community.[53]

According to historian Samuel White, the rise of the UE in Evansville provided "contested terrain" for what unionism meant and was "as much a political event" as it was an "economic and social" event.[54] Employers' opposition to the shop floor struggles during wartime had confirmed a sense of the stakes to many workers. In a meeting of the eighty-four members of the Seeger negotiation committee in 1943, "one worker after another rose to make the same point: that in fighting to maintain our union we are having to fight not just the Sunbeam management but the whole wolf-pack of the [National Association of Manufacturers] and the [Chamber of Commerce]." Activist workers committed to the union drive not only because it sought to have a militant contestation on the shop floor but also because it presented a visionary program of how the union could transform Evansville. In early 1944, Sentner and seventy-five Evansville UE stewards discussed a plan to rebuild employment levels after the war through community planning for "mass housing, civic improvements, schools, recreational centers for teen age groups, hospitals and similar projects," including "continued attention to afford employment opportunities for Negroes." (The Missouri Valley Authority program was obviously less of a draw in Evansville.)[55] By 1945, the UE's base in some shops in Evansville and its work in the local CIO had produced an unemployment center for returning veterans, a price-rollback campaign, a child care program for women workers, a campaign for better commuter services, and other community projects. Its unemployed service center became a community center that avoided the factionalism that occurred in St. Louis. "What we have attempted to do is organize the unemployed workers . . . so they will have an organization to fight for their rights even though unemployed," reported organizer Jim Payne. The movement prevented evictions, kept stores from cutting off credit, and even got local grocers to lobby along with the unemployed for more unemployment compensation. The local gathered signatures on an open letter to Seeger management asking for a wage increase in an effort to "fight the perception issued by management that high wages would keep new industries out of Evansville and thus cause unemployment." Workers paraded in front of the home of a Seeger boss to make their demands—after all, organizer James Payne remarked, the "sidewalks are public thoroughfares." Local 813's CIO-PAC (political action committee) work resulted in the election of its president, Charles Wright, who started work at Seeger as a heat treater in 1936, to the Indiana state legislature in 1944.[56]

Wright was just one of a growing number of workers who strongly identified with this vision of unionism. Among others were Sadelle Berger, a passionate organizer who had come to the UE from the Rural Electrification Administration, where she had become involved in the CIO under the aegis of the United Federal Workers. She signed on as a District 8 organizer during the war and led the district's political campaign for the 1944 congressional elections in the St. Louis area, an effort that helped unseat Bennett Champ Clark, longtime antilabor congressman. In 1946 Sentner persuaded her and her new husband, attorney Sydney Berger, also a former REA staffer, to move to Evansville to help organize the town, joining James Payne who had moved there permanently in 1940. Sydney, drafted in 1942, was outraged as a soldier by segregated eating establishments and developed into a "true idealist." Later both were accused of being CP members, but according to their son they were more aptly described as committed to "social justice rather than the ideology of one party." As the union endured attacks, Sydney earned a reputation as one of the most feisty labor attorneys in the Midwest, pulling old statutes and (according to Logsdon) other "rabbits out of his hat" to defend workers' rights against the intensifying political persecution. Sadelle focused on mobilizing women shop workers as well as the wives and children of workers in Evansville. Sadelle and Sydney saw the workers they helped mobilize as the cardinal instrument for social change in the postwar period. To recognize the kind of personal choices these two made is to realize the great hopes for the postwar era that were embodied in what seemed like a simple union campaign.[57]

With each union campaign, more workers seemed to identify with the goal of social movement unionism, though only a handful officially joined the party. A bitter conflict at Faultless Corporation in 1946, when the entire shop was fired by the boss after a wildcat strike, brought workers such as Ernest Upton and Mary Knable into a closer identity with the Left. Later some Faultless workers admitted that they joined the CP through such struggles and that, indeed, there seemed to be very little difference between the content of CP meetings and the content of discussions of unions in bars and other venues. One such worker later recalled that he simply believed the "Communists were right on economic issues"; that he "wanted to improve the government, not overthrow it"; and that the latter topic was never discussed in the CP.[58] Charles Fridy, Albert Eberhard, and William Nightingale, all charter members of Local 813, survived at Servel during the bitter years when so many activists lost their jobs. Eberhard was among those on the Left who were also Catholic, but their experiences with Sentner taught them that Communists were not "bogeymen," as Eberhard put it.[59]

Organizers were convinced that victory in organizing Servel would transform politics in Evansville. Gearing up for another union election in 1946, the local focused on the large number of returning veterans (one-third of the workforce by 1946). It also set up special committees for the 350 women and 150 black workers in the plant. The local sought to undermine fear and influence that had been so effective for Servel in 1939. As testimony to their evangelical spirit and effort to bring a community presence, the UE erected a revival tent across the street from the Servel plant; it remained in place for years.[60]

Servel's president, Louis Ruthenberg, sought to fortify the company from the campaign in the same way it always had, with conservative community elements as his allies. Now he added a heightened populist anticommunism twist to the mix with a small base consisting of an antiunion war veterans' committee and the War Dads Club, whose Evansville president was the former president of the Servel company union. The Vets Social Committee reminded veterans that they "did not go over there and fight Communists so that Communists can take over Servel as they are trying to do now." Their leaflets cited Click's 1945 election material and asked, "Do you want Americanism or Communism?" In another leaflet they noted that Payne had not denied his affiliation and declared, "Most of us believe in RELIGION of some kind. Communists do not. Russia is Communist. . . . Vote 'no' for Freedom of Religion, Freedom of the Press, Freedom of Speech, Free Enterprise." Ruthenberg simply announced, "A vote for UE is a vote for Communism in America."[61] The union countered by suggesting that red-baiting was designed to take workers' minds off the issues and that Ruthenberg had always denied freedom of speech to workers. It also shot back with its own reminder that Ruthenberg had been appointed to Servel by Swedish industrialist Axel Wenner-Gren, the "notorious fascist" exposed by the State Department in 1942. Workers voted for the union by a significant margin in the March 1946 election.[62]

The victory at Servel turned the tables and put the anticommunists on the defensive. The Servel Organizing Committee unanimously passed a resolution "against red baiting" that they presented to the district convention in Kansas City in March 1946. Charles Fridy, chief shop steward at Servel and one of the charter members of the local, made a passionate appeal to delegates, explaining that in the thirteen years he had worked at Servel, company officials "have hollered Communism and everything else" to defeat the union. But, he "joined this organization where in the preamble in our dues book it says that each and every one of us has the right to our own political belief or religion, etc., regardless of race, creed, color. I thought that was very fine." Recounting in detail the way that the company had used the Click faction charges, he concluded, "My God, what is this, are we union people or are we fighting one another[?]"[63] Joining the offensive, Louis Wagner, Local 1104 (Wagner Electric) president and district secretary, repudiated the notion that because he allied with Sentner he was a dupe, avowing that while he was an "Evangelical and proud of it," he had "been accused of being a Communist." He "def[ied] anyone in Kansas City or St. Louis to prove it." His experiences had taught him that red-baiting "can tear hell out of the organization in one night." As to his relationship with Sentner, he said that "because Bill and I get along, I say hooray for us. When he is wrong and I think he is wrong, I am the first one to tell him he is wrong."[64] Charles Kaplan, a Local 1102 delegate who had nominated Click for district president at the previous October convention, announced that he had changed his position because of his experiences in the previous six months: "I repudiated anything I said" and avowed new respect for the UE constitution. The "kind of practices" engaged in by the Click faction were "unAmerican and undemocratic."[65]

Sentner, in a dramatic moment, framed the resolution: "Let's be frank" about "what we are really doing. . . . We [are] fighting for the rights of Communists to be full-fledged citizens in this union." There "needs to be some sober thought on this continuous battle of whether or not Communist people who believe in scientific socialism who belong to the smallest party in the U.S. and the least effective in the affairs of the nation, shall have the right to belong to a labor union." Sentner pointed to the need for more education and debate about this "growing philosophy of thought" that "dates back to 1848." It was "not a doctrine against religion, or that Communists want to kill people. . . . Why has anybody got any fear of learning about it?" His support for the Soviet Union was not something that should be viewed as subversive: "I am a friend of Russia—I will tell you why. Russia has ushered into the world a new form of system. It is throwing the fear of God into the big money people. I am saying that I believe we should study what they are doing in Russia just as they learned what we were doing in 1776." He asked the delegates to consider why Servel's Louis Ruthenberg might focus on Communists: "Why doesn't Ruthenberg say—watch out for Tommy—he is a Republican?" And he answered that "the people who control those parties are the boys in the same money class with the boys who run our plants. . . . I am not saying that the person who red baits necessarily is stooging for the bosses. Absolutely not." But by joining in the debate on their terms, "we do things that help them . . . because you can use Communism as something very subversive."[66]

Sentner concluded by suggesting that an understanding of socialism should be "part of our trade union education" so that it could not be used to "smear things so as to diffuse real issue[s]." He offered to speak on the issue before the locals' educational committees, "to listen, talk," and "debate," as long as it didn't "interfere with the other work I have." He cautioned that "nobody asked anybody to believe in Socialism. . . . Did I ever stand up before you and say that either you do as I say—that was never said to anybody."[67]

Few delegates spoke against the resolution. Raymond Mertens, a Local 1104 delegate who had been outspoken in Click's camp in October, now seemed on the defensive, objecting colorfully and vociferously to the suggestion that anticommunists were "friends of the bosses": "I know that rather than side with [the] boss, I would rather die. . . . Raymond D. Mertens never sucked ass with the bosses and never will." William Drohan charged that the resolution was a type of "political skullduggery" intended to stifle dissent from Communist control, a sentiment Click seconded. Nevertheless, the resolution passed by an overwhelming margin.[68]

District 8 leadership felt hopeful that they could move on from the factionalism to build the kind of movement that the conditions of the postwar required. Factionalism hurt organizing drives and diminished the Left's ability to build community coalitions—its means of gaining allies and the way it sought to address the problems of the postwar era. The district struggled to cope with the decline in membership in the wake of the postwar layoffs, the most significant of which was the loss of the huge numbers of workers at Small Arms. By 1947, the district held contracts with fifty-five companies covering thirty thousand workers, but membership never again approached wartime levels. At the end of the war, the district had planned to use networks from established plants to build outward from those communities across the region. Their southern organizing strategy was based on the concept of organizing on a community-by-community basis, in direct contrast to the CIO's central-ized campaign for Operation Dixie, which sought to organize with "flying squadrons" targeted at large corporations. Sentner and Logsdon derided the CIO plan as wrongheaded and instead sought to use the Evansville model— entrenching the union in strategic towns and cities—to combat the intense antiunion community forces and slowly build alliances that could help the union build its southern periphery. But they got almost no chance to work on that strategy. District 8 organizers who were in Kentucky and Tennessee were appalled by the Operation Dixie campaign. From their perspective, the entire goal of the CIO was disastrously bound up with using organizers dedicated to keeping the Left from gaining influence. The CIO hired Orville Munzer for the campaign. Logsdon was shocked, writing that Munzer had been the most racist official of Local 825, someone they viewed as an extraordinarily incompetent organizer and "even out of sympathy for anything the CIO stands for." The CIO officialdom held secret meetings that excluded district UE organizers from the meetings. By late 1947, Operation Dixie was in collapse, as Logsdon had pre-dicted. Meanwhile, the CIO gave leads to UE rivals when the district was tied up with working against raids and factionalism. Logsdon listed a number of plants that would have been easily organized had they had the staff resources, which would soon be even more tied up in fighting CIO and AFL raids. Nevertheless, the district *was* expanding southward, able to organize in towns from Cape Girardeau, Missouri, to Tell City, Indiana, Ft. Smith, Arkansas, and Henderson, Kentucky, each step of the way using a community campaign as the basis for organizing.[69]

Using Networks to Make Communism the Issue

But there were countersubversive community and regional networks that intended to thwart the ability of the Left to organize effectively, and these net-works were based both within and outside the union and enhanced by the growing Cold War. Chastened by the District 8 delegates, the anticommunists sought and received support from outside the UE to continue their campaign. Click relied on Father Leo Brown, who by then "was a friend of mine," to arrange a meeting for him in New York with around six others. "The Catholic Church was pretty much involved. In all fairness, that's one of the reasons I went to Brown, other than being a friend. I also knew he had to have connections in other places who were probably interested in doing it, and he did." Brown wrote on Click's behalf to Father Charles Owen Rice of Pittsburgh, the leading anti-communist Catholic in the country, whose own crusade against Communist influence in Pittsburgh and the labor movement nationally had been under way since the 1930s. He cautioned Rice, however, that "if you talk to people about this, please don't mention my name. It would be disastrous here to have suspicion develop that I am interested and active."[70]

With the help of Click's new contacts, UE Members for Democratic Action (UEMDA) was established in Pittsburgh in August 1946, and Click was elected national secretary. A national organization committed to uniting the anticommunist forces in the UE, the UEMDA argued that a "Communist machine" controlled the UE national and district conventions and therefore the policies "did not represent the desires of the rank and file membership." Given an opportunity by referendum, they suggested, the rank and file would "kick out" Fitzgerald, Emspak, and Matles, the top national leaders, as well as those leaders associated with communism at the district level. Since District 8 already had a referendum form of election, there was a clear expectation that a victory by Click in October 1946 could vindicate their criticism.[71]

Anticommunist sentiment in the local and national CIO was an instrument to foster the UE dissident group. The Left's success in St. Louis and Evansville caused oppositional groups within the CIO to form, ready to act to undermine the union. In 1945 Robert Logsdon had become head of the St. Louis body and Charles Wright head of the Evansville CIO, as the UE's numbers and alliances grew at the local level. But by 1946 national CIO policy began to dissolve coalitions, which had always been tenuous. With anticommunist James Carey as secretary-treasurer of the CIO, the right wing in District 8 had a powerful ally. Carey used networks to support the work of the UEMDA. The national CIO targeted control of local bodies by the Left, a campaign solidly under way in St. Louis.[72]

Harold Gibbons of the CIO's United Distribution Workers Union in St. Louis had been a strong ally and was influential in the internal politics of the UE. Gibbons came to St. Louis in 1941 to reorganize the fledgling group of St. Louis warehouse workers. He was strongly influenced by Trotskyist socialists who had long been at odds with the CP. He opposed the no-strike pledge during the war but had little success in organizing enough workers to gain power in the CIO. According to Logsdon, Gibbons "deeply resented" the fact that the UE was the "predominant union" in the area and that Sentner was the leading labor spokesman, and this led him to support Republican Party candidates in order to harm the CIO-endorsed candidates favored by the Left. When the local CIO reaffirmed the no-strike pledge in mid-1943, Gibbons condemned it as evidence of Communist control and withdrew from the body, along with the Textile Workers Union representatives who shared his sentiments and ideological roots. The UE nonetheless built "good relations" with most of the other CIO union delegates during the war, especially in the context of the MVA and political work. UE organizers were given much credit for the election of progressive Democrats. In 1943, the St. Louis CIO council rescinded its 1939 prohibition against Communist participation.[73]

As the war wound down and warehouse and textile workers' unions reaffiliated with the Industrial Union Council (IUC), Logsdon warned that the "line-ups of 1939 and 1940 here are being repeated more and more," with Gibbons "becoming a large center of red-baiters."[74] UE success in organizing would preface control of the CIO local body in the postwar period, and already there were efforts to contest or just ignore CIO jurisdictional boundaries and to intervene to contest elections.[75] Gibbons hired a Local 1102 anticommunist for his staff, and Local 1102 transferred Emerson cafeteria workers it had organized during the war to the warehouse workers' union, making the alliance clear.[76] In September 1945, Gibbons joined Local 1102 and half the delegates from Local 825 in an effort to unseat Logsdon from his position as secretary-organizer of the IUC. Logsdon charged that the campaign, in which he ran against a delegate of the warehouse workers' union, was "not based on the issues but mainly on red-baiting and considerable anti-Negro sentiment. . . . Of course they put out no printed matter on these things so that they could be nailed down." Since Gibbons was a strong advocate of racial justice, this highlights the way that the anticommunist issue produced "strange bedfellows." Logsdon won, despite what he called the "slanderous" reports about him. The "relationship with many CIO unions here is not good," he said simply.[77]

In June 1946, Local 1102 delegates joined Harold Gibbons's forces in bringing the anticommunist issue before the St. Louis body. Accusing Communists of tarnishing labor's image and contributing to the growing reactionary antiunion sentiment, Local 1102's resolution "urged local unions to ferret out proponents of Communism and Fascism within their ranks." Logsdon responded that unions should "emphasize union loyalty, not an individual's political beliefs." Using the roll-call vote method as a strategy (thereby leaving any delegate who voted against it vulnerable to attack as a Communist), the resolution easily passed by a three to one margin.[78] More momentum came in September when Logsdon was defeated in his bid for the IUC presidency, in what the press declared a "major victory for anti-communist forces." Gibbons and Click fielded candidates not only against Logsdon but also against Oscar Ehrhardt, secretary-organizer of the Gas Workers Union and a quiet closet Socialist who was charged with being "soft on left-wingers" for refusing to engage in the attack on Communists. Ehrhardt's narrow victory signaled that those who accepted CP members as legitimate trade unionists would be treated as the enemy. "I had to watch my back from that time on, and I couldn't give any support. It was the beginning of McCarthyism, right there," said Ehrhardt.[79]

With the IUC sanction to "ferret out" Communists, Local 1102 and Local 1108 in late August adopted resolutions recommending the "ouster" of Communists from the union. Harvey Smith was able to get enough workers mobilized in Local 1104 to pass a resolution instructing delegates to vote for an anticommunist UEMDA resolution at the national convention. Though one delegate, Sam Silverman, expressed reservations—"As officers sworn to uphold the constitution, we could not support any attempt to attack members of the union for their political beliefs"—they nevertheless complied. But they voted "with Sentner" on every other issue at the convention, including foreign policy issues, arousing fury and more charges about "Communist" control. Wagner's stewards were still solidly with the Left, but they faced a barrage of baiting on a daily basis, organized by closet Association of Catholic Trade Unionists (ACTU) members who called anyone who opposed Click's faction Communists, and this seemed to have an effect.[80] Click challenged Sentner to a debate on communism, noting Sentner's offer at the March convention. While Sentner relished the challenge, workers on the district executive board and especially the Wagner stewards "threatened to find another candidate" if Sentner allowed Click to make communism the central issue. But Click was then able to use Sentner's refusal to debate to suggest that Sentner had something to hide.[81]

The networks outside of the union became an instrument to build support and contacts in other areas—to solicit, as William Drohan put it, the "out of town Locals, where the membership voted like a machine in favor of Sentner."[82] Father Brown's contacts were also valuable in bringing names of workers who might be willing to work to oust the Left. Two Seeger plant workers, William Debes and Troy James, were motivated by strong anticommunism, discontent with the Seeger contract, Catholicism, and reactionary political views. Hearing of the establishment of the UEMDA, Debes and James felt emboldened to declare publicly that President Charles Wright had turned Local 813 into a front for the CP: "Our union office is cluttered with Communist literature[,] . . . our officers are salesmen for the Communist Daily Worker[,] . . . [and] our local Political Action Committee and contributions are used to further . . . the progress of the Communist Party," though the evidence they cited was flimsy.[83] Bill Debes charged that in 1946 contract negotiations Sentner had "sold us out" when he agreed to a private conference with the company attorney. While it is not possible to know exactly what happened in this case (and it certainly wasn't the view of most Seeger leaders), it demonstrates that within the countersubversive tradition, any disagreement or problem could be attributed to Communist duplicity or malfeasance.[84]

The handful of Evansville UEMDA recruits gained an important ally in Walter Hayden, local UAW leader and editor of the Evansville CIO newspaper, *Labor's Voice*. Hayden's antipathy toward Local 813 was fueled by rivalry between the UE and the UAW and by the national UAW, which had authorized the Evansville

UAW to raid the Servel local in 1944—a precursor to the large-scale raiding activity by the UAW after the Taft-Hartley Act. UAW vice president Richard Frankensteen had discouraged Hayden during the war from working with Local 813 on postwar planning. At the time, Sentner had remarked that "the UAW is . . . watching us like hawks and would like to pounce in for the kill. . . . [T]hey smell blood and are licking their chops." Hayden even organized and led meetings of the UE rump group, which were held at the UAW hall. District 8 would have disputed the assertation that Phillip Murray kept CIO rivals from attacking Left-led unions. Since 1943, District 8 had faced jurisdictional battles launched by other CIO unions, some with authorization by top leadership such as in this case. They had reciprocated on occasion and sometimes had successfully appealed, but at other times they just persevered despite top CIO leadership's complicity, as was made clear in the approach of the CIO to District 8 organizers in Operation Dixie. Little did they know that the worst was yet to come.[85]

Hayden was influenced by the doctrines of the ACTU, which he had helped to establish in Evansville. The ACTU sought to "carry the gospel of Christianity into every labor union" and to combat Communist influences among workers. It asserted that the CIO-PAC was a Communist instrument. When Local 813 president Charles Wright defeated a UAW candidate to become president of the local CIO, Hayden painted it as a Communist attempt to control PAC politics. Hayden helped form the UE Vets Anti-Communist Committee, a group of mostly Catholic veterans.[86] Evansville's Father Charles Schoettelkotte, who had helped establish the Evansville ACTU chapter, personally visited Catholic members of Local 813 and encouraged the notion that local UE leadership "discriminated against Catholics."[87] Schoettlekotte recommended that pastors "foster and spread . . . sound trade unionism based on Christian principles."[88]

Catholic officials' influence was apparent in other parts of the district as well. In a letter sent by William Debes to a contact in Tell City, Indiana (a city with a 70 percent Catholic population, where District 8 had organized a newly transplanted General Electric plant), Debes applauded the important assistance of Father Vollmer, who ensured the distribution of leaflets in the plant. Debes noted, however, that the UEMDA needed to "establish a good contact in Tell City" because "we must quit using the Catholic Rectory to forward our cause" in order to prevent the Left from charging Catholic interference in union affairs.[89] During the 1946 district officers' election campaign, though, the bishop for Tell City instructed Catholics "to get rid of Sentner." When challenged about Church interference, one priest "gave warning that this was the will of the church and must be complied with." In Moline, Illinois, Father Bill O'Conner of St. Ambrose College, another Brown contact, lent his students to Click during the campaign. However, in nearby Washington, Indiana, which had a similarly dense Catholic population, when "a committee of Catholic UE officers visited their priest" there were no further open efforts to influence the election.[90]

As Father Leo Brown's cautionary note to Father Rice indicated, in St. Louis any help from the Catholic Church hierarchy had to be at least low-key if not clandestine, despite (or perhaps because of) the large percentage of Catholics among St. Louis's working class. In a 1948 interview with a Sentner sympathizer who posed as a features reporter, Brown explained that the ACTU was "not active" in the St. Louis area: "Too many working people in this area are skeptical about the church taking an active part in trade union politics. We have our Labor School and that serves to bring in a much wider segment of the trade unionists than any partisan organization could get at this time."[91] Because Brown wanted to remain in the background, Father L. T. Twomey, another priest at St. Louis University, took a slightly more open role in organizing support for the group. Sentner alleged that Twomey gave constant advice during the October 1946 district convention. Logsdon derisively called Twomey's St. Louis University office "red-baiting headquarters" for Gibbons and Click. John Burns confirmed that "you had to be careful because the Communists were using that against us—said we were bringing outsiders into the union, the Catholics."[92] Burns also remembered the difficulty of getting priests in some working-class areas to condemn the UE. In particular he remembered one priest in the Soulard area of St. Louis who suggested that the UE was an ally of working people, a contention that he believed was proof of the influence of "Communist thinking even in the Church" but in fact was evidence of the remnants of an alliance forged over various community issues, from unemployment to the MVA. The influence of Catholic lay societies, such as the Knights of Columbus or Catholic Veterans, was much more of a factor than many priests who declined or refused to get involved. Sentner claimed that at Emerson, Century, and Wagner, the leading anticommunists worked through "small groups of Veterans, most of whom are Catholic," to gain their strongest adherents.[93] Through these associations, Click's faction linked up with explicitly antilabor business forces. They connected through networks built in an earlier era but now reinforced by ties to the FBI.

The veterans' group was run by John Griffin, a banker from St. Louis. Griffin was the national leader of the American War Dads group, whose stated purpose was to organize veterans against communism in American life and to seek to bridge class differences through the military affiliations of many workers. Griffin bankrolled Forum Press, which published *Today's World,* a paper that sought to galvanize Catholic workers to oppose communism in unions and other institutions. Griffin, a prominent Catholic who was knighted by the pope as a Knight of the Holy Sepulcher and was also a leader of the Catholic fraternal group the Knights of Columbus, placed Fred Bender, the antiunion operative who intervened in Maytag and the 1939 Servel strike, to run the press. It is likely that connections with Bender and Griffin had caused Ruthenberg to mobilize the War Dads group against the union drive at Servel in 1946. Though the union had prevailed, veteran and fraternal or civic and Catholic groups remained a key avenue of tapping a populist patriotic anticommunism to contest unionism. By 1947, Click's faction was working with the American Legion to help them "expose the subversives who would wreck America." Through Ernie Stuebinger, an "America Firster" who had opposed Sentner for district presidency in 1941, the Click forces linked up to this paper and its principal backers and apparently drew financial support for their efforts. Stuebinger wrote to Click telling him that *Today's World* had pledged to "help us every way possible"—including "dough" for the Click campaign and a promise to meet with Click. Stuebinger worried that the paper "did us some harm with some of their statements they made in the past," apparently referring to its negative stories about labor, and was relieved that his contact had "suggested that we assign a man to go over such items that affect Labor." But the paper remained overtly suspicious of worker demands, continuing to suggest that Communist subversives fomented labor strife. By late 1947 it was the mouthpiece of the reactionary congressman Hamilton Fish.[94]

The mainstream press was not far behind *Today's World*. The St. Louis and Evansville newspapers, particularly the *St. Louis Globe-Democrat* and the *Evansville Courier*, were essential allies of the anticommunist faction. Bender and Griffin were also closely allied to the publishers and some of the reporters of these papers. There was nary a word in the articles published by these papers suggesting any level of democracy in the UE. Local 1102's charges of "Communist-inspired maneuver[s] intended to muzzle the opposition to the ironclad Communist Clique" were reported as fact.[95] Bold headlines such as "Communists Rule CIO Electrical Union" found their way into print with ease. The *St. Louis Globe-Democrat* assigned two reporters to cover the factionalism, and these reporters worked in close contact with the FBI.[96] As the 1946 election campaign neared, the Click camp was portrayed as a defender of democracy and a crusader against "evil" forces intent on control of the labor movement. The *Globe-Democrat* uncritically adopted Click's clever line about an "iron curtain" having fallen over the UE, with lurid depictions of the UE policy that claimed that Logsdon "helps his boss [Sentner] control U.E. members" in the district and that the district was a "haven for unemployed Communists and their sympathizers."[97] While the *St. Louis Post-Dispatch* was slightly less enthusiastic for red-hunting in its coverage, it nevertheless coined the expression "avowed Communist" as Sentner's "official designation" in every story about the UE. Sympathetic reporters revealed to the UE that the labor reporter was replaced by an FBI agent "turned reporter" to cover a UE story. The *Post-Dispatch* editorials, Sentner bitterly charged, "stunk to high heaven" by uncritically repeating the charge that Communists controlled the union. The Evansville newspapers, Sentner drolly noted, "rated UE Communism fables on a par with news from the White House. And the little town criers of Tell City, Washington, Newton, Moline, chirped a merry little chorus echoing their big city brother liars."[98]

With so many elements having now made "Communism the issue," expectations rose for the 1946 district elections. Click gained a considerable support especially from middle-class and business leaders who wrote praising his "efforts to return American labor to a respectable position in the eyes of the public generally."[99] But when the voting was completed in the closely monitored election in late October, the opposition was stunned. Sentner's ticket had won again. With a higher turnout of eligible voters, Sentner had carried a majority in twelve of the district's sixteen locals.[100] Sentner reveled in the victory: "the re-election of a well-known Communist and Jew as District President must be considered an outstanding victory for progress."[101]

Evaluating the 1946 Victory

How and why did the Sentner ticket win? Assessment of the voting provides a simple answer: members voted along the same lines as the delegates of their local. If the leadership of the local supported Sentner, they convinced the majority of workers in their local through a variety of arguments. In only one case, that of Local 821 (Washington, Indiana) with a high percentage of Catholic members, did the members vote for Click while the leadership supported Sentner. In every other case the presence or dominance of Catholic members did not govern.[102] In a few instances, such as with Otto Miller in St. Louis Local 1128 (Perfection and Benjamin Air Rifle), the local leadership were themselves Communists who had risen through the ranks, but in most cases they were not. They supported Sentner's right to political affiliation and denied that Sentner used the CP in the way that Click alleged.[103] At the October 1946 district convention, delegates had again voted two to one for a resolution supporting the right to political affiliation: "we re-affirm our determination to unite all workers in our industry on an industrial union basis, and through rank and file control, regardless of craft, age, sex, nationality, race, creed or political belief, and pursue at all times a policy of aggressive struggle to improve our conditions."[104] Click's suggestion that the resolution "in effect gives a free hand to Communist Party members" only irritated some of the delegates. Maurice Young of Newton, Iowa, declared, "I'm getting tired of hearing about the red issue at every convention and I'm tired of these people coming into our town to stir up trouble." An Evansville delegate said he had "more to do than worry whether a man is a red, a Jew, a Negro or a Catholic as long as he is willing to fight for better wages and working conditions."[105]

Leaders who supported Sentner also argued that their direct experience with him showed that he was not attempting to exert Communist "control" of the local. William Cuthbert assured Maytag workers: "I have yet to see or hear Bill Sentner using the United Electrical union for purposes of the Communist Party."[106] One of Click's Moline, Illinois, supporters reported that when he attempted to expose Sentner's Communist affiliation to the membership, Charles Burkhardt, president of the Minneapolis-Moline local, averred that "if you had to be a Communist to get a workingman a decent living then he was one of them."[107]

Exposure of some of Click's reactionary alliances also proved effective. When the Evansville UEMDA members invited antilabor Republican congressman Edward Mitchell to a meeting to drum up veterans' support for the anticommunist campaign, according to Sentner "the unholy combination gave off such a stench that no honest veteran would touch it with a ten foot pole."[108] The Click faction's defense of antilabor newspapers was denounced at the October convention, when delegates voted for a resolution condemning St. Louis and Evansville newspapers "for engaging . . . in a campaign to destroy the UE."[109]

Sentner's supporters questioned Click's record on militant unionism. Local 813 published an exposé, widely distributed throughout the district, of "Click's contract" with Emerson, alleging that since the end of the war, rates and conditions had declined because the local refused to work with district leadership on a constructive strategy. They pointed to the sixty-five-cent starting rate for women, to the "low 80% of base rate guarantee for incentive workers," and to an "efficiency" contract clause consented to by Click in 1946 in which the union agreed "to aid in improving the efficiency of the workers. The Union recognizes the company's right to utilize the skills of its employes to obtain increased efficiency." The district's policy had argued against the acceptance of such clauses. Click "agrees to help the company speed-up the workers!" denounced the *Evansville UE News.*[110]

These arguments were persuasive, even in shops with high Catholic membership. For example, Local 810, the amalgamated local of more than fifteen medium- and small-sized shops in St. Louis that totaled two thousand members, was targeted by Click's supporters because of its high number of Catholic members, many of whom were visited at home. On election day, shops with as few as thirty workers were visited by as many as six of Click's supporters.[111] But Local 810 delivered a majority vote for Sentner. Logsdon attributed the victory to the influence of Clarence Bingamon, the elected business agent of the local, and his shop stewards, who were able to counter the barrage of anti-Sentner literature issued during the campaign. Logsdon later described Bingamon as "less sympathetic to Communist Party issues than I was" but as someone who was deeply committed to the UE program and whose trust in Sentner was not diminished by his different political views. Local 810 had won significant wage increases and other shop floor gains in the local shops in the immediate postwar period through innovative campaigns. For instance, workers picketed a manager's home in Ladue (the wealthy suburb of St. Louis) during a strike.[112]

On the other hand, the 1946 district election confirmed the solid base for the UEMDA that was provided by St. Louis Locals 1102 and 1108. Local 1102 employed a steady educational campaign over issues of Communist control. Local 1102 had also clamped down harshly on dissent within its ranks. Logsdon wrote in December 1945 that "Local 1102 is now using tactics employed by [Local] 825 and the Chicago IUC in adjourning meetings before action can be taken which they hope to avert." Local 1102 changed its constitution to prohibit handbilling and caucuses unless approved by the executive board. In early 1946, it suspended Charles Anderson, a member of the local and a district organizer who, though a Catholic, had for years "refused to take part in red baiting," for participation in a caucus opposing the leadership inside Local 1102.[113] Charles Kaplan, the delegate who "repudiated" the right-wing caucus at the March 1946 convention, was left unaided by the local when he was fired by Emerson.[114]

Lloyd Austin, who alleged that the local arranged to get Kaplan fired, recalled the concerted effort to suppress the leftist caucus:

> It really got to be too much. You couldn't win. If you supported Sentner, they'd say, "you're a Communist." If you said no, they'd say, "What's the matter, are you ashamed of it?" If you supported [Sentner], they'd harass you till you couldn't take it anymore. So I had to bite my tongue. Most people, you know, can't take that kind of pressure. We saw what happened to those people who spoke out, how they were threatened—I mean physically threatened. You know they did the things they *said* the Communists did, but I never saw Bill [Sentner] or any of the people who were accused of being Communists act like they did. . . . [T]hey [the Left] never made you feel like you couldn't speak your mind.[115]

Austin's comments were echoed by Bill Reidel, the original "Mayor of Emerson" during the 1937 sit-down, who quietly supported Sentner until it "was impossible. . . . You'd have to be there to understand the atmosphere." Logsdon contended that focus on communism proved a convenient "means of keeping the members of 1102 agitated and to hide [the anticommunist coalition's] inability to meet the problems of the members of that local union," who were experiencing dramatic decreases in pay and speedup in the postwar period amidst the insecurity of increasing layoffs.[116]

The Left still had good indications that it might prevail in the factional battle. Logsdon wrote in January 1947 that the UEMDA in District 8 was "weaker than at any time in the past." Click's supporters in Tell City conceded that they had "enough trouble right now" fighting employers' attempts to roll back conditions; they wanted to put aside the anticommunist campaign to address this. In St. Louis Local 810, officers' elections in January brought a 2–1 vote margin for pro-Sentner candidates. The only chief shop steward sympathetic to the Click faction among the fifteen plants in that amalgamated local was defeated. At the March district convention in Moline, a resolution recommending that the UEMDA voluntarily disband passed solidly 161–56, and a second resolution condemning "red-baiting, witch-hunts and purges" passed by similar margins.

On the heels of the convention, the Wagner local voted 3–1 to declare the UEMDA "injurious to the welfare of our Union." There, a solid core of black workers led by Lee Henry organized effectively as a coalition within the local, and this was a large factor that kept Click's forces from making an inroad in the local.[117]

The UEMDA's fortunes declined more dramatically in Evansville. Though Troy James savored the fact that the "UE got beat" in an organizing drive for a small shop there in December 1946, thus taking "some of the wind out of Payne's and Wright's sails," his own conduct was soon in the spotlight.[118] In January 1947, James told an International Harvester worker "to vote for neither the FE [Farm Equipment Workers] or the UAW [CIO rivals] in the election." When presented with the charge, James threw his UE membership card down and strode out of the meeting, failing to face his accuser.[119] William Debes wrote that "it's a ragged road over here. It is getting worse. . . . We have all been ready to quit because of the lack of interest [of] the membership," and he warned that the contest against Wright in the next election would "be our last attempt. . . . [I]f they still want Wright and his methods far be it from me to stand in their way."[120]

UEMDA members then waited to see if the Left would fail to get a contract at Servel. Servel was planning for strikebreakers, interviewing thousands of them in anticipation of a strike. But the company also watched the tremendous community mobilization strategy that the local was preparing. Certainly the membership was strengthened for the battle: with a 216-member strike strategy committee assigned to examine every detail of the company's contract proposals, a Christmas party and other activities for UE children, a picket squad committee, a special community issue of the Local 813 newspaper, a Veterans Committee, antidiscrimination committee, and a radio show, leaders were "welding together" the membership. Debes "ignored" Wright's pleas for the anticommunists to unite in this effort and relished a description of Sentner as noticeably shaken about what might happen at Servel: "Bill Sentner walked around as in a trance" in a March meeting as a strike loomed, Debes alleged. But Servel capitulated, even to increased protection against speedups, more union control of the shop floor, and wage gains. Debes wrote solemnly to Click that "everything has sure changed here. Servel signed the contract with Local 813."[121]

Then in late May, workers at Bucyrus-Erie (B-E) voted to join the UE. B-E, a producer of digging and construction equipment, was a strong opponent of unionism. Headquartered in Milwaukee, B-E had been an active member of the NMTA and established its labor policies "to fit local circumstance," including the regular use of spies and blacklists to weed out activists. Its Evansville branch, established in 1912, had defeated unions until 1942, when a majority of eight hundred workers voted for the AFL Machinists Union.[122] In October 1945, workers struck the company and for more than three months "maintained aggressive picket lines," but the strike ended "on the company's terms" and workers sought affiliation with the UE. By late 1946, the UE was essentially functioning as the union and won the union election in spring 1947, despite efforts by the UAW, with Walter Hayden's advice, to intervene in the election. Placing its tent across the street, the union had an eighty-member organizing committee for a workforce of just over one thousand. The victory at B-E rounded out a drive that placed Local 813 as the key union in Evansville and the largest local in the district with more than seven thousand members. Now half of District 8's membership was outside of St. Louis.[123]

William Debes wrote to Click in June 1947 that the Evansville group had voted to disband "indefinitely for lack of support." In a June meeting, "[we] took one of the worst defeats we ever got." The meeting condemned U.S. foreign policy as well as the UEMDA, adding to his disgust. Debes was bitter and stated that it was "very vicious and unAmerican and the more unAmerican it was the louder the applause." Debes concluded that "the people got a raise last year and this year and they don't give a dam[n] for anything else including us and our work. The Communist issue is dead at the present time because the Bucyrus Company used it to try to keep the union out recently. . . . We talked to some of the Bucyrus boys and they look at us like we were silly because they have been called communists all through[out] there [sic] organization drive by the company and the company stooges."[124] Jim Payne gave another version of the disbanding of the UEMDA forces. He claimed that Troy James and Tom Wheeler, the key Local 813 anticommunists, resigned "shortly after they were exposed as having made several secret agreements with the Seeger management in violation of the contract." Seeger shop stewards in a special meeting voted to "rescind such agreements and hold the company to the contract."[125] Whatever the primary reason, Debes himself concluded that "we couldn't reach Bill Sentner with a ten foot pole." In Moline, UE representative Rex Wheelock wrote that members of the Click faction were staying in Moline trying to develop allies in the area, saying he had teased one of them that "it was rather humiliating to learn that apparently they feel Moline is about the only fertile field left to them." Though he recognized that they would find allies among Catholic members, he felt it unlikely that the situation could be effectively countered, partly because workers saw the UE as the base of community activities. Ed Swope reported to Click that he had ferreted out some support there.[126]

Reactionary Political Tides

No matter how ruined the UEMDA local fortunes seemed, they enjoyed momentum from seemingly unending coffers as well as reactionary national and international political tides. Click's forces linked their campaign to international developments of the Cold War and its corollary, domestic anticommunism. District 8's experience bears out historian Ellen Schrecker's conclusion that it is "hard to imagine anticommunism succeeding without federal leadership, aid, and legitimization. Sometimes pursuing their own agenda, sometimes reacting to popular anticommunism, sometimes working hand in glove with industrialists, and always espousing the highest patriotism, federal officials waged a battle on every front against left trade unionism." Schrecker observed that "corporations and other unionists had been battling the labor reds for years. Victory came when their efforts were subsumed into the broader national campaign against American Communism. And here the state took the lead."[127]

The passage of the Taft-Hartley Act in 1947, which placed pressure on union representatives to sign the noncommunist affidavits prohibiting both "belief in" and "support" of communism, was key. Those unions whose officials refused to sign the affidavits were denied the services of the NLRB and could not be listed on union election ballots. Charges of unfair labor practices against companies also would not be heard. The CIO's national leaders initially urged all CIO affiliates to refuse to sign the affidavits because of their clear violation of individual political rights and because of the CIO's opposition to the other provisions in Taft-Hartley, which was clearly intended to roll back union power. But by 1948, as anticommunism gripped the CIO, only the Left-led unions were holding out, making them easy prey for raiding by other CIO unions as well as the AFL. As Schrecker points out, the affidavits allowed anticommunists to suggest to workers that the left-wingers' refusal or (as in the case of Sentner) inability to sign the affidavits would have serious consequences for workers' economic well-being.[128] This continual refrain, that Sentner's politics compromised workers' rights, now resonated more deeply.

The House Un-American Activities Committee (HUAC) focus on the UE elevated this impression. In June 1946 HUAC announced witnesses against the UE, and the press identified the UE with communism nationally. Like HUAC, the House Labor Committee and other congressional committees also focused on the Left in the UE. "Clearly the government had become the ally of the anti-Communist forces in the UE," Ronald Filipelli and Mark McCulloch conclude.[129]

Polarization between Left-led unions and the rest of the CIO over political and foreign policy issues continued, ensuring external support of the Click faction's effort to win control of the union's regional leadership. Meanwhile, the leftist leadership in District 8 had little trouble getting resolutions passed that questioned the drift toward the Cold War by the Truman administration. Some historians have contended that UE Communists got these sorts of resolutions passed because workers did not care about foreign policy issues. But it is clear that the issues were discussed and debated in District 8's conventions. These debates suggest that delegates genuinely were persuaded to question the CIO's drift toward unqualified support for Truman and the Democratic Party. But the UEMDA forces portrayed any dissent from the pro-Truman CIO position as the "smoking gun" of Communist control. This issue came to a head in 1948 over the Left-led unions' support for Henry Wallace's Progressive Party, which brought the full repercussions from the national CIO leadership and is viewed as the "suicidal" moment for the UE leadership, the key factor that precipitated the decision to purge the Left from the CIO body. Logsdon claimed that he was a decisive influence in advocating the third party venture, not Sentner, because of his "disgust" with Truman over labor and foreign policy issues, including his betrayal of the MVA proposal. Initially, it didn't seem "suicidal" at all because of the commitment of liberal forces to the campaign. But these "evaporated" as Truman, "that slippery little devil," moved to the left on key issues and as Wallace got tagged with the taint of communism by a concerted campaign.[130]

Finally, the press supported the Click faction openly and kept the issue of "Communist control" on the front pages throughout 1947 and 1948. In February 1947, Logsdon wrote to UE president Albert Fitzgerald, attaching a *St. Louis Post-Dispatch* article that recounted UEMDA allegations. He noted that a reporter who was a "friend of mine . . . advised me that the editor of that paper had issued orders to continue this line of attack on every possible occasion. This is St. Louis's so-called 'liberal paper,'" he added.[131] Within a few weeks, the major papers in District 8 printed an abridged version of a sensational series by the Alsop brothers titled "Will the CIO Shake the Communists Loose?" in *The Saturday Evening Post.* The articles depicted anticommunists as patriotic heroes who were trying to save the UE and the CIO from an "antidemocratic, authoritarian party serving a foreign interest." The article also implied that workers' desire for material gain might lead them to sell out their own country.[132] The St. Louis and Evansville papers refused to print the district's response to the articles. Sentner wrote bitterly to publisher Joseph Pulitzer that only a short time before the UE had been "accorded news space and occasional editorial commendation," but now the only topic the paper covered was "factionalism." But the worst was to come. Blatantly misleading articles, such as the April 1947 *Globe-Democrat* story titled "CIO Attack on Religion Labeled Communistic," twisted district delegates' criticism of the ACTU influence in labor affairs into a charge that the UE was attempting to repress its members' religious beliefs. Reporters admitted that they no longer contacted the district for comment on opposition charges because such would be edited out. Intense distortions of contract negotiations were regular fare in the Evansville press, with newspaper articles increasingly hinting that only violence might take out the Left.[133]

Clear signs of battle-weariness were evident. Sentner relied on the local stewards to defend his right to association. By the October convention, Local 1104 delegates (now members of the second largest local in the district due to Wagner Electric's postwar expansion) joined other delegates to ask Sentner to drop his party membership because it was consuming too much effort and starting to impede their effectiveness on the shop floor. Logsdon recalled that "many of these people began to say to Bill, just drop the party. You don't have to drop talking about socialism, we'll support you on that. You can still say all the things you say now." But Sentner refused.[134]

Nevertheless, Sentner won the 1947 district presidential referendum vote against Frank Lenhardt (Click declined to run, perhaps hoping that another member of their caucus would do better). But the margins of victory had narrowed. At Local 1104 (Wagner) Sentner lost by under one hundred votes, a result of the local leadership's refusal to fully back him.[135] Sentner's victory was clouded by Lenhardt's false charges that the Left had stolen the election, a charge that dominated newspaper headlines for months and fueled notions of an undemocratic cabal.[136] A St. Louis circuit court judge impounded the ballots and ordered that Lenhardt be seated as district president even before the ballots were recounted and the allegations of vote fraud were repudiated. Meanwhile, papers reported the allegations as though they were fact, with headlines such as "Union Defies Court Order, Declares Communist Election Victory."[137]

International events in 1948, especially the "war scare" with the Soviet Union, intensified domestic anticommunism throughout the nation, bringing frenzied pressure against the UE and placing Sentner at the center of charges of a Communist conspiracy to betray the nation. When local newspaper headlines replaced "UE" with "Sentner's Union," Local 1102's leadership grasped the opportunity to expel him from the local for "anti-union activity." The Right's influence in Local 1102 was evident when a well-attended membership meeting voted to expel Sentner on a voice vote, without allowing him to speak to the membership. Sentner was accused of "anti-union activity" for charging that Local 1102 leaders had orchestrated the expulsion of founding member Lou Kimmel. Workers were told that they would get their names and photos in the morning edition of the *Globe-Democrat* if they voted against expulsion. Even loyal Sentner supporters such as Lloyd Austin recalled that he did not object to the vote for "fear of repercussions."[138]

In early 1948, Emerson management transferred three Sentner supporters to lower-paying jobs, citing "national security" reasons. The company's elevated role in defense contracting after 1947 (landing some big contracts from the U.S. Air Force, where Stuart Symington had been named the first secretary) was a factor in securing Click a steady base of support, but those contracts also made "security" issues more directly a practical means of attacking the Left in Local 1102. With headlines such as "Woman Communist Is Found in War Plant Here" appearing in local newspapers, Local 1102 refused to grieve these workers' transfer. Shop steward Opal Cline protested that she was not a party member but had been an outspoken opponent of speedups and of Click's faction in the local and that the transfers were in fact demotions. Matt Randle, a black worker who fought for access to better jobs for black workers, was also among the three fired.[139]

Logsdon and others felt that the right wing had calculated a strategy based on impeding the Left's organizing, shop floor mobilizations, contract negotiations, and community action. The defense case against Lenhardt's election fraud charges in 1947 consumed more than one-fourth of the district's previous six months' income. Because of the decentralized structure of the UE, the locals had more money in their coffers than the district office. In reaction to this, Clarence Bingamon of Local 810 introduced a resolution at the spring 1947 convention to replace referendum voting with delegate convention voting.[140] Sentner objected to rescinding the referendum vote, and the motion died. Logsdon recalled that the referendum "was really Sentner's thing.... He needed to have that because of the charges that Communists weren't democratic.... [T]hat was all well and fine in normal circumstances, but these weren't normal circumstances." At the March 1948 district convention, the resolution was reintroduced, and this time the delegates voted resoundingly 144–79 in favor of it. But the amendment had to be approved through local membership meetings, and Click's forces relished the opportunity to suggest that the Left was antidemocratic (even though he had proposed the same idea a few years before). As the district leadership retreated over the issue, it was clear that Click had scored points.[141]

Evansville: "We'll Turn the Whole Town against the Commies"

The Evansville district remained the tower of support for the Left, but the district leadership became convinced that all of the Evansville power structure as well as "old time labor finks and stool pidgeons [sic] long ago exposed by the La Follette Committee" were gearing up to destroy the UE in Evansville. Martin Arundel, editor of the *UE Reporter,* posed as a reporter for a syndicate features newspaper to interview right-wing figures. Arundel approached the subject skeptically but concluded that reactionary forces were integrally involved in the UEMDA strategy. Fred Bender, the operative who had long attempted to slay the UE, "brag[ged] about being in the Evansville situation" and expressed assurance that "they are going to get that Sentner this time.... [E]veryone in Evansville is with us—the newspaper, radio, the clergy. We got them all lined up. It's a perfect set-up. It took us months to work it out. We'll turn the whole town against the commies." While one could doubt the credibility of Bender's claims—even Arundel stressed that Bender seemed to be "a little on the screwball side, though he talked coherently enough"—they seem to be supported by subsequent events, and the interviews conducted by Arundel were admitted as authentic by some of the parties later. Other evidence, including correspondence in the files of Evansville's Republican congressman Edward Mitchell, suggests that a small cabal was prepared to effectively utilize the international political conflict to its advantage.[142]

Writing to Click in mid-March 1948, Troy James mirrored Bender's enthusiasm about dawning prospects: "the boys got a chance to meet them two people you talked to," James enthused, and "boy are they ready." Were the two Bender and Arthur Robinson, Bender's key liaison in Evansville? Robinson was a member of the UAW, but his main identity was anticommunist Veteran. He told Arundel that he had spied on "Communist activity" for the Republican Party since the 1930s when he was involved in the Workers' Alliance, and it might be surmised that he was a Bender contact at that time. He was associated with the Merrill law firm, which represented major antilabor Evansville companies. Beginning in late 1947, Robinson had offered his services to Mitchell, who had passed the information on to Servel's personnel manager. According to Arundel's interviews, Merrill was using him and his veterans' groups as a means to have a front for their plan of attack on the UE.[143]

The Merrill law firm and Servel were key organizers for the Evansville Council for Community Service (ECCS), a "new civic organization" that formed soon after the UE organized Servel. The UE charged that the ECCS was simply a new version of the discredited Evansville Cooperative League, the antilabor employer organization established in 1936 with the impetus of Servel president Louis Ruthenberg. The ECCS sought to oppose "subversive elements which might uproot" the "American system" and was yet another incarnation of the Citizens' Industrial Alliance, but this time with more intense efforts at organizing all "civic minded person[s]" to oppose "ideals contrary to the United States Constitution." Its board of directors was broader to give it the kind of community respect that had eluded the Cooperative League and to continue to shape the political economy of the area. The major goal of the group was to shore up the role of the local police in labor disputes, a role that had become more neutral since the days of the 1939 Servel strike when the company could virtually command the police to do whatever it wanted. The ECCS suggested that mass picketing was the work of subversive elements in the labor movement. It sought to stave off criticism by including clergy, college officials, and labor representatives such as Walter Hayden of the CIO, but Hayden resigned after the group instituted guidelines for police and state officials that would make mass picketing ineffective. Hayden admitted that the Left's charges that it was a "Ruthenberg-dominated" front were correct. The AFL representative objected that the "ground-rules" did not seek labor input and placed "little in the way of restrictions on employers." Nevertheless, interlinked networks among the ECCS, the company's official operatives, Congressman Mitchell, and a spectrum of anticommunist activists, including Hayden, James, Becker, and Robinson, informed and sometimes coordinated the strategies of each other.[144]

The first event in this showdown was the Seeger strike. Seeger management "demanded a contract giving it the exclusive right to discipline and fire workers, to set and change wage rates at will," and to reduce the effectiveness of shop stewards. On April 1, the day the contract expired and workers walked out, Bender arrived in town. The *Evansville Courier* labor reporter advertised his willingness to "slant" the news to hurt the UE strike. Full-page newspaper ads by Seeger charged "left-wing plots" and "irresponsible union leadership," and management "deluged the homes of strikers with anti-UE letters." Editorials in the *Courier* equated Sentner with Stalin. Meanwhile, the AFL and then the UAW launched a raid on the Seeger local right after the strike began.[145]

Seeger workers determined "to bridge the gap" between their ways and those at Servel sustained a mass picket line throughout the strike and organized a community campaign that drew support for their cause from other Local 813 members, Evansville small business owners, and the public, and this effectively countered the raiding campaign. The union exposed Bender's involvement, thereby deepening workers' resolve. By the end of April, Seeger was ready to bargain, agreeing to a contract that the union later claimed "made greater gains in wage, vacation, holiday, and other contract provisions than any other CIO or AFL union in Evansville." Wage rates at Seeger now approached those at Servel, establishing an "Evansville pattern." The victory there propelled a strike of packinghouse workers and presented a serious challenge to the ECCS, which the Evansville CIO charged was a threat to "human rights." Overall, the local police were not decisively opposed to unions, a fact that dogged the ECCS crowd.[146]

It was this momentum that the UE sought to use, in combination with a rank-and-file national bargaining consortium, to challenge Bucyrus-Erie. As an NMTA company, B-E had held firm against uniform wages and conditions; it sought to use the lowest-paid community wage and conditions as a wedge against demands from other workers in its other locations.[147] District 8 sought to reverse the equation, to use the developing "Evansville wage" as leverage. Since May 1947, the local at B-E had worked without a contract rather than accept company's rates. On March 8, UE Local 813 held a conference in Chicago with local United Steel Workers representatives to plan bargaining for a contract. The group elected Sentner chair and agreed to report to each other and act in a coordinated fashion to attain more rights: "when one plant has problems, the others would be notified." The B-E was paying rates in Evansville that were now falling below what the UE had designated as an "Evansville pattern," and the UE 813 decided that they would make their stand in Evansville, with victory there allowing them the power to challenge the entire B-E system in other areas. They demanded the right to determine work schedules and overtime hours, eliminate the no-strike–no-lockout and management rights clauses that were standard in other B-E plants, and insert the UE's grievance representation structure. This differed from the centralized model that was taking hold in the CIO, where the pattern was negotiated out by national leaders, while the locals were left to work out minor details for their local agreements.[148]

But after the Seeger victory, as if on cue, N. R. Knox, head of B-E, announced that B-E would not negotiate with the UE "because it was dominated by Communists." Another NMTA firm, the Remington Rand Corporation of New York, originator of the Mohawk Valley strategy used in the Maytag strike of 1938, had only recently done the same. More specifically, Knox suggested subversive intent in Sentner's refusal to sign a contract along the same lines as the steelworkers' union in Erie, New York. Knox insinuated that UE demands masked Soviet influence. "What you really want," Knox charged, "is a contract which will give you complete domination over those of our employees who belong to your union and deprive us of the right to manage our business. This we would not agree to last year and we won't now."[149] Knox was "anxious" to avail Click of his letter, as Ed Klingler of the *Evansville Press* noted "confidentially" when he passed the letter along to Click. Troy James wrote excitedly that the UEMDA forces were "going great" after Knox's announcement.[150]

Knox's letter implied that Sentner was the sole obstacle to a contract. When in a meeting of B-E workers Sentner confirmed that he was a member of the CP, some members made "loud demands" that he resign, suggesting that "his leadership is jeopardizing the welfare" of the workers. Al Eberhard responded that workers had the right to vote Sentner out of office as provided by the constitution, but not at the demand of the company.[151] Sentner sent his own open letter to Knox arguing that the wage increases demanded were beneficial to the "welfare of your employees and the community" and that the shop steward system the union was demanding was "industrial democracy." He also demanded a debate "before an assembly of your employees" on the question of whether his "political objectives would help to destroy this country in the interest of a foreign power. This is a charge of treason, and if true would make me subject to prosecution under Federal Law."[152]

The Evansville newspapers stepped up the attack. "Strongman" Sentner had been trying to "get a foothold in Evansville industry" since the late 1930s, the *Evansville Press* insisted, adding that his opponents "say Sentner is an assumed name" and implying a secretive plot by Communists to control the town.[153] The *Evansville Courier* chimed in with a sensational series about a purported former dues collector for the CP of Evansville, Katherine Bell, a Faultless Castor worker who claimed to have been recruited to the party from a picket line. Her picture of intrigue, deceit, and a red network that controlled Local 813 made union demands seem to be part of a larger international conspiracy to betray American democracy and Christianity.[154] A veterans' group dubbed the "Spirit of Kilroy" and led by Arthur Robinson pledged to eradicate the Communist influence in the union. Republican congressman Edward Mitchell joined in, accusing Local 813 president Albert Eberhard of being a "pinko." Eberhard replied that Mitchell was "a dirty liar" and asserted, "I'm a Democrat. Sometimes I vote Republican when I feel the better man is in that party. I'm a Catholic, and I hope a good one. In the face of that the pinko charge is absurd. I'm as good a citizen as Ed Mitchell or anyone else."[155]

Local 813 leaders blasted the attacks as payback for militancy on the shop floor and their challenge to the corporate dominance of Evansville. "From the formula set up by [Troy] James and [Congressman] Mitchell you have to be a sellout artist, a racketeer and a 'red' baiter to be a good American. Your officers refuse to accept this brand of 'Americanism.' We prefer to be the kind of Americans who are loyal to our Country, our union, and our members—and work for the good and welfare of all."[156] Sentner challenged the editor of the *Courier* and Knox to a "traditional American town meeting" to air the "slanderous attack on my loyalty to my country and my union" and to determine whether "Local 813 and its officers have loyally served their country and membership."[157]

In mid-June, Local 813 and Sentner agreed that the best response to the attacks was renewed commitment to "solving every grievance problem that arises in the shop and in the community," since unresolved grievances were the companies' "testing grounds" for such issues as speedup and discrimination. They decided that Local 813 needed to develop its community programs even further, including working to prevent a bus fare increase and demands for a "hospital and outclinic, a day nursery and children's clinic." The local called for the "thirty hour week with no reduction in pay" and developed an educational program to contest the need for "speed-ups and rationalization."[158] Meanwhile, when the ECCS condemned Swift packing workers for mass picket lines, the local CIO began to mobilize its opposition to the Evansville power structure, giving more legitimacy to the UE's own efforts.[159]

At a June membership meeting, UEMDA forces were routed. The most climactic moment of the meeting occurred when Sentner challenged James to a debate over whether he was furthering CP aims. When James refused, the leadership chided, "Imagine if you can a man who has run all over Evansville shouting charges against Sentner and the officers . . . ranting that the officers were afraid to face this issue. When faced with a demand for proof before the members—he flatly refuses to talk!"[160] In early August, the leftist leadership of Local 813 was elected by a two-to-one margin, despite the front-page newspaper admonishments that "Communism Is [the] Issue" in the elections, where Sentner was "still a strongman in the UE."[161]

With B-E management still obstinate in their refusal to bargain, the local voted to strike in July. The union prepared a community campaign similar to the one that had been so effective in the Seeger strike, distributing appeals to small businesses and community groups and using radio broadcasts to publicize its perspective. The appeals stressed that the union had "the welfare of our community at heart. We feel that we are entitled to the same kind of benefits and treatment that the people receive from the other companies in this town." They demanded that B-E raise its minimum rates from $.88 to the community rate of $1.11 and eliminate wage differentials with other plants. Broadcasts depicted well the realities of speedup at the plant.[162] Local 813 member Ralph

Finan condemned the company for its contentions that communism was the key issue. "The company thinks it is going to fool a lot of us people with all its yapping about reds and red plots, but I'll tell you," he exclaimed, "this company doesn't fool me one minute with its propaganda."[163]

For a month, the B-E picket line held, with all the hallmarks of District 8's community campaigns, despite the company's efforts to get a back-to-work movement going. Local 813's ads in local newspapers, for example, were signed by dozens of local businesses and placed the struggle as one of family sustenance versus corporate greed. In frustration, the company sought to ship material to the Atomic Energy Commission to portray the union's mass picketing as a subversive attempt to interfere with the defense program. The union countered by offering to ship the material itself under government supervision.[164] But the company succeeded in getting a restraining order from the county court against "congregating in any group or groups." Soon thereafter, the company sought to use foremen to break the mass picketing while some UEMDA leaders, according to the newspapers, were organizing workers to cross the lines. Striker Ralph Finan, on the front line, announced to those attempting to cross, "To hell with restraining orders. You are strike breakers, scabs. Don't let those sons of bitches in." Sentner agreed, allegedly saying, "Shit on the injunction. . . . We are going to hold this picket line. There wouldn't be enough jails in this city to hold all the pickets." Striker Elbert Cain put himself directly in front of the automobile attempting to cross, just one of many moves that heightened the drama. Sentner and Charles Wright were arrested and charged with contempt of court and disorderly conduct.[165] Troy James sent accounts of the union's troubles to Click, commenting that "boy are the commies on a spot now. Ha ha. I hope they hang every damn one of them, every damn commie is in town for the kill."[166]

Following ECCS guidelines, the local sheriff used the fracas to ask Indiana's governor Ralph Gates to send in state police. Meanwhile, a company-organized back-to-work meeting convened on August 30 to make plans to cross the lines, with 350 people attending and the company warning that it would not rehire anyone engaging in "picket-line violence." The next morning, 140 state police formed a corridor of police cars and officers two blocks long "to prevent mass picketing." When state troopers forced aside 7 women at the plant gates, the women began to fight back, triggering a cascade of events between 200 strikers who sought to break through the line and a cordon of police determined to hold them back, leading to the arrest of some strikers and union leadership. Fifty workers marched on the jail to demand release of some of those arrested.[167]

All those who sought to enter the plant that day did so, but the local had shown spirit and pledged to "defeat their efforts to maintain involuntary servitude in Evansville." Initially it seemed possible that they could pull it off. The local CIO federation now pledged support, even calling a labor holiday, in reaction to the attempt of the AFL to decertify the UE local in the midst of the strike.

Most B-E workers had not attempted to cross the lines, and by September 4, only 30 percent of the regular workforce had done so. B-E workers took their cause to the Evansville neighborhoods, urging residents to shun scabs who were named in leaflets. An indication of the level of community support came when Gold Medal Dairy sent ten dollars to the local in apology because one of its drivers crossed the line. B-E worker Gaither West refused when called to cooperate with a county prosecutor investigating picket line incidents and instead called on a grand jury to investigate "eighty-eight cents an hour rates at Bucyrus-Erie and their effect on our community." Unable to staff the plant, the company sought to operate with prison labor, but the union exposed this and rallied its members. A major blow came on September 7 when the ECCS's own D. Bailey Merrill ruled in an injunction hearing to bar all picketing. Already the union had lost its representation rights because of the Taft-Hartley noncommunist affidavit issue. Then the local learned that a special subcommittee of the House Education and Labor Committee (HELC) would hold hearings in Evansville on "Communist influence in the B-E strike."[168] Recognizing the crisis they were now facing, the union ended the strike because of the "combination of forces" that had "joined hands with the union hating" B-E management.[169]

Modeled after the interrogations of HUAC, the HELC had played a similar role in other strikes, starting with its initiation of such tactics in the Allis-Chalmers plant of Milwaukee, the home location of B-E.[170] The hearings were chaired by antiunion Republican congressman Gerald Landis and led by local Republican congressman Edward Mitchell, who was not even a member of the committee. Mitchell claimed that a letter from William Debes had prompted the hearings, making it appear that the request came from the rank and file. But Mitchell was a longtime associate of Merrill and Ruthenberg, and it is more likely that this hearing was designed with advice from Allis-Chalmers and NMTA. The key witnesses were Katherine Bell, the informant for the earlier *Courier* series about UE; Ernest Rutherford, a Seeger worker and UEMDA member who had run against Seeger shop chairman Clifford Haire and was an outspoken opponent against Local 813 leadership; and Arthur Robinson, the auto worker who identified himself as "a commander of the Spirit of Kilroy" veterans' group. These witnesses named twenty-six people who they claimed were members of the CP or had attended party meetings. Bell testified that she had been recruited to the party by Ernest Upton, the Faultless Castor shop chairman, and Charles Wright, former president of Local 813 and current district secretary of the UE. She claimed that Wright, Upton, and Briggs auto worker Alfred Smith (the first president of Local 1002, the predecessor to Local 813) formed a "three man secretariat" that controlled the party and the unions in Evansville. The dramatic presentation of a few signed membership cards she claimed to have saved from when she was membership director of the local party chapter lent credibility to her charges.[171]

Most of the workers called before the committee refused to answer questions until their counsel, the national UE attorney, could represent them. Regarding this as simply a ploy to evade the committee's questions, Landis and Mitchell attacked each uncooperative witness. At one point Landis retorted that "you guys all quote that little line; you pull that same lingo all the time; hide behind the Constitution that you are out to beat." Tiring of the refusal of witnesses to answer whether they had ever been in the party, Mitchell and Landis were determined to tarnish the character of the witnesses. Mitchell taunted them, "Do you believe in God, Mrs. Smith?" and "Are you a Communist?" And when they continued to respond that they were "not refusing to answer" but "wanted counsel," Mitchell egged them on by continuing to repeat the question, "Wait just a minute. Do you believe in God?"[172] When shop steward Ernest Upton continued to refer to his right to an attorney, Landis railed, "Do you think it would be a violation of your constitutional rights if a group got together and hid behind the constitution and tarred and feathered you birds?" Landis assured reporters that "99%" of uncooperative witnesses at other hearings "have been communists" and asked the press to print the names and addresses of every uncooperative witness so as to "give these people the proper publicity" to "the people next door" so that they know "the kind of termites" they were. "We are not going to stop until we run them down." The names and addresses of the accused were listed in the newspapers. Some workers criticized the hearings, and even some anticommunists called to testify suggested that they did not want the committee's intervention. One worker criticized the Taft-Hartley Act because the government used it to "hurt the common working people" of America or harm "workers who did not want the AFL again." Occasionally a worker in frustration stated that he or she believed in God and went to church, frustrating Mitchell's portrayal of militant workers as under the influence of "godless Communists."[173]

What Sentner described as a "lynch spirit" took hold in Evansville. The *Evansville Courier* opined that a "real American citizen" would not "hesitate to answer" if asked whether he or she was a member of the party. As the accused returned to work, most were forced out by fellow workers acting in a "carefully orchestrated" manner, sometimes through physical threats and violence as the employer looked on or provided assistance. At Faultless, the company set up a "Taft-Hartley affidavit room, asking workers to renounce communism and ask[ing] for their religious affiliations as proof of loyalty," and then fired workers who refused. While few UE members actually participated in the purges, the effect was to silence many who supported the Left.[174] When told of these events, Mitchell responded that "I hope the workers will finish cleaning their own house and then keep it clean." While some of the workers "may not be Communists," he said, "they had their chance to clear their names . . . and wouldn't take it."[175] This sort of pressure led some of the accused to ask to be recalled to the hearings in order to reclaim their jobs. Some disputed Bell's claims that they had been members while others admitted to having once been a member of the party or having attended meetings, but none confirmed the "grand conspiracy" voiced by Bell and the congressmen. Meanwhile, the entire leadership of the Faultless union, all accused of party membership by Bell, resigned in protest, despite having been elected overwhelmingly on the eve of the hearings.[176] At a meeting of Local 813, held one day after the end of the hearings, anticommunists took the lead. Logsdon claimed that during the entire meeting, Father Schoettlekoette was "out on the escape hatch looking in the window . . . [and] shouting at the people what to do." The meeting revoked Sentner's honorary membership in the local and voted to fire Payne, along with Sidney and Sadelle Berger and other office staff (although Bell had only named Payne). Albert Eberhard, the union president, refused to resign, commenting that he was determined to "pull this union together so we can go ahead and fight for a living wage." Logsdon, reacting, appointed Payne "as field organizer in charge of that local. And you should have heard the hollering!"[177] Commenting on the events, the *Evansville Courier* predicted that the hearings marked "the end of Sentner's influence in the UE at Evansville." The *Post-Dispatch* commended workers for "showing Sentner the door."[178] Meanwhile, B-E had fired sixty-five activists, who endured a local blacklist, but when the local sought to publicize it, B-E filed a libel suit to prevent its publicity. Within two weeks, B-E workers voted to join the AFL, and the company signed a four-year contract that ended its labor troubles for the moment.[179]

Just as it seemed virtually certain that Local 813's Left would be annihilated, the union leadership devised remarkable strategies to rouse the membership. Vernon Countryman, a law professor at Yale University, wrote to expose the illegitimate use of a congressional subcommittee (which was limited to investigations regarding law) to weed out union activists. Syd Berger and national UE attorney Arthur Kinoy filed a lawsuit for an injunction against "the congressional subcommittee, the congressmen and the companies," using Reconstruction era statutes designed to protect freed slaves from former slaveholders' conspiracies. Berger and Kinoy charged a conspiracy to destroy Local 813.[180] While they knew they could not win, the strategy encouraged workers. The union invited clergy and the public to its own "UE hearing" where it presented evidence that N. R. Knox, Fred Bender, John Griffith, Don Scism (*Courier* editor), Arthur Robinson, and Walter Hayden had conspired along with Mitchell and Landis to create "mob hysteria" to "black-list the B-E strikers who fought labor's fight against 88 cent wage scales." Through radio broadcasts, they exposed a blacklist that targeted some of the most militant workers at B-E. Ernest Upton, noting that he had been raised in Oklahoma and was from multiethnic "American" roots, remarked, "I'd like to have a greater share of the profits of the company that I work for. I'd like to give my children the benefit of a college education that I didn't have."[181] Within a few weeks, the local was recapturing segments of workers who had initially repudiated the leadership. Jim Payne was reelected president of Local 813. Then in early November, Congressman Mitchell, running on his role against "reds" in the HELC interrogations, lost his seat in the 1948 election.[182]

But the events in Evansville convinced key leaders, especially Wagner Local 1104, to withdraw support for Sentner's election.[183] When the district convention opened on September 25, 1948, Sentner, after a long soliloquy on the struggles of the past and the present, closed with an announcement that both he and Logsdon would not seek reelection to district office. Charging that his opponents were motivated by ambition that did not belong in the trade union movement, he warned that "it is a grievous error to try to make a political organization out of a labor union. It is just as much an error to maintain that a union is nothing but a pure and simple economic organization." He acknowledged those who had "reluctantly voiced the opinion that I should step aside in the interest of the organization. Some of you have told me that you believe that my stepping aside will greatly assist in unifying our membership in the fight against the employers and the enemies of this union. . . . You say that . . . red-baiting and the war hysteria makes it more difficult, if not almost impossible for you to continue your support to me." Sentner noted that "in principle I cannot agree with you because to concede that one's political beliefs bar one from holding office in this union makes concession to those who would change the Constitution of our Union, as well as pervert the basic democratic concepts upon which this nation was founded." Despite his objections, Sentner noted the "sincerity of those who have asked me to consider this matter in the light of the red-baiting war hysteria that has engulfed our nation" and cannot be "ignored."[184]

In a subsequent evaluation of his decision, Sentner reflected when he stepped aside, the "progressive forces" were indeed unified for the rest of the convention. They chose Joe Pogue as their district presidential candidate. Pogue was only twenty-eight years old, but he had been a member of the Wagner local since 1937, when he joined at age seventeen. He ran on a ticket with Albert Eberhard, president of Local 813. A renewed commitment to racial justice was expressed when Lowell Waldron of Wagner Electric withdrew from the executive board in order to elect African American delegate Lee Henry of Local 1104 for his position. The new unity resulted in overwhelming delegate votes "against red-baiting" and other "progressive" resolutions. Local 813 members united behind restoring the jobs of many of the workers blacklisted because of the HELC hearings.[185]

Click approached the election with confidence, given the Evansville events and the growing anticommunist sentiments among workers. He attacked Sentner's "hand-picked" candidates and blasted Pogue for evading the issue of communism, suggesting that he was "more dangerous to the security of his country and the welfare of his union than a dozen Sentners, Emspaks or Matleses."[186] But the Pogue slate, according to Sentner, focused on "basic issues of wage rates, contract conditions, speed-up, [and] rate cutting" and contended that Click was responsible for the fact that women at Emerson received the lowest minimum rates in the district.[187] When Opal Cline, the Local 1102 member transferred as a security risk, contended that she had been fired for protesting the eighty-eight-cent rate she earned after her transfer and that Local 1102 had abandoned her, Click denied that there was such a low rate. Then Cline produced her pay stubs. Click was invited to debate the opposition ticket at Local 813; he "appeared but stayed outside in his automobile." Sentner wrote that this "exposure of Click's yellow streak became the property of the membership and did him no good in the election."[188]

The Pogue slate won by almost two thousand votes. Even in St. Louis, the UEMDA forces showed losses compared to the previous year. In 1947, Click had managed to get 95 percent of Emerson local members to vote, but in 1948, 31 percent refused to vote "despite harassment."[189] In Evansville, the UEMDA forces conceded the hopelessness of their struggle. Shortly after the election, they voted to disband and issued a bitter statement: "The members of our union have shown by a fair referendum vote that they do not wish to rid our union of Communist elements."[190]

Outside Forces and the Triumph of the Right

During 1949, as anticommunism deepened and as recession and unemployment racked the district, the Left fought a rearguard action that allowed little time to advance a positive program. District staff (including Sentner and Logsdon, who were appointed as international representatives) fought off one CIO or AFL raid after another. Certainly it seemed possible to believe that their strategies of militance might prevail in such adversity (Wagner elected large majorities favorable to the Left), but it was difficult to assert a positive program, and signals of the key argument emerged when the Right argued that workers were economically harmed during trying times by the Left's presence. This was the reason that in February 1949, anticommunist forces prevailed in the Moline Local 814 (Minneapolis-Moline Power Tool Company) elections, where the members had elected new delegates including "a dyed in the wool Republican . . . a good rightwinger," as described by one of Click's supporters.[191]

Such comments underscored the ideological differences on trade union issues that underlay the two camps. Though Click was certainly not the advocate of company unionism that Sentner's faction claimed he was, he had constructed an alliance with forces that undermined any effort to establish a unionism that could challenge corporate power. Thus, not only ideology but also factional politics led to polarized loyalties and meaningful differences on key issues.

These distinctions between Left and Right on bargaining issues were particularly apparent at Seeger and were revealed in contract negotiations amidst impending layoffs in the sharp recession of 1949. In late 1948, Sentner calculated that 75 percent of the Seeger shop stewards were favorable to the Left, but this waned as the UAW pounced with a raid on the local. The UE pointed to significant distinctions between its style of unionism and the UAW's, embodied in contract differences. It pointed out that the Evansville UAW's contract at General Motors and at International Harvester allowed the company the right to fire workers for "so-called 'inefficiency'" and "forced workers to submit grievances to the foreman instead of the union shop steward."[192] The UE won the election, but the raid took its toll. It resulted in the right-wing's victory in local union elections; opponents argued that the leftist leadership would bring on continuous raids and distract the union from winning a new contract because they refused to sign noncommunist affidavits.[193]

But the Right's willingness to accommodate with Seeger was soon very apparent. Otto Maschoff found that the company was pushing for a serious rollback in the previous year's contract victories, including "limitations on women's seniority to certain job classes," restrictions on company-wide seniority, rate cutting, and restrictions on the ability of shop stewards to "police" the shop floor, and that the local's right-wing leadership was "inclined to concede" to the company. Maschoff called for a one hundred-person negotiating committee and a membership vote on the company proposals. Seeger's day shift voted "hearty agreement" on both. But by the time of the night shift meeting the Right launched an attack, accusing Maschoff of being the impediment because he was a "communist," and supporters such as "an elderly woman" who "pleaded for company-wide seniority w[ere] shouted down and called all kinds of vile insulting names." Maschoff, "physically prevented" from speaking, was lucky to survive the meeting.[194] Someone attempted to push Maschoff through a third-story window. He was kicked and punched across the hall and beaten while in a kneeling position. He dodged a blow to the head with a chair and then narrowly escaped when a "defender" took blows for him.[195] Maschoff withdrew from negotiations when he was warned that negotiating "would make me subject to physical violence. Threats were made on my life." Maschoff concluded that the Right was dividing the membership along age and gender lines at a time when large layoffs threatened and that in the context of the increasing unemployment situation in Evansville and anticommunism, "desire for job security can be whipped into mob violence."[196]

Shortly after Maschoff withdrew, the right wing signed a contract that contained twenty-two changes with negative effects on workers' wages and rights.[197] The Seeger leadership threatened to deliver the local to the UAW. The UE won, but only by a narrow margin. Afterward, Local 813 leaders allowed Seeger workers to form their own local. A year later the key right-wing leader who had pushed the changes was promoted to foreman.[198]

The Left, where it remained viable, continued to show that its attention to community-based organizing distinguished its style of unionism and could galvanize workers in the midst of unrelenting attacks on its patriotism and effectiveness. By 1949, community-based campaigns around unemployment issues seemed essential. More than ten thousand of the twenty-nine thousand workers the district represented in 1949 were laid off for a significant part of the year, while many others were on reduced hours. The district launched unemployment committees, but they received no support from the right-wing locals. Local 813, where the Left was strongest, organized unemployed workers in the community, reaching beyond its own members. There was also a strong organized protest against the city's bus line fare hike.[199]

This sort of activity was steadily losing ground, however, to the right wing's emerging argument that workers were in danger of losing economic security because of the Left's presence. In 1949, the "Sentner slate" (as Click dubbed the Left), headed by Local 813's Albert Eberhard, won in the closest election ever, with only five hundred votes separating the two slates.[200]

Even before the vote, Click's forces were preparing for an alternative method of taking power. In October 1949 the CIO expelled eleven unions that were charged with being "Communist-dominated" and set up rival unions in their place. The International Union of Electrical Workers (IUE) was now the CIO-affiliated union, backed by an enormous amount of money and support from the national CIO federation. In this context, the argument that workers who remained allied with the Left would endanger their economic livelihood became extraordinarily powerful. "Red meat on the table or red negotiators!!" one leaflet shouted.[201] Now workers would have to choose between remaining in an ostracized union or a union sanctioned and supported by the CIO and the government. The Left had emphasized the need for joint action with other CIO unions. Now it would have to persuade workers otherwise with uneven campaign chests.

Seven months later, in June 1950, Sentner tried to put the best face on the situation by noting that the IUE had failed in its "main objective which was to destroy the UE completely." Nevertheless, the district had been irreparably torn apart. Seven of the district's twenty-five locals, including 1102, 1108, 814, and 805, quickly marched into the IUE by lopsided votes. On the other hand, Locals 810, 813, 1116, and 1110 stayed solidly with the UE. Others, such as Local 1104 (Wagner), where shop stewards voted 81–8 to remain in the UE, were brought into the IUE only after a months-long campaign that included numerous full-time CIO personnel and an unlimited campaign chest. CIO officers distributed anti-UE HUAC material; on the inside of the plant UE supporters were accused of being disloyal to the nation. Hershel Walker years later was certain that the key factor in the defeat of the UE related to threat to workers' jobs, which was "impossible" to counter. Wagner, now the largest employer of the St. Louis independents, had come to rely on defense work in the postwar period, and when the company and the CIO showed workers evidence that the government would deny defense industry subcontracts if they did not vote for the IUE.[202]

The focus on the Communist issue had overwhelmed the Left's efforts to continue an ideological struggle that included commitment to militancy on the shop floor, a challenge to corporate power in the community and the larger political economy, the breaking down of social divisions, and the right of political radicals to have membership in and leadership of unions. The district's campaign at B-E had placed workers' struggle for wages and security as part of a larger struggle for community and workplace control. These were the same sorts of issues that had animated, for instance, the Maytag struggle of 1938, and—a half-century before that—the St. Louis metal trades strike. Workers were clearly prepared to struggle for these aims under leftist leadership, but the campaigns that brought anticommunism to the forefront of American life resulted in a precipitous routing. The ingredients for the anticommunism drive developed at the local level, from a multitude of factors, including principled anticommunists, political reactionaries, employers and revived NMTA networks, labor spies and other operatives, socialist factional enemies, CIO national and local officials, opportunists, priests and Catholic lay societies, veterans organizations, the American Legion, liberals, FBI agents, and antilabor congressmen. These actors came to the project with a variety of motivations, but in the end they resulted in a reactionary outcome. In the name of fighting totalitarian influence in District 8, they destroyed one of the most democratic organizations of working-class life in the Midwest. For the "militant minority" of businessmen who had initiated the crusade in the 1930s, that had been the goal all along. They had played out an agenda of local strategies that made them an important part of the history of the 1930s and 1940s.

Conclusion

District 8 of the United Electrical, Radio and Machine Workers of America (UE) survived through 1955. Its tenacious leadership continued to urge the struggle for worker rights on the shop floor and more community campaigns, struggles for "full and unequivocal civil and job rights for our Negro members," the "fight for increased women's rights," and the defense of the rights of radicals, including Communists, to membership in and leadership of the union. But the Cold War and domestic anticommunism that gripped the nation continued to construct a conspiracy context to every labor and community demand; even picket line solidarity came under suspicion. When Local 813 members picketed with Singer Sewing Machine workers in Evansville, they were harassed and threatened with "bodily harm" by anti-Left forces in the community who suggested that mass picketing and cross-union solidarity were "another Communist plot and trick."[1]

The rival International Union of Electrical Workers (IUE) was not the "company union" that the UE charged it was, but the stifling of the Left mattered critically in approaches to trade union and community issues. Surviving UE District 8 locals continued to advocate wage policies based on solidarity. They argued that unions should combat divisions between skilled and unskilled; men, women, and blacks, and the top of the wage hierarchy and the bottom. Increasing skilled trades' rates in the plants up to prevailing community wage levels of craft unions should be accomplished with the aim of moving up all pay rates in the plant. At the same time, the IUE District 8 applauded efforts to move toward percentage-based increases in wage contracts rather than a "cents per hour" increase that the UE had initiated in 1937, a goal that the local electrical firms had had for years. A leaflet for the Skilled Trades division of the IUE, headed by Click's factional ally Harvey Smith, noted in 1956, "It was not until the IUE had replaced the UE that this special consideration for skilled groups was possible." Emerson worker and leftist ally Lloyd Austin recalled that "we tried to argue about that. We said, 'Why not pay attention to the person at the bottom rather than the person at the top?'"[2]

Distinctions between the UE and the IUE were complicated by a variety of factors. On the one hand, in St. Louis amalgamated UE Local 810 and in Evansville's Local 813, where the Left was strongest and not as susceptible to raiding, shop floor militancy and community-oriented campaigns remained the hallmark of unionism. These two locals in the period 1950–55 sought to eliminate the no-strike clause, incentive pay, and the piecework system and to institute plantwide seniority whenever it had not already been implemented. They made the elimination of gender and racial divisions and other inequalities top priorities. "Stop-and-go" strikes and "work-to-rule" strategies helped to gain contracts and settle issues and grievances. Ray Staeder, an IUE District 8 representative in the 1970s and 1980s, remarked that the most "difficult locals" he had to "contend" with as a business agent were those the Left had influenced through the 1950s. Commenting on some former Local 810 shops, he said that "I never could get it into the heads of the membership that the company needed to make a decent profit" and that "efficiency" was a concern of the union, because "the Communists had made them think that they needed to resist that sort of stuff." It is notable that dissident United Automobile Workers member Jerry Tucker renovated the "stop-and-go" and "work-to-rule" strategies in the 1970s after seeing it in a former UE District 8 local.[3]

These resistance strategies were increasingly isolated from a broader strategy to influence the political economy in the 1950s. By the early 1950s, Evansville Local 813's community campaign goals were lost amidst headlining addresses by Joseph McCarthy and UAW leader Walter Reuther. By the mid-1950s, UE District 8 representative Eve Milton lamented the difficulty of effectively organizing workers in St. Louis in solidarity for sympathy picketing and in breaking down racial and gender barriers in the context of a divided labor movement. Without a cohesive base, any hopes to stanch the runaway shop campaigns that were shaping up as the leading corporate policy died on the vine or amidst a budget shortfall. In Cape Girardeau, Missouri, District 8 had managed to reorganize the runaway Superior Electric shop, and women were in key leadership positions, forging ahead on bargaining over a variety of factors that affected women's low wages. But almost overnight, the AFL's International Brotherhood of Electrical Workers worked on the men's resentment of a woman president, and the union disaffiliated. And even the most loyal members' concerns about effectiveness of the union compared to state- and Congress of Industrial Organization (CIO)-sanctioned unions deepened. Such was the case in the Maytag local, which had been solidly in the leftist caucus in the period of developing anticommunism but abruptly left the district in 1951 to join the UAW, suggesting that it wasn't getting adequate representation. Sentner agreed, writing that the local officers had "curbed the fighting spirit of their membership" against "long-standing grievances" and that the district had gone along because it had taken for granted a membership that had reviled IUE raiding.[4]

Sentner remained a UE international representative until 1954, when the UE decided that it could no longer support an open Communist. He was trailed and harassed wherever he attempted to lead organizing drives during these years. Federal Bureau of Investigation (FBI) informants notified employers of his

Communist affiliation in the small towns and remote areas of Illinois, Indiana, Missouri, and southern states. In 1951, *Newsweek* heightened the stakes when it labeled him the Communist Party (CP)'s top choice to "hurt the United States defense effort." Wherever he went, one newspaper noted, "authorities sought information on Sentner's political affiliations and background because they said he drew attention by making inflationary speeches to workers in those areas."[5] In Mt. Carmel, for example, the Meissner plant had temporarily closed down, but the membership had voted against the IUE resoundingly, and the UE contract was still in effect. When it reopened, however, townspeople led by the mayor and the American Legion met Sentner's train at the station "ready to run him out if he tried to enter" and forced workers into accepting IUE representation.[6]

Still, the vision of social movement unionism that sought to connect union to community was not obliterated, though it was put into practice by only the most committed cadre under isolated and deeply repressive circumstances, hidden beneath the surface of the intense anticommunism of the period. One notable example of the continuing influence of the old visions took place in a struggle almost completely vanquished from the memory of civil rights struggles in the pantheon of St. Louis and was led by Wagner Electric worker and CP member Hershel Walker, one of the original nut pickers' union supporters. A small group of activists under the aegis of the National Negro Labor Council campaigned against Sears Roebuck retail stores, demanding that black women be hired as sales clerks. Their struggle was relentless, lasting nine long months, and involved a core of thirty workers, a number of them white and black workers from the electrical plants. While they did get some support from black clergy and the mayor of Kinloch, they could not get the civil rights organizations of the city involved despite numerous overtures. Their tenacity, despite harassment by the FBI and St. Louis Police Red Squad officials, paid off when Sears, embarrassed about the bad publicity and the police cameras in front of their stores, finally agreed to the demands.[7] Another example took place in Louisville, Kentucky, about 70 miles from District 8's Tell City local, where workers at International Harvester organized under the Farm Equipment Workers (FE) in 1947. District 8 gave steady assistance and advice to the local, especially in constructing a community campaign that continued after the FE merged with the UE in 1952. That campaign developed into a full-fledged effort for job rights in the plant and civil rights in Louisville. Senter urged FE Local 236 and two other Left locals in Louisville to hire Carl and Anne Braden as joint editors their paper. This experience launched the Bradens on a path that led to influence the civil rights movement of the 1950s and 1960, especially among youth. (In his eloquent 1963 "Letter from a Birmingham Jail," Martin Luther King, Jr. cited Anne Braden as one of the cadre of white supporters who recognized the need for strong resistance strategies to racial oppression.) The Sentners and Bradens became close friends as they faced prosecutions based on charges of subversion.[8]

Sentner spent a great deal of time defending himself and his family from relentless persecution. Beginning in 1949, the Sentner family fought the government's attempt to deport Toni Sentner, who had steadily if unsuccessfully sought citizenship papers since the late 1930s but had been denied because of her political activism. Prosecuted under immigration laws and the McCarran Act, she was named "one of the 86 top alien Communists in the United States." Since she had not been active in the CP since the 1930s, government officials targeted her primarily because of her relationship to William Sentner.[9] As William "Red" Davis, a St. Louis CP member, joked years later, Toni Sentner was "charged with associatin' with her husband!" At the time it was no laughing matter. Sentner called it an "unprincipled act of political cowardice" on the part of the government. Because none of the countries asked to accept her would do so (including her native Yugoslavia), she was saved from separation from her family but faced years of legal proceedings, appeals, and government harassment.[10]

In 1952 in the midst of negotiations at Eagle Signal in Moline, William Sentner was arrested and charged under the Smith Act with "conspiracy to advocate the overthrow of the U.S. government by force and violence." This was part of the "red roundup" of "second string" midwestern Communist leaders, who FBI director J. Edgar Hoover declared were among the most dangerous in the country. Eagle Signal management, told that Sentner was due to be arrested, held up negotiations accordingly. Awakening him from his hotel room in the early morning, FBI agents seemed bemused that they found a Missouri fishing license rather than CP paraphernalia in his wallet. "The charge is ridiculous," Sentner said, and he accused the government of intentionally disrupting union negotiations and giving employers ammunition in the nearby Farm Equipment Union strike in which Sentner was also critically involved: "They are going stark mad in Washington when they do this kind of stuff. The only thing I have conspired in is to keep the Eagle Signal Corporation from installing an incentive system at the plant."[11] The trial began in early 1954. Sentner passionately defended his belief in democratic socialism, the U.S. Constitution, and nonviolence, evidence of which was in the FBI files but was withheld from his defense team. His attorney, Sidney Berger, sought to show that the prosecution was "trying to prove that dissent is treason," since they had not shown Sentner guilty of conspiracy to advocate the overthrow of the government. But in the frenzied atmosphere of the times, the jury took little time to find him and the four other St. Louis Smith Act defendants guilty for their beliefs and association. Sentner was sentenced to five years in prison, though he was released pending appeal. The hardships of the series of legal prosecutions were compounded by Sentner's inability to find work. He took odd jobs to make ends meet and eventually obtained a job at Barnes Hospital as a maintenance carpenter, though constant illness left the family in dire circumstances. Still, he continued to remain active in political affairs. When he ran for the Board of Freeholders to revise the city charter, the number of votes he received was high enough to raise alarm about the connections between the St. Louis African American community and the CP.[12]

Despite Sentner's continuing misgivings about the CP, he did not officially resign until early 1957. Clearly, revelations about Stalin made Sentner question his previous efforts to legitimize the party, but he was still deeply committed to the need for a working-class party dedicated to socialist principles, the very impetus that had caused him to cast his lot with the CP more than twenty years before. According to FBI informants, at the time he resigned he expressed regrets about the mistakes he had made after he joined the CP. He spoke somewhat wistfully of workers' urgings that he leave the party, noting their promise that if he would, they would support his right to discuss socialism—"but as long as you are a Communist we are afraid to take a chance." With his resignation, he noted that he might at last expect the "end to government persecution." Sentner did not have much time to enjoy such freedom. Just two months after the Supreme Court's *Yates* decision overturned the Smith Act convictions in 1958, Sentner died of a heart attack at the age of fifty-one. The vast number of people who came to pay their last respects and who helped pay for the cost of the funeral for a family that was penniless were indications of the affection that many held for Sentner, even when they could not feel free to openly express it.[13]

By 1955, the remaining unions of UE District 8 merged with the International Association of Machinists (IAM). Logsdon remembered years later that it was the painful decision of those in the field that led to taking this hard step. Jim Payne wrote in 1954 that "despite the fight put up by the UE and despite the fact that UE working conditions and contracts are far superior to the raiding unions, I fear that the UE will be wiped out or reduced to insignificance as a bargaining agent." The core Evansville cadre met at a tavern near the Servel plant to "say good-bye to their local amidst tears and drink." Logsdon signed on as organizer for the IAM, eventually retiring after a lifetime of organizing that he "liked" but that was a "far cry" from the experiences of the UE. The IAM also hired James Payne, but he had to be "cleared" of charges of communism before the IAM's loyalty committee. The Evansville locals continued the democratic traditions started in the UE, but the impact of the international union's agenda was clearly felt. Many of those in Evansville who had stuck it out with the UE, such as Charles Fridy, Charles Wright, Sadelle and Sydney Berger, and numerous others were under suspicion for years in the town; many others feared the consequences of even discussing those years even in the 1990s after the end of the Cold War. They paid a heavy price indeed for their union commitments.[14]

Factional warfare and cronyism plagued the IUE as James Click, the IUE district director, tried to realign with progressive forces while working with former allies who, he later admitted, were "Neanderthals" as far as unionism was concerned. The anticommunist coalition that had been created at Emerson during the UE period continued to perpetuate a right-wing leadership in the local. In this context, even Click welcomed CP member "Red" Davis's activism in the local. Davis had left Memphis because of red-baiting and took a job at Emerson in 1952. Davis got women worker allies to persuade Click to run for local president against a leading right-winger. Click won the election, and that cemented a relationship with Davis, who continued to work to make "progress" on key issues such as racial and gender problems in the local. According to Davis, "Click wasn't doing anything about blacks' or women's issues, but he didn't mind my doing it. . . . He had gotten trapped in his own anticommunism, but he was for a good strong union." When Local 1102 went on strike in 1954, Davis headed the relief work. He won the respect of a significant section of the new executive board, who refused to take action after the FBI informed them that they had a Communist in their midst. But when Davis was called before the House Un-American Activities Committee St. Louis hearings in 1956 and charged with contempt of Congress afterward, Emerson fired him. Click promised to arbitrate the case but never did.[15]

In the early 1960s, IUE District 8 was still mired in intense factionalism, this time between Click and his former allies. Some, including Harvey Smith and John Burns, decided that Click was a "sell-out" and sought to expose his lackluster performance. Smith, who had been appointed as business representative by Carey only after being continually and resoundingly defeated for various offices in the Wagner union local, even hired someone to take a recorder into the closet of a hotel room where Click was negotiating by himself with management. He played the tape recording to members of the Seeger local, and workers refused to agree to the contract. Click survived that accusation, but he could not survive the machinations of James Carey, president of the IUE, who Click suggested had "gone mad" by the 1960s: "I mean that literally. . . . [H]e used to sit in the office and listen to his speeches on tape. And just cackle, just clap. Do that FOR HOURS! [Of] course that wasn't dangerous, but some other things he did [were]." A faction in the international encouraged Click to contest Carey, but Carey "had enough on five or six members of that group, that they couldn't afford to make a fight. Bad debts, money borrowed illegally, a whole bunch of other stuff. So that quieted them." Carey loyalists included Orville Munzer, the former leader of Local 825 and then lackluster Operation Dixie organizer, now appointed as the IUE Midwest organizing director. Click derided Munzer for having "failed to organize anything or be in any winning campaign in all the years he's worked" in the position, an echo of Logsdon's assessment in 1947. Click complained that William Drohan, West Coast director, had "failed to organize a single shop or be associated with any winning campaign in the past 5 years." Carey sent a number of staff members to the district to organize against Click for the district presidency, and Click had had enough. He resigned from the district presidency and left the IUE, suggesting that the union was a "hopeless mess of dishonesty, confusion and ineffectiveness."[16]

The mainstream union movement was in full retreat from the expansive visions that had animated District 8. One interesting exception was led by Harold Gibbons, Sentner's nemesis, who disaffiliated with the CIO Distribution Workers and led the local members into the St. Louis Teamsters union. Gibbons hired Ernest Calloway, an African American Red Caps (railroad) union member who, like Gibbons, was a former Socialist. Calloway was the soul of the union, as they urged the union movement to integrate the "identities of 'worker' and 'citizen'" in the 1960s and led the union on a mission against the scourge of St. Louis's slums and in other campaigns to connect the union to civil rights issues. Later Gibbons was also among a small cohort of trade unionists who challenged the labor movement's acceptance of U.S. foreign policy, joining Labor for Peace, urging withdrawal from Vietnam, and earning the ire of many local and national labor figures. Perhaps under different political and international circumstances, had the UE survived, the union movement's role in the city might have achieved the kind of social democratic milieu Joshua Freeman has shown animated New York City. But Gibbons had helped to eradicate from the labor movement the very forces that had initially brought civic unionism to the forefront and also operated mostly in isolation from the rest of the labor movement.[17]

Metal and machining workers in the midwestern communities where District 8 had organized were unable to present a unified voice as they faced the disinvestment that reduced unionized jobs from the 1950s through the 1980s. In 1954, management at Emerson, Wagner and Century undertook a campaign to "break the industry pattern," the agreement, won during the war period, that they would follow the wage pattern at General Electric, designed to take wages out of competition. At the time, Sentner wrote that it was evidence that the old National Metal Trades Association (NMTA) "bunch" were still operating collectively, with the same designs they had had since the turn of the century. Emerson was the strategic leader in St. Louis and the Midwest for these developments, and their efforts had global repercussions. Buck Persons, Emerson Electric's new president, provoked the 1954 strike in order "to decide who was going to run the business." After ten weeks of striking, the union agreed to forego wage increases, help eliminate waste, improve quality, and reduce costs. The wage concessions did not prevent the company from deciding shortly thereafter to aggressively pursue a decentralization policy, announcing that its St. Louis workforce would be "employed only if the company could expand its military business." Emerson established its first satellite motor plant in Paragould, Arkansas, where wages were 40 percent below St. Louis's wages and where the local business and government officials not only provided subsidies to build the plant but also pledged support for a "nonunion environment." Lloyd Austin remembered the intense feelings wrought by being unable to confront realistically what was happening and by the glib attitude of the officials of the union he had fought to build. "The company brought those motors back to

St. Louis and had workers put a cover on them so they could get the union label [affixed to the motor]. They paid a few workers real well at the St. Louis plant to do that. I couldn't believe it! And the union went along with it!"[18]

The critical alliance of labor with the military Keynesianism and Cold War Agenda of the Democratic Party facilitated mainstream unionists' acceptance of capitalist disinvestments in this period. Defense contracts from the Cold War military buildup, Korean War, and Vietnam War spending kept many Emerson workers employed even as the company's commercial business left the area, a direct subsidy that took the political heat off the disinvestment campaigns, as was obvious by Emerson's announcement. The subsidy was facilitated by Stuart Symington, whose political clout as air force secretary and then as senator kept contracts coming to Emerson and other St. Louis area companies while he sounded alarms about the "Soviet advantage" and advocated "preventive war" with the Soviet Union.[19] The commercial business decentralization policy was pushed by General Robert Wood of Sears, whose obsession with reducing union influence was revealed in the McClellan hearings, one of the few investigations of employer behavior since the LaFollette Committee. These hearings exposed Sears's financial backing of Labor Relations Associates, a management consulting firm that had ties to the underworld. Fred Bender made an appearance at the hearings, testifying as one of the consulting firm's operatives. The hearings showed that Whirlpool (which took over the Seeger company in 1955) had spent more than $136,000 for antilabor operatives to keep its new plants union-free. But the committee never explored the issue of Wood's role in pushing Sears contractors toward decentralization campaigns. Moreover, the hearings resulted in attention to union, not company, corruption. Meanwhile, similar announcements of decentralization strategies linked to defense spending were made in Evansville, Indiana, where, for instance, Servel garnered U.S. Air Force contracts but gradually transferred its refrigeration line, again influenced by Sears's agenda.

Emerson's profits from the motor division rose sharply because of the combination of runaway shops and increased defense contracts, suddenly making Emerson a major player in the motor business by 1961. By the 1970s, Emerson had overtaken GE as the largest motor manufacturer in the world. It was a political economy that had been fixed with the means to undercut workers' power, even at the height of unionization. Under the leadership of Charles Knight, the new president of Emerson in 1977, Emerson took center stage, determined to use any means necessary to build the company's profits through aggressive decentralization, even of defense production to other countries, and to eliminate the last vestiges of unionism in the motor industry. In every step along the way, from Paragould to Juarez, Mexico, and Seoul, South Korea, Emerson used community alliances to exert a political economy of control. By 1997, Emerson closed its factories in St. Louis.[20]

There was no counterstrategy on the part of labor and no ability to organize around the power struggle that this represented from the mainstream labor movement. This reinforces Steven Rosswurm's conclusions that the crushing of the Left in the labor movement mattered greatly in the lack of clear understanding and strategy toward capitalist disinvestments. By the time the labor movement started to confront this seriously in the 1980s, a full-scale New Right movement had reconstructed cultural politics in the United States. This was a remarkably effective politics of Christian moralism, patriotic nationalism, and only slightly veiled racism that trumped the politics of class. Interestingly, that politics owed a debt to Servel's Louis Ruthenberg, who became a board member of the John Birch Society, the organization that helped give birth to the New Right. The society consructed a popular conservatism that depicted liberal reforms as a masquerade of elite subversion that could only be countered by Christian Americanism. Much of their literature seemed lifted from Servel's community campaign playbook against District 8 from 1946 to 1955.[21]

By the 1980s, memories of District 8's challenge to the employers' class and political power in the earlier era had faded. In light of Charles Knight's draconian labor policies, many in St. Louis were nostalgic for a past that had never really been, of a supposed loyalty of companies to the area, and there was a tendency to blame what were deemed workers' excessive demands and work rules for the decline of the industry. When Stuart Symington died in 1988, there was little discussion of how he had facilitated the integration of St. Louis as part of a larger military industrial complex. Instead, the *St. Louis Post-Dispatch* remembered him as someone with a progressive approach to unions, a memory that had been carefully shaped in his political campaigns by IUE president James Carey, who told a mythical rendition of labor relations for Symington in many campaign stump speeches. Referring to Symington's willingness to deal with the union, the 1988 article claimed that Symington "made arrangements considered almost socialist at that time," a terrific irony indeed given the price that others had paid for their ideas. The article also suggested that the "known communist" whom Symington had to deal with was not "really concerned with the workers" as much as Symington had been. Such distortions, Lloyd Austin remarked when reading the article, were the kind that workers had always been used to. He remarked that "it's all gone now" and that most people have "long forgotten what we did." Still, he hoped that another generation might benefit from the "real story" of what had happened and how the vision of unionism had been lost.[22]

This ending, as well as the beginning of District 8's story, caution us against accepting the conclusion that there is one key story to be told about the labor movement that arose in the 1930s and its relationship to the state and to capitalism, a story that dwells on the accomplishment of the organization of large multiplant corporations. These small players became major determinants of the construction of capitalist accumulation regimes and the politics of the late twentieth century. District 8's story reinforces the work of historians and geographers who remind us that both labor and capital build their power on what David Harvey has called the "spatial fix"—"certain configurations of the landscape . . . in order for them to reproduce themselves . . . from day to day and from generation to generation." Elaborating on this point, Jane Wills has remarked that "just as any characterization of capital as geographically footloose understates the importance of fixed location to the accumulation process, so too workers' traditions are more than simply free-floating ideas. Ideas need to 'take place' in some material sense if they are to be reproduced and reinvented. Ideas can only be reproduced and reinvented in the long term—among workers, at any rate—through being materially grounded in some way."[23]

When Toni Sentner reflected on District 8's development, she spoke thoughtfully of the ideas that took place by being grounded in community-based experiences, of networks between activists on the local, regional, (especially southern periphery) and national level, attempting to convey the spatial and personal relationships from which a movement was built and how those relationships were truncated or destroyed by the anticommunist agenda of the 1940s and 1950s. "It takes a long time to lay the foundation," of "preparing and educating" to build a group of activists who view the labor movement "as their life." Through participation in struggles, a "bond is created." She spoke of the transfer of experiences of a trained cadre from other locations as well as their own layers of experiences, first in local unemployed organizing, building insights with each struggle. Archie Thompson, head of the "union commissariat" during the 1938 Maytag strike conveyed a similar sentiment, even after being forced back to the plant by bayonet. The struggle for "our Civil rights against tremendous odds" developed ties between people and could provide a model for struggle for a "broader and better social and economic life." This network approach was the central practice of the District.[24]

District 8's conceptualization of unionism recognized that any national framework of unionism required building solidarity at the local level and that the union movement needed to be able to address the local structuring of the political economy to confront effectively the power of capital at the national level. This history may be useful to keep in mind given current efforts to formulate an effective labor movement, in that the emphasis on the need for organizing at the national and global level may cause us to lose sight of how important community-level organizing is to the development and sustenance of ideas and bonds of solidarity. The activists who built District 8 were ever mindful of building a national movement, but their insights grew in respect to how the strength of a national movement could be built from a horizontal/networking conceptualization of unionism. Addressing the local political power structures and political economy was essential to building alternative ideas; just as vital was adding one labor activist at a time. Across time and through experience,

District 8 activists used community-based organizing to build outward. Their vision of the union mission went beyond militancy on the shop floor precisely because capitalist power is located beyond shop floor conflicts and is inherently political and ideological. Further the national concerns for loss of control and Communist influence staunched the innovative politics of District 8, from the Maytag challenge, the local campaign for the Industry Councils, a grassroots approach for the Missouri Valley Authority (MVA) plan, the community-based strategy for organizing the South against decentralization, and a community/ decentralized basis for pattern bargaining. In this respect, this study joins other recent work that suggests that the political content to community work was a distinguishing feature of some Left trade union activism in the 1930s and 1940s. It also critically expands on the work of scholars and activists such as Staughton Lynd whose insights into community-based unionism too often has been mis-understood as advocating a parochial or atomized movement. In a similar vein, civil rights movement historian Charles Payne has pointed to the way that the vibrancy of that movement drew on the steady development of an organizing ethos at the local level, one that developed horizontal conceptualizations of organizing and leadership. The agenda of a national movement could some-times be destructive to those impulses.[25]

District 8's story also reinforces the findings of a small group of scholars who have shown that the anticapitalist perspectives of leftist unions led them to have contracts that were distinguishable by their democratic thrust, their quest for power on the shop floor, their attention to racial and gender inequities, and their unwillingness to enter into the CIO mainstream's endorsement of the politics of stability over conflict.[26] District 8's fight for workers' bread and butterwas not something separate from control issues, both on the shop floor and in the larger political economy. As John Buckowczk has written, "Calling for a decent livelihood and workers' rights has been a *radical* prescription fundamentally at odds with the wage-labor system."[27] When we recognize how closely employers tied their control of the shop floor to their ability to control the local community labor market and wage structure, we can better appreciate that District 8's workers were engaged in a longer history of struggle for control, one that carried on the legacy of the Feder-ated Metal Trades Council of St. Louis and Vicinity (FMTC) decades before them; the current local living wage campaigns and campaigns against capitalist disinvest-ment carry on that same tradition. If one can put aside the negative association with the CP, it is possible to see that the "concentration" strategy that led radicals to target political economic relationships on the local level, was conceived in a similar light as that originally conceived by the FMTC, which recognized that the strength of the labor movement might begin at the local level while not being limited to that local level. The capacity of workers to become self-aware and purposeful actors capable of taking on corporate power could take place there, and in fact their abil-ity to have expansive visions of transformation grew from those experiences.

David Montgomery has written that "'history from the bottom up' and the common fixation on great leaders" obscures the "decisive role . . . of the 'militant minority': the men and women who endeavored to weld their workmates and neighbors into a self-aware and purposeful working class." Certainly the Left in District 8 can be better summarized by that description than with the "conventional trade unionists" tag that some historians have assigned to the CIO left-wing activists or by the revived opprobrium of anticommunist scholars who focus on the CP activists' allegiance to the Soviet Union.[28] Some in the "militant minority" were associated with the CP, an authoritarian political party structure, but in the context of a coalitional politics and on the terrain of community, they had organized the most democratic union at the local level, had struggled to make the expansion of workers rights possible, had argued for a decentralized style of democratic regional economic planning, and most importantly, had sought to develop workers' capacity to continue to develop a style of unionism that could be a force for social transformation, with no prescribed or pre-ordained outcome. While it is important to recognize the role that the CP played in District 8's history, it is clear from the record that the style of trade unionism cannot easily be reduced to this relationship. Neither can the style be reduced to the participation in liberal goals as part of the Popular Front. For example, with the MVA, the left carefully steered toward a decentralized campaign style that avoided control by liberal elites, in order to discuss a more democratic participatory style of planning that had not arisen under the New Deal.

The association of the radical union agenda with the CP made the destruction easier than it might have been, because it unquestionably tarnished its democratic impulse and fatally damaged the trust that Toni Sentner recognized was so vital to its development. But those obstacles are only part of the story. District 8's story underscores the dimensions of what Judith Stepan-Norris and Maurice Zeitlin have referred to as the intraclass political struggle that took place in various phases during the twentieth century and was deeply affected by international politics.[29] District 8's Left inherited the terrain that had resulted from the struggles of the previous generation, a terrain with an already deep fissure between the workers' movement and working class radicalism, and this presented difficulties for legitimizing socialist views even before the missteps of, and problems of association with, the CP. The CIO's vaunted "culture of unity" was always tenuous and beyond that, the AFL was a source of further division because of this legacy. The CP's ties to the Soviet Union continued to be a major impediment to District 8's influence in the CIO. In District 8 in particular, the Left faced raids much earlier than is usually recognized—raids encouraged by national union leaders but also geared to ensuring that they would not be able to control the local CIO bodies where it was potentially a significant political and organizational force.

The peculiarities of this intraclass struggle should not cause us to lose sight of employers' role, which gave the struggle its larger consequences. For most of the period, the independents' recalcitrant antiunionism sprang from the same source as its antiradicalism, the desire to create the terrain that would allow them to produce profits on the periphery of the industry. During World War II, capitalists in the St. Louis area were themselves struggling with how to create the spatial terrain for the postwar, and some had come to believe that economic planning might be retained after the war, even as they worried about the potential loss of managerial control. Not only did some countenance dialogue with a Communist over these issues, but St. Louis business had even endorsed the MVA. They were not yet aware of how thoroughly continued defense spending would be a major factor in the city's welfare. It was more than the Truman Doctrine and the Berlin blockade that were involved in the demise of possibilities for alternative modes of economic planning that might have fundamentally altered the political economy of the postwar. Within this context, the groundwork for the attack on ideas associated with economic planning had been laid among local anticommunist and employer networks in the 1930s, and these reemerged as a powerful force in conjunction with the assistance of the Cold War state and the national CIO. Certainly without this assistance the Left in District 8 would have prevailed, continuing to represent workers through the bonds they had established in the earlier era. Anticommunism helped to vanquish ideas that were seriously considered just a few years earlier.

One could suggest that Sentner did himself or District 8 workers no favor by stubbornly refusing to give up Party membership. But while a variety of factors contributed to this decision, it is important to recognize that for Sentner, the canvas of ideas that gave life to District 8 had sprung from a conceptualization of unionism that would incorporate alternatives to the political economy of capitalism, and the feeling that without open articulation of these alternatives, and the ability of radicals to participate openly, the labor movement's vitality would be staunched. The need to connect alternatives to capitalism to trade union policies were something that kept him tied to the CP despite his criticisms of the organization. The fact that much of the core group of activists pleaded with Sentner to renounce the CP but continue to advocate for socialism shows that working class consciousness was not a static canvas in the 1930s and 1940s that automatically rejected more radical ideas. It is also clear that Sentner's open status rather than hidden affiliation reinforced engagement that directed him toward more open dialogue over policies. It was that relationship that led him in the aftermath of the Duclos letter to cry out for making the Party more democratic. The association of socialism with authoritarian states was a devastating blow to the democratic impulses that had made it a vibrant part of the Midwestern and national landscape in the early 20th century. By the 21st century, these ideas, once a vital part of the Midwestern milieu, seemed embarrassing and even archaic to many within labor organizations, given the declaration of capitalist supremacy across the globe after the end of the Cold War. Most of the labor movement had inherited the more static canvas of ideas, unable to imagine or articulate alternatives to a capitalist system that continued to devastate and destroy communities, driving uneven development and uneven distribution of resources and environmental destruction across the United States and the globe.

Sentner recognized that it was not the radical content of his views but rather the Soviet connections of the CP that were rejected by the workers he represented. The "militant minority" that shaped policy development for the District and were elected to leadership positions embraced unconventional trade unionism: the concept of "human rights over property rights;" the use of sit-downs to gain more workplace power; the attempt to make the union a cardinal part of transforming their communities; the assertion that workers should have more democratic control over shopfloor regimes, from pay systems to group grievances; the advocacy of democratic worker role in economic planning, the idea of using the strongest link within the union to build power. Other issues, especially racial and gender justice demands, over time and through activism became a part of the landscape of the possible in the district. Certainly being located within a national structure that endorsed the admission of radicals was an essential part of the success at the community level for the radicals in District 8. Still, concerns for community and bread and butter were not impediments to radical demands but often the source of a new level of consciousness that drove workers' identity with the movement. In light of scholarship that locates the source of workers' conservatism or failure to adequately confront capital mobility and disinvestments in their "parochial" or familial concerns, [30] it is worthwhile to point to workers such as Otto Maschoff, who from local labor activism became a leading advocate in the District of an internationalist, antiracist, gender-conscious rights agenda without moving more than fifty miles from his birthplace. Unlike appeals to patriotic nationalism or to a national culture that some have suggested radicals used to make their agenda palatable in the 1930s and 1940s, civic unionism recognized that the community was a central arena of struggle, one that was a necessary base for the labor movement to be able to counter the effort of capital to take on one group of workers at a time. The development of workers' consciousness that the labor movement could be a force for a larger power struggle took place there, and moved outward in networking that influenced workers in other communities. It was not necessary to "overcome" local concerns as much as it was to learn how to coordinate them with other workers' struggles, the goal in the Bucyrus-Erie pattern bargaining. Sometimes consciousness grew as a result of the reversal of the adage "think globally, act locally."

NOTES

Abbreviations Used in Notes

CPR	Records of the Communist Party, Fond 515, Russian State Archive of Social and Political History, Library of Congress, Washington, D.C.
DMR	*Des Moines Register*
DMT	*Des Moines Tribune*
DW	*Daily Worker*
EC	*Evansville Courier*
EP	*Evansville Press*
FEPC Mic.	*Microfilm Record of the Fair Employment Practices Committee, 1941– 1946* (Glen Rock, N.J.: Microfilming Corporation of America, 1979)
FMCS280	Records of the Federal Mediation and Conciliation Service Files, National Archives II, College Park, Maryland
IAM	International Association of Machinists and Aerospace Workers Records, 1901–74, Wisconsin Historical Society, Madison, Wisconsin
IAM D9	Records of the International Association of Machinists, District 9, Western Historical Manuscripts Collection, University of Missouri–St. Louis
ILHOP	Iowa Labor History Oral Project, Iowa State Historical Society, Iowa City, Iowa
IUER	International Union of Electrical Workers Records, Rutgers University Archives, New Brunswick, New Jersey
JDP	James Davis Papers, Collection 3666, Western Historical Manuscripts Collection, University of Missouri–Columbia
JWCP357	James Weldon Click Papers, Collection 357, Western Historical Manuscripts Collection, University of Missouri–St. Louis
JWCP507	James Weldon Click Papers, Collection 507, Western Historical Manuscripts Collection, University of Missouri–St. Louis
MHS	Missouri Historical Society, St. Louis
NDN	*Newton Daily News*
NLRB25	Records of the National Labor Relations Board, Case Files and Transcripts, Record Group 25, National Archives II, College Park, Maryland
NWLB Mic.	Microfilmed *Papers of the National War Labor Board, 1918–1919* (Frederick, MD: University Publications of America, 1989)
NWLB2	Papers of the National War Labor Board, Record Group 2, National Archives II, College Park, Maryland
NWLB202	Records of the National War Labor Board (World War II), Record Group 202, National Archives II, College Park, Maryland
PP	*People's Press*

RD	Red Dot (unprocessed) files in the United Electrical Workers Archives
SHSI	State Historical Society of Iowa, Iowa City, Iowa
SLGD	*St. Louis Globe-Democrat*
SLL	*St. Louis Labor*
SLPD	*St. Louis Post-Dispatch*
SLST	*St. Louis Star-Times*
T&E	Transcripts and Exhibits files, Entry 156 (see NLRB25 above)
UEA	UE Archives, Archives of Industrial Society, University of Pittsburgh, Pittsburgh, Pennsylvania
UEN	*UE News*
ULP	Urban League Papers, Washington University Archives, Olin Library, St. Louis, Missouri
WHMC	Western Historical Manuscripts Collections, University of Missouri–St. Louis
WSP	William Sentner Papers, Washington University Archives, Olin Library, St. Louis, Missouri

I facilitated the collection and depositing of a number of the collections cited in the notes into archives. I reviewed the files before they were processed. Whenever possible, I have attempted to ascertain the final folder or box location of the material cited as ultimately processed. Sometimes that was not possible. In those cases, I designated the citation as "unprocessed."

Introduction

1. See, for example, Nelson Lichtenstein, *State of the Union: A Century of American Labor* (Princeton, N.J.: Princeton University Press, 2002), 44–45; Robert Zieger, *The CIO: 1935–1955* (Chapel Hill: University of North Carolina, 1995).

2. Lizabeth Cohen, *Making a New Deal: Industrial Workers in Chicago, 1919–1939* (Cambridge: Cambridge University Press, 1989), 7. A different approach is apparent in other studies, such as Elizabeth Faue, *Community of Suffering and Struggle* (University of North Carolina Press, 1991).

3. For the concept of "spatial fix," see David Harvey, *The Limits to Capital* (Chicago: University of Chicago Press, 1982). Thomas Klug has argued that the local labor market became "a terrain of struggle between capital and labor." Recent studies of Philadelphia by Philip Scranton and Howell John Harris have documented the critical importance of the local arena of struggle. Gordon Clark suggested in the 1980s that there has been too much emphasis on national studies of unionization and that local employment relations is the "crucial factor of capital allocation between places." Labor strategies such as modern personnel management and welfare programs were only internal means of control, but employers also concentrated on external or community-based strategies. For an excellent exploration of this dynamic at a national level, see David Robertson's study of the struggle for labor market control in the early twentieth century. Anthony Herod's and Don Mitchell's works have extended Clark's insights and also question historians' lack of attention to the geographical dimensions of labor conflict.

Thomas Klug, "Employers' Strategies in the Detroit Labor Market, 1900–1929," in *On the Line: Essays in the History of Auto Work,* ed. Nelson Lichtenstein and Stephen Meyer,

42–72 (Urbana: University of Illinois Press, 1989); Howell John Harris, *Bloodless Victories: The Rise and Fall of the Open Shop in the Philadelphia Metal Trades, 1890–1940* (Cambridge: Cambridge University Press, 2000); Phil Scranton, *Figured Tapestry: Production, Markets and Power in Philadelphia Textiles, 1885–1941* (Cambridge: Cambridge University Press, 1989). For the interaction of internal corporate strategies of the large packinghouses with the local political economy of Chicago's packing town, see James R. Barrett, *Work and Community in the Jungle: Chicago's Packinghouse Workers, 1894–1922* (Urbana: University of Illinois Press, 1987). David Montgomery, *The Fall of the House of Labor: The Workplace, the State, and American Labor Activism, 1865–1925* (Cambridge: Cambridge University Press, 1989); Gordon Clark, *Unions and Communities under Siege* (Cambridge: Cambridge University Press, 1989), 8; David Brian Robertson, *Capital, Labor and State: The Battle for American Labor Markets from the Civil War to the New Deal* (Lanham, MD: Rowman and Littlefield, 2003); Andrew Herod, *Organizing the Landscape: Geographical Perspectives on Labor Unionism* (Minneapolis: University of Minnesota Press, 1998); Andrew Herod, *Labor Geographies: Workers and the Landscapes of Capitalism* (New York: Guilford, 2001); Don Mitchell, *The Lie of the Land: Migrant Workers and the California Landscape* (Minneapolis: University of Minnesota Press, 1996).

4. Ronald Schatz, *The Electrical Workers: A History of Labor at General Electric and Westinghouse, 1923–60* (Urbana: University of Illinois Press, 1983), 85–86. For a similar argument regarding the organization of auto workers, see Steve Babson, *Building the Union: Skilled Workers and Anglo-Gaelic Immigrants in the Rise of the UAW* (New Brunswick, N.J.: Rutgers University Press, 1991).

5. Levenstein, *Communism, Anticommunism, and the CIO,* 62.

6. Schatz, *The Electrical Workers,* 156, 197.

7. Ronald Filipelli, "UE: An Uncertain Legacy," in *Political Power and Social Theory,* Vol. 4, ed. Maurice Zeitlin, 217–54 (Greenwich, Conn.: JAI Press, 1984), 241, 222, 224. This perspective, repeated in Ronald Filipelli and Mark McCulloch's *Cold War in the Working Class: The Rise and Decline of the United Electrical Workers* (Albany: State University of New York Press, 1995), was introduced by James Weinstein's review of James Matles and Jimmy Higgins, *Them and Us: Struggles of a Rank and File Union* (New York: Prentice Hall, 1973). Weinstein pointed out that by omitting the mention of Communists in the organization of the UE, Matles and Higgins were suggesting that "Communists had no politics of their own beyond left liberalism, no visible political differences with the liberals who ran the CIO." James Weinstein, "The Grand Illusion: A Review of Them and Us," *Socialist Revolution* 6 (1975): 97.

8. David Brody, *Workers in Industrial America* (New York: Oxford University Press, 1980), 132 (first quotation); David Brody, "Radicalism and the American Labor Movement: From Party History to Social History," *Political Power and Social Theory,* Vol. 4, 258 (second quotation). See also Brody's assessment in David Brody, "The CIO after 50 Years: A Historical Reckoning," *Dissent* 32 (Fall 1985): 457–72. For similar assessments, see Cochran, *Labor and Communism,* 278–79, 355, 379; Levenstein, *Communism, Anticommunism, and the CIO,* 40, 334. Nelson Lichtenstein, "The Communist Experience in American Trade Unions," *Industrial Relations* 19 (Spring 1980): 128.

9. See, for instance, Martin Glaberman, "Vanguard to Rearguard," *Political Power and Social Theory,* Vol. 4, 37–42, who argues that Communists were generally less militant than other trade unionists.

10. For the argument about workers' control in the earlier period, see David Montgomery, *Workers' Control in America: Studies in the History of Work, Technology, and Labor Issues* (Cambridge: Cambridge University Press, 1979).

11. John Bodnar, "Immigration, Kinship, and the Rise of Working-Class Realism in Industrial America," *Journal of Social History* 13 (1980): 44–64, and John Bodnar, *Workers' World: Kinship, Community and Protest in an Industrial Society, 1900–1940* (Baltimore: Johns Hopkins University Press, 1982). See also Peter Friedlander, *The Emergence of a UAW Local, 1936–1939: A Study in Class and Culture* (Pittsburgh: University of Pittsburgh Press, 1975); Robert Zieger, "The CIO: Bibliographical Update and Archival Guide," *Labor History* 31 (Fall 1990): 413–40; Daniel Nelson, *American Rubber Workers and Organized Labor, 1900–1941* (Princeton, N.J.: Princeton University Press, 1988); Melvyn Dubofsky, "Not So 'Turbulent Years': Another Look at the American 1930s," *Amerikastudien* 24 (1979): 5–20; Mike Davis, *Prisoners of the American Dream* (London: Verso, 1986); David Brody, "Workplace Contractualism in Comparative Perspective," in *Industrial Democracy in America: The Ambiguous Promise*, ed. Nelson Lichtenstein and Howell John Harris, 176–205 (Cambridge: Cambridge University Press, 1993); David Brody, "Response to Staughton Lynd's 'We Are All Leaders': A Job-Conscious Perspective," paper presented at the North American Labor History Conference, October 1992. But see also the insightful criticism of Bodnar's influential thesis in James Barrett, "The Transplanted: Workers, Class and Labor," *Social Science History* 12 (Fall 1988): 221–31.

12. Gary Gerstle, "Catholic Corporatism, French Canadian Workers, and Industrial Unionism in Rhode Island, 1938–1956," in *Labor Divided: Race and Ethnicity in United States Labor Struggles, 1835–1960*, ed. Robert Asher and Charles Stephenson (Buffalo: State University of New York, 1990), 209; Gerstle, *Working Class Americanism: The Politics of Labor in a Textile City* (Princeton, N.J.: Princeton University Press, 1989), chaps. 8–10; and Michael Kazin, "Struggling with Class Struggle: Marxism and the Search for a Synthesis of U.S. Labor History," *Labor History* 28 (Fall 1987): 502. Schatz's conclusion that skilled workers were the only reliable base for radical ideas is a major foundation for these views.

13. Drawing on David Roediger, *The Wages of Whiteness: Race and the Making of the American Working Class* (London: Verso, 1991), recent studies have also suggested that any progressive direction for the CIO and liberalism was limited by the developing race consciousness of white workers. See especially Bruce Nelson, *Divided We Stand: American Workers and the Struggle for Black Equality* (Princeton, N.J.: Princeton University Press, 2000). But compare this to the possibilities discussed in Michael Honey, *Southern Labor and Black Civil Rights: Organizing Memphis Workers, 1929–1960* (Urbana: University of Illinois Press, 1993).

14. The release of the Venona transcripts has brought an outpouring of literature on the connections between the American CP and the Soviet Union. See, for example, John Earl Haynes, Harvey Klehr, and Kyrill Anderson, *The Soviet World of American Communism* (New Haven, Conn.: Yale University Press, 1999). For a recent summary of the literature in this field, see Bryan D. Palmer, "Rethinking the Historiography of United States Communism," *American Communist History* 2(2) (2003): 139–174.

In key respects, my study joins a small number of recent revisionist studies that have challenged this perspective as well as the notion that there was nothing distinctive about the Left-led unions. These studies are cited in the conclusion, note 26.

15. Montgomery, *The Fall of the House of Labor*, 2. Kim Voss, "Disposition Is Not Action: The Rise and Demise of the Knights of Labor," *Studies in American Political*

Development 6 (Fall 1992): 273–99. Voss draws upon social movement studies and in particular on Scott McNall's assessment of the Populist movement, in which he argues that "in mobilizing, in trying to actually change the economic and political system, people create themselves as a class." However, the group must also have an organization that can be sustained against the onslaught of its opponents in order for people to act. See Scott G. McNall, *The Road to Rebellion: Class Formation and Kansas Populism, 1865–1900* (Chicago: University of Chicago Press, 1988), esp. chap. 1.

Chapter 1: The Militant Minority in the St. Louis Electrical Industry and the Political Economy of Control, 1900–1935

1. David Montgomery, *The Fall of the House of Labor: The Workplace, the State and American Labor Activism, 1865–1925* (Cambridge: Cambridge University Press, 1987), 2.

2. Howell John Harris, *Bloodless Victories: The Rise and Fall of the Open Shop in the Philadelphia Metal Trades, 1890–1940* (Cambridge: Cambridge University Press, 2000); Phil Scranton, *Figured Tapestry: Production, Markets and Power in Philadelphia Textiles, 1885–1941* (Cambridge: Cambridge University Press, 1989). Bonnett's classic study of employers' associations long ago demonstrated that even as they organized at the national level, employers' most potent activity was locally based organizing and ideological drives against labor. Clarence Bonnett, *History of Employers' Associations in the United States* (New York: Vantage, 1956). See also William Millikan, *A Union against Unions: The Minneapolis Citizens Alliance and Its Fight against Organized Labor, 1903–1947* (Minneapolis: University of Minnesota Press, 2001).

3. Ronald Schatz, *The Electrical Workers: A History of Labor at General Electric and Westinghouse, 1923–1960* (Urbana: University of Illinois Press, 1983), 3–27.

4. *A Century Plus of Electrical Progress: History of the Electrical Industry in Metropolitan St. Louis* (St. Louis: Electrical Board of St. Louis, n.d.), 12–15, 20–22; P. B. Postlethwaite, "The Story of the Wagner Electric Corporation: An Address before the St. Louis Stock Exchange," June 21, 1940, MHS; Edward G. Holtzman, "History and Growth of the Electrical Manufacturing Industry in St. Louis," MHS; Mabel Vivian Wood, "Geographic Landscape of the Northwest Industrial District, Metropolitan St. Louis" (Master's thesis, Washington University, 1936).

5. *Emerson Electric: A Century of Manufacturing, 1890–1990* (St. Louis: Emerson Electric Co., 1989), 46–65; William Scott Snead, *Emerson Electric Company: The History of an Industrial Pioneer* (New York: Newcomen Society, 1965); "St. Louis—*the* Electrical Center," *Greater St. Louis,* March 1921, 3; *Forward St. Louis,* April 20, 1914.

6. *A Century Plus of Electrical Progress,* 20; "History of Century Electric Company," Century Electric Corporation Records, Century Electric, St. Louis, Missouri.

7. "St. Louis—*the* Electrical Center"; St. Louis Foreign Trade Committee, *The Foreign Trade of St. Louis* (St. Louis: Business Men's League, 1912); *SLGD,* February 27, 1927.

8. Missouri State Bureau of Labor Statistics, 1899 *Red Book,* "1856–1928 Biographica" Box, Frank O'Hare Papers, MHS; *Emerson Electric: A Century of Manufacturing, 1890–1990,* 46–59; Snead, *Emerson Electric Company: The History of an Industrial Pioneer.* In 1901, Emerson sold its switch and switch bond department to another local firm that recognized the crafts solely because this product line required a higher degree of skill than its other operations and thus made it more vulnerable to trades unions' rules and demands.

9. David Kreyling to Samuel Gompers, September 9, 1917, Reel 88, Frame 424, *The American Federation of Labor Records: The Samuel Gompers Era*, Part II (Sanford, N.C.: Microfilm Corporation of America, 1979); *SLL*, February 14, 1904; Minutes, July 1905, International Association of Machinists, District 9, Box 1, Vol. 2, WHMC; *Open Shop Review*, May 1913.

10. *Golden Jubilee Recollections, September 11, 1937* (n.p., n.d), Tin Room Collection, St. Louis Public Library; Edwin J. Forsythe, "The St. Louis Central Trades and Labor Union, 1887–1945" (PhD diss., University of Missouri, Columbia, 1956), 1–145; David R. Roediger, "Not Only the Ruling Classes to Overcome, but Also the So-Called Mob: Class, Skill and Community in the St. Louis General Strike of 1877," *Journal of Social History* 19 (1989): 219–40; Kim Voss, *The Making of American Exceptionalism: The Knights of Labor and Class Formation in the Nineteenth Century* (Ithaca, N.Y.: Cornell University Press, 1993); *SLL*, January 12 and March 2 and 9, 1929; *Progressive Press*, January 2, 1931.

11. Mary Jane Quinn, "Local Union No. 6, Brewing, Malting, and General Labor Departments, St. Louis, Missouri" (MA thesis, University of Missouri, 1947).

12. "Ludwig Dilger," in *News from the Land of Freedom: German Immigrants Write Home*, ed. Walter D. Kamphoefner, Wolfgang Helbich, and Ulrike Sommer, 492–94 (Ithaca, N.Y.: Cornell University Press, 1991). One example of this influence and continuity was the *St. Louis Labor*, the city's major labor paper and also the organ of the Socialist Party. Socialist Gottlieb Hoehn edited both the *SLL* and its German-language counterpart, *Arbeiter-Zeitung*, from 1898 to 1928. The paper brought union members into contact not only with Socialists but also with local unemployed movements and women's political and social organizations.

13. Quinn, "Local Union No. 6"; *Golden Jubilee Recollections;* Gary Fink, *Labor's Search for Political Order: The Political Behavior of the Missouri Labor Movement, 1890–1940* (Columbia: University of Missouri Press, 1973), 28.

14. John R. Commons and Associates, *History of the Labor Movement in the United States*, Vol. 2 (New York: Macmillan, 1918), 388, fn. 93; Clippings and notes in Folder 58, David Burbank Papers, WHMC; *SLL*, July 22, 1893, and November 3 and December 1, 1894.

15. *Twenty-third Annual Report of the Missouri Bureau of Labor Statistics* (1901): 277; *Twenty-fifth Annual Report of the Missouri Bureau of Labor Statistics* (1903): 280. On the fate of other metal trades federations, see Gary Fink, ed., *Labor Unions* (Westport, Conn.: Greenwood, 1977), 281; and International President, International Association of Machinists to Dear Sir and Brother, October 28, 1900, *The American Federation of Labor Records: The Samuel Gompers Era* (Sanford, N.C.: Microfilm Corporation of America, 1979), Reel 141, Frame 313. On the national/local issue of metal trades unionism and shop committees, see David Montgomery, "New Tendencies in Union Struggles and Strategies in Europe and the United States, 1916–1922," in *Work, Community, and Power: The Experience of Labor in Europe and America*, ed. John Cronin and Carmen Sirianna, 88–116 (Philadelphia: Temple University Press, 1983). Montgomery dates the advent of shop committees to the period around World War I, but in St. Louis metal trades, shop committees already existed in 1900.

16. "Official Circular of the Federated Metal Trades Council of St. Louis and Vicinity," March 18, 1900, Reel 26, Frame 268, *The American Federation of Labor Records: The Samuel Gompers Era* (Sanford, N.C.: Microfilm Corporation of America, 1979).

17. On the importance of the streetcar strike for the revival of unionism in St. Louis, see *SLL*, January 29, 1929.

18. David Montgomery has argued that it is not "helpful to juxtapose 'labor market issues' against struggles for workers' control, as though one explanation excluded the other. No workers fought for collective power just for the fun of it. It was the quest for wages that brought people out to work. Their battles over the pace of work, the length of the work day, authority of overseers, job assignments, and other conditions of employment were all related to earnings. . . . Nevertheless, to abstract market issues from the human interaction in which they were embodied is to define the answer by the manner of posing the question—to lock one's mind inexorably into the conclusion that workers were job-and-wage conscious and nothing more." David Montgomery, "Class, Capitalism, and Contentment," *Labor History* 30 (Winter 1989): 127–28.

19. Montgomery, *The Fall of the House of Labor,* 265; Stenographic Report of Minutes, November 16, 1900, Frames 332–80, Reel 141; Samuel Gompers to J. H. Kaeffer, November 12, 1900, Frames 315–17, Reel 141, *AFL Records* (microfilm edition).

20. *Synopsis of the Proceedings of the Twelfth Annual Convention of the National Metal Trades Association, April 13–14, 1910* (1910): 61–62; Harris, *Bloodless Victories,* 98.

21. H. L. Purdy, *An Historical Analysis of the Economic Growth of St. Louis, 1840–1945* (n.p., 1946); Rosemary Feurer, "Shoe City, Company Towns: The St. Louis Shoe Industry and the Turbulent Drive for Cheap Rural Labor, 1900–1940," *Gateway Heritage* (Fall 1988): 2–17.

22. Scott McConachie, "The Big Cinch: A Business Elite in the Life of a City, St. Louis, 1895–1916" (PhD diss., Washington University, 1976); Jack Muraskin, "Missouri Politics during the Progressive Era, 1896–1916" (PhD diss., University of California–Berkeley, 1969), 70–76, 108; Purdy, *An Historical Analysis,* 11; St. Louis Foreign Trade Committee, *The Foreign Trade of St. Louis* (St. Louis: Business Men's League, 1912); all are from *Greater St. Louis,* November 1919, 1; June 1920, 3; February 1924, 5; *SLPD,* March 25, 1918; *SLGD,* February 27, 1927.

23. On the origins of the local and national CIA, see *Citizens' Industrial Exponent: A Journal of Law and Order* 1 (June 1904): 1–12. Dina M. Young, "The St. Louis Streetcar Strike of 1900: Pivotal Politics at the Century's Dawn," *Gateway Heritage* 12 (Summer 1991): 4; Steven L. Piott, *The Anti-Monopoly Persuasion: Popular Resistance to the Rise of Big Business in the Midwest* (Westport, Conn.: Greenwood, 1985).

24. David Kreyling to Samuel Gompers, September 9, 1917, Reel 88, Frame 424, *The American Federation of Labor Records: The Samuel Gompers Era* (Part II), microfilm edition, Microfilm Corporation of America; *SLL,* February 14, 1904. As David Parry, leader of the national organization, noted at the time, "It is a distinctive name inclusive of ideas conveyed by such names as employers associations and citizens' alliances." *SLL,* February 14, 1904. See William Millikan, *A Union against Unions,* for a brilliant analysis of the CIA in another location.

25. *Square Deal* 11(90) (January 1913): 519; U.S. Senate, Committee on Education and Labor, *Labor Policies of Employers' Associations, Part 1: The National Metal Trades Association,* 76th Cong., 1st session (Washington, D.C.: U.S. Government Printing Office, 1939), 5; *Synopsis of the Proceedings of the Twelfth Annual Convention of the National Metal Trades Association, April 13–14, 1910.*

26. Minutes, April 28, 1904, Box 1, Vol. 1, IAM D9.

27. *SLL,* July 30, 1904.

28. Minutes, February 6, 1902, Box 1, Vol. 1, IAM D9; Minutes, July 13, 1905, Box 1, Vol. 2, IAM D9.

29. *Square Deal* 13(97) (August 1913): 77; *Synopsis of the Proceedings of the Thirteenth Annual Convention of the National Metal Trades Association, April 12–13, 1911* (1911), 215–21; *Open Shop Review,* October 1916. For a discussion of the NMTA blacklist, see James O'Connell to Samuel Gompers, September 19, 1917, Reel 88, 0437, *AFL Papers,* Pt. 2; the blacklist remained extraordinarily effective into the early 1920s. See Robert Saunders' autobiography, WHMC. For the emphasis on legal strategies, see "CIA" folder, Edward Goltra Papers, MHS.

30. *Citizens' Industrial Exponent* 2–7 (1905–10); Citizens' Industrial Alliance brochures and records of events, in "Tin Room" Collections, St. Louis Public Library; *Handbook of the Citizens' Industrial Alliance in St. Louis,* File Collections MHS; Michael Rogin, *Ronald Reagan, the Movie: And Other Episodes of Political Demonology* (Berkeley: University of California Press, 1988).

31. Van Cleave to Edward Goltra, September 20, 1907, "CIA" folder, Edward Goltra papers, MHS; Minutes, August 8, 1907, IAM D9.

32. W. A. Layman, "Some of the Problems Confronting the Engineer as an Industrial Manager," *Journal of the Engineering Club of St. Louis* (1917): 103–11.

33. *SLPD,* September 27, 1916; "Photo of rules for Mr. Lord Premium Allowance," K-342, Wagner Photo Collection, Pictorial Division, MHS.

34. Text on reverse of photo of a championship departmental ballteam, circa 1916, Photo K-425, Book 2, Wagner Electric Collection, Pictorial Division, MHS.

35. C. B. Lord, "How to Deal Successfully with Women in Industry," *Industrial Management* 54 (September 1917): 844.

36. Ibid., 842. On the prevailing rate, see Montgomery, *The Fall of the House of Labor,* 149.

37. *Wagner Electric Aid* 4 (September 1917); C. B. Lord, "Athletics for the Working Force," *Industrial Management* 54 (October 1917): 44–49; W. S. Thomas to Jas. A. McKibben, File #332-19, Welfare Work, 1910–13, Boston Chamber of Commerce Records, Harvard Business School, Boston, Massachusetts.

38. "Industrial Survey by New Committee," *Forward St. Louis,* February 23, 1914, 12.

39. Wm. Hannon to Dear Sir and Brother, January 11, 1917, Folder 43, Box 7, IAM D9; *Proceedings of Hearing Held at Room 208, City Hall, June 14, 1918,* in Wagner Case 170-803, FMCS280; author's interview with Grace Vesper, St. Louis, Missouri, July 9, 1987.

40. Minutes, November 9, 1916, Box 3, IAM D9; Minutes, November 11, 1917, Box 4, IAM D9.

41. *SLL,* January 13, 1917; author's interview with Frank Sulzer, March 22, 1987, St. Louis, Missouri.

42. *SLPD,* March 7, 1918; Christopher Gibbs, *The Great Silent Majority: Missouri's Resistance to World War I* (Columbia: University of Missouri Press, 1988); Wm. Hannon to Dear Sir and Brother, January 11, 1917, Folder 43, Box 7, IAM D9; *SLL,* March 10 and 24, 1917; Lord, "How to Deal Successfully with Women in Industry," 840.

43. *St. Louis Republic,* February 4–7, 1918; Wartime era clippings in Strikes and Riots Scrapbook, MHS.

44. *SLL,* March 2, 9, 16, and 23, 1918; Fink, *Labor's Search for Political Order,* 76.

45. *Proceedings of the Missouri Federation of Labor, 1918,* 54; Fred Richard Graham, "A History of the Missouri State Federation of Labor" (MA thesis, University of Missouri, 1934), 120; Executive Session Minutes, August 27, 1918, 2, Frame 206, NWLB Mic.; W. H. Rodgers to H. L. Kerwin, March 7, 1918, Department of Labor Case File 33-1009, filed in Case 4, Box 1, NWLB2.

46. *SLL,* March 16, 1918.

47. *SLPD,* March 7, 1918; *SLL,* March 16, 1918; Gibbs, *The Great Silent Majority,* 198; *SLL,* March 2, 9, 16, and 23, 1918.

48. Minutes, March 12, 1908, Vol. 3, Box 1, IAM D9; Rosemary Feurer, *Step By Step: The History of Lodge 41, International Association of Machinists,* Video (St. Louis: IAM Lodge 41, 1989). *SLL,* March 31, 1916. On women's influence on the local labor movement, including the electricians, see Rose Feurer, ed., *The St. Louis Labor History Tour* (St. Louis: Bread and Roses, 1994). On the unifying effect of eight-hour-day campaigns, see David Roediger and Philip Foner, *Our Own Time: A History of the Struggle for Shorter Hours* (Westport, Conn.: Greenwood, 1989). Minutes, March 31, 1916, Vol. 4, Box 1, IAM D9; *SLL,* July 14, 1917.

The AFL established a national Metal Trades Council in 1908, and St. Louis had the first MTC chartered under it, but it was solidly under the control of the national union officers and the AFL. Workers needed approval from their international union officers for all decisions. Throughout the war era, local unions sought to reestablish the right to strike in sympathy with other local unions, but the national organizations successfully fought this call. *SLL,* November 18, 1916. Racial exclusion still dominated the perspective of the St. Louis area IAM, which formally excluded African Americans and sometimes denounced employers who hired them; employers could quite effectively incite existing racial divisions by using black strikebreakers, which was done both in the Century strike of 1916 and the Wagner strike of 1918.

49. "Resolution of Mass Meeting" to Woodrow Wilson, undated, Case File 33-1054, Wagner Electric Company, FMCS280.

50. "Stenographers Report of Conference between Representatives of Wagner Electrical Manufacturing Company and a Committee of Striking Employees," May 2, 1918, 2–8, Houts Exhibit 1, July 27, 1918, Untitled folder, Box 1, Case 4, Case Files, NWLB2; "Proceedings of Hearing Held at Room 208, City Hall, St. Louis, Missouri, June 14, 1918," 3, Case File 170-803, FMCS280.

51. "Digest, St. Louis Controversies," Reel 22, Frame 7, NWLB Mic.

52. Stanley King to Felix Frankfurter, June 21, 1918, Box 17, Correspondence of the Chair and of the Executive Secretary, Records of the War Labor Policy Board, Record Group 4, National Archives, Washington, D.C.; *SLL,* April 6, 1918.

53. Wm. B. Northrop to Edmund Leigh, May 9, 1918, Plant Protection Section, Military Intelligence Division, War Department Records; Boyle O. Rodes to Chief of Plant Protection, March 23, 1918, both in Box 117, Record Group 165, National Archives II, College Park, Maryland. The Ordnance Department representative's use of business's definition of the community wage is in Memorandum of Adjustment of Wages in Plant of Commonwealth Steel Company, November 1, 1918, Case File 472, *Hod Carriers Local 397 v. Commonwealth Steel,* NWLB2.

54. William Hannon to Thomas J. Savage, April 17, 1918, Box 1 Case Files, Case 4, NWLB2; Executive Session Minutes, August 27, 1918, 8–10, 17–18, 26, Reel 8, Frames 215–17, 224, 233, NWLB Mic.; Executive Session Minutes, July 25, 1918, 36, 27, 28, Reel 7, Frames 372, 363, 365; Report of Victor Olander, Executive Session Minutes, June 28, 1918, 54, Reel 6, Frame 736; Fink, *Labor's Search for Political Order,* 80. Employers' fears of the uprising's threat to their control of the external labor market is revealed clearly in Commonwealth War Labor Board, Case File 472, NWLB2, and in Report, September 27, 1919, Wagner Case File 170–803, FMCS280.

55. Quote is from O. E. Jennings Testimony, Transcript of Proceedings, St. Louis Controversies, 91, July 24, 1918, Box 1, Transcript files, Docket 4, NWLB2; see also O. E. Jennings to Frank E. Walsh, August 7, 1918, Case 4, Untitled file folder, NWLB2.

56. On the struggles of 1919–22, see Montgomery, *The Fall of the House of Labor,* 370–464; G. Y. Harry to H. L. Kerwin, September 27, 1919, Case File 170-803, FMCS280. Established unions tended to sustain their membership at least through 1922. *SLL,* September 7, 1921, and January 7 and September 9, 1922; Fink, *Labor's Search for Political Order,* 99, fn. 16.

57. As late as fall 1920, ten thousand St. Louis workers rallied against the open shop and cheered when the socialist president of the Missouri State Federation of Labor suggested that American workers needed to have a revolution on the order of the Russian workers. But repression against the various radical sectors was ongoing from 1917 through most of the 1920s. See, for instance, Reel 11, Frames 299–326, Reel 16, Frames 1–600, Reel 19, Frames 335–411, in *U.S. Military Intelligence Reports: Surveillance of Radicals in the United States, 1917–1941* (Frederick, Md.: University Publications of America, 1984). *SLL,* October 1, 1921, January 21, 1922, August 8 and October 20, 1923, May 31, 1924, July 2, 1927, and March 3 and August 18, 1928; Noel Dark interview with David Burbank, November 29, 1972, WHMC. On the impact of these developments nationally, see Montgomery, *The Fall of the House of Labor,* 430–39.

58. *SLL,* July 2, 1927.

59. *SLL,* January 12, 1929; Quinn, "Local Union No. 6," 122–28; Minutes, September 1921–April 1927, Boxes 6–7, IAM D9. The relative positions of the building trades to these industrial unions is amply illustrated through the gradual decline of the leftist labor paper, the *St. Louis Labor,* during the 1920s, while the conservative paper sponsored by the Building Trades' Council, the *Trades Council Union News,* established in 1917, survived and grew. On national unions and AFL control of central labor bodies in the 1920s, see David Montgomery, "New Tendencies in Union Struggles and Strategies in Europe and the United States, 1916–1922," in *Work, Community, and Power,* 99–100.

60. District 9 Minutes, November 9, 1921, Box 6, and Folder 61, IAM D9; *SLL,* January 21 and August 12, 1922; Central Trades and Labor Union Minutes, January 12, 1922, February 26, 1922, June 25, 1922, August 7, 1922, St. Louis Labor Council Minutes, 1913–63, WHMC.

61. *SLL,* August 4, 1923, and May 31, 1924; Central Trades Minutes, February 28, 1926, St. Louis Labor Council Minutes, 1913–63, WHMC; District 9 Minutes, October 18, 1924, Box 8, IAM D9. In June 1922 the Central Trades refused to rent its hall to William Z. Foster, the leader of the TUEL, because he had attacked Samuel Gompers, who had denounced Foster's "amalgamation" campaign. Central Trades Minutes, June 11, 1922, St. Louis Labor Council Minutes, 1913–63, WHMC. Only a delegate of the Metal Trades Council loudly denounced the decision.

62. International President to Wm. Fitzmaurice, February 25, 1927, Reel 76, IAMR; *SLL,* April 9, 1927; author's interview with LeRoy Quernheim, St. Louis, Missouri, May 15, 1989; author's interview with Charles Mirtching, St. Louis, Missouri, August 29, 1989.

63. Author's interview with LeRoy Quernheim; Saunders Autobiography, Part II, WHMC.

64. *Emerson Electric Company: A Century of Manufacturing, 1890–1990,* 70; P. B. Postlethwaite, "The Story of the Wagner Electric Corporation," An Address before the St. Louis Stock Exchange, June 21, 1940. The number of electrical workers increased 375 per-

cent in St. Louis compared to 198 percent nationwide during the period 1914–23. *Executive's Magazine,* April 20, 1929; "St. Louis as an Electrical Center," *American Industries* 26 (October 1925): 29–30.

65. Proceedings, 17–19, Case No. 58, In the Matter of the President's Commission on Fair Employment Practices, ex rel Ollie Haynes, et al., Reel 19, FEPC Mic.

66. *The Factory Labor Situation in the St. Louis Industrial District,* 1, Industrial Club, Chamber of Commerce Pamphlets, MHS.

67. "Industrial Report of St. Louis," 11, Box 4, in American Zinc Company Records, Western Historical Manuscripts Collection, University of Missouri-Rolla.

68. Calculated from Table 1, General Statistics for Industrial Areas, U.S. Department of Commerce, Bureau of the Census, *Fifteenth Census of the U.S. Manufactures: 1929; General Report* (Washington, D.C.: U.S. Government Printing Office, 1930), 242.

69. *Greater St. Louis,* November 1919, 1; *Greater St. Louis,* February 1923, 4; *Greater St. Louis,* April 1924, 6; *Greater St. Louis,* January 1920, 2; *SLGD,* February 27, 1927. This is quite different from John Cumbler's interpretation of a definitive transition from "civic capitalism" to "national capitalism," with local capital's decision-making power being eclipsed by far-flung corporate control. John Cumbler, *A Social History of Economic Decline: Business, Politics and Work in Trenton* (New Brunswick, N.J.: Rutgers University Press, 1989), 93–112.

70. Author's telephone interview with Frank Abfall, November 19, 1987; author's interview with Margaret Entrikin, St. Louis, Missouri, February 24, 1988.

71. Letter from Charles Slezak to author, April 4, 1987; Louis N. Teitlebaum, "The Labor Market in St. Louis" (Master's thesis, Washington University, June 1929), 94; *SLL,* January 1 and March 26, 1927; May 1927 Industrial Report, Box 9, Ser. 4, ULP.

72. David Montgomery, "Thinking about American Workers in the 1920s," *International Labor and Working Class History* 32 (Fall 1987): 3–24, quotation on p. 10.

73. "Preliminary Report," August 11, 1926, Case 170-3576, FMCS280.

74. Author's interview with Roy Hoffman, April 13, 1988.

75. Hoffman interview; author's interview with Frank Abfall, St. Louis, Missouri, July 6, 1987; letter from Charles Slezak to author.

76. Author's interview with Frank Abfall, July 6, 1987; author's interview with Lloyd Austin, July 29, 1986; letter from Charles Slezak to author.

77. Lloyd Austin telephone interview, March 4, 1994; letter from Charles Slezak to author.

78. K-766, K-775, K-932, Wagner Photo Collection, MHS.

79. *SLL,* March 23, 1918; Official Report of Proceedings, Transcript, May 7–10, 1937, 130, 117, 5, 26, Emerson Case 14-c-34, T&E 1903, NLRB25; "Biography," Robert Saunders Papers, WHMC; "History of Century Electric Company," Century Electric Corporation, St. Louis, Missouri.

80. "History of Century Electric Company"; Case No. 83, Executive Secretary's files, NLRB25; author's interview with Henry Fiering, Los Angeles, California, June 18, 1989.

81. Author's telephone interview with Joseph Janofsky, July 8, 1987; author's interview with Robert Rhodes, August 1, 1986; *Emerson Monthly* 16 (September 1919): 7; St. Louis Republic clippings in Compensation Box, unprocessed Alroy S. Phillips Collection, MHS.

82. Author's interview with Charles Seilnacht, St. Louis, Missouri, November 7, 1986; author's interview with John S. Piskulish, July 10, 1987; author's interview with John

Jung, June 25, 1985. None of the walkouts that some surviving workers remembered or that were referred to in the 1930s documentation were reported in the newspaper.

83. Robert Mason to United Electrical Workers Union, July 24, 1936, D8/133, UEA.

84. Author's telephone interview with Lloyd Austin, December 16, 1988.

Chapter 2: A Vision of Unionism Takes Shape

1. The early 1930s is often viewed as simply a training ground for some of the activists who would bring about the later CIO movement, a movement that awaited a nationally coordinated organization to give such impulses any coherence. See, for example, David Brody, "CIO after Fifty Years," *Dissent* 32 (Fall 1985): 457–72; Robert Zieger, *The CIO, 1935–1955* (Chapel Hill: University of North Carolina, 1995), 6–21; Nelson Lichtenstein, *State of the Union: A Century of American Labor* (Princeton, N.J.: Princeton University Press, 2002). But Staughton Lynd and others have argued that we need to take the early 1930s more seriously, to see it as more than an "inchoate prelude" and instead see it as an alternative to what came about with the legally sanctioned CIO. Staughton Lynd, ed., *"We Are All Leaders": The Alternative Unionism of the Early 1930s* (Urbana: University of Illinois Press, 1996).

2. Author's interview with Clessie DeNagle, St. Louis, July 9, 1987; Meeting of the Board of Representatives, May 26, 1932, and March 31, 1932, both in Emerson Case 14-c-34, Board's Exhibit 5, T&E 1903, NLRB25; Century Electric, Case No. 83, Stenographic Transcript, 60, Region 12 records, NLRB25; Meeting of the Board of Representatives, July 23, 1934, 38, T&E 1903, NLRB25.

3. See materials in "Labor" folder 16, Electrical Code Industry files, Box 2114, Record Group 9, National Archives II, College Park, Maryland; Meeting of the Board of Representatives, June 27, 1933, July 6, 1933, Board's Exhibit 5, T&E 1903, NLRB25; Stenographic Transcripts of Records, 54, July 23, 1934, Case 83, Region 12 Pre-Wagner Act Files, NLRB25.

4. Stenographic Transcript of Proceedings, July 23, 1934, 129, 49, Case 83, Executive Secretary's Files, NLRB25; William Fitzmaurice to A. O. Wharton, February 19, 1934, Reel 76, IAMR.

5. Stenographic Transcript, July 23, 1934, 49, 54, Case 83, NLRB25; Nathan Witt, Memorandum to the Board, August 14, 1934, Case 83, NLRB25; *SLGD,* June 30, 1934; *SLPD,* July 1, 1934; William Fitzmaurice to H. F. Nickerson, June 26, 1934, Reel 76, IAMR.

6. *SLPD,* July 7, 13, and 18, 1934; Newspaper articles in Scrapbook 2, Region 12 Pre-Wagner Act Files, NLRB25; Stenographic Transcript of Proceedings, 110, Century Case 83, NLRB25.

7. *SLST,* July 19, 1934; *SLGD,* July 19, 1934; St. Louis Regional Labor Board, Statement of Facts, Findings and Recommendations, Case No. 127, August 2, 1934, NLRB25; *PP,* District 8 ed., April 24, 1937; Samuel B. McPheeters to Lloyd K. Garrison, September 24, 1934, Century Case 127, NLRB25.

8. Memorandum for the Board, August 14, 1934, Case 83, Executive Secretary Files, NLRB25.

9. Valentine H. Schweiss to Franklin Delano Roosevelt, February 26, 1935, Exhibits Files, Century Case 83, Executive Secretary files, NLRB25; "One Who Knows" to Franklin Delano Roosevelt, undated, Exhibits Files, Century Case 83, Executive Secretary files, NLRB25; "In the Matter of Century Electric Company and Employees of the Century Electric Com-

pany," Case No. 83, Decision, September 17, 1934, *Decisions and Orders of the National Labor Relations Board* (Washington, D.C.: U.S. Government Printing Office, 1935), 79–81.

10. Official Report of Proceedings, Transcript, 21–43, Emerson Case 14-c-34, T&E 1903, NLRB25.

11. Official Report of Proceedings, Transcript, 21, 129, Emerson Case 14-c-34, T&E 1903, NLRB25; Minutes, August 4, 1933, Folder 27, Box 6, IAM D9.

12. Official Report of Proceedings, Transcript, 70–72, 134; "General Committee Structural Outline," Board's Exhibit 4; both in Emerson Case 14-c-34, T&E 1903, NLRB25. "Employees Representation Plan," in "Emerson Company Union" folder, Case File, Emerson Case 14-c-34, Entry 155, NLRB25; Official Report of Proceedings, Transcript, 690–94, Emerson Case 14-c-185, T&E 1010, NLRB25.

13. Alroy Phillips, a representative to Emerson's board of directors, helped to put and keep the ERP in place. Phillips was an attorney who helped bring about the workman's compensation plan in Missouri. See Alroy Phillips Papers, Box 271, MHS.

14. Letter from Charles Slezak to author, April 4, 1987; author's interview with Frank Sulzer, March 22, 1987, St. Louis, Missouri; General Committee Meeting, December 3, 1935, Board's Exhibit 5, Emerson Case 14-c-34, T&E 1903, NLRB25; Emerson Electric, *Information and Instructions for Employes* (1920s), original in possession of Ed Fitzgerald, St. Louis.

15. Letter from Charles Slezak to author, April 4, 1987; Minutes, Board of Representatives Meeting, November 22, 1932, January 16, 1934, Board's Exhibit 5, Emerson Case 14-c-34, T&E 1903, NLRB25.

16. Author's interview with Frank Sulzer; Slezak letter to author.

17. Official Record of Proceedings, 118–21, Emerson Case 14-c-34, T&E 1903, NLRB25; *SLPD*, May 11, 1937; author's interview with Frank Sulzer.

18. A few examples of the workers who were involved in both the ERP and the UE drive: Oscar Debus, a fan assembly line worker had been hired in 1920 and was occasionally elected to the ERP to represent his department, would later become UE Local 1102 president; Pete May, employed since 1922, was a board representative and occasionally served as secretary for the ERP. He was the first secretary of Local 1192. Both allied with the leftist caucus but neither remained with the company past 1939. Frank Schlieman, one of the longest-employed workers in the plant and an ERP representative from tool and die, later encouraged skilled workers to join the UE drive. Official Record of Proceedings, 21, 129, 259, in Emerson Case 14-c-34, T&E 1903, NLRB25.

Gerald Zahavi describes a similar tug-of-war in a company union in *Workers, Managers and Welfare Capitalism: The Shoeworkers and Tanners of Endicott Johnson, 1890–1950* (Urbana: University of Illinois Press, 1988).

19. Author's interview with Frank Sulzer; Minutes, Board of Representatives Meeting, March 31, 1932, May 25, 1933, March 29, 1933 (quotation), November 28, 1933, December 28, 1933, Exhibit 5, Emerson Case 14-c-34, T&E 1903, NLRB25.

20. *Emerson Electric: A Century of Manufacturing*, 63–65, 76.

21. Ibid., 75; author's interview with Robert Rhodes, August 1, 1986; author's interview with Marie Strathman, St. Louis, Missouri, June 6, 1994; Progress Report, March 9, 1937, In the Matter of Emerson Electric Company, File 182–2266, FMCS280.

22. *Emerson Electric: A Century of Manufacturing*, 76–81; Rhodes interview.

23. Author's interview with Frank Abfall, St. Louis, Missouri, April 22, 1987; author's interview with Marian Bastionello Barry, June 22, 1989; author's interview with Clessie

DeNagle, St. Louis, July 9, 1987, author's telephone interview with Fern Koch Beck, October 30, 1992; author's interview with Marie Strathman; Report, March 12, 1937, Case 182–2266, FMCS280.

24. General Committee Meeting Minutes, July 28, 1933; Board of Representation Meeting Minutes, June 29, 1933, July 27, 1933, August 31, 1933, September 27, 1933; all in Board's Exhibit 5, T&E 1903, Emerson Case 14-c-34, NLRB25.

25. Minutes, Board of Representation Meeting, January 19, 1934, Board's Exhibit 5, Emerson Case 14-c-34, T&E 1903, NLRB25; Official Report of Proceedings, Transcript, 44–53, 140, Emerson Case 14-c-34, T&E 1903, NLRB25; Slezak letter to author; Robert Mason to James B. Carey, July 24, 1936, D8/133, UEA; Box 6, Folder 27, IAM D9; Memorandum for the Board, August 14, 1934, Case File 83, Executive Secretary files, NLRB25.

26. Official Report of Proceedings, Transcript, 14, 64, 86, 123, Emerson Case 14-c-34, T&E 1903, NLRB25.

27. Minutes, Board of Representation Meeting, November 28, 1933, August 20, 1935, November 27, 1935, December 3, 1935, Board's Exhibit 5, Emerson Case 14-c-34, T&E 1903, NRLB25.

28. Minutes, Board of Representation Meeting, April 25, 1934, November 27, 1934, Board's Exhibit 5, Emerson Case 14-c-34, T&E 1903, NLRB25.

29. Minutes, Board of Representatives Meeting, April 25, 1935, Board's Exhibit 5, Emerson Case 14-c-34, T&E 1903, NLRB25.

30. Minutes, Board of Representatives Meeting, December 28, 1933, January 28, 1933, January 25, 1934; General Committee Meeting Minutes, September 5, 1935, October 3, 1935, November 7, 1935, all in Board's Exhibit 5, Emerson Case 14-c-34, T&E 1903, NLRB25.

31. Official Report of Proceedings, Transcript, 51, Emerson Case 14-c-34, T&E 1903, NLRB25.

32. Minutes, Board of Representation Meeting, October 31, 1935, April 30, 1936, February 22, 1934 (see also November 27, 1934), Board's Exhibit 5, Emerson Case 14-c-34, T&E 1903, NLRB25; Official Report of Proceedings, Transcript, 17, 51, 22, 123, Emerson Case 14-C-34, T&E 1903, NLRB25.

33. Official Report of Proceedings, Transcript, 5, 79–80, Emerson Case 14-c-34, T&E 1903, NLRB25; Ninth Conference, May 8, 1937, 78, Respondent's Exhibit 13, Emerson Case 14-c-34, T&E 1903, NLRB25; Robert Mason (Manewitz) to James Carey, July 24, 1936, D8/133, UEA; Slezak letter to author.

34. Minutes, Employees Representation Plan, July 26, 1933, January 16, 1934, September 5, 1935, December 10, 1936; Minutes, General Committee, July 28, 1933; both in Board's Exhibit 5, Emerson Case 14-c-34, T&E 1903, NLRB25.

35. *SLL*, February 23 and April 28, 1929; Minutes, Central Trades and Labor Union, February 24, 1929, February 9 and 23, 1930, April 13, 1930, St. Louis Labor Council Minutes, 1913–63, WHMC.

36. Author's interview with Fannie Goldberg, St. Louis, Missouri, August 18, 1991; David Burbank interview with Noel Clark, November 29, 1972, WHMC; "Memo," Director of Military Intelligence, Office of Chief of Staff, Washington, D.C., to Recruiting Officer, December 6, 1920, Reel 19, *U.S. Military Intelligence Reports: Surveillance of Radicals in the U.S., 1917–1941* (Frederick, Md.: University Publications of America, 1984); Report, October 27, 1921, Communist Party in St. Louis, Missouri File, 1919–58, File 61-215, FBI-HQ, Washington, D.C.; May 1924 Report, Delo 323, Reel 21, CPR; Minutes,

August 7, 1929, Delo 1773, Reel 135, CPR; Harold Williamson, December 13, 1929, Report, 20, Delo 1776, Reel 135, CPR.

37. Paul Dennis Brunn, "Black Workers and Social Movements of the 1930s in St. Louis" (PhD diss., Washington University, 1974), 167; Alfred Vaughn Taylor, "American Workers' Union" (MA thesis, Washington University, 1938), 5. For the unemployed movement history in other areas, see James J. Lorence, *Organizing the Unemployed: Community and Union Activists in the Industrial Heartland* (Albany: State University of New York Press, 1996); Leab, "'United We Eat': The Creation and Organization of the Unemployed Councils in 1930," *Labor History* 8 (Fall 1967): 300–315; Roy Rosenzweig, "Organizing the Unemployed: The Early Years of the Great Depression, 1929–1933," *Radical America* 10 (July–August 1976): 37–60; Albert Prago, "The Organization of the Unemployed and the Role of the Radicals, 1929–1935" (PhD diss., Union Graduate School, 1976), 87–99. Frank Folsom, *Impatient Armies of the Poor: The Story of Collective Action of the Unemployed, 1808–1942* (Niwot: University Press of Colorado, 1991), links the UC to a longer tradition.

38. Judith Levy, "Historical Analysis of the Community Fund" (MA thesis, Washington University, 1928); Charlotte Ring Fusz, "The Origin and Development of the St. Louis Relief Administration, 1929–1937" (MA thesis, St. Louis University, 1938); *Greater St. Louis,* October 1919, 7; *Greater St. Louis,* January 1920, 3; *Greater St. Louis,* January 1923, 25; *Greater St. Louis,* March 1923, 23; *SLL,* November 22, 1924; Louis Teitlebaum, "The Labor Market in St. Louis" (MA thesis, Washington University, 1929), 80, 157–158; Frank J. Bruno, "The Treatment of the Dependent Unemployed in St. Louis in the Winter of 1931–32: A Community Case Study," *Southwestern Social Science Quarterly* 13 (September 1932): 169–76.

39. *SLPD,* November 21, 1930; *DW,* October 22, 1931; *SLST,* March 9, 1932.

40. Alma Vanek, "A History of the St. Louis Provident Association, 1930–1935" (MA thesis, Washington University, 1938); *SLPD,* November 11, 1930, September 1, 1933, January 14, 1932, and April 2, 1935; Neil Primm, *Lion of the Valley: St. Louis, Missouri* (Boulder, Colo.: Pruett, 1981), 467–68.

41. *SLPD,* March 3 and 6 and November 11, 1930; "Call for Meeting" and "March Against Hunger!" leaflets, in Scrapbook, Bureau for Homeless Men Collection, WHMC.

42. A handful were second-generation radicals from the Jewish radical community. But others, such as John Peer, a thirty-year-old former preacher who became secretary of the UC, were radicalized through the Depression experience. At the first major UC demonstration to city hall in March 1930, the mayor's secretary chided UC activist Delbert Early for having "'foreign' connections." Earley retorted that he was "100 per cent American." Twenty-three-year-old Orville Smith, a UC activist, told a reporter that he was a Communist "because no other party seems to offer a future for young men or even bring about conditions so they can get jobs." George Benz (almost an old timer at age thirty-five in 1932) was a native St. Louisan and a World War I veteran. In explaining how he came to join the CP, he recalled that "when I was discharged from the service I couldn't find a job, and was reduced to living in box cars. Nobody seemed to have room for a serviceman. Finally I got a job when I pretended to have worked at other places, never going to war. I tell you, it made me think." When he again lost his job during the Depression, he was "like a caged lion—nothing to do but think about my troubles." Communism helped him to regain his "mental balance" and "saved me from going mad," because he could focus on "helping others." *SLPD,* March 3, 1930; *SLGD,* January 19, 1933; *SLPD,* January 26, 1930, January 19, 1933, and January 16, 1935 (Benz quotations).

43. *SLPD,* November 14 and 26, 1930, and February 20 and 25, 1931. This is quite different from Harvey Klehr's description of the typical American Communist of the early 1930s as a "white, foreign born male between the ages of 30 and 40"; Harvey Klehr, *The Heyday of American Communism: The Depression Decade* (New York: Basic Books, 1984), 165, 305. Author's interview with Fannie Goldberg.

44. Brunn, "Black Workers and Social Movements," 114–17, 139, 167–68; *SLPD,* October 29, 1931. See Primm, *Lion of the Valley,* 468–70, for a full comparison of black and white unemployment. Harold Williamson, December 13, 1929, report, 20, Delo 1776, Reel 135, CPR. St. Louis's party leadership had a significant proportion of African Americans by 1934 because of the party's involvement in the UC. February 1933 membership report, Delo 3257, Reel 252, CPR; author's interview with Hershel Walker, St. Louis, Missouri, January 8, 1987.

45. Van Gosse, "'To Organize in Every Neighborhood, in Every Home': The Gender Politics of American Communists between the Wars," *Radical History Review* 50 (Spring 1991): 109–41. Despite the title, this article deals only with the period 1930–32. Rosenzweig, "To Organize . . . ," 40, notes that UCs were intended to be set up on a factory basis but in practice were established on a neighborhood basis.

46. Author's interview with Antonia Sentner, June 16, 1989; author's interview with Fannie Goldberg.

47. *DW,* November 24, 1931; "March 7 meeting of section committee in St. Louis," Delo 1773, Reel 222, CPR.

48. *DW,* January 17, 1931; *SLPD,* January 17, 19, and 20, 1931; *SLGD,* January 20, 1931; *SLPD,* October 25, 1931.

49. *SLPD,* October 25 and February 21, 1931, and May 2, 1932.

50. *DW,* June 28, 1932; *SLST,* June 23 and July 1, 1932; *SLPD,* July 6, 1932.

51. *SLPD,* July 2, 1932.

52. *DW,* February 17, March 14, April 11, and July 8 and 12–14, 1932; B. K. Gebert, "How the St. Louis Unemployed Victory Was Won," *Communist* (September 1932): 786–91; *SLPD,* July 8 and 11, 1932; *SLGD,* July 12, 1932; *SLST,* July 8 and 12, 1932; B. K. Gebert, Report on July 8–11, 1932, events, September 1932, Delo 2865, Reel 220, CPR.

53. John Laslett, "Swan Song or New Social Movement? Socialism and Illinois District 12, United Mine Workers of America, 1919–1926," in *Socialism in the Heartland: The Midwestern Experience, 1900–1925,* ed. Donald T. Critchlow, 167–214 (Notre Dame, Ind.: University of Notre Dame Press, 1986); Carl Weinberg, "The Tug of War: Labor, Loyalty and Rebellion in the Southwestern Illinois Coalfields, 1914–1920" (PhD diss., Yale University, 1995). This aspect of coal towns has been well argued in Herbert Gutman's writings on nineteenth-century miners culture; see Herbert Gutman, "The Workers' Search for Power," in *Power and Culture: Essays on the American Working Class,* ed. Herbert Gutman and Ira Berlin, 70–92 (New York: Pantheon, 1987). Author's interview with Antonia Sentner, June 16, 1989. Familial involvement in union efforts was always a politicized and contested issue. John L. Lewis opposed the establishment of women's auxiliaries and rejected the active role of women, long a tradition in mining communities. However, the Progressive Miners, the radical alternative to the United Mine Workers of America in the early 1930s, like the Communist organizers celebrated and encouraged familial involvement, particularly women's involvement. See "Minutes of the Social Justice Commission (On UMWA/Progressive Miners Dispute)," 12, May 15, 1933, Temple Israel, in Record Group 107-37-10, Rev. Wm. Scarlett Papers, Archives of the Episcopal Church, Austin, Texas.

54. B. K. Gebert, "How the St. Louis Unemployed Victory Was Won," *Communist* (September 1932): 791; *DW*, July 22, 1931; author's interview with Antonia Sentner. Shaw had been head of the Yugoslav Educational Committee of the Communist Party in the 1920s, and that explains his close contact with a dissident Illinois coal miner such as Radosovitch, whose daughter Toni came to St. Louis and worked in the packinghouses and quickly became involved with the Croatian Fraternal Union. Radosovitch was married to a railroad worker in a very unhappy marriage but would soon divorce him.

55. William Sentner FBI file, Summary Report, August 22, 1951, 1–4, FBI-HQ, 100-18332-139, and Special Personal Investigation, June 8, 1943, FBI-HQ 100–18332-14 in Box 5, Ser. 4, WSP; "A Yaleman and a Communist," *Fortune* 28 (1943): 213; author's interview with Antonia Sentner, June 16, 1989. While Julius Sentner was a "militant trade unionist," according to Toni Sentner, he was not "politically oriented." His father left the garment trades to become a delicatessen owner by the time Sentner came of age. There is no familial connection to William Sentner's left-wing politics. Sentner's brother volunteered to fight with U.S. forces against Pancho Villa in the American expedition to Mexico in 1916–17. Sentner's father died in 1926; Sentner's mother never understood her son's politics, and most of the rest of the family came to view his politics with some embarrassment, although they never rejected him. Antonia Sentner, letter to author, March 3, 1992; author's interview with Shirley Raven, July 15, 1994.

56. Letter of introduction from Thornley and Pitt, customs brokers, May 25, 1928, and from W. J. Siegrist, November 11, 1931, in William Sentner, Personal Correspondence File, unprocessed WSP; William Sentner FBI file, Special Personal Investigation re War Labor Board, June 8, 1943, 4, FBI 100-18332-14, Box 5, Ser. 4, WSP. On the radical milieu of the merchant seamen, see Bruce Nelson, *Workers on the Waterfront: Seamen, Longshoremen, and Unionism in the 1930s* (Urbana: University of Illinois Press, 1988); and Howard Kimeldorf, *Reds or Rackets? The Making of Radical and Conservative Unions on the Waterfront* (Berkeley: University of California Press, 1988).

57. Antonia Sentner interview; Sol Abrahams letter, May 29, 1931, in William Sentner Personal Correspondence, unprocessed WSP; William Sentner FBI file, Summary Report, August 22, 1951, 29, FBI-HQ 100-18332-139, Box 5, Ser. 4, WSP; Sentner testimony in bound volume of testimony, 353, from case file, *In the Matter of the State of Iowa v. Sentner*, located in Respondents Exhibit 3, Maytag Case 18-c-183, T&E 507, NRLB25. Sentner also managed to attend the Rolla School of Mines, an engineering college, for four months in 1929.

58. "Re: William Sentner," July 30, 1938, Folder 2, Box 5, William Frey Papers, Library of Congress; *DW*, October 10, 1933; *Left Front* 1(2) (September–October 1933), 8–12. On the John Reed Clubs and left-wing artists in St. Louis, see Doug Wixson, *Worker-Writer in America: Jack Conroy and the Tradition of Midwestern Literary Radicalism, 1898–1990* (Urbana: University of Illinois Press, 1994), 272, 295. On the broad implications of the cultural front, see Michael Denning, *The Cultural Front: The Laboring of American Culture in the Twentieth Century* (London: Verso, 1996).

59. Report, December 10, 1931, Delo 2470, Reel 187; March 7, 1933 meeting of section committee, Delo 2833, Reel 222, CPR.

60. Ralph Shaw report, December 10, 1931, Delo 2470, Reel 1872, CPR; *DW*, January 21, 1932; Bill Gebert, "The St. Louis Strike and the Chicago Needle Trades Strike," *Communist* 12 (August 1933): 800–809; Myrna Fichtenbaum, *The Funsten Nut Strike* (New York: International Publishers, 1991), 20; Antonia Sentner interview; *SLPD*, May 18, 1933; R. Shaw, "St. Louis' Biggest Strike," *Labor Unity*, August 1933, 8–11.

61. Ralph Shaw to Williamson, March 1933, Delo 3265, Reel 253, CPR; *SLGD,* May 2, 1933. On the TUUL, see Edward P. Johannigsmeier, "The Trade Union Unity League: American Communists and the Transition to Industrial Unionism: 1928–1934," *Labor History* 42(2) (2001): 160–77.

62. Ralph Shaw, "St. Louis' Biggest Strike," *Labor Unity,* August 1933, 8–11; Ralph Shaw to Williamson, March 1933, Delo 3265, and Ralph Shaw to District Secretariat, May 15, 1933, Del. 3266, both in Reel 253, CPR.

63. Ralph Shaw to District Secretariat, May 15, 1933, Delo 3266, and Ralph Shaw Report, May 25, 1933, Delo 3265, both Reel 253, CPR; Shaw, "St. Louis' Biggest Strike," 11.

64. *SLST,* May 15 and 16, 1933; *SLPD,* May 16, 17, 18, and 19, 1933.

65. John Bronson, "The Nut Pickers Picket," *Left Front* 1(2) (September–October 1933): 8–12.

66. *DW,* May 22, 1933; Shaw, "St. Louis' Biggest Strike," 9; Catherine Risch, "The Effects of Communist Propaganda upon the Negroes of St. Louis" (MA thesis, St. Louis University, 1935); *St. Louis Argus,* May 19, 1933. The strike committee was very egalitarian in its structure, a necessary ingredient of the mass mobilization. "St. Louis Nutpickers' Strike Sets Example," *Party Organizer* 6 (July 1933): 4. Sarah Shaw, a party member, recalled that during the strike Smith used the slogan "A Brick in one hand, a Bible in the other!" Sarah Shaw letter to author, August 26, 1991. Despite the slogan, the strike was nonviolent.

67. *SLST,* May 18, 1933; Fichtenbaum, *The Funsten Nut Strike,* 22–47; *DW,* May 23, 1933.

68. Rabbi F. I. Isserman to Claude Pearcy, May 9, 1933, Private Papers of the Rt. Rev. William Scarlett, RG 107-37-10, in the Archives of the Episcopal Church USA, Austin, Texas. Just prior to the Funsten strike, the newly established Progressive Mine Workers Union of southern Illinois asked the SJC to investigate what they claimed were abuses of civil liberties perpetrated by John L. Lewis's supporters in the United Mine Workers in the southern Illinois coalfields. Scarlett and Isserman were accompanied by Clarence Darrow in the coalfields. *SLGD,* May 1, 1933; the members of the SJC were white. *SLPD,* May 15, 1933.

69. *SLGD,* May 19, 1933; Report, May 25, 1933, Delo 3265, Reel 253, CPR.

70. Author's interview with Fannie Goldberg; *SLGD,* May 18 and 20, 1933; *SLPD,* May 23, 1933; *Argus,* May 26, 1933. Dickmann's committee included Isserman, Urban League executive secretary John T. Clarke, "colored" YMCA executive secretary O. O. Morris, black attorneys Joseph L. McLemore and William H. Parker, Rev. Fr. William Markoe of St. Elizabeth's parish, and Emmett Canty, chief parole officer for the city. The committee was later expanded to include Dean Sidney Sweet of the Christ Church Cathedral, another major figure in the SJC, as well as a few others. *SLGD,* May 24, 1933.

71. *SLPD,* May 23 and 24, 1933; *SLST,* May 23, 1933; *DW,* May 23 and 25, 1933; *Argus,* May 26, 1933; Bronson, "Nut Pickers Picket."

72. Jack Conroy, *A World to Win,* reprint ed. (Urbana: University of Illinois Press, 2000). Conroy obviously based some of the character Sol Abrahams on Sentner (145, 221), with whom he had "frequent contact . . . over the next few years." Wixson, *Worker-Writer in America,* 294.

73. Catherine Risch, "The Effects of Communist Propaganda"; Brunn, "Black Workers and Social Movements," 356–57; Shaw, 11; Ira De A. Reid, "A Study of the Industrial Status of Negroes in St. Louis, Missouri," 1934, 55, in Ser. 4, Box 9, ULP; John Bronson, "Nut Pickers Picket," 16.

74. Shaw, *Labor Unity,* 11; *Daily World,* June 1, 1933; *DW,* September 8, 1933.

75. *DW,* October 4 and 7, 1933; *Argus,* October 13, 1933.

76. See "Re: William Sentner," William Frey Papers; William Sentner FBI file, 100-18332-139; FBI 100-18332-14, 5, Box 5, Ser. 4, WSP; *Argus,* October 13, 1933.

77. *SLST,* October 19, 1933; *SLPD,* October 19, 1933; *SLGD,* October 20, 1933.

78. *DW,* November 29, 1933.

79. *DW,* November 6, 1933.

80. *DW,* June 5, 8, and 12, 1934; *SLPD,* June 16, 1934. On the Lundeen bill and the movement that guided it, see Kenneth Casebeer, "The Workers' Unemployment Insurance Bill: American Social Wage, Labor Organization, and Legal Ideology," in *Labor Law in America: Historical and Critical Essays,* ed. Christopher Tomlins and Andrew King (Baltimore: Johns Hopkins University Press, 1992).

81. Author's interview with Fannie Goldberg.

82. By 1933, the FLWU had won its demand for an unemployment fund paid into by the employer and administered by workers. Philip S. Foner, *The Fur and Leather Workers Union: A Story of Dramatic Struggles and Achievements* (Newark: Nordan, 1950), 381–87. Evidence that the Fur and Leather Workers' experience was known and used by St. Louisans is contained in Taylor, "American Workers' Union," 4.

83. See, for example, Jacqueline Jones, *Labor of Love, Labor of Sorrow: Black Women, Work and the Family from Slavery to the Present* (New York: Basic Books, 1985); Robin D. G. Kelley, "'We Are Not What We Seem': Rethinking Black Working Class Opposition in the Jim Crow South," *Journal of American History* 80 (June 1993): 75–112; Alice Kessler-Harris, "Treating the Male as 'Other': Redefining the Parameters of Labor History," *Labor History* 34 (Spring–Summer 1993): 190–204; Ardis Cameron, *Radicals of the Worst Sort: Laboring Women in Lawrence, Massachusetts, 1880–1912* (Urbana: University of Illinois Press, 1995).

84. *SLPD,* June 12, 1934; *DW,* June 8 and 15, 1934; Risch, "The Effects of Communist Propaganda," 60–80; Brunn, "Black Workers and Social Movements," 365, 368–69.

85. Ira De A. Reid, "A Study of the Industrial Status of Negroes in St. Louis, Missouri," 1934, 55, in Ser. 4, Box 9, ULP; Brunn, "Black Workers and Social Movements," 36; author's interview with Antonia Sentner; author's interview with Hershel Walker. This bears out Edward Johannigsmeier's observation that the TUUL helped to establish a new type and style of Communist unionism, more suited to the organization of African Americans, women, and mass production workers. "The Trade Union Unity League," 161.

86. *DW,* April 17, 1934.

87. Bill Gebert to Earl Browder, September 20, 1934, Delo 3643, Reel 282, CPR; "Workers of Century Electric" leaflet, F. C. Reilly to National Labor Board, July 26, 1934, in Case 127 files, Regional Labor Board, District 12, NRLB25; Brunn, "Black Workers and Social Movements," 364–90. The National Labor Board was created under the NIRA to oversee violations of section 7a.

88. Brunn, "Black Workers and Social Movements," 258; Bill Gebert to Earl Browder, September 20, 1934, Delo 3643, Reel 282, CPR; see other materials in this Delo for the way that factionalism and defection to Pacific Movement may have contributed; *DW,* December 13 and 17, 1934.

89. Harvey Klehr's *The Heyday of American Communism* is the best source for the traditional depiction, but see Bryan D. Palmer, "Rethinking the Historiography of United

States Communism," *American Communist History* 2(2) (2003): 151. Letter from Sarah Shaw to author, September 16, 1991; author's interview with Antonia Sentner; Report, July 16, 1934, Delo 364, Reel 282, CPR.

90. Employees Board of Representation, Minutes, November 22, 1932, December 28, 1933, January 19, 1934; General Committee, Minutes, November 7, 1935, both in Board's Exhibit 5, T&E 1903, Emerson Case 14-c-34, NLRB25.

91. E. H. Brown to Donald Richberg, December 12, 1934, In the Matter of Century Electric Co. and Employees of Century Electric Co., Case File, Case No. 83, Executive Secretary's files, NLRB25.

92. Beyond their influence on the workers' movement, the nut pickers and other struggles among black workers caused a significant change in the local Urban League, reorienting it from its exclusive focus on job facilitation. The Urban League in turn began to focus on union organizing among black workers. The nut pickers' struggles were one factor that prompted the Social Justice Commission to become more oriented to dealing with community racial issues, a factor that continued to be significant into the 1940s in the city. On the other hand, the establishment of the New Deal-era labor boards, with their model of employer and labor representatives, diminished the role of ministers and local academics and lawyers in the settlement of these disputes. When the first labor board was named during the NRA period, there was protest about the lack of African American representation, based on the previous local precedent of black ministers' and lawyers' involvement in the TUUL-era strikes. "Mayor Dickman, and the Mediation Board," *St. Louis World,* Scrapbook, Vol. 1, 1, NLRB Region 12 Pre-Wagner Act files, NLRB25.

93. Alfred Wagenknecht to Herbert Benjamin, May 24, 1935, Delo 3896; October 1935 Sentner Report, Delo 3894, both in Reel 298, CPR; author's interview with Ernest Shay, January 26, 1986.

94. Alfred Taylor, "The American Workers Union." See also American Workers Union folders, in Socialist Party Papers, WHMC; Gas House Workers' *Bulletins,* Gas Workers Collection (OCAW Local 5–6), *Warehouse Workers Bulletins,* all in WHMC.

95. *SLPD,* April 26, 28, and 30, May 9 and 11, 1936, November 26 and 28, and December 15, 1936; *SLST,* March 27 and December 4, 1936; *SLGD,* December 17, 1936; "Unions-AWU, 1934–1936" folder, Box 11, Ser. 4, ULP. Sentner pushed involving the Ministerial Alliance in early 1935. Bill Sentner to Dear Friends, February 1935, Delo 2896, Reel 298, CPR.

96. Author's telephone interview with Toni Sentner, July 22, 1990.

97. Respondent's Exhibit 3, Maytag Case 18-c-183, T&E 507, NLRB25.

98. William Z. Foster, *Organizing Methods in the Steel Industry; Labor Unity,* June 1928 (New York: International Publishers, 1935).

99. Wagenknecht to Herbert Benjamin (ca. 1935), Delo 3896, Reel 298, CPR.

100. Gebert to Earl Browder, September 20, 1934, Delo 3643, Reel 282, CPR; author's telephone interview with Antonia Sentner, July 22, 1990.

101. William Sentner FBI File, August 22, 1951 Report, citing April 12, 1944, Sentner speech, FBI-HQ 100-18332-139, Box 5, Ser. 4, WSP.

102. Sentner interview; Bill Sentner Report, October 1935, Delo 3894 Reel 298, CPR. Kate Wiegand, *Red Feminism: American Communism and the Making of Women's Liberation* (Baltimore: Johns Hopkins University Press, 2001), suggests the wider dimensions of feminism in the party.

103. Elizabeth Faue, *Community of Suffering and Struggle,* 71.

104. William Sentner FBI File 100-18332-139, 12, Box 5, Ser. 4, WSP. This material stressing nonviolence was withheld from Sentner during his Smith Act trial and was initially withheld from his son in an FOIA request.

105. Report, October 1935, Delo 3894, Reel 298, CPR.

106. *SLPD,* May 2, 1936; Robert Logsdon, undated interview with Douglas Wixson, in Wixson's possession, Austin, Texas; Toni Sentner interview; author's interview with Shirley Raven.

107. Monthly Reports, January–December 1935, Industrial Secretary files, Box 4, Ser. 4, ULP; quotation in October 1935 report, Negro Worker Council files, Box 7, Ser. 4, ULP; Antonia Sentner interview. In addition to his labor organizing, Sentner continued to work for the construction firm to keep food on the table; Folder 38, Box 1, Charlotte and Raymond Koch Papers, Reuther Library, Wayne State University; author's interview with Raymond Koch.

108. Regional Case File 14-C-26, In the Matter of Scullin Steel Company and Amalgamated Assn. of Iron, Steel and Tin Workers Local Lodge No. 1062, Entry 155, NLRB25.

109. William Sentner to John Brophy, undated [mid-1936], in unprocessed WSP; Minutes of the 2nd District Convention of the CP, District 21, October 12–13, 1935, Delo 3894, Reel 298, CPR.

Chapter 3: *"Human Rights over Property Rights"*

1. William Sentner, "A Concentration Policy" Draft, December 2, 1955, 1–2, copy in author's possession, original in possession of William "Red" Davis, St. Louis; Minutes of the 2nd District Convention of the CP, District 21, October 12–13, 1935, Delo 3894, Reel 298, CPR.

2. Author's interview with Henry Fiering, Los Angeles, California, June 18, 1989; William Sentner, "A Concentration Policy" Draft, 2.

3. Manewitz testimony, Vol. 2, 1002–3, and Schoemehl testimony, Narrative Statement, Vol. 2, 909, CA.8, *Sentner v. U.S.,* #15097 Crim and 15098 *Forest et al. v. U.S.,* Box 4, Ser. 4, WSP.

4. Robert Logsdon, interview with Dennis Brunn, January 22, 1974, WHMC; author's interview with Fritzi Kimmel, St. Genevieve, Missouri, June 15, 1987; author's telephone interview with Robert Manewitz, November 15, 1989; UE Picnic Book, 1946, unprocessed Lloyd Austin Collection, WHMC; Official Record of Proceedings, 475, Emerson Case 14-c-34, T&E 1903, NLRB25.

5. Author's interview with Robert Logsdon, January 8, 1987. Despite Logsdon's roots in a southern Illinois coal town, that experience did not instill any strong union beliefs. Logsdon, whose father worked as a grain miller, recalled years later that "as far as unions go, I sure didn't get [a prounion attitude] from [my parents]."

6. Author's interview with Robert Logsdon; Robert Mason [Manewitz] to John T. Clark, February 3, 1936, "Unions-AWU, 1934–1936," Box 11, Ser. 4, ULP.

7. Author's telephone interview with Robert Manewitz; William Sentner to James Carey, December 31, 1936, O/1288, UEA.

8. William Sentner to Ray Koch, 1947, unprocessed WSP; author's interview with Lloyd Austin, St. Louis, Missouri, March 3, 1994.

9. Robert Mason [Manewitz] to James Carey, July 24, 1936, D8/133, UEA; Robert Manewitz to James Carey, August 24 and 30, 1936, D8/500, UEA; Official Report of

Proceedings, Transcript, 21, 129, 259, Emerson Case 14-c-34, T&E 1903, NLRB25; Minutes, Board of Representatives, April 28, 1932, Board's Exhibit 5, Emerson Case 14-c-34, T&E 1903, NLRB25; Robert Manewitz to Brothers Carey and Emspak, November 4, 1936, D8/500, UEA.

10. Robert Manewitz to Julius Emspak, September 25, 1936, November 4, 1936, D8/500, UEA; Julius Emspak to Robert Manewitz, December 30, 1936, D8/498, UEA. This counters to the conclusion that skilled workers were the most important component of the industrial union movement. See especially Ronald Schatz, "Union Pioneers: The Founder of Local Unions at General Electric and Westinghouse, 1933–1937," *Journal of American History* 66 (1979): 586–602, where Schatz argues that the UE was "initiated by members of a craft elite"; Ronald Schatz, *The Electrical Workers: A History of Labor at General Electric and Westinghouse, 1923–1960* (Urbana: University of Illinois Press, 1983), 99, fn. 1; Ronald Filipelli and Mark McCulloch, *Cold War in the Working Class: The Rise and Decline of the United Electrical Workers* (Albany: State University of New York Press, 1995), 16–17, 56, 79; and Grace Palladino, in "Building a Union: The Early History of UE Local 610," *Western Pennsylvania Historical Magazine* 67 (January 1984): 1–16. On the other hand, George Alexander Blair, "Struggling for a Union: Electrical Workers in Buffalo, N.Y., 1933–1956" (PhD diss., State University of New York, Buffalo, 1993), 44–63, found that union initiators shared few of the characteristics isolated by Schatz but attributes this difference to the time periods studied. Steve Babson, *Building the Union: Skilled Workers and Anglo-Gaelic Immigrants in the Rise of the UAW* (New Brunswick, N.J.: Rutgers University Press, 1992), suggests similar role for skilled auto workers.

11. Minutes, Board of Representatives, December 1936, Emerson Case 14-c-34, Board's Exhibit 5, T&E 1903, NLRB25.

12. Robert Manewitz to National Office, November 29, 1936, December 6, 1936, D8/500, UEA; author's interview with Marie Strathman, St. Louis, Missouri, June 6, 1994.

13. Robert Manewitz to James Carey and Julius Emspak, November 4, 1936, November 20, 1936, D8/500, UEA; James Carey to Robert Manewitz, December 1, 1936, D8/498, UEA.

14. Robert Manewitz to Brothers Carey and Emspak, November 4, 1936, D8/500, UEA; author's interview with Henry Fiering.

15. Author's interview with Henry Fiering; John Steffanow to Dear Sir, December 27, 1936, D8/607, UEA. For a similar sentiment and the argument that Communists organized with a style distinct from the United Mine Workers of America organizers who were assigned to the SWOC drive, see Max Gordon, "The Communists and the Drive to Organize Steel, 1936," *Labor History* 23 (Spring 1982): 260–65. See Roger Keeran, "The IWO and the Origins of the CIO," *Labor History* (Summer 1989): 385–408, for an elaboration of the role of radicals in the steel campaign.

16. William Sentner to James Carey, December 31, 1936, O/1288, UEA; Robert Manewitz to Julius Emspak, January 11, 1937, D8/500, UEA.

17. Robert Manewitz to Julius Emspak, December 26, 1936, D8/500, UEA; Julius Emspak to Robert Manewitz, December 30, 1936, D8/498, UEA.

18. R. Manewitz to James B. Carey, January 11, 1937, February 13, 1937, D8/500, UEA.

19. National Metal Trades Association, "The St. Louis Meeting on Industrial Cooperation," undated [July 1936], in "Emerson—Statements of Foremen" file, Case File, Emerson Case 14-c-34, Entry 155, NLRB25; U.S. Senate, Committee on Education and Labor,

Labor Policies of Employers' Associations, Part I: The National Metal Trades Association (Washington, D.C.: Government Printing Office, 1939), 37, 53, 150, 156; U.S. Senate, Committee on Education and Labor, *Industrial Espionage* Report No. 46, Part 3, 75th Cong., 2nd sess. (Washington, D.C.: U.S. Government Printing Office, 1938), 88, 96; U.S. Senate, Subcommittee of the Committee on Education and Labor, *Hearings Pursuant to S. Res. 266, Violations of Free Speech and Rights of Labor, Corporations Auxiliary,* 75th Cong., 2nd sess., Part 3, Ex. 392, 1013–14, exh. 398-D, 1036; W. C. Wright testimony, Official Record of Proceedings, Transcript, 308–58, Emerson Case 14-c-34, T&E 1903, NLRB25. Top officials of Wagner and Century were also among the national officers of the NMTA as well as local officers, a rather dramatic representation given that there were only twenty officers; Newman was too new to the industry.

20. National Metal Trades Association, "Vertical Union Squad Very Busy," October 27, 1936, "Emerson-Statements of Foremen" file, 14-c-34, Entry 155, RG 25; Dave Shaw to Benedict Wolf, April 8, 1937, Emerson Case File, 14-c-34, Entry 155, NLRB25; William White to H. L. Kerwin, March 27, 1937, Emerson Electric, Case 182–2266, FMCS280.

21. Diary of Alroy Phillips, February 3, 1937, in possession of David Phillips, Chicago, Illinois; William White to H. L. Kerwin, March 20, 1937, Case File 182–2266, Emerson Electric, FMCS280.

22. Official Report of Proceedings, Transcript, 8, 113, 122, Emerson Case 14-c-34, T&E 1903, NLRB25; "Union Statement on the Layoff," Gladys Slate Collection, WHMC; Emerson Electric management to employees, March 3, 1937, unprocessed William Reidel Papers, WHMC.

23. William Sentner to Julius Emspak, March 6, 1937, Weekly report, WSP; James Carey to William Sentner, March 8, 1937, O/1288, UEA.

24. Ronald Schatz, *The Electrical Workers,* 66; author's interview with Lloyd Austin, March 4, 1994; author's interview with Gilbert Kamp, St. Louis, Missouri, February 24, 1994.

25. Gilbert Kamp interview; author's interview with Lloyd Austin, March 4, 1994.

26. Marie Strathman interview; William Sentner to James Carey, March 8, 1937, O/1288, UEA; William Sentner, Organizing Report, March 20, 1937, Folder 2, Box 5, Ser. 1, WSP; "Sit Downers Take Over Cafe, Scour City to Get Food," newspaper clipping, unprocessed Gladys Slate Collection, WHMC; *PP,* St. Louis edition, April 3, 1937; interview with Marie Strathman; *Emerson Equalizer Strike Bulletins,* unprocessed Lloyd Austin Collection, WHMC; *SLPD,* March 8, 1937; *SLST,* March 9 and 11, 1937; "200 Stay-In Strikers Continue to Hold Emerson Plant," *SLPD,* home edition, clipping in "Emerson Electric Manufacturing Company-St. Louis, Missouri" folder, Emerson Case 14-c-34, Regional Case Files, Entry 155, NLRB25; *SLST,* March 17, 1937; *SLPD,* March 23, 1937; Earl McGrew to James Carey, March 11, 1937, O/836, UEA.

27. William Sentner, Organizing Report, March 20, 1937, Folder 2, Box 5, Ser. 1, WSP; *SLPD,* March 13, 1937, in Folder 2, Box 5, Ser. 1, WSP.

28. Earl McGrew to James Carey, March 11, 1937, O/836, UEA. The trial examiner for the NLRB's case against Emerson Electric found the St. Louis newspapers' treatment of workers' struggles was much more favorable than in other areas of the country. See Frank Bloom to Dave Shaw, May 23, 1937, Case File, 14-c-34, Entry 155, NLRB25.

29. Speech, "Ladies, Gentlemen, Fellow Workers," n.d., Folder 8, Box 5, Ser. 1, WSP.

30. Unidentified newspaper article, March 10, 1937, Gladys Slate Collection, WHMC.

31. William Sentner, Speech, "Ladies, Gentlemen, Fellow Workers," Folder 5, Box 4, Ser. 1, WSP.

32. *SLPD*, March 9, 1937.

33. William Sentner, Organizing Report, March 20, 1937, March 27, 1937, Folder 2, Box 5, Ser. 1, WSP; *SLGD*, March 16, 1937; *SLPD*, March 16, 23, and 24, 1937; *SLST*, March 16 and 19, 1937; William White to H. L. Kerwin, March 27, 1937, File 182–2266, FMCS280; Dave Shaw to Benedict Wolf, April 8, 1937, Emerson Case 14-c-34, Entry 155, NLRB25.

34. *SLPD*, March 24, 1937; author's interview with William Reidel, St. Louis, Missouri, August 10, 1986; author's interview with Marie Strathman, St. Louis, Missouri, June 6, 1994.

35. William Sentner to James Carey, March 8, 1937, O/1288, UEA; Earl McGrew to James Carey, March 11, 1937, O/836, UEA; author's interview with Del Garst, St. Louis, Missouri, June 11, 1987.

36. *SLPD*, March 29, 1937; William Sentner to James Carey, March 30, 1937, O/1288, UEA.

37. William Sentner, Organizing Reports, March 20 and 27, 1937, Folder 2, Box 5, Ser. 1, WSP.

38. William Sentner to James Carey, March 8, 1937, O/1288, UEA; "Strategy Board Formed by Unions in Emerson Strike," Scrapbook, JWCP507; *SLST*, March 18, 1937; William Sentner to James Emspak, May 2, 1937, O/1289, UEA.

39. *SLST*, March 24, 25, 26, 29, 30, and 31, 1937; *SLPD*, March 25 and 31, 1937; *PP*, UE edition, April 10, 1937, 7; *Emerson Equalizer*, April 1 and 2, 1937, unprocessed Lloyd Austin Collection, WHMC; *SLST*, April 2, 1937; *SLPD*, April 7, 1937; *SLST*, April 30, 1937; *SLGD*, April 30, 1937; "Labor Relations," February 1937 Monthly Report, Box 4, Ser. 4, ULP. See also "Report of the Industrial Secretary, April 1937" therein.

40. Phillips diary, March 5 and 7, 1932, May 18, 1932; William White to H. L. Kerwin, March 20, 1937, Case 182–2266, FMCS280. According to White, Newman told him that "he was going to make no effort to evict the sitdown strikers or get into trouble of any kind as he knew at a later date they would all have to work together again and he wanted no hard feelings to exist."

41. Phillips diary, March 19, 1937.

42. Ibid., March 29, 1937. Until March 20, according to federal conciliators, Newman was confident of victory. Progress Report, March 20, 1937, Case 182–2266, FMCS280.

43. Phillips diary, March 15, 1937; William Sentner to James Carey, March 30, 1937, 0–1288, UEA; William Sentner Organizing Report, April 17, 1937, Folder 2, Box 5, Ser. 1, WSP.

44. *SLPD*, March 16, 1937.

45. Phillips diary, March 29, 1937.

46. Author's interview with Henry Fiering; Weekly Report, *Century Electric v. United Electrical Workers Local 1108*, Case File, 14-c-37, NLRB25; *SLPD*, April 16, 1937.

47. Author's interview with Henry Fiering; *PP*, St. Louis UE edition, April 24, 1937; *SLST*, April 19, 1937; *SLPD*, April 20, 1937; *Century Electric v. George Schwartz et al.*, In Equity #15287, St. Louis Circuit Court Records, St. Louis, Missouri.

48. William Sentner, Organizing Report, April 17, 1937, Folder 2, Box 5, Ser. 1, WSP; *Cent-Em Striker*, unprocessed Lloyd Austin Collection, WHMC; Weekly Report, April 17, 1937, Century Electric, Case 14-R-37, Entry 155, NLRB25.

49. *PP*, St. Louis UE edition, April 17, 1937.

50. *Cent-Em Striker,* n.d., unprocessed Lloyd Austin Collection, WHMC; Jim Pope, "Worker Lawmaking, Sit-Down Strikes, and the Shaping of the American Industrial Relations, 1935–1958," *Law and History Review* (forthcoming).

51. *Emerson Equalizer,* March 12, 1937.

52. *SLPD*, April 15, 20, and 23, 1937; William Sentner, Organizing Report, April 17, 1937, Folder 2, Box 5, Ser. 1, WSP; author's interview with Henry Fiering, WHMC.

53. William Sentner, Organizing Report, April 25, 1937, Folder 2, Box 5, Ser. 1, WSP; *SLPD*, April 20, 1937; *Century Electric et al. v. William B. Carey et al.,* 15,287 In equity, Records of the Circuit Court, City Courts Building, St. Louis, Missouri.

54. Phillips diary, April 12, 1937; Weekly Report on Pending Cases, April 17, 1937, Case 14-c-34, Entry 155, NLRB25; *SLPD*, April 18, 1937; *SLST,* April 16, 1937; *SLGD*, April 16 and 18, 1937.

55. Weekly Report on Pending Cases, Week ending April 17, 1937, Emerson Case 14-c-34, NLRB25.

56. *SLGD*, April 12, 1937; *Emerson Equalizer,* April 1 and 2, 1937, unprocessed Lloyd Austin Collection, WHMC.

57. Phillips diary, April 15, 1937; *Emerson Equalizer,* April 1, 1937; Official Report of Proceedings, Transcript, May 14, 1937, 522–35, T&E 1903, Emerson Case 14-c-34, NLRB25.

58. Phillips diary, April 15, 1937; Official Report of Proceedings, Transcript, May 14, 1937, 522, Emerson Case 14-c-34, T&E 1903, NLRB25; Phillips diary, April 21, 1937.

59. *SLST,* April 23, 1937; *SLPD*, April 22, 1937; Conference Transcript, April 22, 1937, Respondent's Exhibit 2; Conference Transcript, April 27, 1937, Respondent's Exhibit 6, 11, T&E 1903, Emerson Case 14-c-34, NLRB25; Phillips diary, April 20–22, 1937; Weekly Report on Pending Cases, April 24, 1937, Emerson Case File, 14-c-34, Entry 155, NLRB25. On the problems Carey created with his less than savvy negotiations style, see Filipelli and McCulloch, *Cold War in the Working Class,* 39.

60. *SLPD*, April 22 and 23, 1937; William Sentner, Organizing Report, April 25, 1937, Folder 2, Box 5, Ser. 1, WSP.

61. Conference Transcript, April 23, 1937, 3, 5, Respondents' Exhibit 5, Emerson Case 14-c-34, T&E 1903, NLRB25.

62. Phillips diary, April 23–27, 1937; Official Report of Proceedings, Transcript, 535, Emerson Case 14-c-34, T&E 1903, NLRB25.

63. Injunction petition, Emerson Electric, Board's Exhibit 16, Emerson Case 14-c-34, T&E 1903, NLRB25; Official Reports and Proceedings, Transcript, 535, May 14, 1937, Emerson Case 14-c-34, T&E 1903, NLRB25; Conference Transcript, April 27, 1937, 5–9, Respondent's Exhibit 6, T&E 1903, NLRB25.

64. *SLPD*, April 28 and 29, 1937; *SLST,* April 29, 1937; *SLGD*, April 29, 1937.

65. Phillips diary, April 27 and 28, 1937; Official Reports and Proceedings, Transcript, May 14, 1937, 535, Emerson Case 14-c-34, T&E 1903, NLRB25.

66. *SLPD*, April 25 and 28, 1937; Sidney Fine, *Sit-Down: The General Motors Strike of 1936–1937* (Ann Arbor: University of Michigan Press, 1969).

67. Conference, Transcript, April 27, 1937, Exhibit 6, Emerson Case 14-c-34, T&E 1903, NLRB25; *SLST,* April 29, 1937; Phillips diary, April 29, 1937; Max Michelson to William Sentner, January 2, 1941, copy in possession of author; Transcript of District 8 Convention, October 6–7, 1945, Folder 5, Box 5, Ser. 1, WSP.

68. Weekly Report on Pending Cases, May 1, 1937, Emerson Case 14-c-34, NLRB25; *SLST,* April 29, 1937. The longest sit-down occurred at the Hercules Motors Corporation, in Canton, Ohio, and lasted fifty-seven days.

69. Official Reports and Proceedings, Transcript, May 14, 1937, 537–39, T&E 1903, Emerson Case 14-c-34, NLRB25; Weekly Report on Pending Cases, May 1, 1937, Case File, Emerson Case 14-c-34, Entry 155, NLRB25.

70. Conference Transcript, April 23, 1937, 5, Respondent's Exhibit 3, Emerson Case 14-c-34, T&E 1903, NLRB25.

71. Official Report of Proceedings, Transcript, April 28, 1937, 14–15, Respondent's Exhibit 7; Official Report of Proceedings, Transcript, April 26, 1937, 10, 12, 14, Respondent's Exhibit 4; both in Emerson Case 14-c-34, T&E 1903, NLRB25.

72. Conference Transcript, April 28, 1937, 14–15, Respondent's Exhibit 7; Conference Transcript, Respondent's Exhibit Nos. 4, 10, 12, 14; both in Emerson Case 14-c-34, T&E 1903, NRLB25.

73. Conference Transcript, April 23, 1937, 20, Respondent's Exhibit 3; Conference Transcript, May 6, 1937, 26, Respondent's Exhibit No. 11; both in Emerson Case 14-c-34, T&E 1903, NLRB25.

74. Conference Transcript, May 8, 1937, 81, Respondent's Exhibit 13, T&E 1903, NLRB25.

75. Conference Transcript, April 26, 1937, 20, Respondent's Exhibit 5; Conference Transcript, May 7, 1937, 30, 35, Respondent's Exhibit 12; both in Emerson Case 14-c-34, T&E 1903, NLRB25.

76. Conference Transcript, April 26, 1937, Respondent's Exhibit 4, 11, T&E 1903, NLRB25. See also Official Report of Proceedings, Transcript, May 14, 1937, 526, T&E 1903, NLRB25.

77. Conference Transcript, May 7, 1937, 30, Respondent's Exhibit 12, Emerson Case 14-c-34, T&E 1903, NLRB25.

78. Conference Transcript, April 26, 1937, 20, Respondent's Exhibit 5, Emerson Case 14-c-34, T&E 1903, NLRB25.

79. Phillips diary, May 6, 1937; Frank Bloom to National Labor Relations Board, May 7, 1937, Emerson Case File 14-c-34, Entry 155, NLRB25.

80. Frank Bloom to National Labor Relations Board, May 7, 1937, Emerson Case File 14-c-34, Entry 155, NLRB25.

81. *SLPD,* April 26 and 30, 1937; Frank Bloom to National Labor Relations Board, May 7, 1937, Emerson Case File 14-c-34, Entry 155, NLRB25.

82. Phillips diary, May 10, 1937.

83. *SLPD,* May 11, 1937.

84. Phillips diary, May 11, 1937; Official Report of Proceedings, Transcript, 541, Emerson Case 14-c-34, T&E 1903, NLRB25.

85. Report on Adjusted Case, May 15, 1937, Emerson Case File 14-c-34, NLRB25. The no-strike clause was a provision likely advocated by Michelson, whose experience in the ACW with marginal employers was influential on Sentner during this period. Later, Sentner deeply regretted agreeing to this provision. In the postwar period, the UE sought to eliminate no-strike clauses and succeeded in some companies.

86. *SLPD,* May 7, 1937.

87. William Sentner, Organizing Reports, April 17 and 25, 1937, May 1, 17, and 25, 1937, June 12, 1937, July 6, 1937, WSP; *PP,* June 12, 1937; *SLPD,* April 21, 1937; Weekly Report of

Pending Cases, May 19 and 22, 1937, Case 14-c-38, NLRB25; *SLPD,* May 19, 1937; *SLGD,* May 29, 1937; "The CIO Scores Another Victory," [June 1937] O/1290, UEA.

88. William Sentner to James Matles, August 20, 1937, O/1292, UEA; William Sentner to James Matles, August 24, 1937, O/1292, UEA.

89. Conference Transcript, Official Report of Proceedings, April 26, 1937, 25, Respondent's Exhibit 5, T&E 1903, NLRB25.

90. See Melvyn Dubofsky, "Not So Turbulent Years: Another Look at the American 1930s," *Amerikastudien* 24 (1980): 5–19, and Lizabeth Cohen, *Making A New Deal,* for examples of reading workers' underlying values and beliefs from the success of the labor movement in the 1930s. My interpretation was influenced in part by social movement literature and especially Kim Voss, "Disposition Is Not Action: The Rise and Demise of the Knights of Labor," *Studies in American Political Development* 6 (Fall 1992): 272–321, who showed how employer repression, not worker consciousness, limited the Knights of Labor.

91. Author's interview with Henry Fiering; the first quotation is from Dubofsky, "Not So Turbulent Years," 19; author's interview with Lloyd Austin, August 10, 1987.

92. Conference Transcript, April 26, 1937, Respondent's Exhibit 6, Emerson Case 14-c-34, T&E 1903, NLRB25.

93. William Sentner, Organizing Reports, June 12, 1937, July 6 and 31, 1937, Folder 2, Box 1, Ser. 1 WSP; William Sentner to James Matles, August 20, 1937, William Sentner to James Matles, August 24, 1937, O/1292, UEA; Robert Logsdon, undated interview with Douglas Wixson, in Wixson's possession, Austin, Texas.

94. Robert Zieger, *The CIO, 1935–1955* (Chapel Hill: University of North Carolina Press, 1995), 70. For the best treatment of the alliances between New Deal political elite and leading CIO officials, see Steve Fraser, *Labor Will Rule: Sidney Hillman and the Rise of American Labor* (Ithaca, N.Y.: Cornell University Press, 1991).

95. Schatz, *The Electrical Workers;* Ronald Filipelli, "UE: An Uncertain Legacy," *Political Power and Social Theory,* ed. Maurice Zeitlin, 4 (1984): 218–21, 225; Ronald Filipelli, "UE: The Formative Years, 1933–1937," *Labor History* (Spring 1976): 351–71.

96. William Sentner to James Emspak, Weekly Report, August 12, 1937, Folder 3, Box 5, Ser. 1, WSP; James Emspak to William Sentner, September 27, 1937, O/1293, UEA; William Sentner Remarks, 45–48, General Executive Board Minutes, December 11–12, 1937, Box 1, Ernie DeMaio Papers, Chicago Historical Society. Until the convention in 1937, St. Louis was still part of the Chicago district of the UE, District 11. Thus, all locals established in this period carried the "11" designation as part of their numbers; that is, Emerson local was 1102, Maytag was 1116, etc. Between December 1936 and August 1937, the national union grew from 33,000 to 120,000 members to become the third largest affiliate in the CIO. The UAW and the Steel Workers were the first and second largest CIO affiliates.

97. Author's interview with Robert Logsdon, WHMC; author's interview with Raymond and Charlotte Koch, November 13, 1993, Chicago, Illinois.

98. *PP,* St. Louis edition, November 20, 1937, May 14, 1938, January 1, 1938 (quote); author's interviews with Raymond and Charlotte Koch; author's interview with Lloyd Austin; author's interview with Willaim Reidel.

99. Sentner, May 22, 1937, Industrial Union Council folder, Folder 3, Box 6, Ser. 1, WSP.

100. William Sentner, Speech, May Day 1937, Industrial Union Council folder, Folder 3, Box 6, Ser. 1, WSP.

101. Lichtenstein and Harris, ed., *Industrial Democracy in America: The Ambiguous Promise* (Cambridge: Cambridge University Press, 1993); Gary Gerstle, *Working-Class*

Americanism: The Politics of Labor in a Textile City, 1914–1960 (Cambridge: Cambridge University Press, 1989), 187–90.

102. Minutes of Sub-District Conference (Iowa) of Missouri-Kansas-Iowa District, July 25, 1937; Minutes of the 1st District Convention, August 8, 1937, Ser. 1, WSP; Educational Committee, "Speakers' Bureau," ca. 1937, D8/220, UEA.

103. Minutes of Sub-District Conference (Iowa) of Missouri-Kansas-Iowa District, July 25, 1937, Ser. 1, WSP.

104. Minutes of Sub-District Conference (Iowa) of Missouri-Kansas-Iowa District, July 25, 1937; Undated article [June 1937], unprocessed WSP; author's interview with Vic Pasche, San Francisco, California, June 17, 1989; William Sentner to Art Meloan, April 1938, O/1297, UEA; Otto Maschoff, Ray Koch, William Steinberg, "Educational Committee Speaker's Bureau," D8/220, UEA.

105. Sentner, notes on steward system, October 14, 1937, in Minutes, Folder 1, Box 5, Ser. 1, WSP.

106. Conference Transcript, April 22, 1937, Respondent's Exhibit 2, Emerson Case 14-c-34, T&E 1903, NLRB25.

107. William Sentner, Organizing Report, June 6, 1937, WSP; *PP*, St. Louis UE Edition, June 12, 1937.

108. *PP*, St. Louis edition, June 19 and 26, 1937.

109. *PP*, St. Louis edition, June 26 and July 3, 1937; William Sentner, Organizing Report, June 19, 1937, Sentner Papers; *NDN*, June 17, 1937.

110. William Sentner, Organizing Report, August 14, 1937, WSP; William Sentner to James Matles, August 17, 1937; Case 14-c-37, In the Matter of Wagner Electric, NLRB25.

111. Official Report of Proceedings, Transcript, May 8, 1937, Emerson Case 14-c-34, T&E 1903, NLRB25.

112. Frederick Ryan to Dorothea de Schweinitz, April 2, 1938, Emerson Case 14-C-185 file, Entry 155, NLRB25; Robert Logsdon to James Matles, August 24, 1938, O/706, UEA.

113. Stenographic Transcripts, May 26, 1938, 580, 690, Emerson Case 14-c-185, T&E 1010, NLRB25; *PP*, August 21, 1937.

114. Author's interview with Henry Fiering; Sidney Williams, Monthly Report, December 1937, 3, Box 4, Ser. 4, ULP.

115. *PP*, St. Louis edition, August 7, 1937; author's interview with Raymond and Charlotte Koch; "News Flashes," May 18, Local 1102, unprocessed Lloyd Austin Collection, WHMC.

116. *PP*, St. Louis edition, October 30, 1937; Official Report of Proceedings, Transcript, May 23, 1938, 34–38, Emerson Case 14-c-185, T&E 1010, NLRB25.

117. Official Report of Proceedings, Transcript, May 28, 1938, 109, Emerson Case 14-c-185, T&E 1010, NLRB25.

118. Official Report of Proceedings, Transcript, May 23, 1938, 313, T&E 1010, NLRB25.

119. Employees Book of Rules, unprocessed Lloyd Austin Collection, WHMC. "Attention Members Local 1102 and all Emerson Workers" Exhibit 19; Karches to Local 1102, February 7, 1938, Exhibit 23; John Driy statement in regard to Rules and Information for Employees, March 1, 1938, Exhibit 27; "Union Demands Adherence to Contract," March 2, 1938, Exhibit 28; all in Emerson Case 14-c-185, T&E 1010, NLRB25; Frederick L. Ryan to Dorothea de Schweinitz, April 2, 1938, Emerson Case File, 14-c-185, NLRB25; Local 1102 Shop Bulletin, March 17, 1938, attached to William White, Progress Report, March 20, 1938, 199-1389, FMCS280.

120. Official Report of Proceedings, Transcript, May 25, 1938, 437, 448, Emerson Case 14-c-185, T&E 1010, NLRB25.

121. "Attention Members of Local 1102" leaflet, undated, Exhibit No. 19, Emerson Case 14-c-185, T&E 1010, NLRB25; Robert Logsdon to James J. Matles, February 5, 1938, O/704, UEA; Robert Logsdon to James Matles, August 20, 1938, O/706, UEA.

122. Official Report of Proceedings, Transcript, May 27, 1938, 580, Emerson Case 14-c-185, T&E 1010, NLRB25.

123. *PP,* St. Louis edition, May 29 and June 12, 1937.

124. *PP,* November 13, 1937, and January 19, May 14, and June 25, 1938.

125. Author's interview with Raymond and Charlotte Koch; author's interview with Orville Leach; author's interview with Henry Fiering; *PP,* UE District 8 Edition, July 10 and November 6, 1937.

126. Author's interview with Raymond and Charlotte Koch.

127. Author's interview with James Click, July 28, 1986. Charles Slezak recalled that some workers, however, resented the presence of the CP in the sit-down strike from the beginning. When CP members came to discuss radical ideas in the sit-down, he was part of a group that "ordered them out." Letter from Slezak to author.

128. Survey is based on profiles of the following workers identified as party members during the 1930s: Dottie Aukamp, Zollie Carpenter, William Cortor, Frank Goforth, Hilda Marsche, Lou Kimmel, George Kimmel, Orville Leach, Tom Maupin, Frank Mier, Helen Musil, John Nordman, and James Payne. This list is not meant to suggest that these workers were reflective of all those who joined the party. However, it does show that unskilled workers with little radical background were attracted to the party within the context of electrical workers' unionism. A much more important point to remember is that many more unskilled workers were also attracted to coalitions that included party and nonparty members attracted to the idea of the union as a vehicle for social transformation. Quote is from Lichtenstein, "Labor and Communism: An Exchange," *Industrial Relations* 19(2) (1980): 126.

129. Author's interview with Orville Leach, Kennett, Missouri, July 22, 1991.

130. Author's interview with Henry Fiering.

131. Official Report of Proceedings, Transcript, 1–19, Emerson Case C-908, T&E, NLRB25; Cortor's testimony, Narrative Statement, CA.8, 774–840, *Sentner v. U.S.,* #15097 Crim and 15098 *Forest et al. v. U.S.,* Box 4, Ser. 4, WSP.

132. Author's interview with James Click, July 28, 1986.

133. Narrative Statement, 1023, *Sentner et al. v. U.S.,* Vol. 2, Box 4, Ser. 4, WSP; *Direct Current,* Labor Day Number, September 1, 1937, JWCP357.

134. Author's interview with Henry Fiering.

135. Ibid.

136. Ibid.

137. Author's interview with Lloyd Austin, July 29, 1986; Lloyd Patrick, "How Communists Are Born," *SLST,* Letter to the editor, August 25, 1938, unprocessed Lloyd Austin Collection, WHMC.

138. Steve Rosswurm critiques this perception in his introduction to *The CIO's Left-Led Unions* (New Brunswick, N.J.: Rutgers University Press, 1992), 6. See also Denning, *Cultural Front.*

139. *SLST,* August 15, 1938.

140. Wixson interview with Logsdon; author's interview with Henry Fiering.

141. Author's interview with Hershel Walker; author's interviews with Marian Bastionello Barry, June 22 and August 10, 1989.

142. Robert Logsdon to James Matles, February 19, 1941, O/718, UEA.

143. William Sentner to Julius Emspak, November 15, 1945, unprocessed WSP. The organizers were mostly men, although as will be discussed in a later chapter, District 8 locals were the first to submit a resolution (in 1939) that the national UE make a commitment to hire blacks and women as organizers.

144. Author's interviews with Raymond and Charlotte Koch; Dennis Brunn interview with Robert Logsdon, WHMC; author's interview with Henry Fiering.

145. Resolution, October 23, 1937, D8/493, UEA; Bill Sentner to James Emspak, November 1, 1937, O/1295, UEA.

146. William Sentner to Oscar Debus, November 10, 1937, "Trotskyists and Lovestonites" file, unprocessed WSP.

147. William Sentner to James Matles, November 5, 1937, WSP; Minutes of the Meeting of St. Louis Joint Board Together with the St. Louis Officers of the District Executive Board, November 3, 1937, attached to William Sentner to James Matles, November 5, 1937, O/1295, UEA.

148. Memorandum, "The History of the Constitution of District 8," D8/192, UEA; "Early 1939" speech, Sentner Papers, Folder 8, Box 5, Ser. 1, WSP.

149. Author's interview with Robert Logsdon.

Chapter 4: "This 'Red' Gave Them a Run for Their Money"

1. Roger W. Ratcliffe, "An Inquiry into the 1938 Strike at Maytag Company, Newton, Iowa" (MA thesis, Drake University, 1964), 1–25; James Thomas, "History of Labor-Management Relations of the Maytag Company, Newton, Iowa," Paper, Iowa State University, 1964, in SHSI.

2. Intermediate Report of the Trial Examiner, *In the Matter of the Maytag Company and United Electrical, Radio and Machine Workers of America, Local 1116*, Case 14-C-118, 5, in RD files, UEA.

3. Ratcliffe, "An Inquiry into the 1938 Strike at Maytag Company, Newton, Iowa," 12.

4. "Maytag Ordeal," *Life Magazine* 5(6) (August 8, 1938), 11; Ratcliffe, "An Inquiry into the 1938 Strike at Maytag Company, Newton, Iowa," 28; May 27, 1939, D8/645, UEA; Bryan Dye, "History of Local 1116, U.E.R.M.W.A.," 1, Local 1116-Maytag Collection, SHSI; Shelley L. Blair, "Crisis in Newton, Iowa: The 1938 Maytag Strike" (Senior thesis, American Studies Department, Grinnell College, May 1976), 4, SHSI; *DMR*, June 30, 1938; Seibert Chestnutt, June 24, 1938, Radio program, in Case File 1, Maytag Case 18-c-183, NLRB25; "Labor Troubles and the Church," *Social Action*, January 15, 1939.

5. *DMR*, July 12, 1938; Steinberger testimony, Exhibit 23, Maytag Case 18-c-183, T&E 507, NLRB25; M. W. Albee testimony, Arbitration Hearings, C-16, Board's Exhibit 9, T&E 507, Maytag Case 18-c-183, NLRB25; Trial Brief, Wilbert Allison, special file, Maytag Case File 18-c-183, Entry 155, NLRB25.

6. Author's interview with Robert Logsdon, January 8, 1987.

7. Dye, "History of Local 1116, U.E.R.M.W.A.," 2; *PP*, July 3, 1937; Virgil Martin interview with Paul Kelso, December 11, 1978, ILHOP.

8. William Sentner to James Matles, October 11, 1937, Weekly reports, Folder 2, Box 6, Ser. 1, WSP.

9. Roxy Ball to K. R. Marvin, April 28, 1938, C-183 folder, "Clip Board file," Maytag Case 18-c-183 file, Entry 155, NLRB25.

10. Ratcliffe, "An Inquiry into the 1938 Strike at Maytag Company, Newton, Iowa," 37; *NDN*, July 11, 13–14, 24–27, 27–29, and 30, August 14 and 26, and September 6–7 and 10–11, 1937.

11. Radio Program, June 20, 1938, file #1, Maytag Case File 18-c-183, Entry 155, NLRB25; Ratcliffe, "An Inquiry into the 1938 Strike at Maytag Company, Newton, Iowa," 33–36; *NDN*, July 2, 1937.

12. Officers' Report to September Meeting of District Council, September 4, 1938, WSP; Dye, "History of Local 1116, U.E.R.M.W.A.," 3.

13. William Sentner to James Matles, February 1, 1938; William Sentner to James Matles, February 7, 1938, O/1296, UEA; William Sentner to James Matles, April 28, 1938, O/1297, UEA.

14. Ratcliffe, "An Inquiry into the 1938 Strike at Maytag Company, Newton, Iowa," 40.

15. Rhodes testimony, Board's Exhibit 51, Maytag Case C-1129, T&E 507, NLRB25.

16. William Sentner to James Matles, April 22, 1938, O/1297, UEA; Blair, "Crisis in Newton, Iowa," 3–4.

17. William Sentner to James Matles, April 29, 1938, O/1297, UEA; *NDN*, April 28, 1938; Wilbert Allison, Radio Program, June 20, 1938, "File #1," Maytag Case File 18-c-183, Entry 155, NLRB25.

18. William Sentner to James Matles, April 29, 1938, O/1297, UEA.

19. Fraser Ottanelli, *The Communist Party of the United States: From the Depression to World War II* (New Brunswick, N.J.: Rutgers University Press, 1991), 115.

20. Resolution, May 4, 1938, Exhibit 127, Maytag Case File 18-c-183, T&E 507, NLRB25; William Sentner to James Matles, May 4, 1938, O/1297, UEA; Ratcliffe, "An Inquiry into the 1938 Strike at Maytag Company, Newton, Iowa," 47, citing *DMR*, October 6, 1938, and October 1, 1938; Virgil Martin interview with Paul Kelso, 15, ILHOP.

21. William Sentner to Robert Wiener, May 31, 1938, Ser. 1, Box 2, Folder 21, WSP; see also *PP*, District 8 edition, May 14, 1938.

22. *DMR*, July 21, 1938; William Sentner to James Matles, May 4, 1938, O/1297, UEA; Ratcliffe, "An Inquiry into the 1938 Strike at Maytag Company, Newton, Iowa," 47, citing *DMR*, October 6 and October 1, 1938; Virgil Martin interview, 15, ILHOP.

23. *PP*, St. Louis UE edition, May 28, 1938; *DMT*, July 13, 1938.

24. William Sentner, Organizer's Report, May 21, 1938, WSP; William Sentner to James Matles, May 26, 1938, O/1297, UEA; *State v. Sentner*, 298 N.W. 813 (Supreme Court of Iowa, June 17, 1941, No. 45227), 4, Folder 2, Box 3, Ser. 1, WSP; Paul Kelso interview with Ezra Cooper, ILHOP.

25. Mrs. Wonders, June 24, 1938, Radio Broadcast, Case File 1, Maytag Case File 18-c-183, Entry 155, NLRB25; *DMR*, June 30, 1938; Ben Henry, 80–81, account of Maytag strike, Folder 2, Collection ZZ 1, SHSI.

26. Quotation on the "formula" is from Roger Keeran, "The International Workers Order and the Origins of the CIO," *Labor History* 30 (Summer 1989): 396. Irving Bernstein, *The Turbulent Years: A History of the American Worker, 1933–1941* (Boston: Houghton Mifflin, 1969), 491, writes that "the essence of the Mohawk Valley formula was the mobilization of local community sentiment and power against the strike." *PP*, UE edition, July 23, 1938.

27. Ellen Schrecker, *Many Are the Crimes: McCarthyism in America* (Boston: Little, Brown, 1998), 48, has elaborated on the reemergence of this tradition in the 1930s in tracing the origins of McCarthyism.

28. Archie Thompson, "Summary of the Activities of the Union Commissary," Maytag Strike of 1938–39 Collection, SHSI; William Sentner, Organizer's Report, May 21, 1938, Folder 2, Box 6, Ser. 1, WSP; William Sentner to James Matles, May 26, 1938, O/1297, UEA.

29. William Sentner, Organizers' Report, May 21, 1938, Folder 2, Box 6, Ser. 1, WSP; William Sentner to James Matles, May 26, 1938, O/1297, UEA; Ratcliffe, "An Inquiry into the 1938 Strike at Maytag Company, Newton, Iowa," 53–54, citing *DMR,* June 4–6, 1938; Intermediate Report, 15, RD 22, UEA; Affidavits, Untitled binder, Maytag Case 18-c-183 File, NLRB25; Blair, "Crisis in Newton, Iowa," 9; *NDN,* June 4, 1938.

30. Blair, "Crisis in Newton, Iowa," 9; *NDN,* June 4, 1938; Exceptions by Local Union, 7, C-1129 Case File 2, Entry 155, NLRB25.

31. *State v. Sentner,* 298 N.W. 831 (Supreme Court of Iowa, June 17, 1941, No 45227), 6, Folder 2, Ser. 1, Box 3, Folder 2, WSP.

32. *State v. Sentner,* 298 N.W. 831, 6, Folder 2, Box 3, Ser. 1, WSP. The statement became a point of contention in a criminal syndicalism case against Sentner, and Sentner denied having said it. However, testimony from several sources credited Sentner with having made the statement, and at other points Sentner asked workers to defy injunctions.

33. Undated newspaper clipping from *NDN,* Maytag Strike of 1938 collection, 1937–39, SHSI; *NDN,* June 17, 1938; *PP,* June 25, 1938.

34. Sentner report, June 18, 1938, WSP; Robert Kirkwood to Julius Emspak, June 20, 1938, D8/644, UEA; *Bulletin,* October 12, 1938, Folder 7, Box 3, Ser. 1, WSP.

35. Equity Case No. 18938, District Court Journal, Jasper County Courthouse Files, Newton, Iowa; Sentner Report, June 18, 1938, WSP; Jack Leaming to Julius Emspak, June 23, 1938, D8/667, UEA; Wilbert Allison to Julius Emspak, June 23, 1938, D8/640, UEA.

36. "Labor Leaders in Maytag Dispute Reveal Main Factors behind Strike," Unidentified article, Folder 20, Box 2, Ser. 1, WSP; Harold Wail affidavit, from Equity no 18938 case, Respondent's Exhibit 3, in Maytag C-1129 case, T&E 507, NLRB25.

37. William Sentner, Organizing Report, June 25, 1938, WSP; Ratcliffe, "An Inquiry into the 1938 Strike at Maytag Company, Newton, Iowa," 63, citing *DMR,* August 2, 1938.

38. John Griffith interview by John Kelso, transcript, 26, ILHOP.

39. Hollis Hall comments, Untitled binder, Maytag Case 18-c-183 file, NLRB25; William Sentner, Organizing Report, June 25, 1938, WSP; *NDN,* June 30, 1938; William Sentner, Organizers' Report, June 18, 1938, WSP.

40. *DMT,* July 30, 1938.

41. Officers Report to September 3 meeting of District Council, District 8, September 4, 1938, unprocessed WSP; Ratcliffe, "An Inquiry into the 1938 Strike at Maytag Company, Newton, Iowa," 51, citing *DMR,* May 16, 1938; Don Harris interview with Merle Davis, 17, ILHOP. *Solidarity and Survival: An Oral History of Iowa Labor in the Twentieth Century* (Iowa City: University of Iowa Press, 1993), 92; John Griffith interview with Paul Kelso, ILHOP; *DMR,* July 6, 1938; *DMR,* June 26 and 28, 1938.

42. William Sentner to James Matles, June 28, 1938, O/1298, UEA.

43. William Sentner, Organizing Report, June 18, 1938, WSP; *NDN,* June 23, 1938; "Radio Program," June 20, 22, 24, 1938, File #1, Maytag Case 18-c-183 file, Entry 155, NLRB25.

44. William Sentner to James Matles, June 29, 1938, O/1298, UEA; *DMR,* June 23, 28 and 30 and July 28, 1938; "Umbreit, V.P. and E. W. Ford Attorney, June 15" notes, file #1, Maytag Case 18-c-183 File, Entry 155, NLRB25.

45. James J. Matles and James Higgins, *Them and Us: Struggles of a Rank-and File Union* (Englewood Cliffs, N.J.: Prentice Hall, 1977); Intermediate Report, 4, RD22, UEA; William Sentner to Jim (James Matles), Thursday night, undated, O/1298, UEA; *NDN,* July 2, 1938, in Maytag Strike Files, SHSI; William Sentner to James Matles, July 20, 1938, O/1299, UEA.

46. July 5, 1938, phone conversation notes, in Maytag Case 18-c-183 file, NLRB25; Intermediate Report, 4, RD22, UEA; William Sentner to James Matles, July 20, 1938, O/1299, UEA; *NDN,* July 6, 1938; Thomas, "History of Labor-Management Relations of the Maytag Company," 8.

47. William Sentner, Organizers' Report, June 25, 1938, WSP; Griffith interview, 26; William Sentner to James Matles, July 20, 1938, Folder 21, Box 2, Ser. 1, WSP.

48. *SLPD,* July 7, 1938; "Sentner, W. D.-Criminal Syndicalism Case," RD22, UEA; *State of Iowa v. William Sentner and Hollis Hall,* District Court of Iowa, Poweshiek County, Case File, Poweshiek County Courthouse, Montezuma, Iowa.

49. *DMR,* July 7, 1938.

50. Fred Bender to Earl Shields, July 7, 1938, Exhibit 7, Maytag Case 18-c-183 file, T&E 507, NLRB25. For Bender's background, see James T. Dunne, Field Examiner, March 22–25, 1939, Servel Case 11-c-540, NLRB25; *SLGD,* September 21, 1961; Case File, File #2, Servel Case 11-c-163, NLRB25; Records of the LaFollette Committee; *DMR,* July 7, 1938; *New York Times,* July 9, 1938; *DMT,* undated, in Folder 17, Box 2, Ser. 1, WSP; Ratcliffe, "An Inquiry into the 1938 Strike at Maytag Company, Newton, Iowa," 82.

51. Ratcliffe, "An Inquiry into the 1938 Strike at Maytag Company, Newton, Iowa," 67–74; *DMR,* July 9, 1938, in Jasper County Historical Society listing, 477; Minutes, Directors' Meeting, The Maytag Co., July 7, 1938, in Mr. Molleck, Labor News Clippings, Book 2, Maytag Co. Archives, in Jasper County Historical Society listing, 476; *DMR,* July 7, 1938.

52. Blair, "Crisis in Newton, Iowa," 26; Robert Weiner to UE, July 9, 1938, in Maytag Case 18-c-183 file, NLRB25.

53. Blair, "Crisis in Newton, Iowa," 29; *NDN,* July 10–13, 1938.

54. *DMR,* July 12, 1938, in Jasper County Historical Society Collections, 481; Board's Exhibit 19, Arbitration Hearings, 20, Maytag Case 18-c-183 file, T&E 507, NLRB25; *DMR,* July 13, 1938; "Labor Troubles and the Local Church," *Social Action,* January 15, 1939.

55. *DMT,* July 15, 1938, in Folder 19, Box 2, Ser. 1, WSP.

56. *DMR,* July 15, 1938.

57. *DMT,* July 12, 1938; *NDN,* July 12, 1938.

58. Blair, "Crisis in Newton, Iowa," 29.

59. William Sentner to Robert Wiener, June 6, 1938, Robert Wiener to UE, July 9, 1938, "c-183, file #1" file, Case File packet, Maytag Case 18-C-183 file, Entry 155, NLRB25; Arbitration Hearings, Maytag Case 18-C-183 File, Entry 155, NLRB25; *DMR,* July 15 and 16, 1938.

60. *PP,* St. Louis UE edition, July 23, 1938.

61. *DMT,* undated, in Folder 17, Box 2, Ser. 1, WSP; Ratcliffe, "An Inquiry into the 1938 Strike at Maytag Company, Newton, Iowa," 82.

62. *DMR,* Extra, July 20, 1938, in Jasper County Historical Society list, 488.

63. *NDN,* July 20, in Maytag Strike 1937–39 ZZ 7 Collection, SHSI; William Sentner to James Matles, July 20, 1938, O/1299, UEA; *New York Times,* July 20, 1938, in 199-1839 Case File, FMCS280; Unidentified AP news clipping, July 20, 1938, in Case File 199-1839, FMCS280.

64. *PP,* St. Louis UE Edition, July 23, 1938.

65. *PP,* District 1 edition, July 23, 1938, in Folder 5, Box 3, Ser. 1, WSP; *DMT,* July 20, 1938, in Folder 17, Box 2, Ser. 1, WSP; Ratcliffe, "An Inquiry into the 1938 Strike at Maytag Company, Newton, Iowa," 82.

66. Ben Henry, strike account, Folder 2, Ben Henry Collection, SHSI; William Sentner to James Matles, July 19 and 20, 1938, Folder 21, Box 2, Ser. 1, WSP.

67. William Sentner to James Matles, July 20, 1938, Folder 21, Box 2, Ser. 1, WSP; account of strike, Folder 1, Ben Henry Collection, SHSI.

68. *DMR,* July 21, 1938; William Sentner to Julius Emspak, July 25, 1938, D8/663, UEA.

69. *NDN,* July 27, 1938, in Mr. Molleck, Labor News Clippings, Book 3, Maytag Company archives from Jasper County Historical Society clipping excerpts, 494, Newton, Iowa.

70. William Sentner to James Matles, July 25, 1938, O/1299, UEA.

71. William Sentner to James Matles, July 19, 1938, Folder 21, Box 2, Ser. 1, WSP. For the CIO and the New Deal Democrats, see Steven Fraser, *Labor Will Rule: Sidney Hillman and the Rise of American Labor* (Ithaca, N.Y.: Cornell University Press, 1991). David Montgomery, "Labor and the Political Leadership of New Deal America," *International Review of Social History* 39 (1994): 335–60, writes that by the late 1930s, the CIO leadership had decided that there was "no other serious game in town" than the "statist orbit of the New Deal" (360).

72. *DMT,* July 30, 1938. On the Iowa Farmer-Labor party, see William H. Cumberland, *Wallace M. Short: Iowa Rebel* (Ames: Iowa State University Press, 1983).

73. *DMR,* July 20, 1938, excerpt, in Jasper County Historical Society Clippings 488, Newton, Iowa; *DMR,* July 28, 1938; Special Orders, No. 62, July 19, 1938, Matthew Tinley Scrapbook, Iowa National Guard Papers, Camp Dodge, Johnston, Iowa.

74. Blair, "Crisis in Newton, Iowa," 30–34; account of strike, Ben Henry Collection ZZ1, Folder 2, SHSI; Robert Hoover and John Hoover, *An American Quality Legend: How Maytag Saved Our Moms, Vexed the Competition, and Presaged America's Quality Revolution* (New York: McGraw Hill, 1993), 142.

75. William Sentner to Julius Emspak, July 31, 1938, Folder 19, Box 2, Ser. 1, WSP; Blair, "Crisis in Newton, Iowa," 33–34.

76. *NDN,* August 2, 1938; *New York Times,* August 7, 1938.

77. *DMR,* August 4 and 5, 1938; William Sentner to James Carey, August 4, 1938, O/1299, UEA; Military commission report, 6, 13, Exhibit 8, Case 18-c-83, NLRB25.

78. Notes, Adjutant General, Folder 8, Nelson Kraschel Papers, University of Iowa, Iowa City; *DMR,* August 5, 1938.

79. William Sentner, WHO Radio Address, August 6, 1938, Folder 8, Box 6, Kraschel Papers, University of Iowa, Iowa City; "Resolution on the Company's Wage Proposal Adopted, Membership Meeting, Local 1116, August 17, 1938," Maytag Strike folder, Box 3, Ser. 1, WSP.

80. *DMT,* August 4, 1938; *New York Times,* August 8, 1938; *New York Post,* August 8, 1938, in unprocessed WSP.

81. Preliminary Report, September 2, 1941, Case 196–5376-1, FMCS280.

82. William Sentner, WHO Radio Address, August 6, 1938, Folder 8, Box 6, Kraschel Papers; *Midwest Daily Record,* November 6, 1938.

83. Clarence Mason et al. to G. T. Watson, February 26, 1934, "Servel, Inc., Official Correspondence, 1933–34," National Labor Board, Pre-Wagner Act Records, Box 31, NLRB25; Servel Case 170–9115, FMCS280. See also, Samuel White, *Fragile Alliances: Labor and Politics in Evansville, Indiana, 1919–1955* (Westport, Conn.: Praeger, 2005).

84. Exhibit 7, Servel Case, T&E 490, NLRB25; "Servel notes," Folder 5, Box 1, Ser. 1, WSP.

85. "Servel notes," Folder 5, Box 1, Ser. 1, WSP.

86. Clarence Mason et al. to G. T. Watson, February 26, 1934; *Labor Forum,* April 27, 1934, in "Servel, Inc.," Official Correspondence, 1933–34, National Labor Board, Pre-Wagner Act Records, Box 31, NLRB25; "File of Workers Testimony," Servel Case 11-c-163, Entry 155, NLRB25.

87. L. E. Dewitt to Gen. Hugh S. Johnson, August 29, 1933, Faultless Castor Case 170–9376, FMCS280; H. B. Dynes to H. L. Kerwin, In the Matter of Servel Inc., 170–9115, FMCS280; *EP,* September 28, 1933; *Labor Forum,* April 6, 1934 (on Sunbeam), in "Servel, Inc.," Official Correspondence, 1933–34, National Labor Board, Pre-Wagner Act Records, Box 31, NLRB25; Arthur W. Meloan to Julius Emspak, January 24, 1938, 0/876, UEA.

88. Clarence Mason et al. to G. T. Watson, February 26, 1934, "Servel, Inc.," Official Correspondence, 1933–34, National Labor Board, Pre-Wagner Act Records, Box 31, NLRB25; "Let's Look at the Record," Exhibit No. 27, T&E 490, NLRB25; In the Matter of Servel, Inc., and United Electrical, Radio and Machine Workers of America, Local No. 1002, Case No. C-488, Decided March 25, 1939, *Decisions and Orders of the National Labor Relations Board* (Washington, D.C.: U.S. Government Printing Office, 1940), 1314.

89. Robert Logsdon, Report, "The CIO in Evansville Indiana from 1936 to 1940," attached to Robert Logsdon to James Matles, January 11, 1940, 0/711, UEA.

90. U.S. Congress, Committee on Education and Labor, *Report of the Committee on Education and Labor: Labor Policies of Employers' Association: Part 1: The National Metal Trades Association* (Washington, D.C.: U.S. Government Printing Office, 1939), 37, 54, 151, 155, 160; U.S. Congress, Committee on Education and Labor, *Report of the Committee on Education and Labor: Industrial Espionage* (Washington, D.C.: U.S. Government Printing Office, 1938), 87. Sunbeam was financially controlled by Servel; Hoosier Lamp was a small family-owned independent based in Evansville. See also "References" and *Evansville UE News,* January 1950, in Misc 813 folder, Box 1, Ser. 1, WSP.

91. "In the Matter of Servel, Inc.," 1320–22; Sam White, "Labor and Politics in Evansville" (PhD diss., State University of New York–Buffalo, 1998), 165.

92. Logsdon, "The CIO in Evansville."

93. William Sentner to James Matles, October 15, 1938, WSP; Art Meloan correspondence in 0/877 and 0/878 files, UEA.

94. Logsdon, "The CIO in Evansville."

95. William Sentner to James Matles, October 15, 1938, WSP; Meloan to Matles, [November 1938], 0/878, UEA.

96. Robert Logsdon to James Matles, February 6 and 7, 1939, 0/706, UEA; William Sentner to James Matles, February 11, 1939, unprocessed WSP.

97. William Sentner to James Matles, October 15, 1938, 0/1300, UEA.

98. Robert Logsdon to James Matles, February 6 and 7, 1939, 0/708, UEA.

99. Ibid.

100. Ibid.

101. Ibid.; Robert Logsdon to James Carey, February 27, 1939, O/708, UEA. Jim Pope, "Worker Lawmaking, Sit-Down Strikes, and the Shaping of the American Industrial Relations, 1935–1958," *Law and History Review* (forthcoming).

102. Logsdon to James Matles, February 6 and 7, 1939, O/708, UEA; William Sentner to James J. Matles, February 9, 1939, O/1302, UEA; Robert Logsdon to James Matles, February 17, 1939, O/708, UEA.

103. William Sentner to James Matles, March 22, 1939, O/1304, UEA; William Sentner to James Matles, February 9, 1939, O/1302, UEA; *EC,* March 12, 1939.

104. Logsdon to James Matles, March 15, 1939, O/708, UEA; Logsdon to James Carey, February 28, 1939, O/708, UEA; *EC,* March 15, 1939; Robert Logsdon to James Matles, March 19, 1939, O/708, UEA; Newspaper articles in Case File 199–3277, FMCS280.

105. Robert Logsdon to James Matles, March 19, 1939, O/708, UEA; *EP,* March 17–18, 1939; Robert Cowdrill to David C. Shaw, April 3, 1939, David C. Shaw to Cowdrill, April 6, 1939, James T. Dunne, Field Examiner, March 22 to 25, 1939, in Servel Case 11-c-163 file #2, Entry 155, NLRB25.

106. Robert Logsdon to James Matles, March 19, 1939, O/708, UEA; *EP,* March 17, 1939; James T. Dunne, Field Examiner, March 22–25, 1939, Servel, Inc., File #2, 11-C-540 Servel 11-C-163 Case File, Entry 155, NLRB25; Robert Logsdon to James Matles, March 23, 1939, O/708, UEA.

107. *EC,* March 15 and 21, 1939; Robert Logsdon to James Matles, March 19 and 23, 1939, O/708, UEA; Statement made in behalf of William Sentner, April 10, 1939, Folder 5, Box 1, Ser. 1, WSP.

108. William Sentner to James Matles, March 22, 1939, O/1304, UEA; Robert Logsdon to James Matles, March 23, 1939, O/708, UEA; Robert Logsdon, "The CIO in Evansville."

109. *EP,* March 20, 1939; James T. Dunne, Field Examiner, March 22–25, 1939, Servel, Inc., 11-c-540, NLRB25; Case File, File #2, Servel Case 11-c-163, NLRB25; *EP,* March 27, 1939.

110. Robert Logsdon to James Matles, March 23, 1939, O/708, UEA.

111. William Sentner to James Matles, March 22, 1939, O/1304, UEA.

112. James Matles to William Sentner, February 8, 1939, O/1303, UEA.

113. William Sentner to Julius Emspak, September 25, 1937, Folder 2, Box 5, Ser. 1, WSP; William Sentner, Speech, January 8, 1938, speech, Convention file, after January 8, 1938, Meeting Minutes, Folder 4, Box 5, Ser. 1, WSP; *PP,* St. Louis UE edition, December 4, 1937; William Sentner, Organizing Report, February 19, 1938, Folder 2, Box 5, Ser. 1, WSP.

114. *PP,* District 8 edition, November 27, 1937.

115. *PP,* District 8 edition, January 22, 1938; *PP,* December 11, 1937; *PP,* January 8, 1938.

116. Author's interview with Henry Fiering, WHMC; *PP,* St. Louis UE edition, November 27 and December 4, 1937.

117. Financial Report, September 3, 1938, Convention Materials, WSP; William Sentner, Organizing Report, February 19, 1938, Folder 2, Box 5, Ser. 1, WSP. James J. Lorence, *Organizing the Unemployed: Community and Union Activists in the Industrial Heartland* (New York: SUNY, 1996), discusses CIO attempts in Michigan at social movement unionism based on alliances between organized labor and the unemployed.

118. Unsigned report on Unemployment Council, February 26, 1938; William Sentner to Hon. Senator LaFollette, March 4, 1938, unprocessed WSP; *SLPD,* March 10, 1938, in

Del Garst Scrapbook, Vol. II, Del Garst Papers, Reuther Library, Wayne State University; News clippings re Cooperative Employment Council News, in Folder 1, Box 6, Ser. 5, WSP; Minutes, January 8, 1938, January 13, 1938, April 4, 1938, "AIM: 1937–1939" folder, Box 86, American Zinc Company Records, WHMC, University of Missouri-Rolla.

119. James Matles speech, Constitutional Convention, January 8–9, 1938, Folder 4, Box 5, Ser. 1, WSP; William Sentner, Organizing Reports, February 19, 1938, March 12, 1938, April 2, 1938, Folder 2, Box 6, Ser. 1, WSP. The quotations are from the March 12 report.

120. *SLPD,* November 27, 1937; *PP,* District 8 edition, November 27, 1937; Knapp-Monarch Shop Bulletin, undated [early 1938], D8/158, UEA; *PP,* District 8 Edition, November 27, 1937; Minutes of District 8 Board Meeting, January 8, 1938, WSP.

121. *PP,* District 8 edition, December 18, 1937, and January 22, 1938; *SLST,* February 5, 1938, in Scrapbook I, Delmond Garst Papers.

122. Sentner Organizing Report, February 19, 1938, Folder 2, Box 5, Ser. 1, WSP; author's interview with John Kociscak, St. Louis, Missouri, March 18, 1987; *Midwest Daily Record,* December 13, 1938; William Sentner Remarks, 45–48, General Executive Board Minutes, December 11–12, 1937, Box 1, Ernie DeMaio Papers, Chicago Historical Society.

123. William Sentner, Report, March 12, 1938, Folder 2, Box 6, Ser. 1, WSP.

124. Officers' Report, Minutes of the District Council Meeting, September 3, 1938, 4, both in "Executive Board, District Eight" folder, Ser. 1, WSP. Resolution on the Union Shop, February 11, 1939, D8/175, UEA.

125. Minutes of the Meeting of All Executive Committees of UE Locals of St. Louis held December 1, 1938, D8/175, UEA.

126. Author's interviews with Henry Fiering; author's telephone interview with Robert Logsdon, November 10, 1988; author's interview with Lloyd Austin, March 4, 1994; author's interview with Orvil Heflin, St. Louis, Missouri, February 22, 1992.

127. Resolution on the Union Shop, February 19, 1939, D8/175, UEA; Minutes of District Council Meeting, September 3, 1938, and attached Officers' Report, "Executive Board, District Eight" folder, Box 1, Ser. 1, WSP.

128. Minutes of a meeting of UERMWA Executive Board of St. Louis, February 18, 1939, D8/175, UEA; Minutes of District Convention, March 26, 1939, D8/14, UEA. On the antagonism by Century Management, see also Minutes of District Council Meeting, September 3, 1938, "Executive Board, District Eight," Box 1, Ser. 1, WSP.

129. Minutes of District Council Meeting, September 3, 1938, "Executive Board, District Eight" folder, Box 1, Ser. 1, WSP.

130. Author's interview with Henry Fiering; "To All Union Men in This Neighborhood" leaflet, O/1302, UEA; *SLPD,* April 1, 1939; *SLGD,* March 14 and 18 and April 2, 1939.

131. Minutes of a meeting of UERMWA Executive Board of St. Louis, February 18, 1939, D8/175, UEA; Minutes of District Convention, March 26, 1939, D8/14, UEA.

132. Minutes of a Meeting of United Electrical Radio and Machine Workers of America Executive Boards, February 18, 1939, D8/175, UEA; Minutes of District Convention, March 26, 1939, D8/144, UEA; author's interview with Lloyd Austin, December 3, 1992.

133. Minutes of District Convention, March 26, 1939, D8/144, UEA; author's interview with Orville Leach, Kennett, Missouri, July 22, 1991.

134. William Sentner to James Matles, March 23, 1939, O/1304, UEA.

135. For criticisms of CIO dues checkoff policies, see Alice Lynd and Staughton Lynd, eds., *Rank and File: Personal Histories by Working-Class Organizers* (New York: Monthly

Review, 1988), xvii–xix and passim; Daniel Guerin, *100 Years of Labor in the USA,* trans. Alan Adler (London: Inklines, 1979), 117–18.

136. Selig S. Harrison, "Poker-Playing Stu," *New Republic,* June 20, 1960, 15; *Emerson Electric: A Century of Manufacturing* (St. Louis: Emerson Electric Corporation, 1989), 96.

137. Selig S. Harrison, "Poker-Playing Stu," 15; Paul I. Wellman, *Stuart Symington: Portrait of a Man with a Mission* (Garden City, N.Y.: Doubleday, 1960), 95–98.

138. This and the description of Symington's background are based on the following sources: *Emerson Electric: A Century of Manufacturing,* 93–99; "Home Front Boss," *Life,* October 2, 1946, 111–18; "Mr. Charm, of Washington," *Collier's,* June 15, 1946; Selig Harrison, "Poker-Playing Stu"; *SLPD,* April 15, 1946; Paul I. Wellman, *Stuart Symington,* 15–123; Ralph G. Martin and Ed Plant, *Front Runner, Dark Horse* (New York: Doubleday, 1960), 265–90.

139. Thomas Ferguson, "The Coming of the New Deal: The Triumph of Multinational Liberalism in America," in *The Rise and Fall of the New Deal Order,* ed. Gary Gerstle and Steve Fraser (Princeton, N.J.: Princeton University Press, 1989), 11.

140. *Emerson Electric: A Century of Manufacturing,* 99–100; William Sentner to Julius Emspak, February 16, 1939, O/1302, UEA.

141. *SLPD,* December 15, 1988. This reputation was reinforced in his most recent James C. Olson, *Stuart Symington: A Life* (Columbia: University of Missouri Press, 2000), 29–40.

142. William Sentner, Organizing Report, October 8, 1938, Folder 1, Box 5, Ser. 1, WSP; *PP,* St. Louis UE edition, October 29, 1938.

143. See Federal Labor Union 18479 and King Colonial Radio Company files, Reel 7, Frames 747–59, *American Federation of Labor Strikes and Agreements Files* Microfilm (Sanford, North Carolina: Microfilm Corporation of America, 1989); Harrison, "Poker-Playing Stu."

144. William Sentner to Julius Emspak, February 16, 1938, O/1302, UEA.

145. Ibid.

146. William Sentner to James Matles, April 29, 1939; William Sentner to James Matles, February 11, 1939; both in Box 1, Ser. 1, WSP. William Sentner to Julius Emspak, February 16, 1939, O/1302, UEA.

147. Resolution on the Union Shop, February 18, 1939, D8/175, UEA.

148. W. S. Symington to William Sentner, February 25, 1939; William Sentner to W. S. Symington, February 27, 1939; William Sentner to James Matles, April 29, 1939; all in Box 1, Ser. 1, WSP.

149. "Good Relationship" leaflet, June 9, 1939, attached to Robert Logsdon to James Matles, June 23, 1939, O/709, UEA.

150. District Council Meeting, March 25, 1939, Box 1, Ser. 1, WSP; William Sentner, Organizing Report, March 25, 1939, Folder 1, Box 5, Ser. 1, WSP; *UEN,* March 4, 1939.

151. William Sentner to James Emspak, March 1, 1939, O/1303, UEA; William Sentner, Organizing Report, March 25, 1939, Folder 3, Box 5, Ser. 1, WSP.

152. *SLGD,* May 5, 1939.

153. Robert Logsdon to James Matles, September 13, 1940, O/716, UEA.

154. William Sentner to James Matles, April 29, 1939, Folder 3, Box 5, Ser. 1, WSP.

155. "Good Relationship" leaflet, June 9, 1939, attached to Robert Logsdon to James Matles, June 23, 1939, O/709, UEA.

156. Robert Logsdon to James Matles, June 10, 1939, O/709, UEA.

157. Ibid.

158. Robert Logsdon to James Matles, June 23, 1939, O/709, UEA.

159. "Resolution Adopted by the Special Membership Meeting of Local 1102," August 7, 1939, D8/493, UEA.

160. President, Local 1102, to Stuart Symington, July 7, 1939, D8/510, UEA; William Sentner, Organizing Report, August 12, 1939, Folder 1, Box 5, Ser. 1, WSP.

161. William Sentner to James Matles, July 5, 1939, D8/543, UEA.

162. William Sentner to John Doherty, October 11, 1939, O/1307, UEA; William Sentner to James Matles, October 11, 1939, O/1307, UEA.

163. *Emerson Electric: A Century of Manufacturing,* 96–97.

164. William Sentner to James Matles, October 11, 1939, O/1307, UEA; *Agreement between Emerson Electric and Local 1102, United Electrical Workers, CIO, Effective 1939,* 2–5, possession of author.

165. William Sentner, Organizing Report, June 12, 1937, Folder 1, Box 5, Ser. 1, WSP.

166. Minutes of District Convention, March 26, 1939, D8/14, UEA; Baldor Electric Case File 199-2962, FMCS280.

167. *SLGD,* January 10, 1939; Case 199–4284, Baldor Electric Case File 199-2962, FMCS280; William Sentner to James Matles, October 16, 1939, O/1307, UEA; Robert Logsdon to James Matles, November 18, 1939, O/710, UEA; William Sentner Organizing Report, December 30, 1939, Folder 3, Box 5, Ser. 1, WSP. For the shoe industry, see Rosemary Feurer, "Shoe City, Company Towns: The St. Louis Shoe Industry and the Turbulent Drive for Cheap Rural Labor, 1900–1940," *Gateway Heritage* (Fall 1988): 2–17.

168. M. J. Heale, *American Anticommunism: Combating the Enemy Within, 1830–1970* (Baltimore: Johns Hopkins University Press, 1990), 122–29; David Milton, *The Politics of U.S. Labor: From the Great Depression to the New Deal* (New York: Monthly Review, 1982); Harvey Levenstein, *Communism, Anticommunism, and the CIO* (Westport, Conn.: Greenwood, 1981), 73–138; Bert Cochran, *Labor and Communism: The Conflict That Shaped American Unions* (Princeton, N.J.: Princeton University Press, 1977), 140–44; Eugene V. Dennett, *Agitprop: The Life of an American Working-Class Radical; The Autobiography of Eugene V. Dennett* (Albany: State University of New York Press, 1990), 106–22.

169. *SLGD,* April 2, 1937.

170. *SLPD,* February 4, 1938.

171. William Sentner Files, 1948, 3–4, American Business Consultants, Inc., Counterattack: Research Files, 27 14-123, Taminent Library, New York; *SLGD,* April 2, 1937; *SLST,* August 15, 1938.

172. *SLGD,* August 25, 1938.

173. Author's interview with John Kociscak.

174. *SLPD,* April 30, 1939; Luther M. Slinkard to William Sentner, April 26, 1939, Industrial Union Council files, Folder 3, Box 6, Ser. 1, WSP; *SLPD,* April 30, 1939.

175. Industrial Union Council Minutes, Folder 3, Box 6, Ser. 1, WSP.

176. Robert Logsdon to James Matles, August 16, 1939, O/710, UEA.

177. *SLGD,* September 29, 1939.

178. Resolution Adopted September 27, 1939, IUC Minutes, September 27, 1939, Folder 3, Box 6, Ser. 1, WSP; *SLGD,* September 28, 1939; "The War against Unionism under the Smoke Screen of the 'Isms,'" attached to William Sentner to James Matles, September 27, 1939, O/1307, UEA.

179. Industrial Union Council, Minutes, September 27, 1939, Folder 3, Box 6, Ser. 1, WSP.

180. Industrial Union Council, Election Results, Folder 3, Box 6, Ser. 1, WSP.

181. William Sentner to James Matles, March 7, 1939, O/1303, UEA; Robert Kirkwood to William Sentner, April 6, 1939, D8/644, UEA; William Sentner to James Matles, September 27, 1939, O/1307, UEA; William Sentner to James Matles, September 27, 1939, O/1307, UEA (two different letters).

182. William Sentner to James Matles, September 27, 1939; William Sentner to James Matles, September 27, 1939 (two different letters), O/1307, UEA.

183. *SLPD*, October 7, 1939; *Abstracts and Arguments*, 230, Iowa 30, Appellants' Abstract of Record, 177.

184. *SLGD*, October 14, 1939; William Sentner to James Matles, October 16, 1939, O/1307, UEA.

185. William Sentner to James Matles, October 16, 1939, Folder 3, Box 5, Ser. 1, WSP.

186. William Sentner to James Matles, October 9, 1939, O/1307, UEA.

187. *Proceedings of the Convention of the Congress of Industrial Organizations, Oct. 10, 11, 12, 13, 1939* (Washington, D.C.: CIO, 1939), 240.

188. James Matles to William Sentner, October 18, 1939, Folder 3, Box 6, Ser. 1, WSP.

189. Hugh Cleland, "The Political History of a Local Union" (PhD diss., Western Reserve University, 1957), 118; *UEN*, October 7, 1939.

190. Dennett, *Agitprop*, 234 (Lewis quote); see also Cochran, 145; Levenstein, *Communism, Anticommunism, and the CIO*, 87–88.

191. *Ten Years in Prison—$5000 Fine: That's the Price in Iowa for Collective Bargaining*, Folder 82, Box 7, and other materials in John C. Lewis Papers, Special Collections, University of Iowa, Iowa City. Bill Sentner to John Connolly, October 20, 1939; Boo Kindig to William Sentner, November 19, 1939; William Sentner to B. Kindig, November 22, 1939; all in Folder 2, Box 3, Ser. 1, WSP. *Des Moines Federationist*, October 18, 1939, and other materials in "Maytag Iowa Trial" folder, Box 3, Ser. 1, WSP.

192. IUC Minutes, October 11, 1939, Folder 3, Box 6, Ser. 1, WSP; undated *Union Labor Advocate* clipping, Folder 82, Box 7, John C. Lewis Papers.

193. William Sentner to James Matles, November 4, 1939, O/1308, UEA; *UE News*, District 8 edition, November 18, 1939.

194. See materials in Folder 82, Box 7, John C. Lewis Papers and materials, in Folder 2, Box 3, Ser. 1, WSP.

195. William Sentner to James Matles, October 30, 1939, O/1308, UEA; James Matles to William Sentner, November 1, 1939, O/1308, UEA.

196. William Sentner to James Matles, December 13, 1939, Folder 3, Box 6, Ser. 1, WSP.

197. Report, February 5, 1940, William Sentner FBI file 100-18332-5, Box 5, Ser. 4, WSP; *Midwest Daily Record*, November 26, 1939, November 28, 1939; William Sentner and Robert Burns Logsdon to John L. Lewis, October 27, 1940, Reel 18, Frame 332, *CIO Files of John L. Lewis, Part 1* (Frederick, Md.: University Publications, 1988).

198. Report, File 65-173, August 27, 1941, William Sentner FBI file, 100-18332-1x2, Box 5, Ser. 4, WSP.

199. William Sentner FBI file, Report, August 22, 1951, FBI-HQ, 100-18332-139, Box 5, Ser. 4, WSP.

200. *State of Iowa v. William Sentner*, Appellant Abstract of Record, *Abstracts and Arguments*, 230 Iowa 30, 177.

201. Author's telephone interview with Robert Logsdon, January 4, 1989; "Memorandum for the File," June 4, 1940, FBI-HQ, 100-18332-x, Box 5, Ser. 4, WSP. Military Intelligence considered Sentner an active Communist in November 1940, along with Toni Sentner. See Estimate of Subversive Situation, 7th Corps, November 18, 1940, Military Intelligence Division, War Department Records, Record Group 165, National Archives II, College Park, Maryland.

202. In early 1940 Sentner tried to join B'nai B'rith, indicating his concern for acceptance in the Jewish community despite the rift over the Nazi-Soviet Pact. His application was turned down. Sentner to Albert Fleishman, January 9, 1940, January 22, 1940, unprocessed WSP.

203. James Matles to William Sentner, October 18, 1939, O/1307, UEA.

204. According to William Sentner Jr.'s unconfirmed suggestion, the December resignation letter was meant for Symington. Sentner, however, was only 2 years old at the time, so at best the information is uncertain.

205. Robert Burns Logsdon to James Matles, December 2, 1939, O/711, UEA; Robert Logsdon to Bill (Sentner), "Sunday" (ca. December 2, 1939), Moving File, WSP.

206. Robert Logsdon to James Matles, December 2, 1939, O/711, UEA.

207. William Sentner to Eustius Brendle, December 23, 1939, "1102-Moving" folder, WSP.

208. Moving items, unprocessed William Reidel Papers, WHMC; "Program on the Emerson Situation," "Moving" File, Ser. 1, WSP.

209. William Sentner, Organizing Report, January 6, 1940, Folder 12, Box, Ser. 1, WSP; see, for instance, the editorial in the *SLST,* December 28, 1939.

210. Eustius Brendle to John Cochran, December 13, 1939, and Special Bulletin, Local 1102, in "Moving—1102" file, Ser. 1, WSP.

211. "Proposed Contract," unprocessed William Reidel Papers, WHMC; "Program on the Emerson Situation," "Moving" File, Ser. 1, WSP. *How a Union Saved 1500 Jobs, a $2,000,000 Payroll and the Business They Create for St. Louis* (St. Louis: Local 1102, 1940), JWCP357.

212. Statement attached to William S. Symington to James Matles, March 7, 1940, D8/527, UEA; *SLGD,* March 8, 1940; author's interview with Morris Levin, St. Louis, Missouri, December 3, 1992. Ironically, it was Symington who got the sole credit for the profit sharing, a memory that achieved folklore status in the 1980s in St. Louis.

213. Symington to James Carey, March 7, 1940, D8/527, UEA.

214. *How a Union Saved 1500 Jobs, DMR,* March 9, 1940.

215. *DMR,* March 9, 1940.

216. Sentner to Matles, March 6, 1940, Folder 3, Box 6, Ser. 1, WSP.

217. William S. Symington to James Matles, March 7, 1940, D8/527, UEA; Robert Logsdon to James Matles, May 21, 1940, O/713, UEA; James B. Carey to W. S. Symington, March 12, 1940; Stuart Symington to James Carey, March 14, 1940, D8/527, UEA. Symington even apparently gave some useful information to the union about the Dies Committee charges.

Sentner never behaved toward Symington with the obsequiousness that James Carey displayed. Carey even suggested that Symington might want to be a union organizer, so strong were his convictions for workers. Symington repaid Carey the compliment by helping to arrange for a biography of Carey. Symington to Carey, May 28, 1940, D8/543, UEA; William S. Symington to Jim, November 18, 1940, D8/543, UEA.

218. Charles W. Anderson to Julius Emspak, May 28, 1940, D8/496, UEA; Julius Emspak to Charles Anderson, June 7, 1940, D8/496, UEA.

219. Author's interview with Thomas Knowles, St. Louis, Missouri, April 14, 1987.

220. *UEN,* December 9, 1939.

221. William Sentner, Organizing Report, March 2, 1940, Ser. 1, WSP; *UEN,* June 29, 1940, June 8, 1940; Robert Logsdon to James Matles, September 13, 1940, O/716, UEA.

222. *St. Louis Labor Tribune,* July 20, 1940.

223. "Century Strike Settled" leaflet, "Century Strike-1940" Scrapbook, Ser. 1, WSP; *SLPD,* July 20 and 25, 1940; *SLST,* July 31, 1940.

224. Robert Logsdon to James Matles, August 2, 1940, O/715, UEA; *SLGD,* July 31, 1940; *SLGD,* July 20, 1940; *SLST,* July 19, 1940; *SLPD,* July 19, 1940.

225. *SLGD,* July 30, 1940; Robert Logsdon to James Matles, August 2, 1940, O/715, UEA.

226. Robert Logsdon to James Matles, August 2, 1940, O/715, UEA; *SLPD,* July 25, 1940; *UEN,* August 3, 1940.

227. *SLGD,* August 14, 1940; *SLPD,* August 2, 14, and 22, 1940; *SLST,* August 22, 1940.

228. *SLST,* August 5, 1940; Robert Logsdon to James Matles, August 2, 1940, O/715, UEA.

229. *SLGD,* July 31, 1940; *SLST,* July 31, 1940.

230. Robert Logsdon to James Matles, September 13, 1940, O/716, UEA; Robert Logsdon to James Matles, August 2, 1940, O/715, UEA. Ironically, this is the period that Lizabeth Cohen describes as a "culture of unity" for the CIO; Cohen, *Making a New Deal,* 233–49.

231. *SLST,* August 1, 1940; *SLPD,* August 1, 1940; Robert Logsdon to James Matles, August 2, 1940, O/715, UEA.

232. Robert Logsdon to William Sentner, September 9, 1940, O/716, UEA; author's interview with Del Garst, St. Louis, Missouri, June 11, 1987.

233. *UEN,* August 31, 1940 (reprint of editorials); *SLPD,* August 6, 1940.

234. Robert Logsdon to James Matles, September 13, 1940, O/716, UEA; *UEN,* October 5, 1940; Robert Logsdon to William Sentner, September 24, 1940, O/716, UEA.

235. Robert Logsdon to James Matles, October 19, 1940, O/716, UEA; Robert Logsdon to James Matles, October 31, 1940, O/716, UEA; "Century Strike Settled" leaflet, "Century Strike" folder, WSP.

236. Robert Logsdon to James Matles, October 31, 1940, O/716, UEA; author's interview with Moris Levin, St. Louis, Missouri, December 3, 1992.

237. *SLGD,* September 30, 1940.

238. *SLPD,* September 26, 1940, in O/1314, UEA.

239. *SLST,* November 15, 1940. Robert Logsdon to William Sentner, January 4, 1940 [actually 1941]; Handwritten notes, undated; both in "Dies Committee—George Apel Case" file, Ser. 1, WSP. William Sentner to James Matles, January 17, 1941, O/1315, UEA; Robert Logsdon to James Matles, March 4, 1941, O/718, UEA; author's interview with Orville Leach. Apel, according to Leach, had originally run for president of the Wagner local in coalition with the Left and joined the CP. But workers revealed his attempt to elect reactionary officers to Leach and Zollie Carpenter, and upon learning this Sentner started his own investigation, which revealed Apel's association with Dies and the evidence that he was a company operative. Apel "got up and flew!" when he learned that this would be exposed to the membership. Years later, as an official of the Department of Labor's Apprenticeship Training, he rejected the Emerson union's complaint that the

State of Missouri was paying training funds for Emerson's runaway shops. *SLPD,* February 5, 1965.

240. *State v. Sentner,* 230 Iowa 590 (1941); "The Applicability of Criminal Syndicalism Legislation to Labor Disputes," *Iowa Law Review* 27 (1941–42): 105–27; William Sentner to C. I. McNutt, June 17, 1941, Box 4u, unprocessed WSP; Convention Minutes, 253–63, September 28, 1941, Folder 29, JWCP 507.

241. William Sentner to James Matles, September 29, 1941, WSP; Wilbert Allison to William C. Reidel, October 4, 1941, unprocessed WSP; William Sentner to James Matles, October 16, 1941, D8/69, UEA; Typed "draft," 1945 District Convention, Folder 6, Box 7, Ser. 1, WSP.

242. Ellen Schrecker, *Many Are the Crimes: McCarthyism in America* (Boston: Little, Brown, 1998), chap. 2; Michael Kazin, *Populist Persuasion: An American History* (New York: Basic Books, 1995), 166–69.

243. Fraser, *Labor Will Rule,* 178–237. In this respect, it is likely that Max Michelson of the Amalgamated had critically affected Sentner's early stance in bargaining with Emerson Electric.

244. Robert Logsdon to James Matles, January 11, 1940, O/711, UEA.

Chapter 5: World War Two and "Civic" Unionism

1. Gary Gerstle, *Working Class Americanism: The Politics of Labor in a Textile City, 1914–1960* (Cambridge: Cambridge University Press, 1989); Nelson Lichtenstein, *Labor's War at Home: The CIO in World War II* (New York: Cambridge University Press, 1982); Mark Leff, "The Politics of Sacrifice on the American Home Front in World War II," *Journal of American History* 77 (March 1991): 1296–318.

2. See especially Kim Moody, *An Injury to All: The Decline of American Unionism* (London: Verso, 1988), 1–41. See Sally M. Miller and Daniel A. Cornford, eds., *American Labor in the Era of World War II* (Westport, Conn: Praeger, 1995). Ronald Schatz has shown that UE leftists' support for increased production did not result in "deteriorating working conditions" during the war but that the union position in the long run made the wage bargain the key agenda of the union. See Ronald Schatz, *The Electrical Workers: A History of General Electric and Westinghouse, 1923–60* (Urbana: University of Illinois Press, 1983), 140–43.

3. Robert Logsdon to James Matles, December 3, 1941, and attached "Proposed Plan," O/722, UEA; see also William Sentner to Lyle Dowling, November 26, 1941, O/1320, UEA.

4. Steven Fraser, *Labor Will Rule: Sidney Hillman and the Rise of American Labor* (Ithaca, N.Y.: Cornell University Press, 1993), 482.

5. Gerald T. White, *Billions for Defense* (Tuscaloosa: University of Alabama Press, 1980), 48; Paul A. C. Koistinen, "The Hammer and the Sword: Labor, the Military, and Industrial Mobilization, 1920–1945" (PhD diss., University of California–Berkeley, 1964), 664.

6. Lichtenstein, *Labor's War at Home,* 41, 88–89.

7. Ibid., 41, 85; Nelson Lichtenstein, *The Most Dangerous Man in Detroit: Walter Reuther and the Fate of American Labor* (New York: Basic Books, 1995), 154–74; Fraser, *Labor Will Rule,* 473–84.

8. Ibid.

9. James Matles to John L. Lewis, July 22, 1940, UE National Correspondence folder, unprocessed WSP.

10. William Sentner to Russ Nixon, January 14, 1942, D8/71, UEA.

11. Fraser, *Labor Will Rule,* 474.

12. Lyle Dowling to William Sentner, January 8, 1942, D8/40, UEA; author's interview with Victor Pasche, June 17, 1989, San Francisco, California.

13. Fraser, *Labor Will Rule,* 480.

14. James Payne to Julius Emspak, August 12, 1941, and attachments, O/1081, UEA; Report of District President, District 8 Convention, September 20–21, 1941, O/1322, UEA.

15. James Payne to Julius Emspak, August 12, 1941, O/1081, UEA; James Payne to Julius Emspak, July 17, 1941, O/1080; William Sentner to James Matles, August 6, 1941, D8/67.

16. William Sentner to James Matles, August 6, 1941, D8/67, UEA; James Payne to Julius Emspak, August 12, 1941, and attachments: resolution and petition, O/1081, UEA.

17. William Sentner to James Matles, August 6, 1941, D8/67, UEA; James Payne to Julius Emspak, August 12, 1941, and attachments: resolution and petition, O/1081, UEA; James Payne to James Matles, August 18, 1941, O/1081, UEA; James Payne to James Matles, August 25, 1941, and attached *Tavern Journal,* O/1081, UEA; Unidentified newspaper clipping, "Union Heads to Air Problems of Job Lay-offs," August 27, 1941, O/1082, UEA.

18. *EC,* September 2, 1941.

19. *UEN,* September 20, 1941; William Sentner, Report on Midwest Emergency Conference on Unemployment Due to Priorities, O/1321, UEA; James Payne to James Matles, September 10, 1941, O/1082, UEA.

20. William Sentner, Report on Midwest Emergency Conference on Unemployment Due to Priorities, O/1321, UEA.

21. William Sentner, Report on Midwest Emergency Conference; *UEN,* September 20, 1941; Robert Logsdon to James Matles, December 3, 1941, O/722, UEA; Donald B. Howard to William Sentner, January 5, 1942, D8/52, UEA. Steven Fraser has shown that the labor advisory committees of the Office of Production Management were Sidney Hillman's "backdoor bureaucratic maneuvering to blockade the 'Murray Plan.'" They "never enjoyed parity with the 'industrial advisory committees' in influencing priority decisions" (Fraser, *Labor Will Rule,* 477).

22. William Sentner, "Report on Midwest Emergency Conference"; William Sentner, Memorandum on Chicago Midwest Emergency Conference, September 12, 1941, O/1321, UEA.

23. William Sentner to James Matles, August 20, 1941, D8/667, UEA; *UEN,* October 25, 1941, October 1, 1941.

24. Report of the District President, 4, District 8 Convention, September 20–21, 1941, O/1322, UEA.

25. William Sentner to Joseph J. Weiner, August 27, 1941, O/1320, UEA.

26. William Sentner to James Matles, October 1, 1941, D8/667, UEA; William Sentner to Julius Emspak, October 20, 1941, D8/69, UEA; Statement by William Sentner to the House Committee Investigating National Defense Migration, St. Louis, November 26, 1941, 7, WSP; "Defense Unemployment in the Industry," Robert Logsdon to James Matles, December 3, 1941, O/722, UEA.

27. (Lyle) Dowling to Bill, October 1941, UE National Office Correspondence folder, unprocessed WSP.

28. William Sentner to Russ Nixon, January 14, 1942, D8/71, UEA; William Sentner to Lyl(e) (Dowling), October 13, 1941, D8/69, UEA; William Sentner to Lyle Dowling, April 20, 1942, D8/75, UEA.

29. William Sentner to James Emspak, February 16, 1943, D8/81, UEA; Russ Nixon to James Emspak, February 18, 1943, D8/132, UEA.

30. William Sentner to Julius Emspak, September 9, 1941, D8/68, UEA.

31. James Payne to James Matles, September 8, 1941, O/1082, UEA. For Carey's split with the UE, see Ronald Filipelli and Mark McCulloch, *Cold War in the Working Class: The Rise and Decline of the United Electrical Workers* (Albany: State University of New York Press, 1995), 62–63.

32. Bill (Sentner) to Jim (Matles), September 14, 1941, D8/67, UEA.

33. Ibid.; James Payne to James Matles, September 17, 1941, O/1082, UEA; William Sentner to Lyl(e) (Dowling), October 13, 1941, D8/69, UEA.

34. *UEN*, October 11, 1941, August 22, 1942; Proceedings of the Annual 1942 Convention UE District 8, September 19–20, 1942, 2, 8, Folder 5, Box 5, Ser. 1, WSP.

35. Report of District President, District 8 Convention, September 20–21, 1941, 4, O/1322, UEA; Brown folder, War Box, Unemployment Due to Priorities Conference, News Article, WSP; see Sunbeam Case File 445-0500, Servel Cases 300-4836, 302-226, 455-1774, 455-4465, 483-372, FMCS280.

36. St. Louis Chamber of Commerce for the Metropolitan Committee on Preparedness for National Defense, *Special Survey of Manufacturing Plants in the St. Louis Industrial Area* (St. Louis: Chamber of Commerce, 1940); Betty Burnett, *St. Louis at War* (St. Louis: Patrice Press, 1987); William Sentner, Statement to the House Committee Investigating National Defense Migration, St. Louis, November 28, 1941, 6, Folder 1, Box 1, Ser. 5, WSP.

37. *Emerson Electric: A Century of Manufacturing,* 106–7.

38. *SLGD,* September 5, 1942.

39. William Sentner to Lyle Dowling, November 26, 1941, O/1310, UEA.

40. Robert Logsdon to James Matles, December 3, 1941, O/722, UEA.

41. Robert Logsdon to James Matles, April 3, 1942, O/790, UEA; William Sentner to James Matles, February 12, 1942, D8/71, UEA; author's interview with Victor Pasche; "Proceedings of the Annual 1942 District Eight Convention," September 19–20, 1942, Folder 1, Box 6, Ser. 1, WSP.

42. Much of the scholarly assessment of the UE rests on the pioneering essay by Donald Critchlow, "Communist Unions and Racism: A Comparative Study of the Responses of the United Electrical Radio and Machine Workers and the National Maritime Union to the Black Question during World War II," *Labor History* 17 (Spring 1976): 230–43, who concluded that the "UE's commitment to racial equality . . . tended to be little more than Popular Front rhetoric" (232). Critchlow suggested that District 8's attention to the issue was due to "the great number of Blacks in the District" (236, n. 18), but he incorrectly suggests that African Americans were 25 percent of UE's St. Louis membership during the war (237, n. 22). The "serious inconsistency" quote is from Marshall Stevenson, "Response: Beyond Theoretical Models: The Limited Possibilities for Racial Egalitarianism," *International Labor and Working Class History* 44 (Fall 1993): 50.

Recently, Judith Stepan-Norris and Maurice Zeitlin have disputed Critchlow's argument, while repeating his evidence, in *Left Out: Reds and America's Industrial Unions* (Cambridge: Cambridge University Press, 2002), 223–24. A more positive report on District 8 is relayed in Andrew Kersten, *Race, Jobs and the War: The FEPC in the Midwest, 1941–46* (Urbana: University of Illinois, 2000), though this work also gets critical information incorrect, suggesting that the left wing capitulated to wartime CP goals and expedient relationship with white workers (as discussed in note 73 below).

43. Author's telephone interview with Robert Logsdon, March 23, 1989. Logsdon's letters to the national office throughout the war period reinforce this suggestion.

44. William Sentner to Sidney Williams, October 30, 1937, Folder 1, Box 5, Ser. 5, WSP. Resistance to their full inclusion also brought a decline in enthusiasm for the union among black workers. By October 1937, out of a total of 300 black workers in the district's shops, only 135 of them were members of the union. The district's total membership at this time was 6,200. Nevertheless there were some "active participants holding offices on the executive boards of three locals and [some were] shop stewards, etc."

45. William Sentner to Lester B. Granger, April 28, 1938, Folder 1, Box 5, Ser. 5, WSP.

46. *UEN,* February 1, 1940, July 6, 1940; William Sentner testimony, Fair Employment Practices Committee, 41, Case No. 63, Reel 20, FEPC Mic.; *UEN,* March 7, 1942; author's interview with Orville Leach, Kennett, Missouri, July 22, 1991; author's interview with Hershel Walker, St. Louis, Missouri, January 8, 1987.

47. Author's interview with Marian Bastionello Barry, June 22, 1989; author's interview with Raymond and Charlotte Koch, November 13, 1993, Chicago, Illinois; author's telephone interview with Robert Logsdon, March 23, 1989; author's interview with Hershel Walker.

48. James Click to James Emspak, June 30, 1941, D8/507, UEA; Robert Logsdon to James Matles, July 2, 1941, O/720, UEA; Robert Logsdon to James Matles, July 12, 1941, O/720, UEA; author's interview with Marian Bastionello Barry, January 12, 1990; author's interview with James Click, July 15, 1986. While it was "CIO policy" to bar racial discrimination, not all unions of the CIO acted on that policy. In particular, the steelworkers and auto workers in St. Louis took no such similar action. See Urban League Industrial Secretary Files, 1941–45, Box 7, Ser. 4, ULP.

49. *UEN,* July 11, 1942; Sullivan testimony, 61, Case 63, Reel 20, FEPC Mic. Around 13 percent of the entire St. Louis metropolitan area during the war was African American, but most plants did not hire blacks in this proportion. Western Cartridge, whose managers dominated the U.S. Cartridge plant, did not practice these policies in its private plant located across the Mississippi in East Alton. Western Cartridge refused to hire any blacks for production work that employed more than thirteen thousand workers during the war. Memo, Will Maslow, February 2, 1944, "Tension" File, Reel 75, FEPC Mic.

50. William Sentner to James Matles, February 12, 1942, and attached plan of organization, D8/71, UEA; Proceedings of the Annual 1942 Convention UE District 8, September 19–20, 1942, Folder 1, Box 6, Ser. 1, WSP; *UEN,* April 25, 1942; author's telephone interview with Betty Raab.

51. William Sentner to Louis V. Clymer, May 10, 1942, UE Exhibit 3, Case 63, Reel 20, FEPC Mic.; *SLGD,* May 17, 1942; William Sentner, "Statement before the FEPC hearings in St. Louis, on August 2, 1944," Folder 2, Box 5, Ser. 5, WSP; William Sentner to Dr. Robert L. Weaver, War Production Board, UE Exhibit 6, Case 63, Reel 20, FEPC Mic.

52. *UEN,* June 20, 1942; Otto Maschoff to R. V. Rickcord, June 13, 1942, UE Exhibit 5, Reel 20, Case 63, FEPC Mic.

53. Otto Maschoff to E. V. Rickord, June 13, 1942, UE Exhibit 5, Case 63, Reel 20, FEPC Mic.; William Sentner to Robert C. Weaver, Chief of the Negro Employment, War Production Board, UE Exhibit 6, Case 63, Reel 20, FEPC Mic.; Sentner, "Statement before the FEPC," 6; *UEN,* June 20, 1942.

54. Louise Elizabeth Grant, "St. Louis Unit of the March on Washington Movement: A Study in the Sociology of Conflict" (MA thesis, Fisk University, 1944), 7–9; Newspaper Articles, ca. June 20, 1942, Theodore McNeal Scrapbook, WHMC.

55. "Racial Conditions in the St. Louis Field Division," January 26, 1944, File #100-135-42-49, 6–11, FBI National Headquarters Files; UE Small Arms News, July 7, 1942, Box 1a, Ernie DeMaio Papers, Chicago Historical Society. David Grant of the MOWM publicly commended UE left-wing activists for taking the lead against segregation at Small Arms, and Military Intelligence reported that Sentner was working with Grant on a plan for integration (FBI File #110-135-42-62, 3). According to the FBI, an interview with leaders of the MOWM "indicated that the group has exercised much care in steering clear of Communist influence, feeling that such association would be detrimental to the best interests of the people it represents" (File #100-135-42-49, 11). Years later, Grant only recalled the MOWM relationship to the UE as worsening during the year and the CP as complicit in a Soviet agenda that led them to forego the struggle on race discrimination. It is true that Sentner sought to suggest that wildcats by black workers, something he felt was encouraged by his factional rivals in the Distribution Workers union, were detrimental to the cause of racial justice, a policy no doubt influenced by the CP wartime line. Richard Resh interview with David Grant, 1970, WHMC.

56. Report, June 3, 1943, U.S. Cartridge Case File, FMCS280; Sullivan testimony, 47, Case 63, Reel 20, FEPC Mic.; Charles Houston to Malcolm Ross, December 1, 1944, Case 63, Reel 20, FEPC Mic. See also "The United States Cartridge Company and Colored Employees," "Tension" File, Reel 75, FEPC Mic.

57. St. Louis Chamber of Commerce, Special Committee of the Labor Training and Labor Supply Committee, "Making Effective Use of Labor Resources in St. Louis," UE Exhibit 1, Case 63, Reel 20, FEPC Mic.; William Sentner, "Statement before the FEPC's Hearings," Folder 6, Box 4, Ser. 1, WSP.

58. William Sentner to William Stead, July 10, 1942, UE Exhibit 2, Case 63, Reel 20, FEPC Mic.

59. Sullivan testimony, 50–57, Case 63, Reel 20, FEPC Mic.

60. *Small Arms News,* August 6, 1943, Betty Raab Papers, WHMC; author's telephone interview with Betty Raab.

61. Sentner testimony before the FEPC, 36, Case 63, Reel 20, FEPC Mic. Initially, the union at Small Arms proposed a contract that allowed for a type of superseniority for black workers because, as the union bargaining committee reasoned, they "were among the last to be employed by the company and thereby have the least amount of accumulative time of service." Thus, the union mandated that in addition to following a general plantwide seniority clause that would protect black workers, layoffs would be made in such a way as to "allow a minimum of ten percent of the plant's working-force to be Negro" (Article V, section g, Draft Contract of Union, U.S. Cartridge Company and UE Local 825, Case 300-4911, FMCS280). However, the union finally settled on a simple plantwide seniority clause and a clause that prohibited discrimination against black workers in employment ("Agreement," Article 4, section 5, Case 300-4911, FMCS280).

62. Otto Maschoff to William Sentner, January 21, 1944, and attached Memo, Exhibit 13, UE Exhibits 14 and 15, in Case 63, Reel 20, FEPC Mic. Memorandum; Will Maslow to Malcolm Ross, April 12, 1944, St. Louis Tension file, Reel 75, FEPC Mic.; Robert Logsdon to James Emspak, January 13, 1944, D8/125, UEA; William Sentner, "Statement before the FEPC's Hearings," 8–11. Sentner charged in August 1944 that more resistance to the implementation of plantwide seniority came from the St. Louis Ordnance District than from the company (Sentner, "Statement Before the FEPC's Hearings," 8–10).

63. Minutes and attached resolutions, Conference on Negro Problems, District 8, May 2, 1943, unprocessed WSP; William Sentner, "Statement before the FEPC's Hearings." District 8 claimed that this was the first conference of its kind by a union in the area.

64. William Sentner to James Matles, June 27, 1942, D8/75, UEA. On separate dances, Minutes, Shop Stewards Meeting, October 11, 1943, Folder 127, Box 12, JWCP357. This type of commitment overall from District 8 could be detrimental to organizing efforts among white workers. In the organizing campaign at Hoosier Lamp in Evansville, Jim Payne reported that "negro baiting" was being used effectively, with the company union "saying that if the CIO wins they will put a big black nigger beside every girl in the plant" (James Payne to James Matles, August 6, 1943, O/1086, UEA).

65. Report of the Negro Committee, May 3, 1945, Interracial Committee Minutes, January 10, 1945, Folder 127, Box 12, JWCP357; Resolutions, Conference on Negro Problems, May 2, 1943, Case 63, Reel 20, FEPC Mic.

66. Robert Logsdon to James Emspak, February 15, 1944, D8/125, UEA; Robert Logsdon Report, September 20, 1945, 2, O/730, UEA; Robert Logsdon Report, May 1945, O/729, UEA.

67. "Local 810," UERWM-CIO, 1943–47 folder, Box 6, Ser. 4, ULP.

68. *Local Review,* May 14, 1943, unprocessed Eugene Paul collection, WHMC.

69. Resolution, Submitted by Thomas A. Barry, Secretary, UE Sports and Social Committee, Adopted May 26, 1942, UE Exhibit 8, Case 63, Reel 20, FEPC Mic.; *UEN,* June 20, 1942.

70. Robert Logsdon to James Emspak, October 25, 1943, D8/125, UEA; Racial Conditions Report, January 26, 1944 Report, FBI-HQ 100-135-42-49, Box 5, Ser. 4, WSP.

71. Sentner, testimony before the FEPC, 71, Case 63, Reel 20, FEPC Mic; Victor Pasche interview. The UE's May 1943 District conference had called upon the mayor to establish a Race Relations Commission, and the UE group pushed this through the CIO.

72. *St. Louis American,* April 2, 1943.

73. Fannie Cook, *Mrs. Palmer's Honey* (New York: Doubleday, 1946); Race Relations Commission Minutes and Correspondence, Box 9, Fannie Cook Papers, MHS; William Sentner to Fannie Cook, April 6, 1946, Folder 1, Box 1, Ser. 6, WSP. Andrew Kersten's suggestion (*Race, Jobs and the War,* 124) that St. Louis's UE leadership tired of the struggle to challenge their rank and file on issues of racial equality is not sustained by the evidence. Kersten confused a conflict at a UAW-represented plant, McQuay Norris, with that of the UE.

74. Minutes, Proceedings of the Annual 1943 Convention, October 2–3, 1943, Folder 1, Box 6, Ser. 1, WSP.

75. *Proceedings,* Fifth Convention of the United Electrical, Radio and Machine Workers, September 1939, 140–45, Reel 53, *American Labor Unions' Constitutions and Proceedings: Parts I & II* (Glen Rock, N.J.: Microfilming Corporation of America, 1979).

76. William Sentner to James Matles, November 23, 1942, D8/79; D. J. Karsch and Charlotte High to James Matles, December 12, 1942, O/583, UEA.

77. Lisa A. Kannenberg, "From World War to Cold War: Women Electrical Workers and Their Union, 1940–1955" (MA thesis, University of North Carolina, Charlotte, 1990), 15; Ruth Milkman, *Gender at Work: The Dynamics of Job Segregation by Sex during World War II* (Urbana: University of Illinois Press, 1987).

78. Proceedings of the Annual 1942 Convention UE District 8, September 19–20, 1942, Folder 1, Box 6, Ser. 1, WSP; *UEN,* May 29, 1943; To the Women of Small Arms [1942], D8/468, UEA.

79. Proceedings of the Ninth International Convention of the United Electrical, Radio, and Machine Workers, 219–23, Reel 53, *American Labor Unions' Constitutions and Proceedings Microfilm; UEN,* October 30, 1943; Kannenberg, "From World War to Cold War," 26.

80. Author's telephone interview with Betty Raab.

81. *SLGD,* July 30, 1942, and February 8, 1943; *Weekly Review,* February 21, 1943.

82. Minutes, Executive Board Meeting, June 26, 1943, D8/7, UEA; *UEN,* October 30, 1943; Ruth Young to William Sentner, November 26, 1943, D8/45, UEA; Kannenberg, "From World War to Cold War," 28–29.

83. Minutes, Regular Meeting of the Executive Board, 19, UE District 8, January 30, 1943, D8/5, UEA; *UEN,* December 30, 1944, August 12, 1944.

84. This interpretation builds on Nelson Lichtenstein, "The Eclipse of Social Democracy," *The Rise and Fall of the New Deal Order,* ed. Steven Fraser and Gary Gerstle (Princeton, N.J: Princeton University Press); the "loopholes" quotation is on p. 125. James Matles to William Sentner, May 4, 1943, D8/471, UEA.

85. William Sentner, "What Helps Labor Helps the Nation" speech, unprocessed WSP; Sentner remarks, 1943 Missouri IUC convention, Folder 42, JDP.

86. Robert Logsdon, Report for District 8, attached to November 22, 1943, D8/213, UEA; Robert Logsdon to Julius Emspak, January 10, 1945, D8/125, UEA; Robert Logsdon, Report, June 1944, D8/181, UEA; Undated Case Report, Emerson Case 7-d-2908, NWLB202.

87. Seidman, *American Labor from Defense to Reconversion,* 129.

88. William Sentner to Lyle Dowling, December 1, 1942, D8/79, UEA.

89. Progress Report, February 8, 1944, Emerson Case 45-470, FMCS280; Undated Brief, Emerson Case 7-d-2908, NWLB202.

90. William Sentner to James Matles, September 7, 1943, D8/84, UEA; Robert Logsdon to Julius Emspak, November 22, 1943, D8/213, UEA.

91. See, for example, the agreement with Local 1116, attached to July 3, 1943 letter, in D8/647, UEA.

92. William Sentner to John Brophy, May 10, 1943, "War" Box, unprocessed WSP.

93. See also Special District 8 council meeting, January 20–21, 1945, Folder 5, Box 6, Ser. 1, WSP. The Communist Party promoted incentive wages as part of its "Production for Victory" campaign to support the war effort. In the UAW this led to serious distance between workers and Communist Party activists in unions (Nelson Lichtenstein, *The Most Dangerous Man in Detroit,* 204). However, Ronald Schatz argues, the issue was not as significant for electrical workers because of the protections against overwork built into the UE's incentive system (Schatz, *The Electrical Workers,* 142).

94. *UEN,* May 29, 1943.

95. "The Yaleman and the Communist," *Fortune,* November 1943, 146–48, 212–21.

96. William Sentner to James Matles, May 23, 1942, D8/76, UEA.

97. Author's interview with Thomas Knowles, St. Louis, Missouri, April 14, 1987.

98. William Scarlett to William Sentner, June 20, 1942, Folder 4, Box 2, Ser. 6, WSP.

99. Edgar Monsanto Queeny to William McClelland, April 8, 1943, Folder 4, Box 2, Ser. 6, WSP.

100. Proceedings, Semi-Annual Meeting, District 8, March 28–29, 1942, 23–24; William Sentner, January 17, 1942, 3; Sidney Hillman had created the labor-management committees as a way of "deflecting sentiment away from the Murray Plan," according to Steven Fraser, *Labor Will Rule,* 477.

101. Regular Meeting of the Executive Board, District Council, UE District 8, January 30, 1943, 3–4, D8/5, UEA.

102. William Sentner to James Matles, May 23, 1942, D8/76, UEA; Robert Logsdon to James Matles, June 26, 1942, O/724, UEA.

103. James Matles to Robert Logsdon, June 29, 1942, O/724, UEA.

104. Robert Logsdon, Report for District 8, attached to November 22, 1943, D8/213.

105. Robert Logsdon to Julius Emspak, April 24, 1944, D8/125, UEA.

106. "The Yaleman and the Communist," *Fortune* 28 (5): 146–48, 212–21.

107. Anna DeCormis to William Sentner, Folder 7, Box 2, Ser. 6, WSP. Symington and Scarlett told *Fortune* that "Sentner gave them the impression that he had ceased to be an active member of the Communist Party." But see also W. S. Symington to William Sentner, November 16, 1943, and William Sentner to W. S. Symington, December 3, 1942, for indications that all parties knew of Sentner's affiliation. The *Fortune* article ran in a condensed form in the *SLPD,* November 7, 1943. Symington probably used his contacts in the publishing world to secure the article and sought to highlight his "modern" management relations.

108. Author's interview with Thomas Knowles.

109. *SLGD,* April 25, 1943; Emerson Case File 302–59, FMCS280, and Case File, Emerson 7-d-298, NWLB202; Memorandum, undated, Folder 161, Box 14, JWC357; See also Local Review files for 1943, unprocessed Jean Paul Collection; author's interview with Thomas Knowles.

110. W. S. Symington to William Sentner, December 6, 1943, Symington Folder, unprocessed WSP.

111. F. M. Karches to Local 1102, December 9, 1943, Symington folder, unprocessed WSP. *Local Review,* April 20, 1945; see Case File, Emerson 7-d-298, NWLB202.

112. *SLGD,* May 11 and 12, 1944; *Local Review,* June 1944; *SLGD,* May 13, 1944; Arthur Hepner, "Wildcat Strikes," *Harper's* 190 (March 1945): 458.

113. "Program for Local 1102," unprocessed JWCP357.

114. W. S. Symington to James W. Click, July 26, 1944, Folder 158, JWCP.

115. Symington to Exec Committee, Local 1102, November 15, 1944, Folder 113, JWCP357.

116. Undated letter, Local 1102 to Symington, Folder 113, Box 10, JWCP357.

117. Author's interview with Thomas Knowles.

118. Robert Logsdon, Remarks to District 8 Semi-Annual Convention, October 14, 1944, Folder 5, Box 5, Ser. 1, WSP; William Sentner to Harry S. Truman, May 29, 1944, D8/88, UEA.

119. *Local Review,* February 5, 1943; *UEN,* March 11, 1944, April 14, 1944; Robert Logsdon to Julius Emspak, March 20, 1944, D8/125, UEA; William Sentner to James Emspak, August 25, 1944, D8/669, UEA.

120. William Sentner to James Matles, July 14, 1944; Russ Nixon to William Sentner, July 23, 1944; both in Folder 3, Box 1, Ser. 6, WSP.

121. *SLGD,* September 7, 1942, in Morgue files, Mercantile Library, St. Louis; *SLGD,* July 12, 1942; District Executive Board Report, January 30, 1945, Folder 5, Box 5, Ser. 1, WSP; *St. Louis American,* April 2, 1943.

122. "30 Hour Week Predicted at Postwar Parley," undated *SLGD* article, in "War Box," unprocessed WSP.

123. *UEN,* August 19, 1944; "Reconversion and Postwar Jobs in Evansville, Indiana," *New Masses,* June 12, 1945, Evansville folder, unprocessed WSP.

124. Transcript, DeSoto (Hotel) Post-War Planning Conference, July 30, 1944, Folder 1, Box 5, Ser. 5, WSP; *SLGD*, July 30, 1944; "Industry Labor Cooperation in Peace Urged," unprocessed WSP; "Civic Leaders Urge Unity in Task of Providing Jobs after War," Unidentified Newspaper Clipping, July 31, 1944, in War Box, unprocessed WSP; *UEN*, August 5, 1944.

125. "Civic Leaders Urge Unity in Task of Providing Jobs after War," Unidentified Newspaper Clipping, July 31, 1944, in War Box, unprocessed WSP. For the interpretation of the CED as a representative of "corporate liberalism," see George Lipsitz, *Rainbow at Midnight: Labor and Culture in the 1940s* (Urbana: University of Illinois Press, 1994), 165–67. For doubts, see Elizabeth A. Fones-Wolf, *Selling Free Enterprise: The Business Assault on Labor and Liberalism, 1945–1960* (Urbana: University of Illinois Press, 1994), 23–34.

126. William Sentner to William McClellan, August 30, 1944, D8/89, UEA.

127. See especially Rexford G. Tugwell and E. C. Banfield, "Grass-Roots Democracy—Myth or Reality," *Public Administration Review* 10 (Winter 1950): 47–55; Edwin C. Hargrove and Paul K. Conkin, eds., *TVA: Fifty Years of Grass-Roots Bureaucracy* (Urbana: University of Illinois Press, 1983); Walter L. Creese, *TVA's Public Planning: The Vision, the Reality* (Knoxville: University of Tennessee Press, 1990). Actually, the TVA perfectly reflected two tendencies that contested for the soul of liberalism in the 1930s and 1940s: the first espoused technocratic solutions to political problems, and the other sought to democratize American life. Some histories have questioned—justifiably, I think—whether the TVA deserves the democratic merits attributed to it. The transfer of power to technocratic experts at the local level, with few mechanisms to include local residents in the planning process, held grave consequences for local residents, many of whom were forcibly displaced by TVA projects. See William Bruce Wheeler and Michael J. McDonald, *TVA and the Tellico Dam, 1936–1979: A Bureaucratic Crisis in Post-Industrial America* (Knoxville: University of Tennessee Press, 1986). Recent analysts have criticized TVA nuclear power projects as mocking TVA claims to environmental stewardship. See William U. Chandler, *The Myth of the TVA: Conservation and Development in the Tennessee Valley, 1933–1983* (Cambridge, Mass.: Harper and Row, 1984). Nevertheless, it is important to understand that, as will be discussed in this section, the advocates for this program in the district, including those associated with the Communist Party, recognized the need for continued community mobilizations even after the passage of such a program.

128. "Memo: Re: M.V.A.," Folder 1, Box 1, Ser. 2, WSP; Marion Clawson, *New Deal Planning: The National Resources Planning Board* (Baltimore: Johns Hopkins University Press, 1981).

129. *New York Times*, May 24, 1944; Henry Hart, *The Dark Missouri* (Madison: University of Wisconsin Press, 1957), 120.

130. *SLPD*, July 17, 1951; John T. Farrell, *Heartland Engineers: A History* (Kansas City: Army Corps of Engineers, 1993).

131. Donald Worster, *Rivers of Empire: Water, Aridity, and the Growth of the American West* (New York: Pantheon, 1985), 268–69; Paul Scheele, "Resource Development Politics in the Missouri Basin: Federal Power, Navigation, and Reservoir Operation Policies, 1944–1968" (PhD diss., University of Nebraska, 1969), 35, 41, 45, 49. Scheele points out that Pick did not bother to explain why any of his proposed "features were necessary either at their proposed size, cost, or location."

132. *SLPD*, May 14, 1944; *SLST*, May 29, 1944.

133. District Executive Board, "MVA Report," Folder 17, Box 2, Ser. 2, WSP; Press Release, March 21, 1944, Folder 2, Box 1, Ser. 2, WSP.

134. *One River, One Plan;* "Post War Planning and the Missouri River Valley Basin," July 13, 1944, Folder 2, Box 1, Ser. 2, WSP; District Executive Board, "MVA Report," August 1944; Untitled fact sheet, Folder 17, Box 2, Ser. 2, WSP.

135. Naomi Ring to Bill McMurphy, September 26, 1944, Folder 1, Box 1, Ser. 2; Wm. McMurphy to Naomi Ring, October 6, 1944, Folder 1, Box 1, Ser. 2; see also, William Sentner to Jerry O'Connal, September 26, 1944, all in WSP.

136. Worster, *Rivers of Empire,* 249–50. Walter E. Packard to William Sentner, July 29, 1944; Paul G. Pinsky to William Sentner, July 18, 1944; William Sentner to Walter Packard, July 22, 1944; Walter Packard résumé, July 18, 1944, all in WSP, Folder 2, Box 1, Ser. 2, WSP.

137. See letters "Correspondence, One River, One Plan," Folder 3, Box 1, Ser. 2, WSP; William Sentner in *The Worker Magazine,* October 8, 1944, Folder 1, Box 1, Ser. 2, WSP; "Statement by James A. Davis before Congress," undated, Folder 798, JDP.

138. "UE Role on M.V.A.," Folder 1, Box 1, Ser. 2, WSP.

139. H. E. Klinefelter to William Sentner, July 21, 1944, Folder 2, Box 1, Ser. 2, WSP.

140. *SLST,* October 18, 1944.

141. *SLPD,* September 11, 1944; "Patton Urges Farm Union to Stand Firm for MVA," Folder 4, Box 1, Ser. 2, WSP; Glenn Talbott to Naomi Ring, August 31, 1944, Folder 2, Box 1, Ser. 2, WSP.

142. Naomi Ring to Kenneth Simons, *Bismarck Tribune* (North Dakota), August 31, 1944, Folder 2, Box 1, Ser. 2, WSP.

143. Naomi Ring to Glenn Talbott, September 5, 1944, reply to Talbott's letter of August 31, 1944; William Sentner to A. M. Piper, September 1, 1944; H. E. Klinefelter to Sentner, August 10, 1944, all in Folder 2, Box 1, Ser. 2, WSP.

144. Naomi Ring to William Sentner, August 18, 1944, Folder 2, Box 1, Ser. 2, WSP.

145. Frances Saylor to William Sentner, July 6, 1944; Naomi Ring to Frances Saylor, July 22, 1944; William Sentner to Frances Saylor, July 29, 1944; all in Folder 2, Box 1, Ser. 2, WSP, giving clear evidence of who wrote the bill. Donald E. Spritzer, "One River, One Problem: James Murray and the Missouri Valley Authority," in *Montana and the West: Essays in Honor of K. Ross Tool,* ed. Rex. C. Myers and Harry W. Fritz (Boulder, Colo.: Pruett, 1984), 125, asserts that the bill was written by Murray and his staff with the assistance of David Lilienthal.

146. *SLPD,* August 18, 1944.

147. *SLST,* November 16, 1944.

148. "MVA Report," September, 1944, Folder 17, Box 2, Ser. 2, WSP; William Sentner to Glenn Talbott, October 12, 1944; William Sentner, "Speech on the Missouri Valley Authority," Folder 6, Box 2, Ser. 2, WSP; *UE News,* January 27, 1945.

149. *SLPD,* October 14, 1944, October 16, 1944; "Patton Urges Farm Union to Stand Firm for MVA," unidentified newspaper article, November 21, 1944, Folder 4, Box 1, Ser. 2, WSP; Spritzer, "One River, One Problem," 127.

150. *SLPD,* November 18, 1944; Spritzer, "One River, One Problem," 128; *SLPD,* November 30, 1944; Walter Packard to Thomas Blaisdell, December 6, 1944, Folder 1, Box 1, Ser. 2, WSP.

151. Spritzer, "One River, One Problem"; Walter Packard to James Patton, December 6, 1944; November 21, 1944, Folder 4, Box 1, Ser. 2, WSP; *SLPD,* November 29, 1944; Douglas S. Smith, "Missouri Valley Authority: The Death of Regional Planning" (Master's thesis,

University of Missouri, 1991), 112; *SLST,* November 16, 1944; *SLPD,* November 29 and November 15, 1944.

152. *Missouri Farmer,* December 1944.

153. Ibid.

154. "Political Action" files, unprocessed WSP; *UEN,* June 17, 1944, November 15, 1944.

155. William Sentner FBI File, FBI-HQ, 100-18332-38, Box 5, Ser. 4, WSP.

156. Bill (Sentner) to Bill (Chambers), December 12, 1944, Folder 17, Box 2, Ser. 2, WSP.

157. "Program for the Development of the Campaign," attached to Williams Sentner to Bill Chambers, December 12, 1944, Folder 17, Box 2, Ser. 2, WSP; William Chambers to H. E. Klinefelter, December 27, 1944, Folder 1, Box 1, Ser. 2, WSP.

158. William Chambers to Clifford McEvoy, December 21, 1944, Folder 1, Box 1, Ser. 2, WSP; William Sentner to Glenn Talbott, Folder 2, Box 1, Ser. 2, WSP; St. Louis Committee for an MVA, "Statement of Principles," January 10, 1945, Folder 794, JDP; *SLPD,* January 21, 1945; William Chambers, "Memorandum" to Bill Sentner and Jack Becker, January 18, 1945, Folder 17, Box 2, Ser. 2, WSP.

159. "Program for the Development of the Campaign"; William Sentner to Bill Chambers, December 12, 1944; William Chambers to H. E. Klinefelter, December 27, 1944; Naomi Ring to Bill McMurphy, September 26, 1944, all in Folder 1, Box 1, Ser. 2; Memorandum, Bill Sentner, William Chambers, January 18, 1945, Folder 17, Box 2, Ser. 2, WSP; Smith, "Missouri Valley Authority," 63–72; Carleton Ball, "What the M.V.A. Proposal Promises for America," *Social Action,* Folder 795, JDP.

160. William Sentner to Francis Saylor, March 31, 1945, William Chambers to William Sentner, January 1, 1945, both in Folder 17, Box 2, Ser. 2, WSP; *SLPD,* February 20, 1945.

161. William Sentner to Frances Saylor, March 31, 1945, Folder 16, Box 2, Ser. 2, WSP; Smith, "Missouri Valley Authority," 67.

162. "Basic Information for Speakers on MVA," January 1945, D8/MVA, UEA; *SLPD,* February 20, 1945.

163. *SLPD,* March 22, 1945; Walter Packard to William Sentner, December 6, 1944, Folder 1, Box 1, Ser. 2, WSP, indicates that Packard revised the MVA bill.

164. Press release, Missouri Conference on MVA, April 16, 1945; Raymond Tucker to James A. Davis, April 30, 1945; both in Folder 794, JDP.

165. "Regional Conference on MVA, July 6–7, 1945," Folder 795, as well as materials in Folder 797, JDP; Correspondence, leaflets, press releases in Folder 8, Box 1, Ser. 2, WSP; "Sponsors of Regional Conference on MVA," D8, UEA; Spritzer, "One River, One Problem," 133.

166. "Political Significance of the MVA movement," Folder 1, Box 2, Ser. 2, WSP.

167. *SLPD,* February 20, 1945; *SLST,* February 17, 1945; Larry Allen Whiteside, "Harry S. Truman and James E. Murray: The Missouri Valley Authority Proposal" (MA thesis, Central Missouri State University, 1970), 77; Spritzer, "One River, One Problem," 129; William Sentner to Jack Becker, May 21, 1945, Folder 8, Box 1, Ser. 2, WSP.

168. Spritzer, "One River, One Problem," 131.

169. *SLPD,* November 29, 1944, and August 4, 1945; Sentner, "Political Significance of the MVA Movement," Folder 1, Box 2, Ser. 2; Spritzer, "One River, One Problem," 132; Scheele, "Resource Development Politics in the Missouri Basin," 41–43.

170. Jack (Becker) to William Sentner, October 13, 1945, Folder 7, Box 1, Ser. 2, WSP; *SLPD,* October 24, 1945.

171. Spritzer, "One River, One Problem," 132; Scheele, "Resource Development Politics in the Missouri Basin," 41–43; Marian Ridgeway, *The Missouri Basin's Pick-Sloan Plan: A Case Study in Congressional Determination* (Urbana: University of Illinois Press, 1955), 215; Sentner, "Political Significance of the MVA Movement"; *Fairfield Iowa Ledger,* September 18, 1945, in Folder 7, Box 1, Ser. 2, WSP; *Kansas City Star,* July 8, 1945, in Folder 8, Box 1, Ser. 2, WSP. For advocates' arguments that the MVA was a clear step toward decentralized government, see Patton quoted in unidentified newspaper article, November 21, 1944, Folder 4, Box 1, Ser. 2, WSP, and William Sentner to A. M. Piper, September 1, 1944, Folder 2, Box 1, Ser. 2, WSP.

172. Statement by James A. Davis before Congress, undated, Folder 798; Press Release, September 21, 1945, Folder 800, both in JDP; Tom Verdot interview with James Davis, Kansas City, Missouri, July 10, 1986, author's possession.

173. "Political Significance of the MVA movement," Folder 1, Box 2, Ser. 2, WSP; William Sentner to C. B. Baldwin, November 3, 1945, Folder 10, Box 2, Ser. 2, WSP.

174. On the way that internal divisions and anticommunism affected the CIO's participation in MVA and on centralization of CIO's activities in Washington, D.C., see William Sentner to Julius Emspak, July 9, 1945, D8/92, UEA; Jack Becker to Phil Murray, July 23, 1945, Folder 8, Box 1, Ser. 2, WSP; Albert Fitzgerald to John Brophy, July 24, 1945, William Sentner to Reid Robinson, August 8, 1945, Folder 7, Box 1, Ser. 2, WSP; Ruth Roemer to William Sentner, July 14, 1947, Ruth Roemer to Robert Logsdon, July 19, 1945, Robert Logsdon to Morris L. Cooke, July 21, 1947, Folder 10, Box 1, Ser. 2, WSP; John Brophy to James A. Davis, April 1, 1948, Folder 819, JDP.

175. The MVA proponents could not get committee hearings. In 1948, the election of a more progressive Congress (including fifteen congressmen and two senators who had won on a pro-MVA platform) renewed hopes among MVA proponents, but a revised bill was unable to make it out of committees still controlled by opponents of the idea. Throughout these legislative attempts, MVA supporters also blamed Truman for torpedoing positive prospects for the bill. Spritzer, "One River, One Problem," 132–36; Benton Stong to Members, November 30, 1948, Folder 823, JDP.

176. Crawford D. Goodwin, "The Valley Authority Idea—The Fading of a National Vision," in *TVA: Fifty Years of Grass-Roots Bureaucracy,* 265.

177. See "River Dreams: St. Louis Labor and the Fight for a Missouri Valley Authority," in *Common Fields: An Environmental History of St. Louis,* ed. Andrew Hurley, 240–41 (St. Louis: Missouri Historical Society Press, 1997).

178. James Matles to William Sentner, July 17, 1944, Folder 3, Box 1, Ser. 6, WSP; author's interview with Victor Pasche, June 17, 1989, San Francisco, California; see Lisa Kannenberg, "The Product of GE's Progress: Labor, Management, and Community Relations in Schenectady, New York, 1930–1960" (PhD diss., Rutgers University, 1999). Robert Logsdon to William Sentner, March 8, 1946, O/732, UEA.

Chapter 6: "To Be Full-Fledged Citizens of This Union"

1. Transcript, District 8 Semi-Annual Convention, March 30–31, 1946, 18, Folder 6, Box 5, Ser. 1, WSP (for title of chapter); *EP,* May 14, 1948.

2. William Sentner to James Matles, August 6, 1941, and attached unidentified newspaper article, D8/67, UEA.

3. Robert Logsdon, "Suggestions on Personnel," attached to Logsdon to James Matles, December 3, 1941, O/722, UEA.

4. Author's interview with Toni Sentner, June 16, 1989.

5. Author's interview with Morris Levin, St. Louis, Missouri, December 3, 1992.

6. Typed transcript, "Minutes of October 6 convention," 63, Folder 5, Box 5, Ser. 1, WSP.

7. William Sentner FBI File, Report, August 22, 1951, FBI-HQ-100–18332-139, Box 5, Ser. 4, WSP.

8. Typed Transcript, Minutes of the District Council Meeting, March 30, 1946, 22, Folder 6, Box 5, Ser. 1, WSP.

9. William Sentner, "Early 1939" speech, Folder 8, Box 5, Ser. 1, WSP.

10. "A Yaleman and A Communist," *Fortune,* November 1943.

11. Author's interview with Vic Pasche, June 17, 1989, San Francisco, California; see also Sentner Testimony in Smith Act Case, 1668, Narrative Statement, *Sentner v. U.S.,* Box 4, Ser. 4, WSP; William Sentner, Speech, March 11, 1945, Box 4 Unorganized, WSP; William Sentner FBI file, FBI-HQ, 100-18332-33, Box 5, Ser. 4, WSP; William Sentner to William Z. Foster, June 25, 1945, Sentner to Committee on Discussion on Resolution, June 25, 1945, Folder 5, Box 1, Ser. 3, WSP. For a discussion of the party's wartime position, see Maurice Isserman, *Which Side Were You On? The American Communist Party during the Second World War* (Middletown, Conn.: Wesleyan University Press, 1982), chaps. 7–9.

12. Isserman, *Which Side Were You On?* chap. 10.

13. William Sentner to William Z. Foster, June 25, 1945, and William Sentner to Committee on Discussion on Resolution, June 25, 1945, Folder 5, Box 1, Ser. 3, WSP. Sentner's criticisms were reiterated in part in a *Daily Worker* letter, July 19, 1945.

14. William Sentner FBI file, FBI-HQ, 100-18332-38, 13, Box 5, Ser. 4, WSP; Isserman, *Which Side Were You On?* 234. Sentner's new position as vice-chair of the Missouri party might have seemed to him an indication of the growing role of trade unionists in the party.

15. William Sentner FBI File, FBI-HQ, 100-18332-219, Box 5, Ser. 4, WSP.

16. *SLGD,* August 27, 1946.

17. Author's telephone interview with Robert Logsdon, March 23, 1989; author's interview with Dennis Brunn, St. Louis, January 22, 1974, WHMC.

18. William Sentner, Undated memo, ca. September 24, 1942, D8/78, UEA.

19. Author's telephone interview with Robert Logsdon, March 23, 1989; Anna DeCormis to William Sentner, Folder 7, Box 2, Ser. 6, WSP.

20. "FBI Interview," December 3, 1943, Folder 2, Box 1, Ser. 6, WSP. The article also may have caused Sentner's investigation. See March 29, 1944, excerpt from House Un-American Activities Committee, unprocessed, JWCP357. Sentner "wanted to fight the inquiry" by the FBI, but was "instructed by the UE National office to retire gracefully" from the NWLB. See 100-18332-20 through 100-18332-27, Box 5, Ser. 4, WSP.

21. Author's interview with James Click, July 28, 1987; author's telephone interview with James Click, July 15, 1987, typed notes. The 1941 switch on foreign policy clearly aggravated some of the leadership in Local 1102 who identified strongly with anticommunist ideology. In December 1941, the local's leadership refused to sign a district letter to President Roosevelt pledging support for the war because it included mention of the Soviet Union as an ally, arguing that the Soviet Union was not an ally of the United States.

22. John Burns, undated notes regarding Interracial Committee Minutes (January 1945), Folder 127, Box 12, JWCP357.

23. Ronald W Johnson, "Organized Labor's Postwar Red Scare: The UE in St. Louis," *North Dakota Quarterly* 48 (Winter 1980): 28–39; Ronald Wayne Johnson, "The Communist Issue in Missouri, 1946–1956" (PhD diss., University of Missouri–Columbia, 1973).

24. *SLGD,* March 11, 1951.

25. Author's interview with Thomas Knowles, St. Louis, Missouri, October 15, 1993.

26. Author's interview with Lloyd Austin, December 3, 1992.

27. Author's interviews with Thomas Knowles, October 15, 1993, Lloyd Austin interview.

28. Click acknowledged that Sentner had tried to "bury the hatchet" and work together, but he contended that he was too principled on the issue of Communist influence to accept such an offer; author's interview with James Click.

29. Author's interview with Robert Logsdon.

30. Author's telephone interview with James Click; *SLGD,* August 28, 1946.

31. Author's interviews with John J. Burns, March 4, 1990; author's interview with William Drohan, March 3, 1990; author's interview with Eugene Paul, May 15, 1990.

32. Resolution, June 15, 1945, UE Local 1102 membership meeting, possession of author.

33. Click interview; see also William C. Pratt, "The Socialist Party and Organized Labor," *Political Power and Social Theory,* ed. Maurice Zeitlin, 4 (1984): 81.

34. Gladys Gruenberg, *Labor Peacemaker: The Life and Works of Father Leo C. Brown* (St. Louis: Institute of Jesuit Sources, 1981); Steve Rosswurm, "The Catholic Church and the Left-Led Unions: Labor Priests, Labor Schools and the ACTU," in *The CIO's Left-Led Unions,* ed. Steve Rosswurm, 119–37 (New Brunswick, N.J.: Rutgers University Press, 1992). Leo Brown's papers at St. Louis University contain no materials regarding the campaign.

35. Author's interviews with John J. Burns and William Drohan.

36. Author's interview with James Click.

37. Robert Logsdon to Julius Emspak, January 13, 1944, D8/125, UEA; Robert Logsdon to Julius Emspak, February 15, 1944, D8/125, UEA; see also issues of *Small Arms Union News,* Folder 31, Box 22, IUER.

38. Robert Logsdon to Julius Emspak, February 15, 1944, D8/125; Vic (Pasche) to Bill (Sentner), undated [September 1944], Betty Raab Papers, possession of author; author's telephone interview with Betty Raab.

39. Robert Logsdon to Julius Emspak, January 13, 1944, D8/125; Robert Logsdon to Julius Emspak, February 15, 1944; Robert Logsdon to James Emspak, January 10, 1945; all in D8/125, UEA. *SLPD,* December 12, 1944; William Sentner FBI File, Report, January 2, 1945, FBI 100-135-42-62, Box 5, Ser. 4, WSP.

40. Robert Logsdon to James Emspak, July 17, 1945, O/729, UEA; "Resolution," Folder 22, Box 31, IUER. For clear evidence of the racist content of two of the anticommunist players, see C. E. Schmick affidavit, December 27, 1945, D8/478, UEA; "Lee Robinson note," December 28, 1945, D8/455, UEA.

41. Robert Logsdon, Report, May 1945, O/729, UEA; Robert Burns Logsdon to James Emspak, August 14, 1945, UEA; Robert Logsdon, Report, September 20, 1945, O/730, UEA; Otto Maschoff to District 8 Appeals Committee, August 17, 1945, "District 8 Appeals, Case of Otto Maschoff," Records of District 8, UE, SHSI; Memo, Harvey Smith,

August 30, 1950, D8/482, UEA; author's telephone interview with Harvey Smith, April 15, 1987.

42. Robert Logsdon to James Emspak, August 14, 1945, O/729, UEA; Robert Logsdon, Report, September 20, 1945, O/730, UEA; William Sentner to All UE St. Louis Local Unions, July 21, 1945, D8/188, UEA; author's telephone interview with Robert Logsdon, March 23, 1989; author's telephone interview with Harvey Smith, January 15, 1990; J. W. Click, et al. (officers of Local 825, 1102 and 1104) to Albert Fitzgerald, September 11, 1945, D8/133, UEA.

43. William Sentner, typed notes on "rank and file control," Folder 5, Box 7, Ser. 1, WSP; William Sentner to Albert Fitzgerald, August 27, 1945, D8/93, UEA.

44. Typed transcript of the October 6, 1945, District Convention Proceedings, p. 55, Folder 5, Box 5, Ser. 1, WSP.

45. Typed transcript, October 6, 1945, District Convention, unpaginated page between pp. 13 and 14, Folder 5, Box 5, Ser. 1, WSP.

46. Minutes of the October 7 Convention, typescript, 30–32, 54, Folder 5, Box 5, Ser. 1, WSP.

47. Typed Transcript, October 6–7, 1945, Convention, 55–65, Folder 5, Box 5, Ser. 1, WSP; "A Statement of Facts" leaflet, undated, Folder 6, Box 5, Ser. 1, WSP; "An Open Letter to James W. Click from William Sentner," October 19, 1945, Folder 6, Box 5, Ser. 1, WSP. On recommendations for staff, see UE National Office Correspondence folder for staff recommendations, including recommendation for Click, Folder 2, Box 11, Ser. 5, WSP.

48. Typed Transcript, October 6–7, 1945 Convention, 61–62, Folder 5, Box 5, Ser. 1, WSP.

49. Typed Transcript, October 6–7, 1945 Convention, 60–63, Folder 5, Box 5, Ser. 1, WSP; "An Open Letter," William Sentner to James Click, Folder 5, Box 5, Ser. 1, WSP; "An Open Letter," October 23, 1945, JW Click to William Sentner, Folder 5, Box 5, Ser. 1, WSP.

50. James Click to William Sentner, November 23, 1945, UEMDA file, unprocessed WSP; Louis Wagner to All Local Unions, November 7, 1945, D8/192, UEA; Bill Sentner to Julius (Emspak), undated, ca. October 1945, D8/94, UEA.

51. Ronald Johnson, "Organized Labor's Postwar Red Scare," 29; Leaflets and campaign information in "1945 Election," Folder 6, Box 5, Ser. 1, WSP; Typed transcript, Special District Executive Board Meeting, November 6, 1945, 13, Folder 5, Box 5, Ser. 1, WSP.

52. Otto Maschoff, Betty Raab, Paul Forrester, *Lawrence Mulvihill v. Local 825 District Appeals Case,* Collection Z 24, unprocessed files of District 8, SHSI; Typed Transcript, Minutes of the District Council Meeting, March 30, 1946, 7–9, Folder 6, Box 5, Ser. 1, WSP; Semi-Annual District Convention, March 30–31, 1946, typed transcript of proceedings, 27, Folder 6, Box 5, Ser. 1, WSP.

53. *EP,* September 15 and 16, 1944; *EC,* September 16, 1944; Servel Organizational Program, May 10, 1944, D8/232, UEA.

54. Samuel White, "Labor and Politics in Evansville, Indiana, 1919–1955" (PhD diss., State University of New York, Binghamton, 1998), 211.

55. *Evansville UE News,* December 17, 1943, D8/312; *EP,* February 22, 1944; "Reconversion and Postwar Jobs in Evansville, Indiana," typed submission to New Masses, Evansville folder, Box 1, Ser. 6, WSP.

56. Typed Transcript, October 6, 1945, District Convention, 9–11, Folder 5, Box 5, Ser. 1, WSP; "Evansville Indiana Area, Report on Organization," September 21, 1945, O/730, UEA; September 24, 1945, Report, unprocessed WSP; *EC,* October 18, 1945; Local 813,

Minutes, First Annual Shop Delegate Conference, July 21, 1946, D8/337, UEA; *Evansville UE News,* December 3, 1943, D8/312, UEA.

57. Author's interview with Charles Berger, Evansville, Indiana, June 8, 1998; UE Org. A–B files, Application for position, Sadelle Berger, March 31, 1944, Organizer files, UEA; William Sentner to David Scribner, March 12, 1946, Personal Correspondence, 1946–47, Box 1, Ser. 6, WSP; William Sentner to Julius Emspak, April 5, 1944, William Sentner to James Emspak, November 5, 1945, Sadelle Berger Organizer file, UEA.

58. House of Representatives, Committee on Education and Labor, *Investigation of Communist Influence in the Bucyrus-Erie Strike: Hearings before a Subcommittee of the Committee on Education and Labor,* 80th Cong., 2nd sess. (Washington, D.C.: U.S. Government Printing Office, 1948), 154; *EP,* September 18, 1948.

59. Unidentified Newspaper clipping, RD22ffle UEA.

60. Jim Payne to James Matles, November 21, 1945, O/1088; "Servel" release, March 13, 1946, Folder 5, Box 1, Ser. 1, WSP.

61. "Election Program—Servel, Inc.," February 24, 1946; Servel Veterans Committee leaflet; "The Latest" leaflet, March 11, 1946, all in Folder 5, Box 1, Ser. 1, WSP; *EC,* March 5, 1946; "Sentner and Other Communists Exposed by Their Own Members" leaflet, March 11, 1946, Folder 5, Box 1, Ser. 1, WSP.

62. Election Program, February 24, 1946; Undated, The History of Wage Increases at Servel; "The Same Old Story" and "It's in the Bag" leaflets; all in Folder 5, Box 1, Ser. 1, WSP.

63. Typed Transcript, District 8 Semi-Annual Convention, March 30–31, 1946, 18–19, Folder 6, Box 5, Ser. 1, WSP.

64. Typed transcript, Minutes of the District Council Meeting, March 30, 1946, 20, Folder 6, Box 5, Ser. 1, WSP.

65. Ibid., 20.

66. Ibid., 20–22.

67. Ibid., 22.

68. Ibid., 18, 19, 22.

69. William Sentner, Annual Report, October 4, 1947, Folder 6, Box 5, Ser. 1, WSP; *SLPD,* July 19 and 24, 1946; *SLST,* July 24, 1946; Robert Logsdon, "Southern Drive" report, November 6, 1946, O/735, UEA.

70. Author's interview with James Click; Leo Brown, S. J. to Rev. Charles O. Rice, June 28, 1946, Reel "C," Charles Owen Rice Papers, Pennsylvania State University Labor Archives. Thanks to Steven Rosswurm for passing these along. For ACTU, see Rosswurm, "The Catholic Church and the Left-Led Unions," and Douglas Seaton, *Catholics and Radicals: The Association of Catholic Trade Unions and the American Labor Movement from Depression to Cold War* (Lewisburg, Pa.: Bucknell University Press, 1981). See also Untitled synopsis of interview with Fr. Leo Brown, Folder 14, Box 1, Ser. 4, WSP.

71. *SLGD,* August 12, 1946; Letters to Click, August 1946, Folder 175, JWCP357.

72. Ronald Filipelli and Mark McCulloch, *Cold War in the Working Class: The Rise and Decline of the United Electrical Workers* (Albany: State University of New York Press, 1995), chap. 4.

73. Harry Vernon Ball Jr., "Case History of a Labor Union: The United Distribution Workers" (PhD diss., Washington University, June 1950), 35–39, 97–110; *SLGD,* August 23,

1943; Minutes, September 27, 1943, Missouri Industrial Union Council, James Davis Papers; Robert Logsdon to James Emspak, October 25, 1943, D8/125, UEA.

74. Robert Logsdon to James Emspak, February 15, 1944, D8/125, UEA; Robert Logsdon, Organizational Report, June 15, 1944, D8/181, UEA.

75. Robert Logsdon, Report for St. Louis, May 1945, O/729, UEA. In the most egregious instance, the steelworkers' director assigned five staff representatives to assist the UAW in a contest with the UE for representation of a shell plant. Though the UAW didn't attack the UE, it was clear that certain CIO officials were placing resources to ensure that the UE would not be the predominant union in the local arena. In another instance, the gas workers, backed by Gibbons and some auto workers, sought to exclude UE from organizing a dry cell battery plant, although it was within the UE's jurisdiction. Robert Logsdon, Report, September 20, 1945, UEA. Meanwhile, at least through 1946, the UE continued to turn over to other CIO unions workers they had organized who fell under other CIO unions' jurisdiction. See Delmond Garst to William Sentner, July 16, 1946, D8/63, UEA.

76. Robert Logsdon to Julius Emspak, September 27, 1945, O/730, UEA; Robert Logsdon to James Matles, August 3, 1946, O/734, UEA.

77. Robert Logsdon, Report, September 20, 1945, O/730, UEA; Robert Logsdon, Report, September 27, 1945, O/730, UEA. Robert Logsdon, November 11, 1945; Robert Logsdon to Albert Fitzgerald, December 17, 1945; both in D8/95, UEA.

78. *SLST,* June 28, 1946; *SLGD,* June 29, 1946; Johnson, "The Communist Issue in Missouri," 31.

79. Johnson, "The Communist Issue in Missouri," 31; *SLPD,* September 26, 1946; *SLST,* September 26, 1946; author's interview with Oscar Ehrhardt, April 16, 1986.

80. *SLGD,* August 28, 1946; *SLPD,* August 14, 1946; Logsdon memo, August 17, 1946, RD 490, Sentner 1945–46, UEA; Logsdon to Emspak, August 22, 1946, "Sentner, 1945–1946" file, RD490, UEA.

81. *Local Review,* June 1946; Eldon Parr to James Click, June 29, 1946, Folder 6, Box 5, Ser. 1, WSP; William Sentner, Memorandum on the District Election, November 3, 1946, Folder 5, Box 5, Ser. 1, WSP; *SLGD,* August 28, 1946.

82. *Local Review,* November 8, 1945; Robert Logsdon to James Emspak, August 22, 1946, "Sentner 1945–1946," RD 490, UEA.

83. Dale Sorenson, "The Anticommunist Consensus in Indiana, 1945–1958" (PhD diss., Indiana University, 1980), 47; William Debes to undisclosed recipient, ca. July 1946, "Sentner 1945–46" file, RD490, UEA; *EP,* June 6, 1946, August 15, 1946, August 29, 1946, August 31, 1946; Robert Logsdon, "The General Situation in the District," May 17, 1946, O/733, UEA; *EC,* May 31, 1948. The charge that the PAC was a Communist front was the common refrain of the Republican Party.

84. Bill Debes to Jim Click, March 30, 1947, Folder 175, Box 15, JWCP357.

85. White, "Labor and Politics," 200–201. Charles Wright to William Sentner, August 16, 1946, D8/300A, UEA; *EP,* July 30, 1946, in D8/319, UEA; see "Organizational Problems" in Thomas Hendricks Collection, University of Southern Indiana, Evansville, Indiana, and Thomas Hendricks interview with Glenda Morrison, copy in Thomas Hendricks Collection, Walter Reuther Library, Wayne State University, Detroit, Michigan.

86. *EP,* July 30, 1946; *EC,* August 30, 1946; Charles Wright to William Sentner, August 16, 1946, D8/300A, UEA; William Sentner, Memo on the District Election, November 3, 1946, Folder 6, Box 5, Ser. 1, WSP. The UE's involvement in third-party politics in Evans-

ville also caused much of the friction. In addition, Wright named Alfred Smith, who had ties to the party, as head of the Evansville PAC.

87. Robert Logsdon, *Disruption in District Eight* (1947), 6, unprocessed Lloyd Austin Collection, WHMC.

88. William Sentner, Memorandum on the District Election, November 3, 1946, Folder 5, Box 5, Ser. 1, WSP.

89. Logsdon, *Disruption in District Eight,* 8, quoting letter from William Debes to Joe Zarrella, September 8, 1946.

90. William Sentner, Memorandum on the District Election, November 3, 1946, Folder 5, Box 5, Ser. 1, WSP.

91. Typescript summary of interview with Father Leo Brown, 1948, Folder 14, Box 1, Ser. 4, WSP.

92. Author's interview with John J. Burns.

93. Untitled summary of interview with Father Leo Brown, "Finks" file, Unorganized WSP; author's interview with John Burns; author's interview with Harvey Smith; Sentner, Memorandum on the District Election, November 3, 1946, Folder 5, Box 5, Ser. 1, WSP.

94. *Today's World,* June 1946, 5; E. J. Stuebinger to James Click, September 2, 1946; Smith to Jim, May 18, 1947; Ivan Adair to James Click, October 9, 1947; all in Folder 175, Box 15, JWCP357. Griffin profile, Bender profile, Folder 14, Box 1, Ser. 4, WSP.

95. Resolution, Local 1102, April 26, 1946, Folder 2, Box 2, Ser. 1, WSP.

96. *Globe-Democrat,* May 5, 1946; *SLGD,* June 25, 1946; Statement Issued by District 8, June 25, 1946, attached to June 28, 1946, Minutes, Folder 6, Box 5, Ser. 1, WSP; *SLPD,* June 26, 1946.

97. *SLGD,* August 27, 1946.

98. *SLGD,* August 14, 1946; *SLPD,* August 14, 1946; William Sentner, Memorandum on the District Election, November 3, 1946, Folder 5, Box 5, Ser. 1, WSP; Robert Logsdon to James Emspak, August 22, 1946, "Sentner 1945–1946," RD 490, UEA.

99. *SLGD,* August 12, 27, and 28, 1946; "Letters from supporters" file, unprocessed JWCP357.

100. William Sentner, "Memorandum on District 8 Election," D8/192, UEA.

101. Ibid.

102. Ibid.

103. Miller was deported under the McCarran Act in the 1950s.

104. *SLGD,* October 6, 1946.

105. *SLPD,* October 6 and 7, 1946; *SLGD,* October 6, 1946.

106. Undated *NDN,* Folder 14, Box 162, JWCP357.

107. Howard Delaney to James Click, Folder 175, Box 15, JWCP357.

108. William Sentner, "Memorandum on the District Election," Folder 5, Box 5, Ser. 1, WSP.

109. *SLPD,* October 6 and 7, 1946; *SLGD,* October 6, 1946.

110. *Evansville UE News,* October 15, 1946.

111. Sentner, "Memorandum on the District Election."

112. Author's telephone interview with Robert Logsdon, March 23, 1989.

113. Robert Logsdon to James Matles, December 24, 1945, O/731, UEA; *Local 1102 Constitution and By-Laws,* 1946, unprocessed Lloyd Austin Collection; Robert Logsdon to James Matles, March 12, 1946, O/732, UEA.

114. *Local Review,* January 1947.

115. Author's telephone interview with Lloyd Austin, January 4, 1993.

116. Robert Logsdon to James Matles, December 24, 1945, O/731, UEA; author's interview with William Reidel.

117. Robert Logsdon to James Matles, January 15, 1947, O/735, UEA; Walter Kleiman Tell City to James Click, January 14, 1947, Folder 175, Box 15, JWCP357; Proceedings of the UE District 8 Semi-annual convention, Moline, Illinois, March 29–30, 1947, Folder 6, Box 5, Ser. 1, WSP; William Sentner to Albert Fitzgerald, April 18, 1947, James J. Matles folder, National UE Material box, unprocessed WSP.

118. Troy James to James Click, December 9, 1946, Folder 175, Box 15, JWCP357.

119. Logsdon, *Disruption in District Eight.*

120. Bill Debes to James Click, January 23, 25, and 26, 1947, Folder 175, Box 15, JWCP357; Logsdon, *Disruption in District Eight,* 4.

121. Charles Wright to William Sentner, January 8, 1947, D8/338, UEA; Bill (Debes) to James Click, March 10, 1947; Bill to Jim, March 14 and 30, 1947, Folder 175, Box 15, JWCP357.

122. Harold F. Williamson and Kenneth H. Myers, *Designed for Digging: The First 75 years of Bucyrus Erie* (Evanston, Ill.: Northwestern University Press, 1955), 127–28.

123. Robert Logsdon, "Organization," December 19, 1946, O/735, UEA; George Lipsitz, *A Rainbow at Midnight: Labor and Culture in the 1940s* (Urbana: University of Illinois Press, 1994), 205; Robert Logsdon to James Matles, May 29, 1947, O/791, UEA; Otto Maschoff to James J. Matles, [May 1947], 11-R-991, RD21, UEA. William Sentner, Annual Report, October 4, 1947, Folder 6, Box 5, Ser. 1, WSP.

124. Wm. A. Debes to James Click, June 21, 1947, Folder 175, Box 15, JWCP357.

125. Jim Payne to Bill, June 23, 1947, Folder 4, Box 1, Ser. 1, WSP.

126. Wm. A. Debes to James Click, June 21, 1947, Folder 175, Box 15, JWCP357; Rex Wheelock to William Sentner, Folder 11, Box 1, Ser. 1.

127. Ellen Schrecker, "McCarthyism and the Labor Movement: The Role of the State," in *The CIO's Left-Led Unions,* ed. Steve Rosswurm (New Brunswick, N.J.: Rutgers University Press), 140.

128. Schrecker, "McCarthyism and the Labor Movement," 147–49.

129. Ronald Filipelli and Mark McCulloch, *Cold War in the Working Class,* 98–104; Schatz, *The Electrical Workers,* chap. 7.

130. Filipelli and McCulloch, *Cold War in the Working Class,* 106. See Convention debates in Folder 6, Box 5, Ser. 1, WSP; Bob McVay, Regional Director of the CIO, to James Click, Folder 175, JWCP357.

Logsdon, who ran for governor on the Progressive Party ticket, insisted that the Progressive campaign was propelled by liberal forces in Missouri who were disappointed with Truman on a range of issues. But as the red-baiting of the Progressives escalated, the Progressive Party quickly disintegrated in Missouri. Political Action correspondence folder, unprocessed WSP; author's interview with Robert Logsdon.

131. Robert Logsdon to Albert Fitzgerald, February 14, 1947, O/737, UEA.

132. Joseph and Stewart Alsop, "Will the CIO Shake the Communists Loose?" *Saturday Evening Post,* February 27, 1947; *Saturday Evening Post,* March 1, 1947; *SLST,* February 19, 1947; *SLGD,* February 13, 1947.; *SLPD,* February 12 and 25, 1947.

133. William Sentner to Joseph Pulitzer, April 12, 1947; William Sentner to E. Lansing Ray, April 10, 1947; reprinted in *When Are You Going to Print Our Side of the Story,* possession of author.

134. Author's telephone interview with Robert Logsdon, March 23, 1989.

135. *SLGD*, October 22, 1947; 1947 Vote Tally, unprocessed JWCP357; author's telephone interview with Robert Logsdon, March 23, 1989.

136. Memorandum, William Sentner to All District EB Members, October 21, 1947, D8/194, UEA.

137. *SLGD*, October 22, 30, and 31, 1947; *SLPD*, November 1 and 3, 1947; Unidentified newspaper article in Folder 159, Box 14, JWCP357; *SLGD*, November 14, 1947.

138. William Sentner to "All Members of Local 1102," D8/96, UEA; William Drohan to James Carey, February 12, 1948, Folder 32, Box 22, IUER.

139. Johnson, "The Communist Issue in Missouri," 53–55; William Sentner to All Members of Local 1102, UE-CIO, October 18, 1948, D8/197, UEA; William Sentner to All Stewards and Officers in District 8, April 23, 1948, D8/538, UEA.

The two women had both been wire inspectors and were transferred to iron piling. Helen Aukamp Sage admitted membership in the party but avowed loyalty to the United States. The UE district and international union appealed the women's demotions to the Industrial Employment Review Board (IERB), which heard cases on loyalty security. Meanwhile, Cline was fired in what she claimed was a setup for continued complaints about speedups. The IERB gave Cline a "partial vindication when it decided she was eligible for back pay." But she didn't get her job back and found that the "taint of disloyalty marked her." Sage initially could not perform her new job of piling iron and had to take time off but then decided to go back to work and endure the new job. See William Sentner to All Stewards and Officers in District 8, April 23, 1948, D8/538, UEA; Johnson, "The Communist Issue in Missouri," 53–55; William Sentner to E. H. Farr, October 5, 1948, D8/100, UEA.

140. *EP*, March 22, 1948; author's telephone interview with Robert Logsdon, March 23, 1989; Bill Sentner to Julius Emspak, October 21, 1949, D8/100, UEA.

141. *Local Review*, May 1948; *EC*, March 22, 1948; Johnson, "The Communist Issue in Missouri," 77–78; *SLGD*, June 2, 1948; Lee Thompson, Local 814 to Jim Click, April 21, 1948, Folder 175, Box 15, JWCP357.

142. Untitled interview with Fred Bender, March 1948, Folder 14, Box 1, Ser. 4, WSP. The authenticity of these interviews was admitted in *SLPD*, October 3, 1948. See, for example, H. O. Roberts to E. A. Mitchell, December 16, 1947, E. A. Mitchell to H. O. Roberts, October 13, 1947, Box 14, Edward A. Mitchell Papers, Indiana Division, Indiana State Library.

143. "Evansville" typescript, 17, Folder 8, Box 1, Ser. 1, WSP; Unsigned, untitled reports on Fred Bender, Walter Hayden, John Griffin, Homer Loomis, Arthur Robinson, and Leo Brown in Folder 14, Box 1, Ser. 4, WSP; Troy James to Jim, March 16, 1948, Folder 175, Box 15, JWCP; *EC*, September 19, 1948; see correspondence between A. W. Robinson and Edward Mitchell, October 13, 1947, December 7, 1947, January 18, 1948, Folder 5, Box 12, Mitchell Papers.

144. "Evansville" typescript, 12, Folder 8, Box 1, Ser. 1, WSP; William Sentner, Memorandum, April 22, 1948, 13, Folder 4, Box 1, Ser. 1, WSP; unsigned April 6 and 8, 1948, typed notes, in "Misc. Local 813, 1948–1954," Folder 8, Box 1, Ser. 1; numerous articles on this subject in Sidney Berger ECCS collection, possession of Charles Berger; F. J. Taggart, Servel special assignments, to E. A. Mitchell, July 27, 1948, Folder 5, Box 12, Mitchell Papers.

145. *UE Reporter*, May 21, 1948; William Sentner, "Memo on Recent Political Developments," April 22, 1948, Folder 4, Box 1, Ser. 1, WSP; Unsigned notes, April 6, 1948, Miscel-

laneous Local 813, 1948–54, Folder 8, Box 1, Ser. 1, WSP; Al Eberhard to Mayor Dress, March 22, 1948, D8/313, UEA; Memorandum on 1948 District Election, D8/196, UEA; William Sentner to Phil Murray, May 20, 1948, D8/99, UEA; Eberhard, et al. to John Bartee, April 7, 1948, D8/303, UEA.

146. *UE Strike News,* April 7, 1948, D8/309, UEA; Unsigned, undated memo, "The Officers . . . ," Folder 4, Box 1, Ser. 1, WSP; *Labor's Voice,* May 14, 1948.

147. Myers, *Designed for Digging,* 128; "Background Report," August 12, 1947, File 473-2021, FMCS280.

148. Conference, March 6, 1948, Morrison Hotel, Chicago, IL, RD22, UEA. For the CIO bureaucratizing method of pattern bargaining, see Kim Moody, *An Injury to All: The Decline of American Unionism* (London: Verso, 1988), 174–75.

149. N. R. Knox to William Sentner, May 3, 1948, Folder 175, Box 15, JWCP; Kamps quoted in Lipsitz, *A Rainbow at Midnight,* 206; Progress Report, August 27, 1947, File 473-2021, FMCS280.

150. Ed Klingler to James Click, May 5, 1948, Folder 175, Box 15, JWCP357; Troy James to Jim Click, May 9, 1948, Folder 175, Box 15, JWCP; *EP,* May 4, 1948.

151. *EP,* May 11, 1948; *EC,* May 11, 1948.

152. "An Open Letter," William Sentner to N. R. Knox, May 15, 1948, D8/216, UEA.

153. *EP,* May 14, 1948.

154. *EC,* May 21–27 and 31, 1948. Bell's newspaper account hints that she was a spy in the party from the beginning.

155. *EP,* May 14 and 19, 1948.

156. Albert J. Eberhard et al. to All Local 813 Members, May 27, 1948, Folder 4, Box 1, Ser. 1, WSP.

157. Ibid.; William Sentner to Don Schism, June 4, 1948, Folder 4, Box 1, Ser. 1, WSP.

158. Program of Organization for Local 813, June 17, 1948, Folder 4, Box 1, Ser. 1, WSP.

159. *Labor's Voice,* May 19, 1948.

160. *Evansville Courier-Press,* June 20, 1948, in Folder 4, Box 1, Ser. 1, WSP; Albert J. Eberhard et al. to All Local 813 Members, undated, Folder 4, Box 1, Ser. 1, WSP; *SLST,* June 21, 1948.

161. *EP,* August 2, 1948; *EC,* August 6, 1948; "Report on the 1948 District 8 Elections," October 27, 1948, D8/197, UEA.

162. Lipsitz, *A Rainbow at Midnight,* 207, suggests the strike may have been called in an effort to discredit leadership, but it is clear from private correspondence that the UE District leadership endorsed a strike. Ernest Snodgrass et al. to "Dear Friend," July 31, 1948, Folder 7, Box 1, Ser. 1, WSP; James Payne to Albert Fitzgerald, July 27, 1948, D8/296, UEA.

163. Ads in Clippings Files on the Bucyrus-Erie Strike, possession of Charles Berger, Evansville, Indiana; Finan quotation in Lipsitz, *A Rainbow at Midnight,* 207–8.

164. "Beware of Neighborhood of Scabs" leaflet, B-E Libel Suit File, RD 21, UEA; *EC,* August 20 and 22, 1948; "The Real Facts at Bucyrus," September 4, 1948, B-E Libel Suit file #377, RD21, UEA.

165. Edward Countryman, Draft, 4, B-E Blacklist folder, RD 527; "Rule to Show Cause," *B-E v. Snodgrass,* RD 21, UEA; *EC,* August 28, 1948; "Tag" (F. J. Taggart) to E. A. Mitchell, July 27, 1948, Folder 5, Box 12, Edward Mitchell Papers; *EC,* August 29, 1948; *EP,* August 30, 1948.

166. Troy James to James Click, August 28, 1948, unprocessed JWCP357.

167. Lipsitz, *A Rainbow at Midnight,* 208–9; *EP,* August 21 and 25 and 27 and 31, 1948, September 9, 1948; *EC,* August 29, 1948; *EP,* August 31, 1948.

168. "Beware of Neighborhood of Scabs" leaflet, BE Libel Suit file #327, RD31, UEA; *UE Strike News,* September 3, 1948, September 4, 1948, in B-E Libel Suit 377, RD 21, UEA; Countryman draft, 4, and B-E Blacklist file, RD 527, UEA.

169. *EP,* September 9, 1948.

170. Stephen Meyer, *Stalin over Wisconsin: The Making and Unmaking of Militant Unionism, 1900–1950* (New Brunswick, N.J.: Rutgers University Press, 1992), 199–210.

171. House of Representatives, Committee on Education and Labor, *Investigation of Communist Influence in the Bucyrus-Erie Strike: Hearings before a Subcommittee of the Committee on Education and Labor,* 80th Cong., 2nd sess. (Washington, D.C.: U.S. Government Printing Office, 1948), 69–85; *EP,* September 13 and 14, 1948; *EC,* September 12, 1948. Witness Arthur Robinson "commended" the hearing, applauding the congressmen who conducted it and the "Taft-Hartley law as a Protection to working men." As a result, UAW Local 265, of which he was a member, announced that he "doesn't speak for the union." *EP,* September 16, 1948, RD 527 notes. HELC hearings had broken strikes in Dayton, New York, and other cities.

172. *Investigation of Communist Influence,* 50.

173. Vern Countryman, "BE Blacklist" file, 6, RD 527, UEA.

174. *EC,* September 12, 1948; Lipsitz, *A Rainbow at Midnight,* 211; Samuel White, "Labor and Politics," 223; *UEN,* September 25, 1948; *UEN,* December 11, 1948.

175. *EC,* September 16, 1948.

176. Unidentified newspaper article, "Witnesses Face Contempt Citation," September 11, 1948, D8/173, UEA; Unidentified newspaper article, "UE officers at Faultless Plant resign," Folder 9, Box 1, Ser. 1, WSP; *EC,* September 14 (Mitchell comments), 15, 16, and 18, 1948.

177. *EP,* September 20, 1948; *EC,* September 20, 1948; Unidentified newspaper article, Folder 9, Box 1, Ser. 1, WSP; William Sentner to Joseph Pulitzer, September 21, 1948, D8/100, UEA; *SLPD,* September 19, 1948; *SLGD,* September 20, 1948; Sorenson, "The Anticommunist Consensus," 73; September 19, 1948, press release, Local 813, BE Blacklist file, RD 527, UEA; author's interview with Robert Logsdon. Sentner still had an honorary membership in Maytag Local 1116.

178. *EC,* September 15, 1948; *SLPD,* September 20, 1948.

179. White, "Labor and Politics in Evansville," 223. Albert J. Eberhard and Alvis King to Lines, Spooner, and Quarles, October 29, 1948, *B-E v. Local 813 et al.,* RD 21, UEA; *B-E v. Snodgrass* file, RD 21, UEA.

180. Arthur Kinoy, *Rights on Trial: The Odyssey of a People's Lawyer* (Cambridge: Harvard University Press, 1983), 68.

181. *EC,* September 17, 1948; "UE On the Air," September 27, 1948, BE Libel Suit 377, RD 21, UEA.

182. *EC,* November 5, 1948; Mitchell ads, B-E Blacklist folder, RD 527, UEA.

183. "Memorandum on 1948 District Elections," Undated, D8/196, UEA.

184. William Sentner, Annual Officers' Report, September 25, 1948, District 8 Executive Board, Folder 6, Box 5, Ser. 1, WSP.

185. "Report on the 1948 District Eight Election," October 27, 1948, D8/197, UEA; "Unionism vs. Bossism" leaflet, D8/160, UEA.

186. Ibid.; H. A. Anderson to James Click, November 2, 1948, Folder 175, Box 15, JWCP. Click was apparently very well funded. Sentner estimated that the lost-time pay for Click was $4,500 but that seventy-five Local 1102 shop stewards and officers also received lost-time payments. His Moline campaign supporters sent him a bill for $879 for election day alone.

187. Leaflets in Folder 3, Box 6, Ser. 1, WSP; "Unionism vs. Clickism" leaflet, D8/160, UEA; "The Real Issue" leaflet, D8/166, UEA.

188. "Report on the 1948 District Eight Convention," October 27, 1948, D8/197, UEA; *EC,* October 14 and 18, 1948; James W. Click to James B. Carey, March 1, 1949, Folder 32, Box 22, IUER.

189. "Report on the 1948 District Eight Convention," October 27, 1948, D8/197, UEA; *EP,* October 23, 1948; *UEN,* November 16, 1948; Robert Logsdon to James Matles, October 16, 1948, D8/125, UEA.

190. *EP,* September 20, 1948, October 23, 1948, November 1, 1948; quote from Sorenson, "The Anticommunist Consensus," 73.

191. Henry A. Anderson to James Click, February 15, 1949, Folder 175, Box 15, JWCP357.

192. "The Officers . . ." untitled statement, March 1949, Folder 4, Box 1, Ser. 1, WSP.

193. *UE Seeger Shop Reporter,* Local 813, May 1949; Undated broadside, "posted on May 16 and 17," both in Folder 4, Box 1, Ser. 1, WSP. "March 24" untitled typewritten notes on spring negotiations, Box 1, Ser. 1, WSP.

194. Otto Maschoff to Albert Fitzgerald, June 17, 1949, Folder 4, Box 1, Ser. 1, WSP.

195. Robert Logsdon to All Local Unions, June 12, 1949, Folder 4, Box 1, Ser. 1, WSP; Otto Maschoff to Albert Fitzgerald, June 17, 1949, Folder 4, Box 1, Ser. 1, WSP.

196. Robert Logsdon to All Local Unions, District 8, UE-CIO, June 12, 1949, Folder 4, Box 1, Ser. 1, WSP; Otto Maschoff to Albert Fitzgerald, June 17, 1949, Folder 4, Box 1, Ser. 1, WSP.

197. *UE Reporter,* July–August 1949; Joseph Pogue to Glenn Like, July 12, 1949, Folder 4, Box 1, Ser. 1, WSP.

198. Agreement, Re Separate Charter, Seeger, August 31, 1949, D8/339, UEA.

199. *UE Reporter,* September 1949; Robert Logsdon, Report for Month of January 1949, Report for February 1949, Report for March 1949, in Folder 3, Box 6, UE District 8 Records, SHSI.

200. "Vote for Militant American Unionism" leaflet, undated, and "Here Are Your Candidates" leaflet, both in D8/163, UEA; Bill Sentner to Julius Emspak, undated, ca. October 1949, D8/100, UEA.

201. William Sentner, "Report on the Status of UE in District 8 to District Executive Board Meeting," June 24, 1950, attached to minutes, D8/12, UEA; "Red meat" leaflet, folder 19, District 8 files, SHSI.

202. William Sentner, "Report on the Status of UE in District 8 to District Executive Board Meeting," June 24, 1950, attached to minutes, D8/12, UEA; author's interview with Hershel Walker; Johnson, "The Communist Issue in Missouri," 88–94.

Conclusion

1. William Sentner, Remarks, 1952 District 8 Convention, unprocessed WSP; John Schulze to William Sentner, September 10, 1949, Box 1407, D8/304, UEA.

2. William Sentner, "Remarks on Labor Unity," 1955, unprocessed WSP; *An Analysis: Progress of the Skilled Trades 1950–1956, St. Louis, MO Area,* unprocessed JWCP357; author's interview with Lloyd Austin, December 16, 1988.

3. Robert Logsdon, Organizational Report to UE District 8 Annual Convention, October 31, 1954; *Evansville UE News,* May 19, 1954; Ray Staeder, remarks to author, St. Louis, March 13, 1992; Jerry Tucker, remarks to author, ca. 1990.

4. Eve Milton to Don Harris, March 31, 1952, Box 2, UE District 8 Papers, SHSI; Local 806 (Cape Girardeau) materials in Folder 2, Box 1, Ser. 1, WSP; "The Disaffiliation of Local 1116 from U.E.," Folder 30, Box 28, Ser. 3, UE District 8 files, SHSI.

5. William Sentner FBI File, FBI-HQ, files 100-18332-149 to 154, Box 5, Ser. 4, WSP; *Newsweek,* March 8, 1951. *Kansas City Star,* September 17, 1952, unprocessed WSP.

6. "A Report to District Council 8" by James Click, undated, District 8, 1941–48 folder, Box 51, IUE District 8, 1950–53, IUER; William Sentner to James Matles, Don Harris, Elmer Ralph, September 6, 1951, D8/627, UEA.

7. Author's interview with Hershel Walker; Rosemary Feurer, *The St. Louis Labor History Tour* (St. Louis: Bread and Roses, 1994).

8. Author's interview with William Sentner Jr., November 23, 1999; Catherine Fosl, *Subversive Southerner: Anne Braden and the Struggle for Racial Justice in the Cold War South* (New York: Palgrave, 2002); Toni Gilpin, "Left by Themselves: A History of the United Farm Equipment and Metal Workers Union, 1938–1955" (PhD diss., Yale University, 1992).

9. Mrs. Sentner had filed for citizenship in 1939, 1942, and 1945, each time admitting that she had been a member of the party until 1938. *SLGD,* September 3, 1942, and October 7, 1949.

10. Author's interview with William "Red" Davis, September 10, 1993; author's interview with Toni Sentner, June 16, 1989; *UEN,* May 26, 1952; *SLPD,* November 16, 1951.

11. William Sentner FBI file, September 29, 1952, report of arrest, FBI-HQ 100-18332-160, Box 5, Ser. 4, WSP. *Des Moines Tribune,* September 7, 1952; *Moline Daily Dispatch,* September 17, 1952; *Rock Island Argus,* September 17, 1952; *Davenport Daily Times,* September 17, 1952; *Kansas City Star,* September 17, 1952; *New York Times,* September 18, 1952; all in "Defense-W.S." Clippings file, RD 271, UEA.

12. Narrative Statement, CA.8, 1537–1637, *Sentner v. U.S.,* #15097 Crim and 15098 *Forest et al. v. U.S.* in Box 4, Ser. 4, WSP; *EC,* May 5, 1954; *SLPD,* April 12 and 14, 1954. The most startling point of the trial was the testimony by William Cortor, who had been on the defense committee until the day he testified and who professed to have a "family" relationship with Sentner until he took the stand, describing Sentner and his family as "wonderful people." Cortor had been reporting defense strategy to the government up until that very morning. "Red" Davis claimed that Cortor told him later that he did so under intense pressure from the FBI and regretted turning in names of his "close personal friends" so that he could obtain work on the riverfront (Narrative statement, 774–870). Years later, when William Sentner Jr. requested his father's FBI files, some of the material redacted was the evidence that Sentner deeply believed in nonviolence. On appeal, some of this material was released and is contained in the FBI files in the WSP.

13. William Sentner FBI file, FBI-HQ 100-18332-227–230; quote in February 4, 1957, report, 14, 100-18332-228, Box 5, Ser. 4, WSP; *SLPD,* December 13, 1958; *EP,* December 13, 1958. "Red" Davis insisted that Sentner never left the St. Louis party, despite what the FBI reports suggested.

14. Samuel White, "Labor and Politics in Evansville," 262–63; "Terms and Conditions of Affiliation IAM-AFL" and *The Voice of District 153,* April 11, 1958, in Esther Ziemann collection, Special Collections, University of Southern Indiana, Evansville, Indiana; *St. Louis Labor Tribune,* February 9, 1956.

15. Author's interview with "Red" Davis. On Davis's background, see Michael Honey, *Southern Labor and Black Civil Rights: Organizing Memphis Workers* (Urbana: University of Illinois Press, 1993).

16. Author's interview with James Click; "The Charges against Carey" and "What's behind the Staff Discharges," Executive Board Files, Box 126E, IUE District and Local Files, IUER; *SLGD,* June 26, 1963.

17. Robert Bussel, "A Trade Union Oriented War on the Slums"; Harold Gibbons, "Ernest Calloway and the St. Louis Teamsters in the 1960s," *Labor History* 44(1) (2003): 49–67; Joshua Freeman, *Working Class New York: Life and Labor since World War II* (New York: New Press, 2000).

18. William Sentner, Memo, September 30, 1954, unprocessed WSP. On GE and West-inghouse's decentralization policies, see Ronald Schatz, *The Electrical Workers,* chap. 8; *Emerson Electric: A Century of Manufacturing* (St. Louis: Emerson Electric Corporation, 1990), 148–55; author's telephone interview with Lloyd Austin, December 16, 1988.

19. *Emerson Electric,* 153–55; Selig Harrison, "Poker Playing Stu," *New Republic,* June 20, 1960. Symington abandoned his hawkish sentiments in some areas after he saw the debacle of Vietnam. Author's telephone interview with Lloyd Austin, December 16, 1988.

20. *Emerson Electric,* 129, 198; *SLPD,* December 16, 1950; Robert Michael Smith, *From Blackjacks to Briefcases: A History of Commercialized Strikebreaking and Unionbusting in the United States* (Athens: Ohio University Press, 2003), 99–101. *SLGD,* October 31, 1957; *EC,* June 27, 1954.

21. Steven Rosswurm, *The CIO's Left-Led Unions* (New Brunswick, N.J.: Rutgers University Press, 1992), 15; *New York Times,* April 1, 1961; Lisa McGirr, *Suburban Warriors: The Origins of the New American Right* (Princeton, N.J.: Princeton University Press, 2001).

22. *SLPD,* December 15, 1988; author's telephone interview with Lloyd Austin, December 16, 1988; see Carey speeches in Box 225, Ser. 18, James Carey Papers, Walter Reuther Library, Wayne State University. Symington later switched from "hawk" to "dove." See James Olson, *Stuart Symington: A Life* (Columbia: University of Missouri Press, 2004).

23. David Harvey, *Spaces of Hope* (Berkeley: University of California Press, 2000), 24–31; Andrew Herod, *Labor Geographies: Workers and the Landscapes of Capitalism* (New York: Guilford, 2001), xiii; Andrew Herod, ed., *Organizing the Landscape: Geographical Perspectives on Labor Unionism* (Minneapolis: University of Minnesota Press, 1998). Wills quotes in Herod, *Organizing the Landscape,* 147.

24. Author's interview with Antonia Sentner, June 16, 1989; Archie Thompson, Summary of the activities of the Union Commissary, Maytag strike of 1938–1939 Collection, SHSI.

25. James Lorence, *Organizing the Unemployed: Community and Union Activists in the Industrial Heartland* (Albany: State University of New York Press, 1996); Robert Rodgers Korstad, *Civil Rights Unionism: Tobacco Workers and the Struggle for Democracy in the Mid-Twentieth-Century South* (Chapel Hill: University of North Carolina, 2003); Zaragosa Vargas, *Labor Rights Are Civil Rights: Mexican American Workers in Twentieth Century America* (Princeton and Oxford: Princeton University Press, 2005); Michael

y, Southern Labor and Black Civil Rights: Organizing Memphis Workers, 1929–1960 (Urbana: University of Illinois Press, 1993); Michael Goldfield, "Race and the CIO: The Possibilities for Racial Egalitarianism during the 1930s and 1940s," *International Labor and Working-Class History* 44 (Fall 1993): 1–32; Staughton Lynd, ed., *"We Are All Leaders": The Alternative Unionism of the Early 1930s* (Urbana: University of Illinois Press, 1996). Charles Payne, *"I've Got the Light of Freedom": the Organizing Tradition and the Mississippi Freedom Struggle* (Berkeley: University of California Press, 1995).

26. Judith Stepan-Norris and Maurice Zeitlin, *Left Out: Reds and America's Industrial Unions* (Cambridge: Cambridge University Press, 2003); Toni Gilpin, "Left by Themselves: A History of the United Farm Equipment and Metal Workers Union, 1938–1955" (PhD diss., Yale University, 1992); Stephen Meyer, *Stalin over Wisconsin: The Making and Unmaking of Militant Unionism, 1900–1950* (New Brunswick, N.J.: Rutgers University Press, 1992); Mark McColloch, "The Shop-Floor Dimension of Union Rivalry: The Case of Westinghouse in the 1950s," in *The CIO's Left-Led Unions,* ed. Steve Rosswurm, 183–200 (New Brunswick, N.J.: Rutgers University Press, 1992). See also an earlier comparison of the influence of the Left in Howard Kimeldorf, *Reds or Rackets: The Making of Radical and Conservative Unions on the Waterfront* (Berkeley: University of California Press, 1988).

27. John Bukowczk, "Immigrants and Their Communities," *International Labor and Working Class History* 25 (Spring 1984): 54.

28. David Montgomery, *The Fall of the House of Labor: The Workplace, the State and American Labor Activism, 1865–1925* (Cambridge: Cambridge University Press, 1987), 2; David Brody, "The CIO after Fifty Years: A Historical Reckoning," *Dissent* 32 (Fall 1985): 457–472. For the interpretation that focuses on Soviet influence, see John Earl Haynes, Harvey Klehr, and Kyrill Anderson, *The Soviet World of American Communism* (New Haven, Conn.: Yale University Press, 1999). For a recent summary of the literature in these fields, see Bryan D. Palmer, "Rethinking the Historiography of United States Communism," *American Communist History* 2(2) (2003): 139–174.

29. Stepan-Norris and Maurice Zeitlin, *Left Out,* 32.

30. Gary Gerstle, *Working Class Americanism: The Politics of Labor in a Textile City* (Princeton, N.J.: Princeton University Press, 1989), chaps. 8–10; Gary Gerstle, *American Crucible: Race and Nation in the Twentieth Century* (Princeton, N.J.: Princeton University Press, 2002); Jefferson Cowie, *Capital Moves: RCA's 70-year Quest for Cheap Labor* (Ithaca, N.Y.: Cornell University Press, 1999), 182–83, 192; Michael Hardt and Antonio Negri, *Empire* (Cambridge: Harvard University Press, 2000), 206.

INDEX

Abfall, Frank, 18, 19, 20, 29
ACTU. See Association of Catholic Trade
  Unionists
ACWA. See Amalgamated Clothing Workers
  of America
AFL. See American Federation of Labor
African Americans, 5, 23, 31, 160, 247n48,
  284n49; as activists, 12, 32–33, 37, 40, 83,
  147–48, 190, 205, 209, 227; and the CIO,
  151, 284n48; and the CP in St. Louis,
  31–64, 254n44; discrimination against, 79,
  82, 148, 284n44,; effect of the Great
  Depression on, 32–33; in electrical and
  metals industry, 5, 12, 16–17, 30, 146, 150;
  and the Left, 40, 85–86, 146, 230; and representation on labor boards, 258n92
  "superseniority" for, 285n61; and unemployed activism, 31–33, 39, 40, 43, 53 ;
  union membership of, 46, 146–48, 283n42,
  284n44. *See also* District 8, activism on
  behalf of African Americans; District 8,
  black membership of; Emerson Electric,
  Employees Representation plan and;
  March on Washington Movement
  (MOWM); nut pickers' union; Urban
  League; U.S. Cartridge;
Allison, Web, 93–94
Amalgamated Association of Iron and Tin
  Workers, 50
Amalgamated Clothing Workers of America
  (ACWA), 37, 63, 135; influence of, on Sent-
  ner, 73, 264n85
Amalgamated Metal Mechanics, 5
America First, 134, 201
American Federation of Labor (AFL), 4,
  13–14-15, 36, 41, 42, 43, 46, 60, 68, 88 95,
  104, 120, 121, 160, 166, 177, 195, 212, 215, 220,
  226; see also Iowa AFL. *See also* Interna-

tional Association of Machinists, Metal
  Trades Council
American Labor Party, 15
American Legion, 108, 109, 122, 128, 134, 201,
  223, 227
American Rolling Mill, 115
American Telephone and Telegraph
  (AT&T), 115
American War Dads, 193, 200
American Workers Union (AWU),
  42–43, 50
Anderson, Charles, 130
anticommunism, xviii, 14, 103, 121, 137,
  177–78, 192–93, 225, 234, 267n127, 292n174;
  of the Catholic Church, 186, 195–96,
  200–201; as a cover for racist sentiment,
  186–87, 294n42; debate concerning,
  188–90; origins of, 178–88; in the press,
  200–201, 208, 213; and reactionary politi-
  cal tides, 206–10; triumph of, 220–23; use
  of networks by anticommunists, 195–202.
  See also countersubversive tradition;
  Evansville, Indiana, anticommunist
  movement in; House Un-American
  Activities Committee (HUAC); Taft-
  Hartley Act (1947)
Apel, George, 133, 280–81n239
Applebaum, Joe, 122–23
Arbitration, 38, 97, 98–99; management
  views of 76, 78, 90, 116, 132, 154, 177; *see*
  NMTA, and arbitration; District 8, griev-
  ance and arbitration of
Arnold, L. T., 76–77
Arundel, Martin, 210
Associated General Contractors, 172–73
Association of Catholic Trade Unionists
  (ACTU), 198, 199, 200, 208
AWU. See American Workers Union

78, 95, 105, 108, 111, 114, 120, 132, 177, 205, 212–213, 216, 222–223, 231, 246n29, 261n19; arbitration and, 6, 78, 95, 177; and the Maytag Corporation, 89, 90, 95; spies and strikebreakers and, 10, 11, 20, 24, 25, 54–55, 56, 61, 205, 223; see also community based company strategies, NMTA and

National Negro Labor Council, 227
National Recovery Administration (NRA), 23, 29; orders William Sentner's arrest, 38, 39, 42; Labor Board of, 25, 257n87, 258n92
National Resources Planning Board (NRPB), 163
National War Labor Board (NWLB), 14, 138, 143, 247n54; use of to challenge managerial control of wage patterns, 152–53
Nelson, Donald, 142, 144, 156
Nelson, N. O., 9
New Deal, the, 87, 99, 100, 110; New Deal elites, 135
New Right movement, 233
Newman, Joseph, 28–29, 62–63, 66, 68, 262n40; and the NMTA, 78
Newton Daily News, 89; accusations of against W. Sentner, 93
Newton, Iowa, 87–88. *See also* Local 1116 (UE)
Nightingale, William, 192
NIRA. *See* National Industrial Recovery Act
Nordman, John, 80
NRA. *See* National Recovery Administration.
nut pickers 42, 53, 59, 74, 111, 151, 155, 227, 258n92; strike, 36–40 see also Food Workers Industrial Union; Funsten
NWLB. *See* National War Labor Board

O'Connor, Bill, 199
O'Hare, Frank, 5
Office of Production Management (OPM), 141, 282n21
One River, One Plan, 165, 167; response to, 166
open shop labor campaigns, 7–10, 14, 25
"open the books" demands, 38, 67, 132–133
Operation Dixie, 195, 199
organizing, community-based, xiii, xvii—xviii, xix, 6–7, 59, 31–34, 89, 91–92, 139–45, 190–95, 234; and criticism of blitz cam-

paigning, 135, 195; developed in early 1930s, 31–41, 43; influence on national organization, 175–176; and District 8 unemployed relief campaigns and, 56, 59, 92–94, 106, 110–13, 140–142, 187, 191, 221–22, 230

Packard, Walter, 165–66, 168
Parker, Herbert, 2
Parry, David, 245n24
Pasche, Victor, 74, 175–76
pattern bargaining, 178, 231, 301n48; *see also* District 8, contract bargaining style of
Patterson, James, 168
Paul, Eugene, 185
Payne, James, 80, 85–86, 139–40, 191–92, 193, 218; 206; 229
Peer, John, 253n42
Perfection Company, 69
Persons, Buck, 231
Phillips, Alroy, 60, 62, 63, 65, 68, 251n13
Pick, Lewis, 164, 289n131
Pick Plan, 164
Pick-Sloan Bill (1944), 169, 173
Pickett, A. J., 122
Pogue, Joe, 219, 220
police in labor disputes, 9, 12, 13, 32, 33, 34, 37, 43, 45, 58, 61, 62. 64, 68, 70, 89, 91, 93, 97, 106–109, 123, 126, 131, 132, 133, 211, 212, 215, 227
political economy, xvii, 1, 36, 40, 46, 226, 234; as basis for organizing electrical plants, 50; during World War II, 138–45; of control corporate, 1, 15–17, 23, 31, 36, 41, 47, 106, ; new critique of, 145–52, 160
Pope, Jim, 61, 107
Popular Front, see Communist Party, Popular Front and
Populist movement, the, 8, 45, 170, 242–43n15
postwar planning conferences, 160–63
"Prevent Evansville from Becoming a Ghost Town" campaign, 140
Printers Union (St. Louis), 15
Priorities Unemployment Plan, 141, 143
Progressive Era, 8, 11; and the "cult of the expert," 174
Progressive Mine Workers Union, 59, 254n53, 256n68

Progressive Party, the, 208, 299n130; "red-baiting" of, 299n130

Queeny, Edgar, 155

Raab, Betty, 148, 149, 187
radicalism, 47, 121, 154, 236; and skilled work-ers, xv, xvi, 80, 242n12, 260n10, 267n128; and wage demands, xv, xvii, 6, 73, 77, 78, 90, 91, 102, 103, 152–53, 223, 235, 245n18
radicals:14–16, 121–27, 133–35; and commu-nity-based organizing, 43, 190–95, 221–22; democracy and, xiii xviii, xix, 43; role of in the 1930s labor movement, xv–xvii, 10, 43, 80–83, 175, 250n1, 283n42. *See also* civil rights and right to association Commu-nist Party (CP); Socialists; unionism/unionization, radical
Radio Corporation of America (RCA), 115
Radosovitch, Toni, see Sentner, Antonia
Ramige, E. A., 98
Randle, Matt, 209
Ranken Technical, 9
Reconstruction Finance Corporation, 34
Red Caps, (United Transport Employees Union), 231
Red Squad (of the St. Louis Police), 123, 126, 227
Reidel, Bill, 65, 204
Republican Party/Republicans, 94, 196
Reuther, Walter, 138–39, 181, 226
Rice, Charles Owen, 196
Riethmeyer, Fred, 62, 80
rights-based unionism, 61, 70, 72–73, 75, 76, 77, 78, 82, 86, 89, 99–100, 103, 107, 124, 130, 137–38, 145, 152, 153, 157, 158, 162, 177, 212, 225, 238; *see also* civic unionism; District 8, challenges to the community wage and management rights; human rights in labor campaigns
Ring, Naomi, 165, 167, 168
Robertson, David, 240–41n3
Robinson, Arthur, 211, 213, 216, 218, 302n171
Rodgers, W. H., 12
Rogin, Michael, 9–10
Roosevelt, Franklin D., 138, 145
Rosswurm, Steve, 186, 233
runaway shops, see decentralization policies and runaway shops

Rural Electrification Administration (REA), 167–68
Russell, R. J., 111
Rustless Iron and Steel Company, 115
Ruthenberg, Louis, 104, 105, 106, 111, 120, 192–93, 194, 200, 211, 216, 233
Ryder, Mary, 15, 31

Sage, Helen Aukamp, 300n139
St. Louis: African American population of, 284n49; electrical industry of, 2–4; ethnic neighborhoods of, 31; flooding of, 163; labor market of, 17; low immigration to, 7; number of electrical workers in, 248–49n64; relief system of, 32, 33–34; slums of, 231; streetcar strike (1900), 7–8; streetcar strike (1918), 12; wages of, 17, 36, 49; wartime production in, 143–44; work-ing class formation and 80, 145, 196. *See also* labor movement, in St. Louis; open shop campaign
St. Louis Chamber of Commerce, 17, 114, 128, 143; attitudes toward African Ameri-cans, 148; position on the MVA, 171, 173
St. Louis CIO-PAC, 170, 199
St. Louis Globe-Democrat, 201, 208, 209
St. Louis Interracial Victory Council, 150–51
St. Louis Labor, 12, 244n12, 248n59
St. Louis Labor College, 46, 52, 57
St. Louis League of Women Shoppers, 131
St. Louis Post-Dispatch, 164, 201, 208, 218
St. Louis Race Relations Commission, 151
St. Louis Small Arms Plant. See U.S. Car-tridge
Samuel, August, 2
Sarnoff, Dave, 115
Scarlett, William, 37, 76, 155, 157, 182, 256n68
Schatz, Ronald, ix, 56, 281n2, 287n93
Scheele, Paul, 289n131
Schlieman, Frank ("Pop"), 26, 27, 52–53, 147, 251n18
Schoettelkotte, Charles, 199, 218
Schrecker, Ellen, 206–7
Schwedtman, Francis C., 2, 4, 8, 9
Scism, Don, 218
Scranton, Philip, 240–41n3
Scullin Steel, 46
Sears, Roebuck, Inc., 104, 115–117, 120, 227, 232; see also Robert "General" Wood

ROSEMARY FEURER is Associate Professor
at Northern Illinois University.

THE WORKING CLASS IN AMERICAN HISTORY

Worker City, Company Town: Iron and Cotton-Worker Protest in Troy and Cohoes, New York, 1855–84   *Daniel J. Walkowitz*

Life, Work, and Rebellion in the Coal Fields: The Southern West Virginia Miners, 1880–1922   *David Alan Corbin*

Women and American Socialism, 1870–1920   *Mari Jo Buhle*

Lives of Their Own: Blacks, Italians, and Poles in Pittsburgh, 1900–1960   *John Bodnar, Roger Simon, and Michael P. Weber*

Working-Class America: Essays on Labor, Community, and American Society   *Edited by Michael H. Frisch and Daniel J. Walkowitz*

Eugene V. Debs: Citizen and Socialist   *Nick Salvatore*

American Labor and Immigration History, 1877–1920s: Recent European Research   *Edited by Dirk Hoerder*

Workingmen's Democracy: The Knights of Labor and American Politics   *Leon Fink*

The Electrical Workers: A History of Labor at General Electric and Westinghouse, 1923–60   *Ronald W. Schatz*

The Mechanics of Baltimore: Workers and Politics in the Age of Revolution, 1763–1812   *Charles G. Steffen*

The Practice of Solidarity: American Hat Finishers in the Nineteenth Century   *David Bensman*

The Labor History Reader   *Edited by Daniel J. Leab*

Solidarity and Fragmentation: Working People and Class Consciousness in Detroit, 1875–1900   *Richard Oestreicher*

Counter Cultures: Saleswomen, Managers, and Customers in American Department Stores, 1890–1940   *Susan Porter Benson*

The New England Working Class and the New Labor History   *Edited by Herbert G. Gutman and Donald H. Bell*

Labor Leaders in America   *Edited by Melvyn Dubofsky and Warren Van Tine*

Barons of Labor: The San Francisco Building Trades and Union Power in the Progressive Era   *Michael Kazin*

Gender at Work: The Dynamics of Job Segregation by Sex during World War II   *Ruth Milkman*

Once a Cigar Maker: Men, Women, and Work Culture in American Cigar Factories, 1900–1919   *Patricia A. Cooper*

A Generation of Boomers: The Pattern of Railroad Labor Conflict in Nineteenth-Century America   *Shelton Stromquist*

Work and Community in the Jungle: Chicago's Packinghouse Workers, 1894–1922   *James R. Barrett*

Workers, Managers, and Welfare Capitalism: The Shoeworkers and Tanners of Endicott Johnson, 1890–1950   *Gerald Zahavi*

Men, Women, and Work: Class, Gender, and Protest in the New England Shoe Industry, 1780–1910   *Mary Blewett*

Workers on the Waterfront: Seamen, Longshoremen, and Unionism in the 1930s   *Bruce Nelson*

German Workers in Chicago: A Documentary History of Working-Class Culture from 1850 to World War I   *Edited by Hartmut Keil and John B. Jentz*

The University of Illinois Press
is a founding member of the
Association of American University Presses.

_____

Composed in 10.5/13 Minion
by BookComp, Inc.
at the University of Illinois Press
Manufactured by Thomson-Shore, Inc.

University of Illinois Press
1325 South Oak Street
Champaign, IL 61820-6903
www.press.uillinois.edu